CIVIL JUSTICE IN THE AGE OF HUMAN RIGHTS

Civil Justice in the Age of Human Rights

JOSEPH M. JACOB
London School of Economics and Political Science, UK

Routledge
Taylor & Francis Group
LONDON AND NEW YORK

First published 2007 by Ashgate Publishing

Published 2016 by Routledge
2 Park Square, Milton Park, Abingdon, Oxon OX14 4RN
711 Third Avenue, New York, NY 10017, USA

Routledge is an imprint of the Taylor & Francis Group, an informa business

British Library Cataloguing in Publication Data
Jacob, Joseph M., 1943-
Civil justice in the age of human rights
1. Great Britain. Human Rights Act, 1998 2. Civil procedure
- England 3. Civil procedure - Wales 4. Human rights -
England 5. Human rights - Wales
I. Title
347.4'205

Library of Congress Cataloging-in-Publication Data
Jacob, Joseph, M., 1943-
Civil justice in the age of human rights / by Joseph M. Jacob.
p. cm.
Includes index.
ISBN 13: 978-0-7546-4576-4
ISBN 10: 0-7546-4576-2
1. Civil procedure--Great Britain. 2. Civil rights--Great Britain. 3. Due process of law--Great Britain. I. Title.

KD7325.J325 2006
347.42'05--dc22

2006025032

ISBN 13:978-0-7546-4576-4 (hbk)

Contents

Table of Statutes

Table of Statutory Instruments

Table of Cases

Preface

This book relates English civil procedural law to that of the European Convention on Human Rights and Fundamental Freedoms and its court at Strasbourg. With many, if not most, before me, I had supposed that our legal system complied with international ideas of what is just and fair. This book argues that this is not so. To comply with those ideas, if we want to, there is much to do. Maybe, we do not want to. Maybe, we like the way we do things. Maybe, in any legal system – international, human rights, domestic – without a context, any idea of what is just or fair defies definition. This book, then, also compares the British and Strasbourg case law, each with itself. Human rights thinking demands principle. Modern civil justice is founded on convenience. This book is not on message. It gives priority to principle over expediency.

This is a law book. I have set aside wider considerations of political or social scepticism about, or enthusiasm for, the human rights project. Of course, law reaches beyond itself. It can be only part of ourselves. This book is limited. It does not expressly touch our constitutional arrangements except where driven to by the Human Rights Act (1998). More importantly, it also avoids wider considerations of human rights philosophy, jurisprudence, of human equality and dignity or policy (including, social, economic and environmental). International human rights law beyond the European Convention and mechanisms beyond the courts are not discussed. I have not even begun to assess whether this type of protection is a good thing. My concern is with human rights law, its internal consistency and what the British courts make of it.

An apology is however owed to my readers. Long monographs are bad manners. My subject has, of course, infinite scope: books, it is said, speak to books, and cases speak to cases. My task is to bring the subject within reasonable bounds. This work is longer than I would wish because it provides the evidence to justify the conclusions that have surprised me. It is also old-fashioned: contrary to the modern way, it is not bulked up by extensive summaries at the beginning, or end, of each section or chapter. Chapter 1 does, however, contain something of an overview, if not of the argument, at least of its scope. Chapter 6 brings the discussion together.

This book is largely a static picture along (procedural) law's journey into the modern world, now for us both European and global. Most journeys have a sense of destination. But this one is odd. It has no such idea. This is a journey informed only by its sense of where it started. History does this too, but history seeks to explain. This book is no history: it is an account. It is my hope that somewhere along the road we may get a notion of the kind of world we have entered and of the kind of universe in which we are going to live. It is my hope too, and despite all experience, that by gaining some idea of what this journey is about we may get to a better place than perhaps we would otherwise.

I do not dwell long on matters of public law or public law procedure. The reason is both once easy and contrary. English civil procedure largely built its processes for private law. And yet, the new procedures adopt many ideas, not least in the control or supervision of discretion, taken from our administrative law. The common law is holistic. Public lawyers will find much that is familiar although they will not find their knowledge re-done.

Acknowledgements

I would like to thank everybody who has helped in the writing of this book but, although most do not know it, there are too many. Two sources have been especially important. Neil Andrews, *English Civil Procedure* and Adrian Zuckerman, *Civil Procedure*, each provide a major chapter on the effect of the European Convention on civil processes.[1] For the rest, let it suffice that some of those to whom special gratitude is owed are thanked, in a small way, by having a gratis copy. I am mean. My masters' classes in civil litigation at the LSE (and, indeed, before them, my undergraduate students) have also been special but they do not have free copies. None is answerable for my route.

As usual but still in earnest I thank LAWTEL and LexisNexis for their daily updating services and LexisNexis and WestLaw for access to their data bases. Such help is essential to the legal academic enterprise.

I have written on the basis that the Constitutional Reform Act 2005 is fully in force. That is not due until 2009. Apart from that the law is stated as I see it at Easter 2006.

Bossolasco (CN)
Piedmonte
Joe Jacob

The Method of Citation

Partly in the interests of economy and party because most of my sources are electronic, the notes give the neutral citations for English authorities where they apply and only dates for Strasbourg.

The table of cases gives the neutral citations and application numbers and dates.

1 Andrews, *English Civil Procedure: Fundamentals of the New Civil Justice System*, Oxford: Oxford University Press, 2003; Zuckerman, *Civil Procedure*, London: Butterworths Law, LexisNexis, 2002.

Chapter 1

Introduction

The Issue

I have spent roughly three score years in and around the law. But it has been the English common law and I can live in the sure and certain knowledge that the more essential a principle is expressed to be, the more easily it can be abandoned: like every Englishman and Englishwoman, the common law knows no fundamentals. Nor, indeed, despite a century and half of largely noble, academic endeavours,[1] does it know with any accuracy of any classification that can explain its past or its present. It is a homogenous whole to be understood, not in pieces, but as a single unity. It is not a historical progression but a living organism. Post-decision classification by black-letter legal academics certainly helps understanding but it does not explain. Even the simplest division, say between civil and criminal law, fails to withstand the reality of actual rules.[2] To the common law, it really is sufficient that where there is a (legal) wrong there is a legal remedy.[3] It does not even mind the apparent tautology.

Suddenly, at the end of the most brutal century in history, our legal system began to absorb and even create principles (in civil procedure the most obvious

---

1 See Sugarman, 'Legal Theory, the Common Law Mind and the Making of the Textbook Tradition', in Twining (ed.) *Legal Theory and Common Law* (1986).

2 See, e.g. Parpworth, Thompson and Jones, 'Environmental offences: utilising civil penalties', *Journal of Planning and Environment Law* [2005] 560 and Kennedy, 'Justifying the civil recovery of criminal proceeds', *Comp Law* [2005] 137, references there cited. And see also: *In the matter of D (Interim Receiver Order: Proceeds of Crime Act (2002)* [2004] All ER (D) 90 (Dec) and *Director of the Assets Recovery Agency v Ashton* [2006] All ER (D) 477 (Mar) QBD (Admin). So also anti-social behaviour orders are civil, *R (on the application of W) v Acton Youth Court* [2005] EWHC 954 (Admin), as are fixed penalties imposed to induce the production of documents under Taxes Management Act 1970, *Sharkey v Revenue and Customs Commissioners* [2006] All ER (D) 147 (Feb). Committal proceedings are civil in that hearsay evidence is admissible but the contempt must be proved to the criminal standard of beyond reasonable doubt, *Daltel Europe v Makki* [2006] EWCA Civ 94. Potter LJ in *Han v Commissioners of Customs and Excise*; *Martin v Commissioners of Customs and Excise*; *Morris v Commissioners of Customs and Excise* [2001] EWCA Civ 1040, [26] explained the autonomous Convention meaning of a 'criminal charge'.

3 The difficulty is explained in Maitland, *The Forms of Action at Common Law*, 1909, lecture I. These lectures themselves were published posthumously and have been republished many times, including now, in several web addresses. And see dissenting opinion of Judge Zupančič in *Roche v UK*, 19 October 2005, discussed at p. 19 below.

are contained 'the overriding objective' set out in Civil Procedure Rules, Part I, but our judges were and are often searching for others and across a wider front) as well as a host of human rights and fundamental freedoms.[4] To be sure, each of the legal systems of the modern world that has adopted these ideas has applied them to all economic actors and not only living, breathing people. Companies, however large, have human rights, but apparently only inchoate duties! That is to be expected. It would be to ask too much for law to reflect humanism as well as justice.[5]

The end of the last century saw two major events: the Civil Procedure Rules (the CPR) came into force[6] and the Human Rights Act 1998 (HRA) gave effect to the European Convention on Human Rights (the ECHR).[7] This book assesses the effect of the Convention on the Act.

Thinking about human rights in general is, in part, an attempt to identify a rational system for the recognition of human dignity and equality. Modern civil justice is concerned with expediency and efficiency. If there is any justification for this book, it is twofold. It attempts to reconcile these sometimes opposing approaches or at least to identify the conflicts. Secondly, it seeks to find out how far the imposition of each of these new ideologies and these (for us) novel methods of analysis affect what the law always takes for justice,[8] assuming (as we must) that justice is something different from majesty, from mere Royal will.[9] It is an uncomfortable assumption but one which is becoming more real. As we shall see, modern judges are expected to satisfy the litigants before them, if need be, by giving reasons for their decisions. The judges have become another subject of our democratic age. Yet, because they, like the law itself, have come from a past whose practices were better explained by habit than sense, the giving of reasons is sometimes the object of tortuous explanation.

---

4 Most importantly, in legal terms, from the European Convention on Human Rights and Fundamental Freedoms, made part of British law by the Human Rights Act 1998.

5 Corporate human rights used to annoy me. Now it is clear that they are parasitic on rights for human beings: they have no life of their own. The rights enjoyed by companies are no more, even if not much less, than rights accorded to people. It is this which results in companies having no duties.

6 The new Rules were introduced in 1998. They are commonly referred to as the *Woolf reforms*. Elsewhere, Jacob, *Civil Litigation: practice and procedure in a shifting culture*, 2001, I argued that much of its genesis was in the case law of the previous two decades.

7 I do not (yet) see the Court at Strasbourg adopting wider ideas of the content of human rights culled from modern international law, but see Booth and du Plessis, 'Common Wealth', (2003) 66 MLR 837, where it is, for example, argued that the Convention on the Rights of the Child can be read into domestic law.

8 My concern is not with any abstract justice or with any philosopher's idea: my concern is what judges as practical men and women have made of the idea.

9 When there was mere majesty (and, for centuries, our judges were the living embodiment of Royalty itself), obedience and acceptance were all that were required. In origin, our modern rights come from writs issued by medieval clerks in the Royal chancellery. Their discretion was expanded and limited as Royal power waxed and waned. Maitland (n. 3 above).

Writing in 1990 Cappelletti observed:[10]

> The human rights philosophy has been *the* most important contribution not only of the West, but of humankind generally, to political science and moral philosophy. What is new in our epoch, however, is the full recognition of the insufficiency of a mere philosophy of human rights – the recognition, that is, that *adequate machinery and processes* are needed to make those rights effective.

This, he said, is the 'most challenging revolution of which all proceduralists are … the most militant revolutionaries'. Proceduralists know about means. To Cappelletti the good ones among them never lose sight of the ends, and the end he had in mind is access to justice for all.

This book is about the weapons available to our contemporary revolutionaries. In doing so, one objective is to increase awareness of the possibility and utility of this most modern perspective on civil trial processes. More importantly, it is a search for socially relevant purposes within the apparent dryness of how things are done. Civil procedure has often been compared to the rules of a game – football, cricket, tennis. This book is written in the conviction that it is more, maybe far more. Procedure is not just rules. It is the means by which society expresses its underlying meaning.

The principles I see in the ECHR, in the CPR and in the case law both of the European Court of Human Rights at Strasbourg (the ECtHR) and Britain which are at issue in this book, are fourfold:

1. trials must be open to the public;
2. there shall be equality of arms between maybe unequal disputants;
3. the tribunal shall be impartial; and,
4. a decision shall be given in a reasonable time.

Of these, the first three have most troubled the English courts. It is clear that systemic delay is one of the biggest problems across the Council of Europe as a whole,[11] and,

---

10 Cappelletti, 'Human Rights and the Proceduralist's Role', in *International perspectives on Civil Justice*, Scott (ed.), at p. 2. Italics in original. Later, at p. 10, he quoted Dante, *Purgatorio* I, 71–72:

Libertà vo cercando ch'é sí cara come sa chi per lei vita rifiuta.

He translated this as:

For liberty I am striving, which is so precious
As he who refuses her refuses life.

11 It is also one of the biggest problems facing the ECtHR itself. Lord Woolf, *Review of the Working Methods of the European Court of Human Rights*, December 2005, on the Court's website, said: 'The number of applications registered in Strasbourg in 1981 was 404. By 1997, this had risen to 4750' and '44,100 new applications were lodged last year, and the number of cases pending before the Court – now at 82,100 – is projected to rise to 250,000 by 2010'. He pointed out that '800 million European citizens have the right of individual petition'. Much of the problem, he said, is caused by the 'enlargement of the Council of Europe after 1990 … what is saving Strasbourg … is that people still do not know about it'. He endorsed the use

that we have nothing be complacent about. Nevertheless, for us, each of the first three has caused the deeper and more intractable problems. I shall argue that of these four issues, the first is the most important if only because if the public cannot see what is being done, the adherence to the rule of law achieved by the others matters less.

Daniels v Walker[12] was decided in the early days of the new civil procedure regime and shortly before the HRA came into force. Having cited Part 1 of the CPR Lord Woolf said[13] these 'provisions … make it clear that the obligation on the court is to deal with cases justly', and added:[14]

> If the court is not going to be taken down blind alleys it is essential that counsel, and those who instruct counsel, take a responsible attitude as to when it is right to raise a Human Rights Act point ... It would be unfortunate if case management decisions … involved the need to refer to the learning of the European Court on Human Rights in order for them to be resolved … I hope that judges will be robust in resisting any attempt to introduce those arguments ... When the 1998 Act becomes law, counsel will need to show self restraint if it is not to be discredited.

This book is thus concerned with the effects of the HRA on civil procedure and in particular its effects on the CPR.[15] It asks whether Lord Woolf was right to worry that the new civil procedure regime could be susceptible to numerous HRA challenges. (I leave aside any discussion of the constitutional propriety of the guidance to future judges and advocates – their role, on the one side, is not to be robust in resisting anything it is to decide according to law and, on the other, fearlessly to put a client's case as effectively as possible.)[16] More specifically this book asks whether there

---

of the distinction between pilot judgments and repetitive cases first applied in *Broniowski v Poland*, 28 September 2005 (Friendly Settlement). A potential difficulty is a classification that a case is repetitive may spawn satellite litigation.

12 *Daniels v Walker*, Also known as *D (A Child) v Walker* and *D v Walker* (Practice Note) [2000] 1 WLR 1382, CA. It was concerned with the question of what happens when one party is unhappy with the report of a jointly appointed expert.

13 At [24].

14 At [23] and [26]. In *Brown v Stott* [2003] 1 AC 681, Lord Steyn set out the objectives of the convention: he contrasted it with the categorical language of the United States Constitution:

> The convention requires that where difficult questions arise a balance must be struck. Subject to a limited number of absolute guarantees, the scheme and structure of the convention reflects [a] balanced approach. It differs in material respects from other constitutional systems but as a European nation it represents our Bill of Rights.

15 Bratza, 'The Future of the European Court of Human Rights' (Lincoln's Inn Lectures on European Human Rights Law), July 2003 (cited in Lester, 'The utility of the Human Rights Act: a reply to Keith Ewing', [2005] PL 249) discussed the converse, the effect of HRA and its case-law on the court at Strasbourg.

16 As regards this last, see Erskine in *R v Paine*, State Trials 22, 1783–1794, 357 and for a modern statement Lord Hobhouse in *Medcalf v Mardell* (Wasted Costs Order) [2002] UKHL 27, [52]-[53] discussed below at p. 149.

are differences between the CPR and ECHR ideas of what constitutes a fair or just decision and between their ideas of proportionality. How far, if at all, do decisions on the meaning of one influence decisions on the other?[17]

To anticipate part of the argument, Lord Woolf could take comfort for his position from the Civil Procedure Act 1997. Section 1(3) charges the Rules Committee to: 'make Civil Procedure Rules ... with a view to securing that the civil justice system is accessible, fair and efficient.' Under this power the Rules Committee has made the CPR.

The CPR themselves open with the declaration of their Overriding Objective. Sedley LJ described its importance:[18]

> A generation ago, Blain J, giving judgment in a long forgotten interlocutory matter, said that litigation was not to be conducted as if it were warfare. In those days the remark represented no more than a fleeting triumph of hope over experience. It is only with the introduction of the Civil Procedure Rules that the hopes of Blain J and many others like him have become reality. The Civil Procedure Rules are not, as at times the Rules of the Supreme Court seemed to be, a sort of Hague Convention regulating the worst excesses of warfare, which litigants were otherwise free to conduct as they saw fit. The overriding objective makes this plain.

The Overriding Objective says[19] the rules are to enable '1.1(1) ... the court to deal with cases justly', defined to include '(2)(d) ensuring that [a case] is dealt with expeditiously and fairly'. It is unclear why the draftsman of rules departed from the terms of the Act – that requires the rules be *fair*, etc., whereas the rules open by speaking of cases being dealt with *justly* and does not mention *fairness* until (2)(d) – but it is doubtful whether anything will ever turn on this drafting.

Both the CPR and the HRA make unusual provision for interpretation. In the CPR the Overriding Objective is to be used in interpreting any rule and applying any discretion. And, overarching even this, s. 3(1) of the HRA says: 'So far as it is possible to do so, primary legislation and subordinate legislation must be read and given effect in a way which is compatible with the Convention rights'. S. 2 requires the UK court to 'have regard' to the Strasbourg jurisprudence.[20]

Thus far, Lord Woolf's position seems to be confirmed.

Article 6(1) of the ECHR says:

---

17 In 'Is the High Court the *Guardian* of Fundamental Constitutional Rights?', [1993] PL 59, Laws asked 'whether ... the common law is today able to accord a priority to fundamental rights ... by incremental decision-making in which apparently new principles belong to a continuum whose starting point is uncontentious and well-established'. The answer was (at p. 67) 'the Convention jurisprudence is a legitimate aid to establish what the policy of the common law should be'.

18 *Kesslar v Moore and Tibbits* [2004] EWCA Civ 1551, [27].

19 As amended to take account of the Prevention of Terrorism Act 2005, SI 2005 No.2005/656.

20 Discussed below, p. 67.

> In the determination of his civil rights and obligations … everyone is entitled to a fair and public hearing within a reasonable time by an independent and impartial tribunal established by law. Judgment shall be pronounced publicly but the press and public may be excluded from all or part of the trial in the interests of morals, public order or national security in a democratic society, where the interests of juveniles or the protection of the private life of the parties so require, or to the extent strictly necessary in the opinion of the court in special circumstances where publicity would prejudice the interests of justice.

The ECHR Art. 6 has a different emphasis from CPR Part 1. Both instruments talk of the need for a fair or just trial. The Convention is, however, of 1950.[21] It is concerned with a static idea, the public determination of rights. To the ECHR, justice is an absolute, but, as its court recently said: it[22]

> has repeatedly stated that its judgments in fact serve not only to decide those cases brought before it but, more generally, to elucidate, safeguard and develop the rules instituted by the Convention, thereby contributing to the observance by the States of the engagements undertaken by them as Contracting Parties.

Lord Steyn's description of the ECHR as,[23] an 'ageing charter of fundamental rights' is open to misunderstanding. As he more accurately said:[24] 'The logic of dynamic interpretation is inexorably that the meaning of a statute may change over time. It is a fairy tale to think otherwise.' The CPR is concerned with the efficient disposal of disputes that might or might not involve the determination of rights and (at least on the face of Part 1) need not be in public. Elsewhere I have argued that the CPR reflect, and I could have said in ways unimaginable in 1950, ideas of consumerism and management.[25] As much as anything, the concern now is not the pursuit of any absolute justice but of fairness and efficiency. That concern, I argue, reflects a dominance of real-life commercial interests over less definitive ideas of justice within our community. Indeed, one of the reasons behind the 1997 Act[26] is the maintenance of London as the forum of choice for the settlement of disputes.[27]

---

21 See Nicol, 'Original Intent and the European Convention on Human Rights', [2005] PL 152.

22 *Capital Bank AD v Bulgaria*, 24 February 2006, [79].

23 Lord Steyn, 'Deference: a tangled story', [2005] PL 346.

24 Lord Steyn, 'Dynamic Interpretation Amidst an Orgy of Statutes', [2004] EHRLR 245.

25 Jacob, *Civil Litigation: practice and procedure in a shifting culture*, 2001.

26 And of the 1996 Arbitration Act, see notes on both Acts in Current Law Statutes and also *City of Moscow*, pp. 65-58. below.

27 Woolf, *Access to Justice*, Final Report, Sect. I para. 5. In 1997, Hope, *Expenditure on Legal Services*, LCD Research Series, estimated that legal services generally (which includes non-contentious business) amounted to around 1½% of GNP. Lord Falconer, *Doing Law Differently*, April 2006, said in 2004 'the legal services market generated £1.9 billion of revenues, almost 2% of our GDP'. While, of course contentious business is by far the smaller part of legal work, it lies at its heart. Its procedures are therefore important to the economy as

There is, however, one central question: does the different emphasis in the CPR and ECHR mask anything more? Lord Woolf was right only if the answer is in the negative. And, it is only if he was right, that the two instruments are not on collision course. If, however, they are in harmony, does the HRA add anything to the CPR?

The Structure of the Argument

Life, however, does not give simple answers to such questions. Both the CPR and ECHR come with baggage. The CPR open by saying 'These Rules are a new procedural code with the overriding objective of enabling the court to deal with cases justly'. Whatever else the CPR changed, the same judges who apply them were largely in office before and they are in no position to imagine that they had not been deciding cases justly for years before the commencement. I shall argue that in case of doubt it is necessary to refer back to its original text of the CPR rather than rely on precedent. Nevertheless, behind both the text and any earlier case-law there is and generally always has been an underlying sense of justice. The new text is to be read with that, and with sensed impediments to justice in the old law, in mind.

The Long Title to the Human Rights Act says it is to give 'further effect to rights and freedoms guaranteed under the European Convention'. The expression 'further effect' recognizes that the Convention had some effect before 1998. In particular, individuals in the United Kingdom had a right of individual petition to Convention machinery to enforce Convention rights for 30 or so years before the Act. This right of petition is untouched. At bottom, the Act is about jurisdiction not rights. It gives the United Kingdom courts a job of considering the Convention which they did not have before. Individuals have no new rights but they do have easier access to them.

The concern in this book is with the two new streams of procedural justice, the code of the CPR and (mainly) Art. 6 of the ECHR. The question of what the HRA adds to the CPR becomes: are the two streams stronger than either alone?

This Chapter sets out some foundational issues, including the not always clear scope of the linkage between the CPR and the ECHR. It begins by describing the argument. It assesses the problems raised by the facts that the jurisdiction of the ECtHR is supervisory and not appellate and that the Convention obligations are owed to other member States of the Council of Europe and not to individual citizens. It considers the scope of what the ECtHR calls the margin of appreciation, that is the scope of discretion member states have to give national meaning to the Fundamental Freedoms defined in the Convention. It notes that Art. 6 which requires a fair trial applies to the whole of the proceedings. A doctrine of proportionality is expressed in the CPR and central to much of the case-law at Strasbourg. In that context, this Chapter assesses it in both regimes.

The chapter then identifies seven difficulties to which my enquiry is subject. To be brief, the central issue is to understand how far, if at all, the domestic incorporation

---

a whole. These figures relate to the income of the profession. They make no allowance for the effect of the application of the rule of law on the wider economy, see further p. 27 below.

of much of the United Kingdom's international obligations under the Convention has affected our civil litigation processes. Some of the problems can be stated shortly, others are more intractable. The flexibility of both the CPR and the ECHR make it difficult to identify the effect of one upon the other. Both instruments are subject to unusual methods of interpretation.

Both s. 3(1) of the HRA, which requires the UK courts to interpret UK statutes as far as possible as if they are Convention compliant and, if that cannot be done, the fallback s. 4 which permits to courts to issue a declaration that an Act of Parliament is incompatible, create a crucial problem. What is meant by compatible?

So also, the old way is to articulate and use analogies from one case to another. The modern way, which contains, a new open recognition of judicial law making, is to use principles. It provides technical challenges to our ways of understanding the law. This is as true in the field of civil processes as it is elsewhere.

Assuming that in the great majority of cases the English and Strasbourg courts have similar conceptions of a fair trial, the question arises whether this is caused by the Convention (or HRA) or whether British judges have their own ideas uninfluenced by such external considerations. Either conclusion provokes questions.

The HRA in s. 2 requires our courts to 'have regard to' the Strasbourg jurisprudence. The section leaves open the questions of when they should cite that material and, more importantly, what is now a binding authority. I shall take issue with the remarkable decision in *Price v Leeds City Council*. That says that our courts should follow English authority, merely noting contrary ECHR case law. I shall also take issue with the conception of legal consistency that the case implies.[28]

Finally, this Chapter notes there are undoubted differences between the common and civil law systems. It notes the special role of the jury and some of the ways its influence continues long after its effective abolition. It asks what has caused these ways, what effect do they have on the application of the Convention and is there any coming together with other European legal systems.

Open justice is discussed in Chapter 2. It is the longest of my chapters. The reason it takes it first, and gives it so much emphasis, is simple. Open justice is, I argue, law's contribution to freedom of expression. This freedom is a reflection of more than the means of mere settlement of disputes between individuals and reflects the values of our culture. It is an essential part of our liberal, tolerant democracy. This book thus gives the basis of our prevailing political creed priority over more strictly legal considerations. This emphasis is not because I want to write about political philosophy but because this aspect of my subject informs so much else. Much of what follows either provides exceptions to it or tests the strength of its principle.

In outline, the chapter traces the roots of open justice and assesses how and why the law recognizes it and how the law thus makes a special contribution to the wider debate on freedom of expression. The chapter describes the extent to which the court both at trials and in interim hearings insists on the right of the public to be present. It assesses exceptions to the openness of justice based on the idea that publicity

---

28 *Lambeth LBC* v *Kay*; *Price v Leeds CC* [2006] UKHL 10.

would destroy the subject of the case. Beyond this, as the chapter recognizes, there are exceptions caused by the choice of private settlement and an inconsistent recognition of a party's right to waive this common law and Convention right. The chapter describes the relation between the courts and arbitration. It is critical of the confusion it sees in prioritizing the supposed right of a party over that of the public.

The chapter then turns to two issues, a modern problem and a modern innovation. The idea of the openness of justice was developed in days when most of the civil process was oral. Today, much is conducted on paper. The chapter notes the concerns of the rules and the court to replicate the former capacity of the public to understand what is happening. So also, appeal courts today insist that they and trial courts give reasons for decisions. It assesses the extent of that duty and the reasons for it. It is in harmony with the Strasbourg jurisprudence but most probably, I suggest, is a result of the growth and application of ideas taken from our administrative law. The chapter ends with a long but necessary examination of the relation between open justice and dispute disposal outside the court, so-called Alternative Dispute Settlement.

Art.6 of the ECHR gives effect to two fundamental principles of the common law, if not all legal systems worthy of the name: the principles that both sides shall be heard and that nobody shall be a judge in their own cause. I discuss how the CPR and ECtHR apply the first of these in Chapter 3 (where I use in its title *equality of arms*, an expression far more familiar in civilian jurisprudence than in the common law) and continue the discussion in Chapter 4. I discuss the second principle in Chapter 5.

Equality of arms is an omnibus term embracing a number of separate rights. On a stricter analysis, some of these are better seen as disparate and only sometimes loosely associated with the term. Chapter 3 addresses various issues as access to the court including the extent that court fees may lawfully impede it (in Chapter 5, I return to discuss the broader issue of State funding for the system of civil justice). Chapter 3 discusses other apparent restrictions on the right of access, including the powers to strike out a claim and the related power to give relief from sanctions. It worries about the effect of time, both after the issue of a claim and before (including statutes of limitation). It addresses special problems, relating those who seek to litigate too much without cause (vexatious litigants), to power to require a party to give security for costs and, on the grander scale, restrictions on access to our courts imposed by international law.

Access is one thing. The right to be heard is another. Chapter 3 discusses it and how far it involves a right to an oral process, what can courts decide on paper. It begins to deal with the opposite, when can courts make decisions in the absence of one party, *without notice hearings*? I say begins because the issue reappears elsewhere, in the consideration of when documents or evidence should be withheld from a party or the court on a substantive hearing. It asks when one side's request for an adjournment may or should be granted. Chapter 3 concludes by asking when a party is entitled to representation, the extent of the obligation on States to provide it and whether the system in England and Wales does so.

Chapter 4, in effect, adds more to the discussion of equality of arms. It discusses the peculiarly common law device of disclosure. This requires all parties to litigation to disclose to the others all the documents they have relating to the case. The chapter notes the very limited extent to which a party can refuse even on grounds of confidence. It discusses the importance to a fair legal system of legal professional privilege and the privilege against self-incrimination. It notes the statutory intrusions on them under the guise of the State's desire to protect itself against money-laundering.

The chapter then describes the relation between the presentation of evidence and fairness. Some space is taken describing what is now known as public interest immunity because of far reaching recent changes. Under this relevant, probative and otherwise admissible evidence is excluded because of some greater public interest in non-disclosure. The chapter traces the invention of the court's power to inspect and the consequent problems that have ensued. These include the fact that in exercising the discretion the court may hear only one side. The solutions are not happy. In some cases, the problem may be mitigated by the appointment of special counsel, but that has created its own problems. The judge may be contaminated by access to information unknown to one side.

Chapter 5 is concerned with the rule against bias, the second of the principles of the common law and of Art. 6. It is the most commonly cited example of the influence of the ECHR on domestic law. For what it is worth, the chapter is also the one that has caused me the most trouble, not I hasten to add because the concept of *bias* is complex. The difficulty is that because any suggestion of it goes to the heart of the integrity of the judges, they tend to view it personally even when deciding an appeal. Every man and woman, especially the honest, is and ought to be sensitive to any imputation that they are not, and when dealing with complicated issues it can easily arise. There is no simple case either in the UK or at Strasbourg where a decision has been quashed because a judge has taken a bribe. Rather the case law is concerned with their conduct before and during legal proceedings and with the structure of the system in which they find themselves. The case law displays both sincere anguish and inconsistency.

The chapter argues that it is necessary to distinguish partiality from independence. Both partiality and independence bite on appearances as well as realities. Briefly, the chapter describes the development of the modern test for bias. It assesses the impact of the judicial oath and moves to discuss what it calls partiality for interest. Going beyond the cases it distinguishes an *advantageous concern* from being merely *interested*. On the basis of principle and authority, it doubts whether *Pinochet* (No.2)[29] is still good law.

It suggests that there is now a rule prohibiting or at least discouraging enquiries by losing litigants about the activities of their judges. One concept is central to the whole discussion. It is the idea of the 'fair-minded and informed' observer, what he or she might think and how perceptions have changed. The chapter notes that the

29 *R v Bow Street Metropolitan Stipendiary Magistrate, ex p Pinochet Ugarte* (No.2) [2000] 1 AC 119.

decisions of a biased court are voidable not void, and that bias is capable of being, and commonly is, waived. It discusses the tone of the language judges should use both in court and outside: how blunt they can be.

Armed with this introduction, the chapter discusses when a judge should recuse him or herself, and when they should not, both for matters arising within the case and because of some previous judicial on non-judicial relationship with the parties.

All these matters go to the question of whether a judge is or is not impartial. As I have suggested there is now a second issue, is the judge independent? It can be a constitutional or structural question bound into ideas of the separation of powers. It can be a systemic issue if senior members of the judiciary are allowed to lean on more junior colleagues with a view to influencing either a decision in a particular case or possibly an understanding of the law. The question of independence can also be a problem that can affect an individual judge, as where his or her previous involvement in legislation under consideration sometimes has been said to produce an appearance of a lack of independence.

The rest of the chapter is concerned with more directly constitutional, structural and organizational questions. Some have received judicial consideration in the UK. These include issues relating to appointment and tenure. Others are the subject of judicial concern in other parts of the Commonwealth, for example, those relating to listing and similar considerations. The last two matters considered in the chapter have yet to be the subject of judicial comment in court. They are the funding of the civil justice system and, curiously, the making of rules for civil procedure. There is, however, enough in the previous argument to place them on the table for discussion and resolution. Both relate to possible apparent influence by the executive of the judiciary.

Chapter 6 pulls all this together. It revisits the questions put at the beginning of this chapter.

There is, no doubt, much else that I could discuss – finality, committal and the protection of the court, the inherent jurisdiction, costs and conditional fee arrangements, problems relating to service, interim injunctions, wasted costs orders, and other of funding, and the enforcement of money judgments – among them. More could be said about evidence of fact and by experts (and the curious idea of judicial notice). Indeed, more could be said even about all the topics I have touched. But this not a text and there is enough to sustain my thesis that the Strasbourg jurisprudence has affected much of what we do but that we have done much without it.

The Jurisdiction of the Human Rights Court

By far the greater number of cases heard at Strasbourg are complaints by individuals (and corporations). Art. 35(1) of the Convention qualifies the right of access to the ECtHR. It provides:

> The Court may only deal with the matter after all domestic remedies have been exhausted, according to the generally recognized rules of international law, and within a period of 6 months from the date on which the final decision was taken.

Its purpose, the Grand Chamber explained in *Pizzati v Italy*,[30] 'is to afford the Contracting States the opportunity of preventing or putting right the violations alleged against them before those allegations are submitted to the Court'. It explained more systematically in *Lukenda v Slovenia*:[31]

> Normal recourse should be had by an applicant to remedies that are available and sufficient to afford redress in respect of the breaches alleged. The existence of such remedies must be sufficiently certain not only in theory but also in practice, failing which they will lack the requisite accessibility and effectiveness ... It is incumbent on the Government pleading non-exhaustion to demonstrate to the Court that the remedy was an effective one available in theory and in practice at the relevant time, that is to say, that it was accessible, capable of providing redress in respect of he applicant's complaints and must have offered reasonable prospect of success ... Although each of the available remedies may not prove to be effective, the aggregate of the available remedies may satisfy the criteria set forth by the Convention ... Once this burden of proof has been discharged, it falls to the applicant to establish that the remedies or the aggregate thereof advanced by the Government was in fact exhausted or was for some reason inadequate and ineffective in the particular circumstances of the case or that there existed special circumstances absolving him or her from the requirement ... Finally, the Court has previously held that the rule of exhaustion of domestic remedies must be applied with some degree of flexibility and without excessive formalism.

We shall note occasions where it may be difficult or even impossible for an individual to complain to the ECtHR because he or she has acquiesced in a breach of the Convention (as sometimes with the right to a public trial) or because, for example, domestic remedies cannot be exhausted because the individual cannot afford either the court fees or the costs. It is my argument that beyond this, where there are systemic breaches, it is open to any other member State to complain to the Court. Of course, this is rarely done, but the ECtHR has jurisdiction to hear complaints from other States. In *Ireland v UK* the Court said:[32]

> A practice incompatible with the Convention consists of an accumulation of identical or analogous breaches which are sufficiently numerous and inter-connected to amount not merely to isolated incidents or exceptions but to a pattern or system; a practice does not of itself constitute a violation separate from such breaches.

---

30 *Pizzati v Italy* 29 March 2006, [38]. And see, e.g. *Markin v Russia*, 30 March 2006.

31 *Lukenda v Slovenia*, 6 January 2006 (and see: *Lukenda v Slovenia* (No.2), 13 April 2006; *Prekorsek v Slovenia*, 6 April 2006, [43]-[45]. It cited the Resolution of the Committee of Ministers of the Council of Europe (DH Res. (2004)3) 12 May 2004 on judgments revealing an underlying systemic problem, [28].

32 In *Ireland v UK*, 18 January 1978, [159].

And it explained:

> The concept of practice is of particular importance for the operation of the rule of exhaustion of domestic remedies. This rule … applies to State applications in the same way as it does to 'individual' applications … when the applicant State does no more than denounce a violation or violations allegedly suffered by 'individuals' whose place, as it were, is taken by the State.[33]

But:

> On the other hand, and in principle, the rule [concerning the exhaustion of domestic remedies] does not apply where the applicant State complains of a practice as such, with the aim of preventing its continuation or recurrence, but does not ask [for] a decision on each of the cases put forward as proof or illustrations of that practice.

However, in *Cyprus v Turkey* it qualified this, saying:[34]

> The exhaustion rule is inapplicable where an administrative practice, namely a repetition of acts incompatible with the Convention and official tolerance by the State authorities, has been shown to exist and is of such a nature as to make proceedings futile or ineffective.

The duties under the Convention are, at bottom, owed to other member states of the Council of Europe and not to private litigants. But, I say, adjudication is not necessary for there to be a breach of a rule of domestic or international law. That which is illegal does not need a court to decide it is illegal. Illegality is not defined by what a transgressor can get away with. Even if not litigated the duties under the Convention are binding. The duties on public authorities under the HRA, for example, s. 6, that they shall apply the Convention, are likewise binding even if they too cannot be litigated.

The Scope of the Engagement

We can start with two obvious points. Quite apart from the ECHR, if a rule in the CPR is outside the powers granted by the 1997 Act (perhaps as modified by HRA interpretation) it is void. Having spoken of the system being 'accessible, fair and efficient' the Act, in Sched. 1, goes on to say: 'Among the matters which Civil Procedure Rules may be made about are any matters which were governed by the former Rules of the Supreme Court or the former county court rules'.[35] In *General*

---

33 As, for example, in *Denmark v Turkey*, 5 April 2000.

34 *Cyprus v Turkey*, 10 May 2001, [99]. It also held that the 6 months rule applies (Para. 104) and that 'is incumbent on the respondent Government claiming non-exhaustion to satisfy the Court that the remedy was an effective one available in theory and in practice at the relevant time' [116].

35 It is extended to include power to amend rules of evidence, sched. 1 para. 4. It is possible, but unlikely, that there could be a challenge to the terms of sched. 1. In order to

Mediterranean Holdings v Patel,[36] the court condemned a rule in the CPR because it said it affects substantive rights – the 1997 Act only permitted the alteration of rules which affected procedure, practise and evidence.

So also, the application of the Convention is limited in two ways. First, the ECtHR is a court of review, it is supervisory: there will almost always be some margin of appreciation, some licence, left to national courts and legal systems.[37] Fredman, in an important article, explained:[38]

> It is only because the ECHR presupposes a full-blooded role for national courts that national authorities enjoy a margin of appreciation. Instead, courts and academic commentators have variously referred to the 'discretionary area of judgment' or 'latitude' which should be given to elected or official decision-makers.

Thus, in *Pizzati v Italy* the court adopted an idea from the 14th Protocol:[39]

> Under Article 1, which provides: 'The High Contracting Parties shall secure to everyone within their jurisdiction the rights and freedoms defined in Section I of this Convention,' the primary responsibility for implementing and enforcing the rights and freedoms guaranteed by the Convention is laid on the national authorities. The machinery of complaint to the Court is thus subsidiary to national systems safeguarding human rights.

---

satisfy the principle of legality, the ECtHR has required that a rule should be adequately accessible, *Sunday Times*. Legislation by reference is never this, particularly if the reference is to provisions otherwise repealed. S. 84 of the 1981 Act says 'the matters about which rules of court may be made under this section include all matters of practice and procedure in the Senior Courts which were regulated or prescribed by rules of court immediately before the commencement of this Act'. The previous jurisdiction of the High Court was defined by s. 18 of the 1925 Consolidation Act. That was in similar terms to s. 16 of the 1873 Act which said 'there shall be transferred to and vested in the High Court the jurisdiction which at the commencement of this Act is vested in a capable of being exercise by the following courts' and there is a list of the old courts including those of equity and common law. Given the lack of contemporary knowledge, even among lawyers, of nineteenth Century procedure, there may be doubt whether this reference is sufficiently precise to satisfy the principle of legality.

36 *General Mediterranean Holdings v Patel* [2000] 1 WLR 272. And see *Goode v Martin* [2001] EWCA Civ 1899 where the terms of CPR Part 17.4(2) (amendments to a statement of case after the expiry of a limitation period) were modified by the interpretative powers of HRA s. 3, discussed below.

37 For example, *Escolano v Spain*, 25 January 2000, [33]; *Brualla Gómez de la Torre v Spain*, 19 December 1997, [31], and, *Edificaciones March Gallego SA v Spain*, 19 February 1998, [33].

38 Fredman, 'From Deference to Democracy: the Role of Equality Under the Human Rights Act 1998', (2006) 122 LQR 53. And see Singh, Hunt and Demetriou, 'Is there a Role for the "Margin of Appreciation" in National Law after the Human Rights Act?' [1999] EHRLR 15.

39 *Pizzati v Italy* 29 March 2006 [GC], [37]. And see Report of the Committee on Working Methods, 1 July 2005.

Nevertheless, perhaps coming out of this idea of subsidiarity, at times but inconsistently the court has been surprisingly and unnecessarily differential for example, the Grand Chamber said in *Roche v UK*:[40]

> Where ... the superior national courts have analysed in a comprehensive and convincing manner the precise nature of the impugned restriction, on the basis of the relevant Convention case-law and principles drawn therefrom, this Court would need strong reasons to differ from the conclusion reached by those courts by substituting its own views for those of the national courts on a question of interpretation of domestic law ... and by finding, contrary to their view, that there was arguably a right recognized by domestic law.

The intention of the Convention is to enforce minimum standards, not either common general principles or convergence in national rules of civil procedure. As Lord Hope put it in *ex p Kebilene*:[41]

> Difficult choices may have to be made by the executive or the legislature between the rights of the individual and the needs of society. In some circumstances it will be appropriate for the courts to recognize that there is an area of judgment within which the judiciary will defer, on democratic grounds, to the considered opinion of the elected body or person whose act or decision is said to be incompatible with the Convention ... It will be easier for such an area of judgment to be recognized where the Convention itself requires a balance to be struck, much less so where the right is stated in terms which are unqualified. It will be easier for it to be recognized where the issues involve questions of social or economic policy, much less so where the rights are of high constitutional importance or are of a kind where the courts are especially well placed to assess the need for protection.

An example occurred in *Kehoe*[42] where the court considered the Child Support Act 1991. That Act removed a parent's personal right to claim maintenance through a

---

40 *Roche v UK*, 19 October 2005 [GC], [120]. But see the dissenting opinion of Judge Loucaides joined by Judges Rozakis, Zupančič, Strážnická, Casadevall, Thomassen, Maruste and Traja.

41 *R v DPP, ex p Kebilene* [1999] 3 WLR 972, 993–4 (drawing on a phrase in Lester and Pannick, *Human Rights Law and Practice*, para. 3.21) the discretionary area of judgment. Sedly LJ cited the passage by in *B v Secretary of State for the Home Department* [2000] HRLR 439.

42 *R (on the application of Kehoe) v Secretary of State for Work and Pensions* [2005] UKHL 48, [2004] EWCA Civ 225. In the Court of Appeal Ward LJ remarked, [80 (iii)] 'We are all used to coming to conclusions as a matter of impression. We sometimes rely on our "feel" for the case. This is imprecise but it works'.

His judgment also contained an extensive review of the history of child support arrangements. *R v R* (rape: marital exemption) [1992] 1 AC 599 was not discussed. There, the House of Lords held that 'the status of women, and particularly of married women, has changed out of all recognition in various ways which are very familiar and upon which it is unnecessary to go into detail. Apart from property matters and the availability of matrimonial remedies, one of the most important changes is that marriage is in modern times regarded as court (which had existed only under statute, consent arrangements were maintained) and gave it to the new Child Support Agency. The Court held that the statutory scheme did not engage Art. 6.

Secondly, Art. 6 itself is confined to the *determination* of rights, which excludes rules of substantive law[43] and, if is not the same thing, the limitation of rights.[44] The rights with which it is concerned are *civil* and not, for example, derived from public law or a liability to a public charge or tax.[45] It also excludes an application by trustees for 'directions' and no doubt similar administrative decisions of a court.[46] As Judge De Meyer put it:[47]

> Any right which a citizen (civis) may feel entitled to assert, either under national law or under supranational or international law, has indeed to be considered as a 'civil' right within the meaning of Article 6(1) of the Convention which enshrines a right which is so prominent that there can be no justification for interpreting [it] restrictively.

Civil rights do, however, include the right to practise a profession.[48] For us, the language is curiously difficult because the common law has no clear idea of a public or state realm that corresponds to these civilian classifications. In *Göç v Turkey*, a

---

a partnership of equals'. It may be that the rationale of Ward LJ's history is gone. If so, the reforms of the 1991 Act may not be what they appear. If, in retrospect (because *R v R*, like all case law, speaks retrospectively), a wife always has had an enforceable right to maintenance, the Act purports to remove it. That may indeed engage Art. 6.

43 *Z v UK*, 10 May 2001 [87]. And see: *James v UK*, 21 February 1986, [81]; *Lithgow v UK*, 8 July 1986, [192]; *Benthem v The Netherlands*, 23 October 1985, [32]; *The Holy Monasteries v Greece*, 9 December 1994, [80]. And note also Lord Bingham in *Matthews v Ministry of Defence* [2003] UKHL 4, [3], citing *König v Federal Republic of Germany*, 28 June 1978, [88] itself citing *Neumeister v Austria*, 27 June 1968, [18]; *Wemhoff v Germany*, 27 June 1968, [19]; *Ringeisen v Austria*, 16 July 1971, [110]; and, *Engel v Netherlands*, 28 June 1976, [81].

44 *DP & JC v UK*, 10 October 2002; *Wilson v First County Trust* (No 2) [2003] UKHL 40. But see *Osman v UK*, 28 October 1998 and the criticism in, e.g. Gearty, 'Unravelling *Osman*', (2001) MLR 159, and '*Osman* Unravels', (2002) MLR 87. And, for a criticism of Gearty's position, Hickman, 'The "uncertain shadow": throwing light on the right to a court under Article 6(1) ECHR', [2004] PL 122. See further p. 116 below.

45 In *Pellegrin v France*, 8 December 1999 [GC] the Court sought to end 'the margin of uncertainty' as to whether claims by civil servants were public or private. And see text and notes in Craig, 'The Human Rights Act, Article 6 and Procedural Rights', [2003] PL 753, at 754–759. Typically, and unfortunately, in academic writings, this piece, despite its title, ignores general civil litigation. It is almost exclusively concerned with administrative procedure. It does not mention the CPR nor even the Overriding Objective. See also Herburg, Le Sueur and Mulcahy, 'Determining civil rights and obligations', in Jowell and Cooper, *Understanding Human Rights Principles*, 2001, at 91.

46 *Re Trusts of X Charity*; *Y v Attorney General* [2003] EWHC 1462 (Ch), [12].

47 *Gustafson v Sweden*, 1 July 1997, Concurring Opinion.

48 *Le Compte, Van Leuven and De Meyere v Belgium* and *Albert and Le Compte v Belgium* 10 February 1983. And see *Tehrani v United Kingdom Central Council for Nursing,*

case not cited in *Roche v UK*, the ECtHR repeated its view[49] that the concept 'must be considered "autonomous"'.

Art.6 includes the whole of the proceedings including the determination of costs[50] and the enforcement of judgments.[51] The ECtHR has held that Art. 6 does not require any right of appeal, but that if there is an appeal, the guarantees of the Article apply.[52] This is itself surprising in view of the fact that most if not all states of the Council of Europe (and thus the European Union), with exceptions in some few specific cases, make provision for appeal against first instance decisions.[53] The Article bites only on determinations by courts so that if a body is constituted under private law and determines obligations by way of contract, it is outside the scope of the article and the HRA. The most common type of such private determination is arbitration, but the principle has been applied to an attempt to review the operations of Lloyd's of London.[54] The extent to which a review of such a determination is itself subject to Art. 6 is discussed later.

The first requirement – that the ECtHR is supervisory – gives Art. 6 a similar, but by no means identical, scope to the rights of appeal against case management decisions under the CPR. The second requirement – that the ECHR is concerned with determinations – has the effect of freeing a number of administrative procedures from the scope of Art. 6. The effect is that, although such procedures are largely outside the projection given by Art. 6, challenges to them, for example, by way of

---

Midwifery and Health Visiting [2001] IRLR 208, *R* (Wayne Thompson) v *Law Society* [2004] EWCA Civ 167, [83].

49 *Göç v Turkey*, 11 July 2002, [41].

50 *Robins v UK*, 23 September 1997, [28]-[29] (the total delay was 4 years which included periods when the state authorities acted on a mistaken impression of the facts and inactivity in the appeals office). And see: *Obermeier v Austria*, 28 June 1990, at [66]-[67]; *Silva Pontes v Portugal*, 23 March 1994, at [33]-[36]; *Di Pede v Italy*, 26 September 1996, *Zappia v Italy*, 26 September 1996, [24] (enforcement is part of the original process); *Duclos v France*, 17 December 1996, [55]; and, *Frydlender v France*, 27 June 2000, [27].

51 *Hornsby v Greece*, 19 March 1997 [40]-[41], *Iatridis v Greece*, 25 March 1999 [GC], [58]; *Immobiliare Saffi v Italy*, 28 July 1999, ECtHR [GC] [74]; *Prodan v Moldova*, 27 April 2004; *Voytenko v Ukraine*, 29 June 2004; *Croitoru v Moldova*, 20 July 2004; *Timbal v Moldova*, 24 August 2004; *Mancheva v Bulgaria*, 30 September 2004, [54]; and, *Wasserman v Russia*, 18 November 2004.

52 *Belgian Linguistics case*, 23 July 1968, [9]; *Tolstoy Miloslavsky v UK*, 13 July 1995.

53 See Evershed, Supreme Court Practice and Procedure, Final Report (Cmnd 8878, 1953) para. 473 quoted by Jolowicz in Cappelletti and Tallón (Eds), *Fundamental Guarantees of the Parties in Civil Litigation* 1973, at 170; Le Seuer, 'Access to Justice the United Kingdom', [2000] EHRLR 457, 460 n. 19 quoting Recommendation No. R (95) 5 of the Committee of Ministers (of the EU). The answer was given by Morritt V-C in *Colley v Council for Licensed Conveyancers* [2001] EWCA Civ 1137, [31] 'Rights of appeal are not so much rights of access to a court, as rights to have the opportunity of persuading a higher court that the first instance decision is wrong'.

54 *R (on the application of West) v Lloyd*'s *of London* [2004] EWCA Civ 506 per Brooke LJ [36]-[37] *Hautanemi v Sweden*, 11 April 1996.

judicial review or appeal are within it.[55] This again corresponds with the scope of the CPR. As Lord Bingham said in *Matthews v Ministry of Defence*:[56]

> The Strasbourg jurisprudence has distinguished between provisions of domestic law which altogether preclude the bringing of an effective claim and provisions of domestic law which impose a procedural bar on the enforcement of a claim. The European Court of Human Rights has however recognized the difficulty of tracing the dividing line between procedural and substantive limitations of a given entitlement under domestic law, acknowledging that it may be no more than a question of legislative technique whether the limitation is expressed in terms of the right or its remedy.

He added in *Runa Begum v Tower Hamlets LBC*:[57]

> The narrower the interpretation given to 'civil rights,' the greater the need to insist on review by a tribunal exercising full powers. Conversely, the more elastic the interpretation given to 'civil rights,' the more flexible must be the approach to the requirement of independent and impartial review if the emasculation (by over-judicialisation) of administrative welfare schemes is to be avoided.

There is, as Lord Rogers discussed in *Wilson* (No.2),[58] a fundamental distinction between substance and procedure but, as Lord Hoffmann put it in *Matthews v Ministry of Defence*,[59] it 'is a slippery one'. But as the Grand Chamber said:[60] 'fine as it may be in a particular case [it] remains determinative of the applicability and, as appropriate, the scope of the guarantees of Article 6.'

As with so many fundamental distinctions it is not always easy and sometimes not even important in its application.[61] Because substantive rights can only be determined after the application of procedural law, the former delimits substantive law. In practice, there are only a few, but within their terms important, occasions when the distinction matters.[62]

---

55 Thus, in *Bryan v UK*, 22 November 1995, the ECtHR held that the UK planning process whereby decisions of inspectors are subject to challenge in the national courts on the grounds that they are either perverse or irrational renders the process Art. 6 compliant. See further the discussion of paper decisions at pp. 138ff.

56 *Matthews v Ministry of Defence* [2003] UKHL 4.

57 *Runa Begum v Tower Hamlets LBC* [2003] UKHL 5, [5].

58 *Wilson v First County Trust* (No 2) [2003] UKHL 40.

59 *Matthews v Ministry of Defence* [2003] UKHL 4, [33]. He cited Dicey and Morris, *The Conflict of Laws*, 13th edn (2000), p. 157f, paras. 7–004: 'The distinction is by no means clear-cut. In drawing it, regard should be had in each case to the purpose for which the distinction is being used and to the consequences of the decision in the instant context.'

60 *Roche v UK*, 19 October 2005, 119.

61 See Gearty, 'Unravelling *Osman*', (2001) MLR 59, at 176–178.

62 Among them is that the protection given to information under the doctrine of legal professional privilege is substantive. Before the CPR, the law of evidence was substantive.

The dissenting opinion of Judge Zupančič in *Roche v UK* is more sophisticated and more understanding of common law way of argument. He described the distinction as 'fictional' and 'artificial'. He argued:

> At its inception it perhaps made political sense that an international instrument such as the European Convention on Human Rights should attempt to limit its effect to what was seen as a mere procedural means. The establishment of a substantive right would then, at least seemingly, remain in the sovereign domain of the domestic law. With time, however, this imagined tectonic boundary between what is substantive and what is 'merely' procedural has developed into a seismic fault-line. It generates hard cases … which make bad law.

And:

> It is ironic that we should, precisely in British cases, build on the distinction between what is procedural and what is substantive. While the Continental legal systems have, for historical reasons, traditionally maintained the strictness of the distinction, it is precisely the common-law system which has always considered the right and the remedy to be interdependent. Is the remedy something 'substantive'? Or is it 'procedural'? Is the legal fiction 'the Crown can do no wrong' – and the consequent blocking of action (immunity) – merely procedural? Or has the substantive right of the plaintiff simply been denied? As we move from one British case to another the dilemma appears in cameo.

He said: 'It is becoming clear that we need to resort back to common sense'. And he asked 'What then is a right? Is it not true that a "right" – including a "human right" – becomes something legally relevant, paradoxically, only when it is alleged to have been denied?'. He concluded:

> Human relations in society may be saturated with all kinds of potential rights. Nevertheless, in most cases they remain unasserted either because they are not violated in the first place or because the aggrieved person omits to pursue them procedurally. Moreover, a right without a remedy is a simple recommendation ('natural obligation'). It follows that a right is doubly dependent on its concomitant remedy. If the remedy does not exist a right is not a right; if the remedy is not procedurally pursued the right will not be vindicated. The right and its remedy are not only interdependent. They are consubstantial.
>
> To speak of rights as if they existed apart from their procedural context is artificially – say for pedagogical, theoretical or nomo technical reasons – to separate what in practical terms is inseparable. A substantive right is not a mirror image of its procedural remedy.
>
> A substantive right *is* its remedy.
>
> It is ironic that so often common sense and common law should come into direct collision. It is doubly ironic that the majority should speak of avoiding mere appearances and sticking to realities when the distinction the judgment is built upon is pure legal fiction. We may have muddled through another case but the underlying false premise remains. The dilemma is certain to come back.
>
> The way to address this dilemma is, obviously, to cease subscribing to the false premise. It is difficult to address this in the abstract. However, at least in cases in which the fault-line is potentially decisive, where it collides with justice and common sense, since we are a Court of Human Rights, we should opt for an autonomous meaning of 'substantive due process'. Intellectual honesty demands no less.

The terms of Art. 6 have caused confusion. It speaks of the *determination* of rights. This is loose and even, at least in a common law context, deceptive language and in *Osman* it lead to error. The court held that a declaration that the scope of the tort of negligence is limited somehow conferred an immunity. A true immunity is a procedural protection and may well engage Art. 6. A limitation of substantive liability is outside its scope. The problem is that, although the common law still apples its declaratory theory, it is unfashionable to say so. Nowadays, it is usual to refer to the theory as if courts make or determine rights. This use of the word *determine* is, of course, not the same as that in Art. 6.[63] The one is general and the other case specific. To it put another way, in the civil law, a court *determines* the outcome of a dispute: in common law, the equivalent word is *decide* or *dispose of*. There is no place for a civilian court to do what a common law judge does when he or she determines the law. The reason lies in the different role of the judge in the two systems that, as we shall see later in this chapter, van Caenegem describes.

The idea that Art. 6 includes the whole of the proceedings has had effects. A defect at some point in the proceedings may but, only may, be cured, for example, by an appeal tribunal with power to decide all the questions of fact and law at issue or to remit the case to a tribunal that does. As the Grand Chamber put it in *Kingsley*:[64]

> Even where an adjudicatory body determining disputes over 'civil rights and obligations' does not comply with Article 6(1), there is no breach of the Article if the proceedings before that body are "subject to subsequent control by a judicial body that has full jurisdiction and does provide the guarantees of Article 6(1).

The converse is also true. If a non-judicial authority has power to vary or not apply a decision, the whole process is not compliant.[65] More importantly, in *Ryabykh v Russia* the ECtHR said:[66]

> Article 6(1) secures to everyone the right to have any claim relating to his civil rights and obligations brought before a court or tribunal ... However, that right would be illusory if a Contracting State's domestic legal system allowed a final, binding judicial decision to remain inoperative to the detriment of one party. It would be inconceivable that Article 6(1) should describe in detail procedural guarantees afforded to litigants – proceedings that are fair, public and expeditious – without protecting the implementation

63 Or as Lord Browne-Wilkinson put it in *Barrett v Enfield LBC* [2001] 2 AC 550:

Although the word 'immunity' is sometimes incorrectly used, a holding that it is not fair, just and reasonable to hold liable a particular class of defendants whether generally or in relation to a particular type of activity is not to give immunity from a liability to which the rest of the world is subject. It is a prerequisite to there being any liability in negligence at all that as a matter of policy it is fair, just and reasonable in those circumstances to impose liability in negligence.

64 *Kingsley v UK*, 7 November 2000, [51]. The ECtHR repeated the passage in *Porter v UK*, 8 April 2003, Notice Inadmissible.

65 *Van de Hurk v The Netherlands*, 19 April 1994.

66 *Ryabykh v Russia*, 24 July 2003, [55].

> of judicial decisions; to construe Article 6 as being concerned exclusively with access to a court and the conduct of proceedings would be likely to lead to situations incompatible with the principle of the rule of law which the Contracting States undertook to respect when they ratified the Convention.

This was applied in *Volkova v Russia*[67] where an appeal a year after judgment was held to violate the Convention and in *Popov v Moldova* (No.2), where the court said:[68]

> Legal certainty presupposes respect for the principle of *res judicata* ... that is the principle of the finality of judgments. This principle insists that no party is entitled to seek a review of a final and binding judgment merely for the purpose of obtaining a rehearing and a fresh determination of the case. Higher courts' power of review should be exercised to correct judicial errors and miscarriages of justice, but not to carry out a fresh examination. The review should not be treated as an appeal in disguise, and the mere possibility of there being two views on the subject is not a ground for re-examination. A departure from that principle is justified only when made necessary by circumstances of a substantial and compelling character.

Ryabykh was also applied in *Smarygin v Russia* where a successful supervisory review initiated by the President of the Regional Court was held to violate the requirements for legal certainty.[69]

An appeal court is not allowed to admit fresh evidence where it was reasonably available before the original hearing.[70] So also where the appeal was made by a non-party:[71]

> The right of a litigant to a court would be equally illusory if a Contracting State's legal system allowed a judicial decision which had become final and binding to be quashed by a higher court on an application made by a State official.

The principle of legality also embraces certainty and finality. Its breach may also violate Art. 1 of the First Protocol (the protection of property).[72]

---

67 *Volkova v Russia*, 5 April 2005.

68 *Popov v Moldova* (No 2), 6 December 2005, [45], repeating a passage in *Rosca v Moldova*, 22 March 2005, [25].

69 *Smarygin v Russia*, 1 December 2005. And *See Tregubenko v Ukraine*, 2 November 2004.

70 And see *President of Equatorial Guinea v Royal Bank of Scotland International* [2006] UKPC 7 (Gue).

71 *Ryabykh v Russia*, 24 July 2003, [56].

72 *Asito v Moldova*, 8 November 2005.

Proportionality

There may be two other general ways in which the HRA affects civil litigation. Even if, as I shall argue is possible, almost all the cases where it has been cited would have been decided in the same way without it, that does not end the enquiry. One major difference between the ECHR jurisprudence and domestic interpretation is that under the former, once a right is engaged, it is often necessary to look to the legislative purpose, if only to know the scope of what is proportionate. In domestic law, whether the purpose of the legislation is relevant can itself often be a major debate. But it can now be let in, so to speak, through the backdoor of the Strasbourg jurisprudence.

Both the CPR and the ECHR rest on ideas of *proportionality*. Under the European Convention, the doctrine asks whether the objective of a state's national statute is proportionate to its supposed purpose. I say 'supposed', not in any derogatory sense, but because intent only rarely appears on the face of a statute.[73] Lord Lester has described this method of applying the HRA:[74]

> The first question the courts must ask is: does the legislation interfere with a Convention right? … It is at the second stage, when the Government seeks to justify the interference with a Convention right, under one of the exception clauses, that legislative purpose or intent becomes relevant. It is at that stage the principle of proportionality will be applied.

As Wilson put it in the Canadian context:[75]

> The relevance of legislative purpose or intent arises as the second stage of the inquiry … when a rights violation has already been found to have occurred and the government is seeking to justify the violation on the basis of some overriding social obligation which the legislation is designed to achieve.

Feldman suggested that the case law establishes a series of stages before proportionality comes into play in the Strasbourg jurisprudence. He said these are:[76]

> 1. *Analyse the act, rule or decision which is said to violate a Convention right …*
>
> 2. *Decide whether the act, rule or decision actually interferes with [it] …*

---

73 But see: Klug, 'The Human Rights Act 1998, *Pepper v Hart* and All That', [1999] PL 246; Steyn '*Pepper v Hart*; A Re-examination', (2001) 21 O.J.L.S. 59.

74 Lord Lester, 'The Act of the Possible-Interpreting Statutes under the Human Rights Act' [1998] EHRLR 665 at 674, cited by Lord Steyn in *R v A* (No.2) [2001] UKHL 25, [37].

75 Wilson, 'The Making of a Constitution: Approaches to Judicial Interpretation' [1988] PL 370 at 371–372. She cited *R v Big M Drug Mart* [1985] 1 SCR 295.

76 Feldman 'Proportionality and The Human Rights Act 1998', in *The Principle of Proportionality in the Laws of Europe*, ed Ellis, 1999, p. 117, 122–123, italics in the original. And see Fordham and de la Mere, 'Identifying the Principles of Proportionality', in Jowell and Cooper EDS, *Understanding Human Rights Principles*, 2001, p. 89 et seq.

3. If a Convention right is implicated, assess whether, and if so how, the act, rule or decision in question interferes with the right ...

4. If the act, rule or decision interferes with a Convention right, evaluate any justification which the public authority offers for the interference in terms of the permitted justifications ... At this point proportionality may become an issue in relation to those Convention rights which expressly or impliedly permit interferences ... by showing that the interferences are directed to achieving a legitimate purpose ... and are not disproportionate to that purpose ...

5. Only if the justification ... satisfies any prior conditions for justifiability ... do we reach the proportionality test.

He reminded us that proportionality[77] 'is the final factor the Strasbourg authorities take into account in determining whether an interference with a right is necessary', and added:

> The question is whether the interference is disproportionate to the legitimate aim pursued. If it is not proportionate, it is not necessary, and the justification fails.

As Sedley LJ said:[78]

> In essence it amounts to this: a measure which interferes with a Community or human right must not only be authorized by law but must correspond to a pressing social need and go no further than is strictly necessary in a pluralistic society to achieve its permitted purpose; or, more shortly, must be appropriate and necessary to its legitimate aim.[79]

Thus, in *Air Canada v UK*[80] the ECtHR upheld non-criminal proceedings *in rem* against an aircraft (that is, its seizure) by Commissioners of Customs and Excise under powers designed to encourage carriers to take effective measures to prevent the illegal import of drugs.

Within the CPR, proportionality is wider in its possible application.[81] It may apply to case management, costs, interim remedies, and disobedience to court orders.

---

77 Quoting Harris, O'Boyle and Warbrick, *Law of the European Convention on Human Rights*, 1995, at p. 300.

78 *B v Secretary of State for the Home Department* [2000] HRLR 439.

79 He cited: Schwarze, *European Public Law*, chap. 5; Tridimas, *The General Principles of EC Law*, 89–93; Lester and Pannick, *Human Rights Law and Practice*, para. 3.10; Grosz, Beatson and Duffy, *Human Rights*, 112–4; Starmer, *European Human Rights Law*, 169–180; Mountfield and Wadham, *The Human Rights Act 1998*, pp. 13 et seq.

80 *Air Canada v UK*, 5 May 1995.

81 Laws, 'Is the High Court the *Guardian* of Fundamental Constitutional Rights?', [1993] PL 59, at 72, suggested that proportionality involves a discussion of merits and, at 75, this involves knowing the reasons for decisions. See further below at p. 78.

The obligation to act proportionally is express.[82] Reflecting the bias of the CPR the emphasis is on money, but it accommodates other considerations. Having required the court to decide cases justly, it says:

> (2) Dealing with a case justly includes, so far as is practicable –
>
> (c) dealing with the case in ways which are proportionate –
>
> (i) to the amount of money involved;
>
> (ii) to the importance of the case;
>
> (iii) to the complexity of the issues; and
>
> (iv) to the financial position of each party.

Beyond this, proportionality prevents the court looking to more general considerations. For example, in considering what to do about breach of an 'unless order', the court should not have regard to its own dignity. Thus, in *Skalka v Poland* the ECtHR said:[83]

> The phrase 'authority of the judiciary' includes, in particular, the notion that the courts are, and are accepted by the public at large as being the proper forum for the settlement of legal disputes and for the determination of a person's guilt or innocence on a criminal charge. What is at stake as regards protection of the authority of the judiciary, is the confidence which the courts in a democratic society must inspire in the accused, as far as criminal proceedings are concerned, and also in the public at large.

In *Balogh v St. Albans Crown Court* Stephenson LJ explained, referring to contempt powers which are:[84]

> To be used reluctantly but fearlessly when, and only when, it is necessary to prevent justice being obstructed or undermined – even by a practical joker. That is not because judges, jurors, witnesses and officers of the court take themselves seriously: it is because justice, whose servants they are, must be taken seriously in a civilized society if the rule of law is to be maintained.

---

82 In *Maltez v Lewis*, 27 April 1999, One party complained that the other had a leader whereas she did not. Neuberger J thought it was also envisaged by CPR Part 1.2(2)(a), that is to say, ensuring 'the parties are on an equal footing'. He held the rule does not extend to depriving a party of its fundamental right to be represented by counsel or solicitors of its choice. See further p. 145 below and also *Piglowska v Piglowski* [1999] 1 WLR 1360 where the House of Lords was concerned that the costs of ancillary proceedings had eaten the whole of the matrimonial assets.

83 *Skalka v Poland*, 27 May 2003 [40].

84 *Balogh v St. Albans Crown Court* [1975] QB 73.

Sales and Hooper have examined the Convention's use of proportionality. They argued that:[85]

> a law's fact sensitivity is the degree to which the outcome of applying it depends on the detailed factual context in which it is applied ... Fact sensitive laws are generally more capable of resulting in proportionate interferences with Convention rights.

This tells us that generally the discretions in the CPR are compliant, not that proportionality is the same between the two instruments.

Art.6 itself is constructed differently from later Convention rights, the so-called 'political rights'.[86] In each of Art. 8 (Right to respect for private and family life), Art. 9 (Freedom of thought, conscience and religion), Art. 10 (Freedom of expression), and Art. 11 (Freedom of assembly and association) a general right in clause one is qualified by limitations in clause 2. On its face, the first sentence of Art. 6 does not limit the scope of the rights it gives, but the language is elastic. As the court put it in *Golder v UK*:[87]

> Art.6(1) does not state a right of access to the courts or tribunals in express terms. It enunciates rights which are distinct but stem from the same basic idea and which, taken together, make up a single right not specifically defined in the narrower sense of the term ... It would be inconceivable ... that Art. 6(1) should describe in detail the procedural guarantees afforded to parties in a pending lawsuit and should not first protect that which alone makes it in fact possible to benefit from such guarantees, that is, access to a court. The fair, public and expeditious characteristics of judicial proceedings are of no value at all if there are no judicial proceedings.

And in *Ashingdane v UK*:[88]

---

85 Sales and Hooper, 'Proportionality and the Form of Law' (2003) 119 LQR 426, cf. Marshall, 'Things we can say about rights', [2001] PL 207 speaking of 'simple (or relatively simple) and complex rights'. And see Thompson, 'Community law and the limits of deference', [2005] EHRLR 243, discussing proportionality in the context of EU law.

86 Laws LJ in *Carson*, [34].

87 *Golder v UK*, 21 February 1975, [38] and [35]. It added at [36]:

Taking all the preceding considerations together, it follows that the right of access constitutes an element which is inherent in the right stated by Art.6(1). This is not an extensive interpretation forcing new obligations on the Contracting States: it is based on the very terms of the first sentence of Art.6(1) read in its context and having regard to the object and purpose of the Convention, a lawmaking treaty.

88 *Ashingdane v UK*, 28 May 1985, [57]. *Ashingdane* has been followed in, among other cases: *Lithgow v UK*, 8 July 1986, [194]; *Bellet v France*, 4 December 1995; and *Fayed v UK*, 21 September 1994, [65]; and also by the Court of Appeal in *J and PM Dockeray (a firm) v Secretary of State for the Environment, Food and Rural Affairs* [2002] EWHC 420 (Admin) (14 days was sufficient in which to lodge an appeal against a valuation of cattle culled in a foot and mouth outbreak).

> Certainly, the right of access to the courts is not absolute but may be subject to limitations; these are permitted by implication since the right of access 'by its very nature calls for regulation by the State, regulation which may vary in time and in place according to the needs and resources of the community and of individuals' ... In laying down such regulation, the Contracting States enjoy a certain margin of appreciation. While the final decision as to observance of the Convention's requirements rests with the Court, it is no part of the Court's function to substitute for the assessment of the national authorities any other assessment of what might be the best policy in this field ... Nonetheless, the limitations applied must not restrict or reduce the access left to the individual in such a way or to such an extent that the very essence of the right is impaired.

In *Lithgow v UK* it added:[89]

> A limitation will not be compatible with Art. 6 if it does not pursue a legitimate aim and if there is not a reasonable relationship of proportionality between the means employed and the aim sought to be achieved.

The court concluded in *Cavanilles v Spain*:[90]

> Such limitations will not be compatible with art 6 (1) if they do not pursue a legitimate aim or if there is not a reasonable relationship of proportionality between the means employed and the aim sought to be achieved.

Laws LJ put it this way:[91]

> It may be said that this is so by force of the Strasbourg court's doctrine of 'margin of appreciation'. I prefer to say that in the real world there are inevitably shades and degrees of every one of the variables in art 6: fairness, publicity, delay, independence, impartiality.

Brooke LJ summarized the effect of the Strasbourg jurisprudence on the CPR saying:[92]

> Provided that judges make their decisions in these cases within the general framework provided by rr.3.9 and 1.1, they are unlikely to fall foul of the ECHR in this regard.

One is left to wonder what he meant by 'fall foul of the ECHR'. Did he mean that it is the job of the British judge to seek a meaning that would be immune from challenge

89 *Lithgow v UK*, 8 July 1986, [194 (c)].

90 *Cavanilles v Spain*, 28 October 1998, [44], cited in *J and PM Dockeray (a firm) v Secretary of State for the Environment, Food and Rural Affairs* [2002] EWHC 420 (Admin). And see *Immobiliare Saffi v Italy*, 28 July 1999, [49]. It was speaking specifically of permitted interference with the right to property in Art. 1 of the 1st Protocol.

91 *Carson* [35].

92 *Woodhouse v Consignia* [2002] EWCA Civ 275, [43]-[44]. He cited: *Ashingdane v UK*; and *Tinnelly v UK*. He himself cited the passage in *Price v Price (trading as Poppyland Headware)* [2003] EWCA Civ 888, [34].

in the ECtHR? Or, by contrast, merely that the court should seek to comply with its obligations under the HRA?

To return to the ECtHR, in *Andersson v Sweden* the ECtHR said:[93]

> A law which confers a discretion is not in itself inconsistent with this requirement, provided that the scope of the discretion and the manner of its exercise are indicated with sufficient clarity, having regard to the legitimate aim in question, to give the individual adequate protection against arbitrary interference.

In the *Sunday Times* it had began to clarify a number of issues. First, the court said where the Convention uses the expression 'necessary in a democratic society' it implies a 'pressing social need' something indispensable between and useful.[94] Secondly, it said practice in other states may be relevant but, particularly where there is a margin of appreciation, it cannot be conclusive.[95] Thirdly, the court concluded, whether any interference is Convention compliant depends on whether it corresponds to a 'pressing social need', whether it is proportionate to a legitimate aim, and whether the reasons given by the national authorities to justify it are 'relevant and sufficient'.[96] We may also note that it said where the Convention uses the expression 'prescribed by law' it includes unwritten law, including the common law.[97] What is required is that:[98]

> The law must be adequately accessible: the citizen must be able to have an indication that is adequate in the circumstances of the legal rules applicable to a given case. Secondly, a norm cannot be regarded as a 'law' unless it is formulated with sufficient precision to enable the citizen to regulate his conduct: he must be able – if need be with appropriate advice – to foresee, to a degree that is reasonable in the circumstances, the consequences which a given action may entail.

Most, but perhaps not all, of the common law is Convention compliant.

Some General Problems with the Central Question

There are at least seven difficulties. Because both the CPR and ECHR have been held to be flexible it is not always easy to see the effect of one on the other or how far either is affected by wider shifts in approaches to disputes and litigation.

---

93 *Andersson v Sweden*, 25 February 1992, [75], cited in *Tolstoy Miloslavsky v UK*, 13 July 1995, [37]. And see: *Chorherr v Austria*, 25 August 1993; and, *Domenichini v Italy*, 15 November 1996.

94 *Sunday Times* 26 April 1979, [59].

95 *Sunday Times*, [61]. It cited *Case 'Relating to Certain Aspects of the Laws on the Use of Languages in Education in Belgium' v Belgium (Merits)*, 23 July 1968.

96 *Sunday Times*, [62].

97 *Sunday Times*, [47].

98 *Sunday Times*, [49].

Both the CPR and the ECHR contain the nugget of an idea, but in any particular case each may be too elastic to expose any difference between them. The decisions on the CPR establish that in the case of doubt it is necessary to refer back to its original text, rather than rely on precedent.[99] It is too soon to say whether the interpretation of the CPR will vary over time. The idea seems to be that the decisions on the CPR are either illustrative of the meaning of the text (each illustration carrying the same validity as any other) or a decision is used as a means of explaining (commonly, but not always, for the benefit of practitioners) the way things should be done.[100] On some occasions, the court, even the Court of Appeal, uses a judgment to indicate future lines of development that may, should or will be taken up by the Civil Procedure Rules Committee.[101] No doubt also, in private, judges raise problems they find in the rules with each other and with the Head of Civil Justice. Certainly, the rules and their associated Practice Directions are frequently updated.[102]

As regards the ECHR we cannot do better than to cite Lord Bingham in *Brown v Stott*. He said:[103]

> In interpreting the convention, as any other treaty, it is generally to be assumed that the parties have included the terms which they wished to include and on which they were able to agree, omitting other terms which they did not wish to include or on which they were not able to agree ... This does not mean that nothing can be implied into the convention. The language of the convention is for the most part so general that some implication of terms is necessary, and the case law of the European Court shows that the court has been willing to imply terms into the convention when it was judged necessary or plainly right to do so. But the process of implication is one to be carried out with caution, if the risk is to be averted that the contracting parties may, by judicial interpretation, become bound by obligations which they did not expressly accept and might not have been willing to accept. As an important constitutional instrument the convention is to be seen as a 'living tree capable of growth and expansion within its natural limits',[104] but those limits will often call for very careful consideration.

---

99 See, e.g. *Hamblin v Field*, 11 April 2000; *Austin v Newcastle Chronicle and Journal* [2001] EWCA Civ 834; and, *Audergon v La Baguette* [2002] EWCA Civ 10, [107]. Associated with this are the attempts reduce the numbers of cases cited and reported, below p. 91.

100 E.g. *Tanfern v Cameron-Macdonald* [2000] 1 WLR 1311, describing the meaning of or the then new restraints on appeal, *Scribes West v Anstalt* [2004] EWCA Civ 835, describing the changes to be introduced the next day to the Appeals Practice Direction, and *Bhamjee v Forsdick* (No.2) [2003] EWCA Civ 1113, discussed below p. 126, describing vexatious proceedings and civil restraint orders.

101 See, e.g. *Jolly v Jay* [2002] EWCA Civ 277, [41].

102 The 41st Update was published in March 2006 (print) and April 2006 (web).

103 *Brown v Stott* [2003] 1 AC 681 (PC).

104 The quotation is from Lord Sankey LC in *Edwards v Attorney General for Canada* [1930] AC 124 at 136.

He seemed to want to approach the Convention as he would any contract or international agreement.[105] He was only partly right. The Human Rights Convention is not like any other treaty. The Court at Strasbourg has recognized rights which those who signed it could not have imagined, and it has done so in recognition of changes in the social and cultural makeup within member states. So too, the ECHR cases establish that the Convention text is flexible.[106] To take examples from outside the scope of our enquiry, in 1950 no one could have anticipated the meanings now given to Arts 2 and 3, nor the Convention's recognition of the sexual revolution that has taken place the last 50 years: in *Tyrer v UK* the ECHR said[107] 'the Convention is a living instrument which ... must be interpreted in the light of present day conditions'. The Strasbourg court looks, so to speak, to the intent of the successors of those who signed the original instrument.

Secondly, as we have seen, s. 3(1) of the HRA says: 'So far as it is possible to do so, primary legislation and subordinate legislation must be read and given effect in a way which is compatible with the Convention rights'. Many see a link between the section and s. 4. This permits the court to make a declaration of incompatibility. S. 4 is said to preserve Parliamentary sovereignty. Maybe it does but instances where the British government has not responded to an adverse finding at Strasbourg or a British court making such a declaration are few and far between. In practice Parliament is not free to ignore human rights law.[108] In *R v A* (No.2) Lord Steyn explained the scope of s. 3:[109]

> In accordance with the will of Parliament as reflected in s. 3 it will sometimes be necessary to adopt an interpretation which linguistically may appear strained. The techniques to be used will not only involve the reading down of express language in a statute but also the implication of provisions.

---

105 See Berman, 'International Treaties and British Statutes', [2005] 26 SLR 1.

106 See, e.g. *Tyrer v UK*, 25 April 1978; *Olsson v Sweden* (No.1), 24 March 1988; *Rees v UK*, 17 October 1986; *Goodwin v UK*, 11 July 2002.

107 *Tyrer v UK*, 25 April 1978, [31].

108 Leach,'Beyond the Bug River-a New Dawn for Redress Before the European Court of Human Rights?', [2005] EHRLR, discussed what the ECtHR can do beyond a declaration.

109 *R v A* (No.2) [2001] UKHL 25, [44] and see Lord Hope, [58] and Lord Hutton, [162]. S. 3 was applied in *R (on the application of Middleton) v West Somerset Coroner* [2004] UKHL 10 to modify the Coroners' legislation. Ekins, 'A critique of radical approaches to rights consistent statutory interpretation', EHRLR [2003] 641, was critical. And see: Young, '*Ghaidan v Godin-Mendoza*: avoiding the deference trap', PL [2005] 23, discussing *Ghaidan v Godin-Mendoza* [2004] UKHL 30; Starmer, 'The Human Rights Act: review of the year: 2004-2005', [2006] EHRLR 1, noting '"the Convention rights" referred to in s.3 HRA are not those Convention rights enforceable under s.6, but the rights enforceable against the United Kingdom in international law', and, Kavanagh, 'Unlocking the Human Rights Act: the "radical" approach to section 3(1) revisited', [2005] EHRLR 259.

But, as he said extra-judicially,[110] 'Inherent in the language of s.3(1), and in particular the words "so far as it is possible to do so", is a limit beyond which the courts may not use the interpretative power'. Or, as Lord Woolf put it in *Poplar Housing and Regeneration Community Association v Donoghue*:[111]

> It is difficult to overestimate the importance of Section 3 ... Subject to the section not requiring the court to go beyond that which is possible, it is mandatory in its terms ... when Section 3 applies, the courts have to adjust their traditional role in relation to interpretation so as to give effect to the direction contained in Section 3. It is as though legislation which predates the Human Rights Act 1998 and conflicts with the Convention has to be treated as being subsequently amended to incorporate the language of Section 3 ... Unless the legislation would otherwise be in breach of the Convention Section 3 can be ignored (so courts should always first ascertain whether, absent Section 3, there would be any breach of the Convention) ... If the court has to rely on Section 3 it should limit the extent of the modified meaning to that which is necessary to achieve compatibility ... Section 3 does not entitle the court to legislate (its task is still one of interpretation).

And,

> The most difficult task which courts face is distinguishing between legislation and interpretation. Here practical experience of seeking to apply Section 3 will provide the best guide. However, if it is necessary in order to obtain compliance to radically alter the effect of the legislation this will be an indication that more than interpretation is involved.

Two cases may help, *Cachia v Faluyi* and *Goode v Martin.*[112] *Cachia v Faluyi* was concerned with s. 2(3) of the Fatal Accidents Act 1976 which provided: 'Not more than one action shall lie for and in respect of the same subject matter of complaint.' It was held that, given the injunction in s. 3 of the HRA, the word 'action' in the section meant 'served process' rather than 'initiated process', because the purpose of the section was to prevent a defendant having to respond to two separate claims. The new interpretation gave effect to that purpose and was proportionate.

In *Goode v Martin* the issue was transformed in the Court of Appeal. There it concerned the power in CPR Part 17 to allow an amendment to a claim after the end of a limitation period. On its face the rule seemed confined to issues alleged

---

110 Lord Steyn, 'Deference: a tangled story,' PL [2005] 346.

111 *Poplar Housing and Regeneration Community Association v Donoghue* [2002] QB 48. And see: Lord Lester, 'Developing Constitutional Principles of Public Law', [2001] PL 68; and Marshall, 'The lynchpin of parliamentary intention: lost, stolen or strained?', PL [2003] 236.

112 *Cachia v Faluyi* [2001] EWCA Civ 998, esp [17]-[20] and *Goode v Martin* [2001] EWCA Civ 1899. This last was applied in *Hemmingway v Roddam (a firm)* [2003] EWCA Civ 1342 and *Mersey Docks Property Holdings v Birse Construction* [2004] EWHC 3264 (TCC). It is surprising that the Rules Committee has not adjusted the wording of the rule to bring it in line with its HRA meaning. And see Scott, 'Access to justice; Limitations; Right to fair trial; Statutory interpretation. Convention compatible interpretation of procedural legislation', (2002) 21 CJQ 88.

in the claimant's statement of case so that it excluded a claim based on a pleaded defence. The court held there was no legislative purpose, or none that advanced justice, in the apparent meaning, but that by applying HRA s. 3 a just meaning could be achieved. The limitation period of itself impeded access to the court but, by a strained interpretation,[113] the court found a meaning that did not. A claim based on facts alleged in the defence was allowed. As Brooke LJ said:[114]

> We now possess more tools for enabling us to do justice than were available before April 1999. Since then, the CPR and the provisions of the 1998 Act have come into force. By the former we must seek to give effect to the overriding objective of dealing with cases justly when we interpret any rule (see CPR 1.2(b)). By the latter we must read and give effect to subordinate legislation, so far as it is possible to do so, in a way which is compatible with the convention rights set out in Sch. 1 to the Act (see S. 3(1) of the 1998 Act). It is commonplace that the claimant must not be impeded in her right of access to a court for the determination of her civil rights unless any hindrance to such access can be justified in a way recognised by the relevant Strasbourg jurisprudence.

Golder v UK[115] is the most important of these. There the ECtHR held 'The fair, public and expeditious characteristics of judicial proceedings are of no value at all if there are no judicial proceedings' but 'the right of access to the courts is not absolute'. In *TP and KM v UK*[116] it amplified this saying:

> It may be subject to legitimate restrictions, for example, statutory time-limits or prescription periods, security for costs orders, regulations concerning minors and persons of unsound mind. Where the individual's access is limited either by operation of law or in fact, the Court will examine whether the limitation imposed impaired the essence of the right and in particular whether it pursued a legitimate aim and there was a reasonable relationship of proportionality between the means employed and the aim sought to be achieved.

The third general problem for our enquiry is that, although I have articulated principles I see underpinning the case law, I acknowledge that hitherto this is not the way we have done things. Hitherto the English common law has argued from the particular to the particular. Now, increasingly its mode of argument, and not only in human rights matters, is to begin with some general statement. The change is subtle but profound. Probably, it is at least in part caused by a variety of factors: by what

---

113 See *R v A* (No.2) [2001] UKHL 25, [44].

114 *Goode v Martin* [2001] EWCA Civ 1899, [35]-[36]. *Smithkline Beecham v Horne-Roberts* [2001] EWCA Civ 2006 and *Kesslar v Moore and Tibbits* [2004] EWCA Civ 1551 are possible additional examples but in both these the Court of Appeal seemed to prefer to interpret the rules on substitution of parties (Part 19.5) with the aid of the Overriding Objective rather than s. 3.

115 *Golder v UK*, 21 February 1975, [35], [38]. It was not expressly mentioned in the judgments in either case (although it does appear in the list of cited cases in *Cachia v Faluyi*).

116 *TP and KM v UK*, 10 May 2001, [98].

Lord Steyn called[117] 'an orgy of statutes', by the efforts of the courts in Brussels and Strasbourg and by the contemporary fixation with all things modern.

Fourthly, connected with this, in some rather indeterminate way, both the CPR and the HRA herald a new era of open judicial law making, the CPR out of the wide discretions it bestows and the HRA because of the broad language of the ECHR it has imported. The mechanisms are unclear and it is too much to say these alone have caused the new law making.[118] Nevertheless, if they are not the only source of this novel assertion of judicial power, they have helped the seeds to germinate. One problem with this new way of arguing is precisely that it is different. In the old way of course there was judicial creativity and to an extent that was sometimes denied.[119] But it was a creativity that was controlled by technique engendered by law's discipline. In the new way, discipline has yet to be found.

The fifth difficulty for our enquiry arises from the role of the Strasbourg institutions. It is supervisory.[120] They ensure compliance with minimum standards. We should expect, and we shall see it is indeed the case, that there are numerous occasions where the UK courts exceed those minima, and by a margin! For example, after the ECtHR endorsed the British search order in *Chappell v UK*,[121] the British courts and now the CPR have added further safeguards. The question arises whether compliance is caused by the Convention or HRA or whether British judges have their own ideas of fairness uninfluenced by such external considerations. Lord Hope has said:[122]

> The requirement of procedural fairness is part of the common law. It is a requirement that applies to bodies in this jurisdiction which have the characteristics of a court ... Common law procedural fairness as such is not a convention requirement. But the convention can and does inform the common law, and the common law informs the convention.

117 Lord Steyn, 'Dynamic Interpretation Amidst an Orgy of Statutes', [2004] EHRLR 245, taking his phrase from Calabresi, *A Common Law for the Age of Statutes*, 1982, p. 1.

118 Among other factors is the novel willingness of the court to permit, and even encourage, non-party interveners, e.g. *Halsey v Milton Keynes General NHS Trust*; *Steel v Joy and Halliday* [2004] EWCA (Civ) 576 where The Law Society, the Civil Mediation Council, the ADR Group and CEDR each made submissions. And see p. 36 n. 136. On occasion, the Court of Appeal has assumed the role of a mini parliament behaving like a Standing Committee on a Private Bill rather than an adjudicator (as to this see generally Blackburn and Kenyon, 2nd edn, *Parliament*). By indulging in this kind of law-making the judges make it harder to preserve the separation of powers. If they do the work of politicians, politicians will seek to do theirs. For an alternative view see Arshi and O'Cinneide, 'Third-party interventions: the public interest reaffirmed', [2004] PL 69. In any event, it gives the ordinary courts in England some of the characteristics of some civilian Constitutional Courts.

119 Sometimes it was said that judges do not make law. But, to take one example, no one ever denied Dicey's view that 'with us the constitution is judge-made'.

120 *Turek v Slovakia*, 14 February 2006, [114].

121 *Chappell v UK*, 30 March 1989.

122 *R (on the application of Smith) v Parole Board*: *R (on the application of West) v Parole Board* [2005] UKHL 1, [74].

A further difficulty for our analysis is that at times the British courts cite ECtHR decisions, but it is not always clear that they do so in order to supplement a conclusion rather than decorate their reasons. The injunction in HRA s. 2 to 'have regard to' the Strasbourg jurisprudence does not of itself require that British judgments make express reference to that material if in doing so it would add nothing except embellishment. Nor are our problems helped when they ignore relevant material from that source. An example may be *ex parte Lightfoot* which I discuss later.[123] I argue that relevant Strasbourg case law was not mentioned.

The case also raised an even more difficult question. *Lightfoot* was a decision of the Court of Appeal. It ought to be binding. What then if, again as I argue, subsequent Strasbourg case law is incompatible with such a binding decision in Britain. Were it not for a curious decision in the House of Lords I would suggest that s. 2 provides a further exception to those set out in *Young v Bristol Aeroplane* and the later cases.[124] In *Price v Leeds City Council* the House sat with seven members. Lord Bingham, in a speech with which all the others agreed on this point, said:[125]

> The mandatory duty imposed on domestic courts by Section 2 of the 1998 Act is to take into account any judgment of the Strasbourg Court and any opinion of the Commission. Thus, they are not strictly required to follow Strasbourg rulings, as they are bound by Section 3(1) of the European Communities Act 1972 and as they are bound by the rulings of superior courts in the domestic curial hierarchy ... That Court is the highest judicial authority on the interpretation of those rights, and the effectiveness of the Convention as an international instrument depends on the loyal acceptance by member states of the principles it lays down.

And:

> The effective implementation of the Convention depends on constructive collaboration between the Strasbourg court and the national courts of member states. The Strasbourg court authoritatively expounds the interpretation of the rights embodied in the Convention and its protocols, as it must if the Convention is to be uniformly understood by all member states. But in its decisions on particular cases the Strasbourg court accords a margin of appreciation, often generous, to the decisions of national authorities and attaches much importance to the peculiar facts of the case. Thus, it is for national authorities, including national courts particularly, to decide in the first instance how the principles expounded

123 Below p. 111.

124 *Young v Bristol Aeroplane* [1944] KB 718 (CA). *Young* said that, subject to some exceptions which it sets out, the Court of Appeal is bound by its own decisions. The other cases include: *Boys v Chaplin* [1968] 2 QB 1; *Davis v Johnson* [1979] AC 264; *Limb v Union Jack Removals* [1998] 1 WLR 1354; and now, *Cave v Robinson Jarvis and Rolf* (*a firm*) [2001] EWCA Civ 245 reversed on other grounds at [2002] UKHL 18. Prime and Scanlan, in their otherwise helpful discussion, '*Stare Decisis* and the Court of Appeal; Judicial Confusion and Judicial Reform?' [2004] 23 CJQ 212, do not discuss this s. 2 point.

125 *Lambeth London Borough Council v Kay*; *Price v Leeds City Council* [2006] UKHL 10, [28] and [40]-[45], and see Lord Nicolls, [50], Lord Hope, [62], Lord Scott, [121], Lord Walker, [177], Lady Hale, [178], Lord Brown, [213].

> in Strasbourg should be applied in the special context of national legislation, law, practice and social and other conditions. It is by the decisions of national courts that the domestic standard must be initially set, and to those decisions the ordinary rules of precedent should apply.

But, he added:

> Adherence to precedent … has been a cornerstone of our legal system … [A] degree of certainty is best achieved by adhering, even in the Convention context, to our rules of precedent. It will, of course be the duty of judges to review Convention arguments addressed to them, and if they consider a binding precedent to be, or possibly to be, inconsistent with Strasbourg authority, they may express their views and give leave to appeal ... Leap-frog appeals may be appropriate. In this way, in my opinion, they discharge their duty under the 1998 Act. But they should follow the binding precedent.

It is difficult to see how merely facilitating an appeal is compatible with 'the loyal acceptance by member states of the principles' the Strasbourg court lays down nor how it fully takes these decisions into account. We have seen that in *Roche v UK* the court said:[126] that 'Where … the superior national courts have analysed in a comprehensive and convincing manner the precise nature of the impugned restriction, on the basis of the relevant Convention case-law and principles drawn therefrom'. The resurrection of the domestic doctrine of precedent cannot aid this analysis. Nor does it advance the ECtHR position in *Pizzati v Italy* that[127] 'The machinery of complaint to the Court is … subsidiary to national systems safeguarding human rights'.

Hard cases, it is said, make hard law. This was a hard case. It concerned a type of action that is very common in county courts – possession actions. The House was anxious to provide a simple, relatively inexpensive procedure for local authorities seeking to re-claim possession of land. It was faced with a decision of its own which it was argued was not compatible with a subsequent decision at Strasbourg. The rationale of *Price* is understandable. So also is the desire to create as much certainty as possible. Lord Bingham's statement leaves no room for doubt: the doctrine of precedent prevails over s. 2 of the HRA.

Nevertheless, there are difficulties.

1. There is no discussion of the relevance, if any, of s. 3 that statutes should be

---

126 *Roche v UK*, 19 October 2005 [GC], [120]. But see the dissenting opinion of Judge Loucaides joined by Judges Rozakis, Zupančič, Strážnická, Casadevall, Thomassen, Maruste and Traja.

127 *Pizzati v Italy* 29 March 2006 [GC], [37].

interpreted as far as possible to avoid conflict with the Convention.

2. There is no discussion of the flexibility that the ECtHR itself sees in the Convention and particularly what happens where there is a later Strasbourg decision.[128]
3. There is no discussion of the possible constitutional nature of the HRA.[129]
4. In the older sense of the expression there is no clear authority on the precedent value of Privy Council decisions in devolution matters. In many of its HRA cases, the House of Lords has cited non-binding decisions from Scottish courts, from itself in Scottish cases and from the Privy Council in both devolution, and Commonwealth appeals. In the Privy Council its members have also been prepared to use appeals from other United Kingdom jurisdictions to state and correct its own statements of English law.[130] *Price* creates uncertainty as to that practice and extends the possibility of different meanings of Convention rights in different parts of the United Kingdom.[131] It is possible that Lord Bingham can take comfort from the CRA, 2005. S. 41 provides:

> (2) A decision of the Supreme Court on appeal from a court of any part of the United Kingdom, other than a decision on a devolution matter, is to be regarded as the decision of a court of that part of the United Kingdom.
>
> (3) A decision of the Supreme Court on a devolution matter –
>
> (a) is not binding on that Court when making such a decision;
>
> (b) otherwise, is binding in all legal proceedings.

This preserves the previous arrangements for the final appeal court (the old Judicial Committee of the House of Lords in its various guises) for the jurisdictions of the Kingdom. As far as I know it is the only attempt ever at enacting the doctrine of precedent.[132] Nevertheless, the possibility of different meanings of Convention

128 As Potter LJ pointed out in *Han v Commissioners of Customs and Excise*; *Martins v Commissioners of Customs and Excise*; *Morris v Commissioners of Customs and Excise* [2001] EWCA Civ 1040 there is no doctrine of precedent at Strasbourg.

129 Masterman, 'Taking the Strasbourg Jurisprudence into Account: Developing a "Municipal Law of Human Rights" Under the Human Rights Act', (2005) 54 ICLQ 907, and cases cited there. And see: Masterman, 'Section 2(1) of the Human Rights Act 1998: Binding domestic courts to Strasbourg?' [2004] PL 725.

130 *Attorney General for Jersey v Holley* [2005] UKPC 23. Lord Hope said on behalf of the majority 'This appeal, being heard by an enlarged board of nine members, is concerned to resolve [a] conflict and clarify definitively the present state of English law, and hence Jersey law, on this important subject'. The Board sat with 5 members who also sat in *Price*. There were three dissents but none on this point.

131 A majority found different meanings in Scotland and England in *Attorney-General's Reference* (No. 2 of 2001) [2003] UKHL 68. The House sat with 9 members.

132 It is a nice question whether this affects the obligation in s. 6 for public authorities, including courts, to comply with the Convention. I hazard the view that it will not because the HRA is something like the 1972 ECA. For that, not only is there no doctrine of implied repeal,

rights in different parts of the United Kingdom remains. It is disturbing. So also, it may be that subs.(3)(b) will cause problems in relation to the obligation to 'have regard' to the Strasbourg jurisprudence in s. 2 of the HRA.

5. As we shall see in *Porter v Magill*[133] the House of Lords adopted with a minor modification a test for judicial bias suggested by Lord Phillips in the Court of Appeal *in re Medicaments and Related Classes of Goods* (2)[134] in defiance of the then existing House of Lords authority in *R v Gough*.[135] If Lord Bingham is right the law of bias is in disarray.[136]
6. Lord Bingham cited Lord Hailsham LC in *Broome v Cassell* as saying 'in legal matters, some degree of certainty is at least as valuable a part of justice as perfection'.[137] But in that case the Court of Appeal described a previous decision of the House as 'unworkable'. Here there was no such conflict. If a lower court departs from an otherwise binding authority it does so, not on the basis, to use Lord Hailsham's phase, that it 'disagreed with the earlier decision' but because in the light of a Strasbourg decision it thinks it is no longer good law. That does not undermine certainty any more than that implied by the enactment of the HRA.
7. The invitation to facilitate an appeal does not mean that an appeal is inevitable. If it is the Court of Appeal that issues the invitation and it is not accepted, a further binding but incompatible authority will be added to the case law.
8. The decision is also an invitation to add to expense. In *Broome v Cassell* the House was concerned that the approach of the Court of Appeal, in Lord Reid's words, 'has greatly increased the expense to which the parties to this case have been put' and to complete the quotation from Lord Hailsham of which Lord Bingham gives part:

> Litigants would not have known where they stood. None could have reached finality short of the House of Lords, and, meantime, the task of their professional advisers of advising them either as to their rights, or as to the probable cost of obtaining or defending them, would have been, quite literally, impossible. Whatever the merits,

---

it is very doubtful if any partial express repeal can be successful. With the HRA my view is that only any partial repeal must be express but the doctrine of implied repeal, beyond any allowable derogation, does not apply. The reason is the same as with the ECA. The schemes are international and the UK is either or out.

133 *Porter v Magill* [2001] UKHL 67.

134 *Re Medicaments and Related Classes of Goods* (2) [2001] 1 WLR 700. Contrary to Lord Bingham's view it is probably the HRA and the recognition of changing fairness that enabled him to depart from an otherwise binding authority.

135 *R v Gough* [1993] AC 646.

136 In the House of Lords *Wilson v First County Trust* (No 2) [2003] UKHL 40 is odd, and possibly unique: neither the appellant nor the respondent appeared or were represented. The Secretary of State was joined in the Court of Appeal and there was a friend of the court and three interveners. On Lord Bingham's view it could not become a binding authority because there was no decision between the parties, in which case what was the House doing?

137 *Broome v Cassell* [1972] AC 1027, and see Lord Reid in the same case.

> chaos would have reigned until the dispute was settled, and, in legal matters, some degree of certainty is at least as valuable a part of justice as perfection.

The last word on what the Convention means is at Strasbourg. The sooner the House of Lords, or the Supreme Court, revisits this anomaly the better. Among other things it gives no meaning to Lord Slynn in either *Alconbury*:[138]

> Although the Human Rights Act 1998 does not provide that a national court is bound by these decisions it is obliged to take account of them so far as they are relevant. In the absence of some special circumstances it seems to me that the court should follow any clear and constant jurisprudence of the European Court of Human Rights. If it does not do so there is at least a possibility that the case will go to that court, which is likely in the ordinary case to follow its own constant jurisprudence.

Or *Amin*:[139]

> In my opinion, even if the United Kingdom courts are only to take account of the Strasbourg Court decisions and are not strictly bound by them … where the Court has laid down principles ... United Kingdom courts should follow what the Court has said. If they do not do so without good reason the dissatisfied litigant has a right to go to Strasbourg where existing jurisprudence is likely to be followed.

Lord Hope in *Attorney-General's Reference* (No. 2 of 2001) is difficult to understand. He held that there is an 'unfortunate' divergence of view between the two jurisdictions but said:[140]

> The right of application to the European Court under article 34 … by persons claiming to be the victim of a violation of the Convention rights has not been abolished ... The last word as to its meaning must, of course, lie with Strasbourg. The doors of that court remain open to those who believe that, as a result of the decision in this case, they have not been provided in this jurisdiction with an effective domestic remedy.

The truth is that, although no doubt all legal systems strive for consistency, it is folly to assume they always succeed or that they should. We may note that the Grand Chamber in *Pizzati v Italy*[141] said it 'welcomes the Court of Cassation's efforts to bring its decisions into line with European case-law' by its 'departure from precedent'. In both the fields with which we are concerned there are inconsistencies, sometimes even in the judgments of the same judge. The broad ways in which the rules are expressed and the novelties of the ground they cover

---

138 *R (on the application of Alconbury Developments) v Secretary of State for the Environment, Transport and the Regions* [2001] UKHL 23, [26], cited by Laws LJ in *Carson v Secretary of State for Work and Pensions* [2003] EWCA Civ 797, [40].

139 *R (on the application of Amin) v Secretary of State for the Home Department* [2003] UKHL 51, [44].

140 At [52], [108].

141 *Pizzati v Italy* 29 March 2006 [GC], [42].

make this inevitable. No doubt patterns develop but there is little reason to suppose that courts get each point right first time. The doctrine of precedent is, at least in our higher courts and at times, but only at times, mutating into a less rigid doctrine of consistency. The problems are to see which decisions actually represent the dominant trends and which are most in accord with the underlying objectives of the CPR and the Convention. In both these fields decisions are fact driven[142] and variations in discretion in case management and in the interpretation of rules are consequences of the uncharted terrains of civil justice and human rights.[143] The judges, here and at Strasbourg, should be well aware that justice is not well served by a slavish adherence to the vagaries of which case was litigated first.

Certainty and predictability are indeed, as Lord Bingham said, desirable elements of justice but not the only ones. There is no question but that the meaning of the Convention changes overtime. I have suggested that maybe the CPR will. Maybe however, the ease with which it, and its Practice Directions, can be amended will prevent the judges feeling any need to do so by way of their judgments.

The last difficulty for this book is more complex. The ECHR was drafted, in part, by British lawyers acting under their understanding of what our law was in 1950. We should expect that the lawyers advising the other signatory states were also satisfied that their systems were compliant with the Convention.[144] In Britain, the CPR were written with the ECHR and its associated jurisprudence in mind.[145] Conflict was not intended and is not to be expected. Speaking specifically of one right protected by the Convention, but his dictum is applicable to much else, Laws J said:[146] 'Freedom of expression is as much a sinew of the common law as it is

142 In *Gaskin v Liverpool CC* [1980] 1 WLR 1549 Lord Denning MR bluntly gave his view of the merits saying:

> The history shows that this young man is a psychiatric case, mentally-disturbed, and quite useless to society. His solicitors now want to see all the reports so as to bolster up a claim for damages. Though what good damages would do him, I do not know.

143 Sedley used a different metaphor, 'The Rocks or the Open Sea: Where is the Human Rights Act Heading?', (2005) 32 *Journal of Law and Society*, 3.

144 The original signatory states were: Denmark, Germany, Iceland, Ireland, Luxembourg, Norway, Sweden, and the United Kingdom. France was not an original signatory because it considered its law was wholly compliant, by the end of the 1950s the ECHR had come into force in a further five countries.

145 In *Less v Benedict* [2005] EWHC 1643 (Ch) Warren J said: 'It should be remembered that the CPR were drafted with the ECHR in the background and were clearly intended to be compliant with it'. As noted earlier, much of the CPR either consolidates long term policies or, more immediately, trends well established in the decade or so before their introduction.

146 *R v Advertising Standards Authority, ex p Vernons Organisation* [1992] 1 WLR 1289, 1293.

of the European Convention for the Protection of Human Rights and Fundamental Freedoms.'

It might be nice to leave this difficulty at this point but we cannot. The fact that conflict between the two modern instruments is not to be expected is a surprising outcome of a past that 'still rules us from its grave',[147] and which cannot be ignored. And the history is not only of law but of much else besides. To paraphrase an aphorism from elsewhere: 'What does he of law know who only law knows?'[148] I assume, although there is always interplay between politics and law, when push comes to shove, politics prevails.[149] Law is the compliant, but sometimes inventive, mistress of polity.[150] Specifically here, the explanatory history is in some places of politics and in others of ideas, most importantly of religion and the secularization of traditions derived from it. This seventh difficulty in approaching our principal question is thus multi-faceted. It is necessary to sketch, even if briefly, some of these faces. For one thing there are undoubted differences between the common and civil law systems. Our question is not, if such a question has any meaning in the modern world, whether one is better than the other. Our question revolves around how these differences interact when mixed together in the ECHR.[151]

---

147 Cf. FW Maitland, *The Forms of Action at Common Law*, 1909, lecture I. Maitland was referring to the fact that modern causes of action have their origin in the old forms. I am referring to the differences between the common law and civilian worlds discussed later.

148 The saying is usually attributed to CLR James relating to cricket.

149 Griffith, 'The Political Constitution', (1978) 42 MLR 1. Here, we need not enquire whether law is best characterized merely as the technical expression of policy.

150 For example, in *R (on the application of Morris) v Westminster CC and First Secretary of State* [2004] EWHC 1199 (Admin) the court allowed an action to continue although none of the relief sought would have any practical impact on the claimant, the claim could continue because the development of the law would be enhanced and clarified by the courts rulings on the issues that arose in the instant case. So also, in *Hughes v Richards (t/a Colin Richards) v Hughes* [2004] EWCA Civ 266 it was held that where the relevant area of law on which a claim is based was still developing and was subject to some uncertainty, and where it was highly desirable that the facts should be found so that any development of the law should be on the basis of actual and not hypothetical facts, that case would be inappropriate for striking out on a summary application.

151 Our culture, I assert, is based on a secularization of a hotchpotch of beliefs and rituals of Roman Catholic and a variety of Protestant sects (including the Church of England). In deference to this idea, it is sometimes called the Judeo-Christian tradition. My point is not of origins (when I would also have to consider the influence of ancient Greece and Rome and no doubt much else besides), but specifically of secularization. We shall touch on this as we discuss freedom of expression, at p. 48 et seq below. Others examples of secularized ideas include the acknowledgement of individual rights, including most recently, as Capelletti said, human rights. More generally, the assertion that much of the democratic and human rights agenda has a religious origin is an assertion that, in modified form, the values of Western liberalism are at bottom theocratic. If this is so, it reduces the supposed gap between that approach (philosophy is too specific a word) and contemporary Islamic states whose legal systems are based on the Koran.

It is convenient to name some of the differences between the common law and civilian systems. The common law builds towards a day in court, civilian procedures towards a decision. The common law is characterized by a system of now modified orality, the civilian by text. Before a common law trial, there is extensive activity by the parties and their lawyers defining the scope of the dispute, giving disclosure of relevant documents, and exchanging statements of witnesses of fact and of experts. The role of the judge has increased but is nevertheless limited. In civilian systems, none of this applies. Once courts have cognizance of disputes, judges control the path. They, possibly at the parties' or their lawyers' suggestion, require the production of such documents as they think fit. They call the witnesses and they examine them. They engage any expert witnesses. Lawyers, if they speak at all, do so only to the judge. The judge, and not the lawyers, asks questions of the witnesses. So also, although a common law appeal is said to be a re-hearing, witnesses are not reheard. In civilian systems a first level of appeal may re-examine the witnesses or require the trial judge to do so. The final court often only has jurisdiction to decide questions of law.

I have suggested the 1950 Convention is expected to be at least broadly compliant with each of the legal systems it governs. Thus, despite all of these differences, all these procedures are Convention compliant. Van Caenegem[152] has sought to understand the causes of these differences. The inhabitants of both England and Western Europe came from similar Germanic tribes.[153] Some sort of jury system was common to most of them. To Van Caenegem, the differences lay in the earlier economic strength and military power of the King in England and the creation of royal judges with nation-wide writs. There were two important features of these judges. They were based in London but travelled. The jury remained. These Royal judges were created a hundred years before the re-discovery of the full text of Justinian's *Digest* in Italy at the end of the twelfth century and its consequent reception throughout the rest of Western Europe, that is, the area of the Holy Roman Empire. The basis of our law was laid before then. In Europe, the *Digest* was used as a root of legal discourse, but it was

---

The theological base of Western Liberalism, including the social contract, was express in one its founding texts, Buchanan, The *Powers of the Crown in Scotland, being a translation, with notes, of George Buchanan's* 'De jure regni apud Scotos', Arrowood, (ed.) 1949, Austin: University of Texas Press (the assessment is by Laski, 'Introduction to Languet', *Vindiciae Contra Tyrrannos – A Defense of Liberty Against Tyrants*, P. 5), discussed in Jacob, *The Republican Crown*, p. 306 et seq. Buchanan wrote to justify the forced abdication of Mary Queen of Scots. A hundred years later Locke adopted similar, but more secular, arguments. On the whole, this seems a more likely explanation of British civil rights than those based solely in the rationalizations of the Enlightenment. Among other things, the constitutional settlement of the late seventeenth century, including the Bill of Rights and the independence of the judiciary, pre-dated any British Enlightenment.

152 van Caenegem, *Judges, legislators and professors: chapters in European legal history*, CUP, 1987.

153 As to the Celtic influence, see Holdsworth, *A History of English Law*, vol. II, p. 13, esp n. 1.

open only to scholars. The judges of Europe either were, or differed to, the clergy (particularly the bishops). This gave the one unified Church of Western Europe a role not mirrored in England. In aiding the settlement of disputes, the Church naturally applied its text-based culture. Such a culture did not require, and indeed would be hindered by, a single day in court. The jury on the continent was replaced by[154] 'the system of proofs contained in Roman-canonical "learned" procedure which is first practiced in the Church courts and afterwards in those of kings and other princes'.

By contrast, by the end of the seventeenth century, and in the wake of our Reformation, the English proclaimed a fear of the re-importation of spiritual or (what often amounted to the same thing) temporal absolutism. The dyke holding that at bay was the jury. And by the end of that century, the dyke itself was protected by the Royal judges who became independent of the Crown. The 'day in court' became the dominant characteristic of the English civil process. We placed it in contrast to what we deliberately and pejoratively call the 'inquisitional' processes of the rest of Europe. Deep into the 20th century, English judges continued to place the English ways in contrast to *despotism*, *tyranny*, *absolutism* and *inquisitorial trials*, all of which were (at least until very recently), to them, much the same thing.

To the British the common law and civilian civil processes were thus placed in contrast. Notably, the ECtHR insists that Art. 6 requires adversarial proceedings.[155]

The history of Europe after the end of the seventeenth century saw a coming together. Whatever the reason for the convergence, general agreement places it in the Allied Victory of 1945: but much was in place before that. Certainly, there was enough in common for British lawyers to play a full part in the drafting of the ECHR in 1950. However, the English do not have a monopoly of virtue nor are they alone in having a sense of fair play.[156] Western Europe does not have civil processes that

---

154 van Caenegem, *op cit*, 36-7.

155 *Hirst v UK* (No.2), 6 October 2005 [GC], [71]; *Capital Bank AD v Bulgaria*, 24 February 2006, [118]. The problem is still with us; see the discussion of found. at p. p. 160 below.

156 Lord Denning MR in *R v Secretary of State for the Home Department ex p Hosenball* [1977] 1 WLR 766 said: 'In some parts of the world national security has on occasions been used as an excuse for all sorts of infringements of individual liberty. But not in England.' He was repeating a view of England he expressed in a case concerning the choice of forum, *The Atlantic Star* [1973] QB 364, where he said: 'You may call this "forum shopping" if you please, but if the forum is England, it is a good place to shop in, both for the quality of the goods and the speed of service.'

On the appeal in that case Lord Reid gave the rejoinder: 'that seems to me to recall the good old days, the passing of which many may regret, when inhabitants of this island felt an innate superiority over those unfortunate enough to belong to other races, – or, as Kipling more forthrightly phrased it, "lesser breeds without the law".' Lord Diplock adopted Lord Reid's view in *The Abidin Daver* [1984] AC 398.

Nevertheless, the insularity is not dead. For example, Lord Hoffmann in *A (FC) v Secretary of State for the Home Department* [2004] UKHL 56 remarked, [88] ... Freedom from arbitrary arrest and detention is a quintessentially British liberty, enjoyed by the inhabitants of this country when most of the population of Europe could be thrown into prison at the whim of are in contrast to the rest of its political philosophy.[157] There are now common values between the CPR, the ECHR (and HRA and on a wider stage of the EU, including its Charter of Fundamental Rights. The Preamble to the Charter refers to Europe's 'spiritual and moral heritage' and the 'indivisible, universal values of human dignity, freedom, equality and solidarity'.[158] In Britain fear (and even knowledge) of any inquisition is gone. The old term of abuse has lost its meaning. Our question – what differences are there between the CPR and the ECHR – is dependent on the residue of this history.

Be all that as it may, the common law for a long time was centred on the existence of the jury. By the middle of the 19th century the first and most important step was taken to dispense with that device in civil cases.[159] They became optional and then over the next hundred years gradually obsolete. The role of the judges correspondingly was transformed from umpires to adjudicators. For a long time this change was masked by the language they use. They spoke of 'directing' themselves. They remained passive.[160] The day in court remained. The civilian systems look on with some admiration at the efficiency (as measured by the speed of final determination) of the common law. The rise of written proceedings in the British system was a much slower affair, always obscured by the need for a day in court and the reluctance to recognize the changed role of the judge.[161] Finally, the CPR confirmed a range of new powers for the judge.

We have seen Part 1 begins by proclaiming the Overriding Objective. In 1.4 it requires the court to further it by 'active case management'. Other powers include those to regulate the giving of evidence. All this is combined, as we shall see, with an unprecedented reliance on written materials. The sum gives the judge powers to dispense with each or both of two previously fundamental principles of common

---

their rulers. It was incorporated into the European Convention in order to entrench the same liberty in countries which had recently been under Nazi occupation. The United Kingdom subscribed to the Convention because it set out the rights which British subjects enjoyed under the common law. And, [93] 'The institutions of some countries are less firmly based than those of others. Their Communities are not equally united in their loyalty to their values and system of government'. France took time to ratify because it thought that the Convention added nothing to French liberty. And see Dyzenhaus, 'An unfortunate outburst of Anglo-Saxon parochialism', (2005) MLR 68 673.

157 Cf. Gearty, ed, *European Civil liberties and the European Convention on Human Right*, 1997, and Colvin and Vigoretti, 'Transnational Civil Proceedings in Italy', (2004) 23 CLQ 38.

158 It also refers to respect for 'the diversity of the cultures and traditions of the peoples of Europe as well as the national identities of the Member States'.

159 The Common Law Procedure Act 1854, s. 1.

160 See: *Yuill v Yuill* [1945] P. 15 per Lord Greene MR who referred to the 'dust of conflict', *Jones v National Coal Board* [1957] 2 QB 55; *Fallon v Calvert* [1960] 2 QB 201.

161 See Sir G Lightman, 'The Case for Judicial Intervention', Speech to the London Solicitors' Litigation Association, 9 November 1999, at the DCA website ... /judicial/speeches/9-11-99.htm.

law procedure – orality and party control of the action.[162] The rise in express judicial law making has been associated with many judgments in the appellate courts being expressed to be that 'of the court to which all members have contributed', that is, anonymous judgments. We have moved towards the previously feared inquisitorial systems of the rest of Europe. However much else the United Kingdom has in common with the USA, all this places it at variance with that State's common law system. Despite attempts, there is little chance in the US of such coming toward our idea of efficiency. The Eighth Amendment to the US Constitution povides:

> In Suits at common law, where the value in controversy shall exceed twenty dollars, the right of trial by jury shall be preserved, and no fact tried by a jury, shall be otherwise re-examined in any Court of the USA, than according to the rules of the common law.

That Constitution thus enshrines two elements of the common law to which we nowadays attribute little importance and which, it can be argued, stand in the way of efficiency: the distinction between law and equity and the civil jury. For our current purposes the more important is the jury. And to repeat the point, where there is a jury there has to be a day in court. Where there is writing, it is often less efficient and more costly to insist that all aspects of a case be tried together. The UK common law and the civilian civil processes have come towards each other, and, in the case of the UK, away from the USA. That jurisdiction is left in its own parochial time capsule defined by old struggles of ours that we have forgotten.[163] Increasingly, we have less to learn from the USA and what we can learn can only be done by appreciating the differences.[164]

It follows from all this that we should not be surprised at the increasing convergence between the UK common law and civilian processes. The UK is in a position to learn, on its own terms, if not from civil procedure in other parts of Western Europe, at least from the jurisprudence of the Court at Strasbourg. This book, then, does two things. It describes those aspects of civil procedure which do, or might engage, Convention rights, and it assesses how far the rules of civil litigation are affected by them. As David Steel J said:[165]

> The tentacles of the Human Rights Act, 1998 reach into some unexpected places. The Commercial Court, even when exercising its supervisory role as regards arbitration, is not immune.

---

162 Sir Jack Jacob, *The Fabric of Civil Justice*, 13–15, 19–21. Party control is still expressed to be one of the foundations of the modern law of arbitration, Arbitration Act 1996 s. 1(a).

163 For a different and more hopeful view see Booth and du Plessis, 'Home Alone? – The US Supreme Court and International and Transitional Judicial Learning', [2005] EHRLR 127.

164 It is with some success, for example, that the CPR have (in Part 19.4) introduced the group action based on lessons learnt from the restrictive British class action and its more expansive US cousin.

165 *Mousaka v Golden Seagull Maritime* [2002] 1 WLR 395, 1.

Our questions are then: what is the reach and what are the effects of these tentacles?

Chapter 2

Open Justice

The Justifications for Openness

It is my argument that open justice is the keel which gives both stability and direction to the legal system. It is the foundation of the whole. It, and the beliefs behind it, provide the means, if not to answer many other problems, at least to articulate them. We shall come to some of these answers in later chapters. Before getting to the law, it is helpful to consider the source of the idea. On any reflection, the need for open justice is not self-evident and may conflict with other values, for example, decorum, candour, privacy, expediency, or efficiency.

It is worth spending a little time with these values. Decorum was at issue in *Scott v Scott*, the leading case establishing the need for justice to be done openly. The case began as a petition for nullity on the ground of the alleged impotence of the respondent. The petitioning wife was found to be a virgin. The trial was in camera. After the decree she sent copies of the transcript to the father and sister of the respondent, and to one other person, to vindicate her character because the respondent was believed to have misrepresented what had happened. Bargrave Deane J said:[1]

> It is manifest that the reason for trying such unhappy cases as this in camera is the protection of both parties, inasmuch as the details of evidence are of a very delicate and private character. The medical evidence and the evidence of the petitioner in particular is of such a nature that it ought to be kept absolutely private and not disclosed to any one.

He found there had been a contempt of court. The Court of Appeal sat with six members. The discussion focused on whether there was jurisdiction to hear the appeal at all because, it was argued, contempt was a criminal matter and at that time there was no appeal via a civil court.[2] As we shall see in the House of Lords the case

1 *Scott* (otherwise Morgan) v *Scott* [1912] p. 4.

2 *Scott* (otherwise Morgan) v *Scott* [1912] p. 241 (CA). Buckley LJ, for example, reasoned:

> An order for hearing in camera of a suit such as this is not an order to enforce any civil right arising as between the parties. It is an order which the Court thinks proper to make for two reasons, first, that the parties may not be deterred from coming forward to seek relief and giving their evidence in the matter (a consideration which proceeds upon the necessity of ensuring the proper administration of justice); and, secondly, that upon grounds of morality and public decency a public hearing, resulting in a publication of details such as are relevant in such a suit, shall be excluded.

took a more dramatic and far less technical turn. Apart from the majority in the Court of Appeal, the issue throughout was whether an intimate, or perhaps even a prurient, subject matter was sufficient to require or permit the judges to do their business behind closed doors and in secret.[3]

Candour is a requirement of due process. Unless justice is aided by open and honest evidence it is difficult to see how it can be achieved. In a sense it is more important than all other requirements. It exceeds the need for equality of arms or an impartial tribunal that we shall consider in later chapters. We shall see it provides the justifications for most of the exceptions to open proceedings (that is, all except waiver) we shall look at in this chapter. Quite simply if a court does not have facts on which it can rely it can make no sensible assessment of any issue it is asked to decide. A procedure which not only inhibits candour but prevents it must be self defeating. Generally, however, beyond the exceptions we shall come to, the courts are satisfied that other devices, among them the rules on contempt, perjury and abuse of process, are sufficient to reconcile candour and openness. Candour is also the rationale for legal professional privilege we shall come to in Chapter 4.

Privacy is protected by the Convention and is thus, in law, a fundamental freedom. Nevertheless, it is a right which is subject to the limitations set out in Art. 8(2). Courts must be mindful of it but are required to balance it with other rights, including those in Art. 6.

Expediency is the court reaching for pragmatic answers. Efficiency lies at the heart of much of the CPR. Openness stays on stage because the courts are directed to deal with cases justly and in its explanation of what this entails in Part 1.1(1) the CPR use the word 'includes' – a formula that suggests the list that follows is not exclusive. I am arguing that the openness is too important to be written out of the script simply because other and newer values have received clearer definition. On the other hand, the new values do receive express mention. Part 1.1(2)(d) requires the court to ensure cases are 'dealt with *expeditiously* and fairly' and Part 1.4(2), having required the court to 'further the overriding objective by actively managing cases', says that this includes '(l) giving directions to ensure that the trial of a case proceeds quickly and *efficiently*' (in both cases my emphasis).

These, then, are other values that the law cannot and does not ignore. Each is important. The questions arise as to why, even against them, openness can get priority. What is the source of that idea and how do the courts respond it? It is these that I seek to answer in this Chapter. Given that efficiency and expediency are new, they are also fashionable. As we shall see, they are at the centre of a changed question. Whereas, once we asked how do we end disputes justly, we now ask how

---

The decision was by majority, with Fletcher Moulton LJ giving a powerful and in places principled dissent. He distinguished the privacy of a hearing from the privacy of what transpired at it.

3 The even more prurient facts of a later case led to the passing of the Judicial Proceedings (Regulation of Reports) Act 1926, see Lord Simon in the *Ampthill Peerage Case* Committee for Privileges [1977] AC 547.

do we dispose of them efficiently. The result is a conflict between ordinary open litigation and other mechanisms for dispute resolution. Because these last are largely secret, this Chapter examines the clash.

The roots of openness then. Within the common law world, there were three: the jury; ideas of freedom of expression and the rule of law; and, the influence of the Enlightenment. This is not the place to elaborate on them because that would take the discussion beyond our primary concerns. But we can be brief. It is unnecessary here to add anything to what I have already said about the jury[4] – because that required a day in court distinct procedures are still required for trial.

There is, in my argument, a historical as well as an ideological link between freedom of expression and open justice. We can follow Mayhew[5] as regards the history of the freedom. He began his account with the mediaeval Roman Catholic doctrine of the *Communion of the Saints*. He traced a line from that, through its Protestant adaptation of *sharing the spirit*, to the movement from congregation to public, the consequent rise in the printing of sermons, and ultimately to the *trade of truth*. Here, the only form of opinion, on mercantile and State as well as religious matters which was reliable is that which was in the public sphere. It is yet another example of the secularization of previously religious ideas.[6] It is this movement which linked openness in public affairs with our modern democracy. When the Human Rights Convention uses the expression 'democratic society', it does so in this more inclusive sense rather than merely referring to majoritarian government. This wider sense also includes political toleration, a concept itself derived from the necessary toleration of one Protestant sect by others.[7]

---

4 Above p. 40 et seq.

5 Mayhew, *The New Public: Professional Communication and the Means of Social Influence*, Cambridge University Press, 1997, p. 157 et seq.

6 The need for public debate was why Kings (and, now, ministers) ought not to have private counsellors and why they should rely exclusively on Parliament. It was said, only in a genuine Parliament people can speak without hidden motives and then only provided what is said there is not subject of any penalty from outside, see Art. 9 of the Bill of Rights 1689.

7 See *Spycatcher* (*The Observer and The Guardian v UK*, 26 November 1991, [59] and *Lingens v Austria*, 8 July 1986. And see Jacob, *The Republican Crown, Lawyers and the Making of the State*, 1996, p. 56f and references there cited. One of the permanent legacies of Cromwell's Commonwealth was the toleration of Jews. Toleration of Roman Catholics came far more slowly. Even the general nineteenth century Catholic emancipation did not include the right to enter the older universities nor affect the limitation to protestants of the office of Lord Chancellor (itself not clearly abolished until the 1974 by the Lord Chancellor (Tenure of Office and Discharge of Ecclesiastical Functions) Act), nor yet the Crown.

The continuing difficulties of Roman Catholics were illustrated in 1948. The Pope in a statement to the 'Italian Catholic jurists' warned Roman Catholic judges hearing divorce cases. The Lord Chancellor responded by threatening not to appoint Catholics to the bench and only relented when the Papal Nuncio explained the limited scope of the doctrine of Papal Infallibility. The affair appears in PRO LCO2/4228. For two centuries, Protestant suspicions of the Roman Church have been less justified than paranoid.

Mayhew linked this dependency on public debate and democracy to a second idea from the same epoch, the *Rule of Law*. In effect, he suggested that in addition to its usual role of protecting individual rights, the *Rule of Law* plays a crucial part in integrating society.[8] Because law's institutions are independent of other sections of society, it can act as a yardstick by which each of us, and each sector of society, can be measured. Law stands apart from the hurly-burly of public debate, from its shifts and variations. Its value is in its stability, not in its modernity nor even in general acquiescence to it.[9] It is only a small step to join these ideas. Public debate and the rule of law combine to form the idea that justice should be done in public. The argument is that the more that can be seen of the way the courts behave, the more (potential) respect this essential cement of society can earn.

The third and separate root of public justice is a contribution to the Enlightenment project. It joins opposition to absolute state power with that movement's conception of objective truth. This idea is reflected in Bentham's aphorism that 'whatever is done by anybody, being done before the eyes of the universal public' is the 'grand security of securities'. Echoes of that resonate in the case law.

The General Freedom of Expression

As I have said, I see an ideological link between freedom of expression and open justice as well as this history. Again, to be brief with freedom of expression (for it is not our main concern) and staying with the way the courts handle it, we can note Lord Bridge's dissent in *Spycatcher*. The majority had held that there was a power to injunct the publication of the autobiography of a former member of the Security Service. Lord Bridge said that his 'confidence in the capacity of the common law to safeguard the fundamental freedoms essential to a free society [is] seriously undermined by' the decision. He argued:[10]

> Freedom of speech is always the first casualty under a totalitarian regime. Such a regime cannot afford to allow the free circulation of information and ideas among its citizens. Censorship is the indispensable tool to regulate what the public may and what they may not know.

---

8 Mayhew, *The New Public*, 1997, p. 11. And see Parsons, 'Law as an Intellectual Stepchild', *Sociological Inquiry* (1977) 47: 11–57.

9 As Lord Mansfield put in *R v Wilkes* (1770) 4 Burr, 2527, 2561–2; 98 ER 327, 347, 'We must not regard political consequences ... if rebellion was the certain consequence, we are bound to say *fiat justicia ruat cœlum* (let justice be done though heaven falls)'.

10 *Attorney General v Guardian Newspapers* [1987] 1 WLR 1248, 1286F.

Where Laws J referred[11] to freedom of expression as a sinew both of the common law and the Convention he ignored what was almost Lord Bridge's anguish. Elsewhere, in *ex p Simms*, Lord Steyn explained that:[12]

> In a democracy it is the primary right: without it an effective rule of law is not possible. Nevertheless, freedom of expression is not an absolute right. Sometimes it must yield to other cogent social interests. Freedom of expression is, of course, intrinsically important: it is valued for its own sake. But it is well recognized that it is also instrumentally important. It serves a number of broad objectives. First, it promotes the self-fulfilment of individuals in society. Secondly, in the famous words of Holmes J (echoing John Stuart Mill), 'the best test of truth is the power of the thought to get itself accepted in the competition of the market'.[13] Thirdly, freedom of speech is the lifeblood of democracy. The free flow of information and ideas informs political debate. It is a safety valve: people are more ready to accept decisions that go against them if they can in principle seek to influence them. It acts as a brake on the abuse of power by public officials. It facilitates the exposure of errors in the governance and administration of justice of the country.[14]

When *Spycatcher* got to the ECtHR, the court sought to describe the scope of Art. 10. It said:[15]

> Freedom of expression constitutes one of the essential foundations of a democratic society … it is applicable not only to 'information' or 'ideas' that are favourably received or regarded as inoffensive or as a matter of indifference, but also to those that offend, shock or disturb.

In *Lingens v Austria* the Court referred to:[16] 'that pluralism, tolerance and broadmindedness without which there is no "democratic society"'. And in *Spycatcher*, it went on:[17]

> The adjective 'necessary', within the meaning of Article 10 para. 2, implies the existence of a 'pressing social need'. The Contracting States have a certain margin of appreciation in assessing whether such a need exists, but it goes hand in hand with a European supervision, embracing both the law and the decisions applying it, even those given by independent courts.

To Judge Pekkanen this last was too loose:

---

11 *R v Advertising Standards Authority, ex p Vernons Organisation* [1992] 1 WLR 1289, 1293, cited at p. 38 n. 146 above.

12 *R v Secretary of State for the Home Department ex p Simms* [2000] 2 AC 115, [126]. And see his remarks in *Re S (a Child)* [2004] UKHL 47, esp [30].

13 *Abrams v US* (1919) 250 US 616 at 630 per Holmes J (dissent).

14 He cited Stone, Seidman, Sunstein and Tushnett, *Constitutional Law* (3rd edn, 1996), 1078–1086.

15 *The Observer and The Guardian v UK*, 26 November 1991, [59].

16 *Lingens v Austria*, 8 July 1986, [41]; *Hertel v Switzerland*, 25 August 1998.

17 The passage also appears in *Skalka v Poland*, 27 May 2003, [32], where the court cited *Janowski v Poland*, 21 January 1999, [30].

> The use of prior restraints must be based, in my opinion, on exceptionally relevant and weighty reasons which clearly outweigh the public's legitimate interest in receiving news and information without hindrance.

Judge de Meyer[18] adopted the views of Justice Black:[19]

> The press must be left free to publish news, whatever the source, without censorship, injunctions, or prior restraint ... in a free and democratic society there can be no room, in time of peace, for restrictions of that kind, and particularly not if these are resorted to, ... for governmental suppression of embarrassing information [Judge de Meyer himself added 'or ideas'].

Human rights are always easy when majorities benefit. They become hard when they help minorities against majorities and are tested to the full when the minority is small and objectionable.[20] Discussing *A v Secretary of State for the Home Department*, Fredman concluded:[21]

> The House of Lords recognized the need for a more sophisticated understanding of democracy than accountability to the electorate and majoritarianism. Previously, courts tended to see democratic decision making as broadly utilitarian, whereby the function of accountable representatives is to weigh the public interest against that of the individual.

---

18 Joined by Judges Pettiti, Russo, Foighel and Bigi.

19 Joined by Justice Douglas, *New York Times v US* and *US v Washington Post* (1971), 403 US 713, at 717, 723–724, the *Pentagon Papers* case.

20 Lord Steyn said in *R (on the application of Roberts) v Parole Board* [2005] UKHL 45, [84]:

> in *US v Rabinowitz* (1950) 339 US 56, 69, Frankfurter J observed: 'It is a fair summary of history to say that the safeguards of liberty have frequently been forged in controversies involving not very nice people.' Even the most wicked of men are entitled to justice at the hands of the state.
>
> So also, Baroness Hale has emphasized in *Ghaidan v Godin-Mendoza* [2004] UKHL 3:
>
> It is a purpose of all human rights instruments to secure the protection of the essential rights of members of minority groups, even when they are unpopular with the majority. Democracy values everyone equally even if the majority does not.

And see: in the context of the need for representation at trial, the remarks of Lord Hobhouse in *Medcalf v Mardell* (Wasted Costs Order) [2002] UKHL 27, [52]-[53], discussed below at p. 149.

21 Fredman, 'From Deference to Democracy: the Role of Equality under the Human Rights Act 1998', (2006) 122 LQR 53; *A v Secretary of State for the Home Department* [2004] UKHL 56. And see Lord Steyn, 'Dynamic Interpretation Amidst an Orgy of Statutes', [2004] EHRLR 245: 'A core characteristic of a constitutional democracy is the protection it offers to the rights of individuals against the majority view as reflected by an elected government.' But see: Hickman, 'Constitutional dialogue, constitutional theories and the Human Rights Act 1998', PL [2005] 306; Ewing, 'The futility of the Human Rights Act', [2004] PL 829 (he referred to 'rights' evangelists'); and, Lord Lester, 'The utility of the Human rights Act: a reply to Keith Ewing', [2005] PL 249.

> *A* signals a judicial appreciation of human rights, not as counterdemocratic forces, but as constitutive of democracy itself.

Or as the Preamble to the Universal Declaration of Human Rights expressly and more pragmatically asserts: 'it is essential, if man is not to be compelled to have recourse, as a last resort, to rebellion against tyranny and oppression, that human rights should be protected by the rule of law'.

In *Steel and Morris v UK* the ECtHR applied the freedom of expression (perhaps extended is a better word) to the distributors of a potentially defamatory pamphlet.[22] We should never underestimate the temptation of our authoritarian tendencies. Art. 10 is one defence against them.

Nevertheless, in *Markt Intern and Beerman v Germany*, a case lacking the high drama of *Spycatcher* and *Steel and Morris*, the ECtHR said:[23]

> In order to establish whether the interference was proportionate it is necessary to weigh the requirements of the protection of the reputation and the rights of others against the publication of the information in question. In exercising its power of review, the Court must look at the impugned court decision in the light of the case as a whole. In a market economy ... the specialized press must be able to disclose facts which could be of interest to its readers and thereby contribute to the openness of business activities. However, even the publication of items which are true and describe real events may under certain circumstances be prohibited: the obligation to respect the privacy of others or the duty to respect the confidentiality of certain commercial information are examples ... it is primarily for the national courts to decide which statements are permissible and which are not.

Markt Intern and *Spycatcher* are not in conflict. The first was a commercial case and the court could take into account the kind of considerations it offered as examples.[24] *Spycatcher*, by contrast, went to the nature of the relation between the security services and the press.

In a sense, as we shall see, Art. 6 is, in part, a specific application of freedom of expression.[25] There is an obligation on the State to ensure that those who wish to hear

22 *Steel and Morris v UK*, 15 February 2005. Unlike the Convention, Section 12 of the HRA expressly refers to journalism. Given the equation now made between the rights of the press and the rights of pamphleteers, it is probable that the section itself needs to be amended.

23 *Markt Intern and Beerman v Germany*, 20 November 1989, [34]-[35]. And see: *Bladet Tromsø and Stensaas v Norway*, 20 May 1999 [GC]; and in England, *R (on the application of British American Tobacco) v The Secretary of State for Health* [2004] EWHC 2493 (Admin).

24 Gearty, p. 125 fn. 25/6 cited Smyth, *Business and the Human Rights Act*, 2000, as saying 'the European Convention jurisprudence fails to confer upon commercial speech the same measure of protection that it confers on political speech'.

25 See, e.g. *Sutter v Switzerland*, 22 February 1984.

what transpires in courts have sufficient access to them. In this connection Sedley LJ has considered Article 17, which provides:

> Nothing in this Convention may be interpreted as implying for any State, group or person any right to engage in any activity or perform any act aimed at the destruction of any of the rights and freedoms set forth herein or at their limitation to a greater extent than is provided for in the Convention.

Sedley LJ said:[26]

> It … brings the Article 6 right to a fair trial into the same frame as article 10 (1), and by doing so denies the right of free expression a clear run where it comes into conflict with the right to a fair trial. It does the reverse too. A proper balance has in each case to be found between the two.

This is but one example of a theme that runs through the Convention and the Strasbourg jurisprudence, the search for balance between apparently conflicting provisions.

Openness of Proceedings

Jaconelli[27] has provided the most extensive discussion of open justice. He suggested that as an ideal it includes the provision of adequate facilities for the attendance of the members of the public and the print media. Secondly, he said, there is a consequent right to report. Thirdly, documents that have come into existence for the trial should be available for inspection.[28] Fourthly, the names of the personnel – parties, judges, witnesses – should be openly available. And, fifthly and sixthly (for he was writing also about the criminal process), the trial should take place in the presence of the accused and he or she should be able to confront the accusers. Throughout his analysis he distinguished between the *dramatis personae* of the trial and spectators. He searched for a rationale behind the idea. It has some affinity with, but is not the same as, the public law concept of natural justice. It provides a disciplinary role for judges and witnesses.[29] And, it provides an investigatory aspect in that further

26 *Cream Holdings v Banerjee* [2003] EWCA Civ 103, [82] Sedley LJ dissented. The majority was reversed at *Cream Holdings v Banerjee* [2004] UKHL 44.

27 Jaconelli, *Open Justice: A Critique of the Public Trial*, OUP, 2002. And see also Department for Constitutional Affairs, *Consultation Paper: Broadcasting Courts* (CP 28/04) 15 November 2004, summarized by Langdon-Down, 'Lights, Camera, Law' LS Gaz, 30 September 2004, 22, and the Department for Constitutional Affairs, *Consultation Response: Broadcasting Courts*, 30 June 2005. The Constitutional Reform Act 2005, s. 47, permits photography in the new Supreme Court.

28 His meaning is different from that used to delimit legal professional privilege, see p. 160 below.

29 At pp. 36–7. He cited: Bentham, the *Rationale of Judicial Evidence* in Bowring (ed.) *The Works of Jeremy Bentham*, vol.vi (1843) 355; Hale, *The History of the Common Law of*

witnesses may come forward. There is also an educational role for the community to know the quality of the administration of the laws made on its behalf.[30]

Part 39 of the CPR says:[31] 'The general rule is that a hearing is to be in public.' With limited exceptions, it applies to all hearings and not merely trials so that, for example, interim applications are generally covered. It thus goes beyond Art. 6.[32] Other provisions of the CPR also affect the public nature of proceedings.[33] A decision, however, that can be taken without a hearing is not, of course, within the scope of Part 39, but, if it determines civil rights, might be within the scope of Art. 6. Within the CPR there is little formal obligation for the giving of reasons[34] but, as we shall see, both the common law (most commonly by some implicit analogy with public law control of discretion) and the Strasbourg jurisprudence (by an implication extending the terms of Art. 6) increasingly require that decisions be justified. Both at common law and at Strasbourg the attempt is to enhance or maintain confidence in the administration of civil justice.

It is helpful to look at the language the courts have used to explain the need for open justice. It is close, at times very close, to that used to justify freedom of expression. Later, we shall come to the occasions when the courts have seemingly ignored the basic principle and at least some of the exceptions. The leading case is, as I have said, *Scott v Scott*.[35] As we consider the exceptions to openness, we shall come to *Department of Economics, Policy and Development of the City of Moscow v Bankers Trust*.[36] *Scott* remains important because of its assertion of the basic principle of open justice and because it recognized the possibility of limited exceptions. In *the City of Moscow* the Court of Appeal set the issue in a modern context and discussed the current scope of the exceptions. It also clarified the distinctions between in camera, *secret*, *in chambers*, and *private* hearings.

In *Scott v Scott* the House was concerned with the validity of the original order. It rested its decision on factors beyond mere law and beyond the convenience or wishes of participants. This way of justifying openness is important because, as I

England (6th edn 1820) 343–4; and, Wigmore, *Evidence*, Vol.6 (Chadbourn Revision, 1976) Chapter 62.

30 At p. 39 he was sceptical, citing Johnson (ed.), *An Orator of Justice: A Speech Biography of Viscount Buckmaster* (1932) 239. If education is a true rationale, why are the public apparently only interested in the salacious?

31 CPR Part 39.2(1).

32 In principle interim proceedings (relating to for example, case management) do not determine civil rights and thus, under the Convention, need not be in public, but see further pp Error! Bookmark not defined. et seq below.

33 In particular para. 4.1 of the Practice Direction to CPR Part 27 and the other provisions of para. 1 of the Practice Direction to Part 39, discussed at p. 62 et seq. below.

34 Brief reasons are required in small claims.

35 *Scott* (otherwise Morgan) v *Scott* [1913] AC 417. In *Three Rivers Council v Bank of England* (Application for Judgment in Private) [2005] EWCA Civ 933 Rix LJ described it as still the 'leading authority'. As with many 'leading cases' it is better known than read.

36 *The City of Moscow*, discussed at p. 65 below.

have said, openness generally trumps other values. A few quotations give the tenor of the decision. The one thing that stands out in the speeches is the absence of strictly legal argument. Thus, Lord Haldane LC:

> The mere consideration that the evidence is of an unsavoury character is not enough, any more than it would be in a criminal Court, and still less is it enough that the parties agree in being reluctant to have their case tried with open doors.

Or Lord Halsbury: 'every Court of justice is open to every subject of the King. I believe this has been the rule, at all events, for some centuries'.[37] And Lord Loreburn:[38]

> English justice must be administered openly in the face of all men ... Courts of justice, who are the guardians of public liberties, ought to be doubly vigilant against encroachments by themselves ... a Court may not be so jealous to do right when its proceedings are not subject to full public criticism.

Lord Shaw gave the most elaborate defence of open justice:[39]

> [The] result, which is declared by the Courts below to have been legitimately reached under a free Constitution, is exactly the same result which would have been achieved under, and have accorded with, the genius and practice of despotism ... To remit the maintenance of constitutional right to the region of judicial discretion is to shift the foundations of freedom from the rock to the sand.

He quoted Bentham, as he said, 'over and over again':[40]

---

37 He cited Emlyn, Preface to the second edn of *State Trials*, in six volumes folio, 1730, at p. iv, 'In other countries … the Courts of justice are held in secret; with us publicly and in open view' and Barrington (1766) who said that the Courts were not open as of right in the time of Edward I, even in England. Barrington said 'I do not recollect to have met in any of the European laws with any injunction that all Courts should be held ostiis apertis, except in those of the republic of Lucca'.

38 In the Court of Appeal Fletcher Moulton LJ had said:

> The Courts are the guardians of the liberties of the public and should be the bulwark against all encroachments on those liberties from whatsoever side they may come. It is their duty therefore to be vigilant. But they must be doubly vigilant against encroachments by the Courts themselves. In that case it is their own actions which they must bring into judgment and it is against themselves that they must protect the public.

39 In the Court of Appeal Vaughan Williams LJ had said: 'the hearing of trials in public is so precious a characteristic of English law that it is important that the power to hear cases in camera, even by consent, should be limited by express specific limitations and not left to the unfettered discretion of the Court or judge.'

40 Jaconelli, op. cit. helpfully cited Postema, *Bentham and the Common Tradition* (1986) 358 esp pp. 363–4.

In the darkness of secrecy, sinister interest and evil in every shape have full swing. Only in proportion as publicity has place can any of the checks applicable to judicial injustice operate. Where there is no publicity there is no justice.

Publicity is the very soul of justice. It is the keenest spur to exertion and the surest of all guards against improbity. It keeps the judge himself while trying under trial.

And this from Hallam:[41]

Civil liberty in this kingdom has two direct guarantees; the open administration of justice according to known laws truly interpreted, and fair constructions of evidence; and the right of Parliament, without let or interruption, to inquire into, and obtain redress of, public grievances. Of these, the first is by far the most indispensable; nor can the subjects of any State be reckoned to enjoy a real freedom, where this condition is not found both in its judicial institutions and in their constant exercise.

Lord Shaw continued:

The right of the citizen and the working of the Constitution in the sense which I have described have upon the whole since the fall of the Stuart dynasty received from the judiciary – and they appear to me still to demand of it – a constant and most watchful respect ... I should most deeply regret if the law were other than what I have stated it to be. If [it were otherwise], then an easy way would be open for judges to remove their proceedings from the light and to silence for ever the voice of the critic, and hide the knowledge of the truth. Such an impairment of right would be intolerable in a free country ... Had this occurred in France, I suppose Frenchmen would have said that the age of Louis Quatorze and the practice of lettres de cachet had returned.

Nearer to our own time, in 1975 in the *Socialist Worker Printers* case, Lord Widgery CJ said:[42]

The great virtue of having the public in our courts is that discipline which the presence of the public imposes upon the court itself. When the court is full of interested members of the public ... it is bound to have the effect that everybody is more careful about what they do, everyone tries just that little bit harder and there is a disciplinary effect on the court which would be totally lacking if there were no critical members of the public or

41 Jaconelli, op. cit. at p. 34, and again helpfully, gave the source as Hallam, *Constitutional Law*, Vol.1 (7th edn 1854) pp. 230–1. Farwell LJ, with the majority in the Court of Appeal, cited the passage. He also described open justice as 'the salt of the Constitution'.

42 *R v Socialist Worker Printers, ex p Attorney General* [1975] QB 637. Counsel included Gordon Slynn and Harry Woolf on one side and Stephen Sedley on the other. Lord Widgery applied *Attorney General v Butterworth* [1963] 1 QB 696 where Lord Denning MR was dealing with one consequence of open justice: 'It may be that there is no authority to be found in the books, but if this be so, all I can say is that the sooner we make one the better. For there can be no greater contempt than to intimidate a witness before he gives his evidence or to victimise him afterwards for having given it.'

> press present. When one has an order for trial in camera, all the public and all the press are evicted at one fell swoop and the entire supervision by the public is gone.

In *Home Office v Harman*, Lord Diplock said:[43] 'The reason for the rule is to discipline the judiciary – to keep the judges themselves up to the mark.' To which in the 1990s, Potter LJ offers the rejoinder:[44] 'He might well have added that it also reduces risk of corruption or any semblance or suspicion of it.' Hitherto much family litigation has been conducted in private. In *Re O (children)* Wall LJ said:[45]

> Unlike lay magistrates, professional judges are not subject to appraisal by their colleagues. The argument that such appraisal is unnecessary often relies on the fact that judges sit in public. Thus, their every word can be reported and, if necessary, publicly criticized. But this is not, of course, true of cases involving children, which are, currently, invariably heard at first instance in private. The fact that cases are heard in private in order to protect the identities of the children concerned, and the fact that they deal with highly sensitive material are, in our judgment all the more reason for judges to be astute to ensure that at all times they behave judicially and in particular that they remain both courteous and calm.

In *ex p New Cross BS* Donaldson MR said:[46]

> It is fundamental to British justice … that the Queen's courts are open to all. And when I say that they are open to all, I do not limit this to those who have business in the courts ... No one is more entitled than a member of the general public to see for himself that justice is done.

Following this, in *Harb v His Majesty King Fahd Bin Abdul Aziz*[47] the Court of Appeal was careless whether the public's interest is in the law or the parties.[48] The case concerned a claim for matrimonial maintenance. That would be heard in private but the prior question of sovereign immunity, particularly in relation to private rather than governmental acts, was one of legitimate public interest and debate.

To return to the main issue, in Jacob J *Forbes v Smith* said:[49] 'The concept of a secret judgment is one which I believe to be inherently abhorrent.' It was not

---

43 *Home Office v Harman* [1983] 1 AC 280, 303. And see *Attorney General v Leveller Magazine* [1979] AC 440, 450. He acknowledged a limitation to the principle as regards 'a trial within a trial', as to which see *Independent Publishing v The Attorney General of Trinidad and Tobago* [2004] UKPC 26.

44 *Gio Personal Investment Services v Liverpool and London Steamship Protection and Indemnity Association* (FAI General Insurance intervening) [1999] 1 WLR 984.

45 *Re O (children)*: *Re* W-*R (a Child)*: *Re W (children)* [2005] EWCA Civ 759, [51].

46 *R v Chief Register of Friendly Building Societies ex p New Cross BS* [1984] QB 227.

47 *Harb v His Majesty King Fahd Bin Abdul Aziz* [2005] EWCA Civ 632.

48 See further Public Access to Documents, p. 78 et seq. below.

49 *Forbes v Smith* [1998] 1 All ER 973, approved in *Hodgson v Imperial Tobacco* [1998] 1 WLR 1056.

only mere control of the courts. He described *Scott v Scott*[50] as 'wholly and almost emotionally in favour of the notion that the administration of justice is a matter of public concern' and held that chambers proceedings were generally held in smaller rooms for administrative convenience. They are public in the sense that decisions, orders and judgments are not secret or restricted to, for example, only the parties. In *Hodgson v Imperial Tobacco* the Court of Appeal endorsed this approach and held that the court has no power to order the parties to refrain from commenting to the media about the terms of such a judgment. Nevertheless:

> Hearings in private in chambers already make an important contribution to the administration of justice. They allow issues to be determined informally and expeditiously ... They allow matters to be discussed which the parties might not wish to discuss in open court. They encourage openness. They are less intimidating to litigants which is particularly important in the case of the small claims jurisdiction ... in the normal way the parties and, in particular, their legal advisers recognize that it is desirable to treat in a confidential manner what occurs in chambers, because it is in accord with the 'chambers culture' ... However it remains a principle of the greatest importance that, unless there are compelling reasons for doing otherwise ... The best way of avoiding ill-informed comments in the media ... when the interest of the public is high, is for the court to be as open as is possible and practicable, not only in relation to the trial but also in relation to the [interim] proceedings which have to take place prior to that trial.

In re P Sir Christopher Staughton,[51] having quoted Lord Haldane LC in *Scott v Scott*, commented:

> That last point is reflected in another decision which I am afraid I cannot recall the name of, where it was said that when both sides agree that information should be suppressed from the public, that is the occasion when the court must be most vigilant to see that it is a proper case for doing so.

The only case in Lexis which uses the phrase 'suppressed from the public' is the *Socialist Worker Printers* case,[52] but there Lord Widgery rejected a suggestion by counsel that a judge had no power by order to give effect to an agreement between the parties that the names of witnesses should be suppressed from the public. Nevertheless, in *ex p Kaim Todner*, Lord Woolf referred to this passage and concluded:[53]

> The need to be vigilant arises from the natural tendency for the general principle to be eroded and for exceptions to grow by accretion as the exceptions are applied by analogy to

50 Particularly the speech of Lord Loreburn.

51 *Re P* CA (Civ Div) *The Times* 31 arch 1998 (Transcript: Smith Bernal) 4 March 1998.

52 Lexis contains none, other than *Re P* itself, using the phrase 'the court must be most vigilant'.

53 *R v Legal Aid Board ex p Kaim Todner* [1999] QB 966, [4]-[5].

existing cases ... Any interference with the public nature of court proceedings is therefore to be avoided unless justice requires it.

It may be, and I argue is, that Sir Christopher Staughton and Lord Woolf were right, but the authority they cited does not support their position.

The principle has been applied in other areas. Thus, Lightman J said of professional discipline:[54]

(a) the public have an interest in the maintenance of standards in the investigation of complaints of serious professional misconduct against practitioners;

(b) public confidence in the GMC and the medical profession requires, and complainants have a legitimate expectation, that such complaints (in the absence of some special sufficient reason) will be publicly investigated by the PCC; and

(c) justice should in such cases be seen to be done. This must be most particularly the case where the practitioner continues to be registered and to practise.

Ex p Wagstaff was concerned with whether the enquiry into the Shipman murders should be held in public. Kennedy LJ said:[55]

There are positive known advantages to be gained from taking evidence in public. Namely:

(a) witnesses are less likely to exaggerate or attempt to pass on responsibility;

(b) information becomes available as a result of others reading or hearing what witnesses have said;

(c) there is a perception of open dealing which helps to restore confidence;

---

54 *R v General Medical Council, ex p Toth*, 23 June 2000, unreported. Layout adjusted.

55 *R v Secretary of State for Health, ex p Wagstaff*; *R v Secretary of State for Health, ex p Associated Newspapers* [2001] 1 WLR 292. He cited, among other authorities: *Crampton v Secretary of State for Health* [1993] CA Transcript 824 and in Strasbourg as *Taylor v UK* [1994] 18 EHRR CD 215; Lord Chancellor, 'Disasters and the Law: Deciding the form of inquiry', (1991) published in Clarke LJ, *Thames Safety Inquiry: Final Report*, Annex D, 2000 (Cm 4558). See now: Blom-Cooper, 'Public interest in public inquiries', [2003] PL 578–579; Department for Constitutional Affairs, *Consultation Paper: Effective Inquiries*, 6 May 2004; Steele, 'Judging judicial inquiries', [2004] PL 738; and the Inquiries Act 2005.

And see also, e.g. Brooke LJ in *R (on the application of Khan) v Secretary of State for Health* [2003] EWCA Civ 1129 (where the agents of a state bore potential responsibility for the loss of a human life, the holding of the inquest would not satisfy that obligation, as the claimant was in no fit state to take part in it himself, unless there was legal representation). These is now, a considerable body of case-law, both domestic and at Strasburg as to the public character of inquiries, see, e.g. Straw and Thomas, 'Human rights and the inquest', (2005) NLJ Vol.155, 630, discussing *R (on the application of Middleton) v West Somerset Coroner* [2004] UKHL 10.

(d) there is no significant risk of leaks leading to distorted reporting.

At least at times, the ECtHR has been emphatic. Thus, in *Sutter v Switzerland*[56] and in *Axen v Germany*[57] it said:

> The public character of proceedings before the judicial bodies protects litigants against the administration of justice in secret with no public scrutiny; it is also one of the means whereby confidence in the courts, superior and inferior, can be maintained.

So also, it went on:

> By rendering the administration of justice visible, publicity contributes to … a fair trial, the guarantee of which is one of the fundamental principles of any democratic society, within the meaning of the Convention.

We shall see the common law has developed a considerable jurisprudence concerning the balance between openness, efficiency and confidentiality in relation to the device of compulsory disclosure. It has also refined non-party access to material used in litigation. This said, it has been troubled by the conflicts that arise between the principle of openness and rules such as those relating to 'without prejudice' negotiations and legal professional privilege (not least as regards wasted costs orders). We shall come to them. Nevertheless, the fundamental principle is that justice in democratic societies (in the wider sense of the phrase which includes toleration as well as majority rule) should be open and should yield only to necessity and not convenience. The rule operates, so to speak, over the heads of all the participants.

The effect of access by the press to the court has been described by Donaldson MR:[58]

> The media are the eyes and ears of the general public. They act on behalf of the general public. Their right to know and their right to publish is neither more nor less than that of the general public. Indeed it is that of the general public for whom they are trustees. If the public interest in the safety of the realm, or other public interest, requires that there be no general dissemination of particular information, the media will be under a duty not to publish. This duty is owed to the public as much as to the confider.

So also, as Lord Nicholls put it in *Reynolds v Times Newspapers*:[59]

---

56 *Sutter v Switzerland*, [26], discussed at p. 72. *Sutter* was applied in *Szücs v Austria*, 24 November 1997, [45]. And see *Gautrin v France*, 20 May 1998, [42].

57 *Axen v Germany*, 8 December 1983, [25]. This passage was cited by Lord Steyn in *Re S* (A Child) [2004] UKHL 47, [15] where he also cited *Malhous v The Czech Republic*, 12 July 2001; *Bakova v Slovakia*, 12 November 2002. And see *Diennet v France*, 26 September 1995.

58 *Attorney General v Guardian Newspapers* (No 2) [1990] 1 AC 109, 183, in the Court of Appeal.

59 *Reynolds v Times Newspapers* [2001] 2 AC 127, 200 G-H.

> It is through the mass media that most people today obtain their information on political matters. Without freedom of expression by the media, freedom of expression would be a hollow concept. The interest of a democratic society in ensuring a free press weighs heavily in the balance in deciding whether any curtailment of this freedom bears a reasonable relationship to the purpose of the curtailment.

All this is, of course, different from where the court uses publicity and the press to give greater efficacy to its decisions. Thus, in *Stanley, Marshall and Kelly* the Court approved of publicity of an Anti-Social Behaviour Order.[60]

Exceptions

Generally

It is necessary to re-emphasize a point I made earlier. Open justice can conflict with other values. Left to themselves very often one or both the parties might prefer cloistered adjudication. Usually, but not always, these wishes are irrelevant. Art. 6 describes the allowable exceptions:

> The press and public may be excluded from all or part of the trial in the interests of morals, public order or national security in a democratic society, where the interests of juveniles or the protection of the private life of the parties so require, or to the extent strictly necessary in the opinion of the court in special circumstances where publicity would prejudice the interests of justice.

This is in line with *Scott v Scott* where Lord Haldane LC said:

> If there is any exception to the broad principle which requires the administration of justice to take place in open Court, that exception must be based on the application of some other and overriding principle which defines the field of exception and does not leave its limits to the individual discretion of the judge.

But as he put it:[61] 'But the exceptions are themselves the outcome of a yet more fundamental principle that the chief object of Courts of justice must be to secure that justice is done.' Among the exceptions Lord Haldane LC mentioned were the interests of 'wards and lunatics' (or, as we now say, children and mental patients) where, the court's involvement is more administrative than judicial[62] (and where the exceptions can now probably be justified by reference to Art. 8) and 'litigation as to a secret process, where the effect of publicity would be to destroy the subject-

---

60 *R (on the application of Stanley, Marshall and Kelly) v Metropolitan Police Commissioner* [2004] EWHC 2229 (Admin).

61 *Scott v Scott* [1913] AC 417, 437–438, cited by Buxton LJ in *Lilly Icos v Pfizer*, No. 2 [2000] EWCA Civ 2 [18].

62 In *Re Trusts of X Charity; Y v Attorney General* [2003] EWHC 1462 (Ch) Sir Andrew Morritt V-C applied the exception to an application by trustees for directions.

matter. There it may well be that justice could not be done at all if it had to be done in public'. Lord Haldane went on:

> But the burden lies on those seeking to displace its application in the particular case to make out that the ordinary rule must as of necessity be superseded by this paramount consideration. The question is by no means one which, consistently with the spirit of our jurisprudence, can be dealt with by the judge as resting in his mere discretion as to what is expedient. The latter must treat it as one of principle, and as turning, not on convenience, but on necessity.

In *ex p New Cross BS*,[63] Donaldson MR concluded that *Scott v Scott* established the only exception is where it 'be shown that a public hearing is likely to lead, directly or indirectly, to a denial of justice'. Where publicity would destroy the alleged right, for example to confidential information, the proceedings can be closed. In *Z v Finland* the ECtHR said:[64]

> The protection of personal data, not least medical data, is of fundamental importance to a person's enjoyment of his or her right to respect for private and family life as guaranteed by Article 8[65] ... the interests of a patient and the community as a whole in protecting the confidentiality of medical data may be outweighed by the interest in investigation and prosecution of crime and in the publicity of court proceedings where such interests are shown to be of even greater importance[66] ... a margin of appreciation should be left to the competent national authorities in striking a fair balance between the interest of publicity of court proceedings, on the one hand, and the interests of a party or a third person in maintaining the confidentiality of such data, on the other hand. The scope of this margin will depend on such factors as the nature and seriousness of the interests at stake and the gravity of the interference.

Within that margin of appreciation, *Scott v Scott* leaves little room for discretion by UK judges to recognize a necessity to counter its general principle.[67]

Much of the litigation has concerned the scope of these exceptions and the burden of displacing a public trial. Outside the rules relating to disclosure before trial (discussed below that there is a general duty, subject to limitations, to disclose to the other side documents which are relevant to the action), principle is not always easy

---

63 *R v Chief Register of Friendly Building Societies ex p New Cross BS* [1984] QB 227.

64 *Z v Finland*, 25 February 1997, [95], [97], [99].

65 It cited Article 3 paras. 2(c), 5, 6 and 9 of the Convention for the Protection of Individuals with Regard to Automatic Processing of Personal Data, European Treaty Series No. 108, Strasbourg, 1981.

66 It cited Article 9 of the 1981 Data Protection Convention.

67 But note: *H (a healthcare worker)* v *N (a health authority)* [2002] EWCA Civ 195 where an interim injunction to prevent publication of the name a health worker with HIV was upheld; and, *Family of Bennett (Appellant) v Officer A (Respondents) and HM Coroner (Interested Party)* [2004] EWCA Civ 1439 where the anonymity of a witness at a coroner's court was approved.

to discern. It took time for the importance of *Scott v Scott* to be appreciated. Early on, in *Local Government Board v Arlidge* the House of Lords held that, where a decision is to be taken by an administrative body ultimately responsible to Parliament, there was no requirement that it should follow the practice of the courts. As Lord Shaw put it:[68]

> Judicial methods may, in many points of administration, be entirely unsuitable, and produce delays, expense, and public and private injury … that the judiciary should presume to impose its own methods on administrative or executive officers is a usurpation.

Scott v Scott was, perhaps unsurprisingly, not cited.

In *ex p Doyle*, Lord Reading CJ was happy to uphold a secret trial (that is, a trial from which the public were excluded) leading to a death sentence (later commuted) on one of the participants in the Dublin Easter Rising of 1916.[69] He said: 'it is in my judgment plain that inherent jurisdiction exists in any Court which enables it to exclude the public where it becomes necessary in order to administer justice.' Whether, on its facts, *Doyle* is still good law is an open question.[70]

The Exceptions in CPR Part 39 and Related Matters

CPR Part 39, the trial, lists a number of exceptions to its general rule that all hearings shall be in public. It says:

> (3) A hearing, or any part of it, may be in private if –
>
> (a) publicity would defeat the object of the hearing;
>
> (b) it involves matters relating to national security;
>
> (c) it involves confidential information (including information relating to personal financial matters) and publicity would damage that confidentiality;

---

68 *Local Government Board v Arlidge* [1915] AC 120.

69 *R v Governor of Lewes Prison, ex p Doyle* [1917] 2 KB 254. The other members of the Divisional Court agreed. Capturing the spirit of the moment, but not the tranquillity on which justice thrives, Darling J observed: 'It appears to me really incongruous that, before the echoes of this rebellion have died away, we should meet here solemnly to consider such points as have been argued before us.'

70 It was cited by Lord Woolf in *Hodgson v Imperial Tobacco*, as if it still had authority. It may however be safer to follow Lord Pearce in *Conway v Rimmer* [1968] AC 910:

> In theory any general legal definition of the balance between individual justice in one scale and the safety and well-being of the state in the other scale, should be unaffected by the dangerous times in which it is uttered. But in practice the flame of individual right and justice must burn more palely when it is ringed by the more dramatic light of bombed buildings. And the human mind cannot but be affected subconsciously, even in generality of definition, by such a contrast since it is certainly a matter which ought to influence the particular decision in the case.

Similarly *Doyle* was a war-time decision.

(d) a private hearing is necessary to protect the interests of any child or patient;

(e) it is a hearing of an application made without notice and it would be unjust to any respondent for there to be a public hearing;

(f) it involves uncontentious matters arising in the administration of trusts or in the administration of a deceased person's estate; or

(g) the court considers this to be necessary, in the interests of justice.

(4) The court may order that the identity of any party or witness must not be disclosed if it considers non-disclosure necessary in order to protect the interests of that party or witness.

The Practice Direction, but not Part 39 itself, has given a broad meaning to the phases *so require* and *strictly necessary* in Art. 6 so that more can be held in private than is perhaps to be expected. It says:

1.4 The decision as to whether to hold a hearing in public or in private must be made by the judge conducting the hearing having regard to any representations which may have been made to him.

Uncontroversially, but unnecessarily, it enjoins the judge to have regard to Art. 6(1)[71] and then in para. 1.5 sets out a number of cases which have in common that specific questions of confidential financial information are at issue.[72] The Practice Direction continues, in para. 1.6, to include 'the approval of a compromise or settlement on behalf of a child or patient or an application for the payment of money out of court to such a person' and in para. 1.7 to draw attention to the practice direction which supplements Part 27 (hearings of claims in the small claims track). It goes on: '1.8 nothing in this practice direction prevents a judge ordering that a hearing taking place in public shall continue in private, or vice-versa.' And other provisions deal with the effect of signs that the proceedings are private and the publicity for private orders.

The Practice Direction to Part 27 (small claims) says:

4.1 (1) the general rule is that a small claim hearing will be in public.

---

71 Para. 1.4A. As to being unnecessary compare Sullivan J in *R (on the application of Ewing) v Department for Constitutional Affairs* [2006] EWHC 504, [24]: 'Just as it is unnecessary to teach one's grandmother how to suck eggs, so it is unnecessary for the Heads of Division to remind High Court judges that, in exercising their discretion under the Practice Direction, they should be guided by the overriding objective'.

72 And see Practice Direction 1.15 'Where the court lists a hearing of a claim by a mortgagee for an order for possession of land under paragraph 1.5(1) above to be in private, any fact which needs to be proved by the evidence of witnesses may be proved by evidence in writing.'

(2) The judge may decide to hold it in private if:

(a) the parties agree, or

(b) a ground mentioned in rule 39.2 (3) applies.

CPR Part 1.4, having provided that the court must further the overriding objective by actively managing cases, adds that this includes: '(j) dealing with the case without the parties needing to attend at court [and] (k) making use of technology.' It is not surprising that these last powers have not attracted much attention from the appellate courts. Where the hearing is by video-link or particularly telephone or web conferencing there may be formidable practical difficulties in making it public.

Other powers to sit in private have been discussed by the courts. Thus, in *ex p Pelling* Keene J noted that the 1997 Act s. 1(3) provides 'The power to make Civil Procedure Rules is to be exercised with a view to securing that the civil justice system is accessible, fair and efficient'. He offered some sort of explanation for secrecy in small claims:[73]

> Justice may well be more accessible if, in cases of that kind, they are heard in private because, in many instances, there will not be lawyers representing one or both of the parties, and parties who are not used to litigation may well be more willing to represent themselves and to speak about their complaints if they are not on public display.

What he said is also largely applicable to the types of hearing listed in the Practice Direction to Part 39. But the question, as put in *Scott v Scott*, is not convenience or whether the parties are more or less willing to use the court. It will be recalled that Lord Haldane LC expressly discussed the possibility of reluctance by the parties to use the court at all. The question is whether privacy is 'necessary' or as Art. 6 puts it 'strictly necessary'. We saw in *Scott*, Lord Shaw spoke about: 'There is no greater danger of usurpation than that which proceeds little by little, under cover of rules of procedure, and at the instance of judges themselves.' Are not these Practice Directions examples of such usurpation? Of course, the CPR prevail over any rule in *Scott v Scott* – unless that is, the apparent meaning of the rule is not compatible with the ECHR. I am arguing that s. 1 of the 1997 Act must be read subject to Art. 6 of the Convention. The accessibility and efficiency of the system is subject to the overarching requirement that justice must be done in public.

In one of his several attacks on the rules and the way they are implemented Dr Pelling sought a declaration that Part 39 is *ultra vires*.[74] As Buxton LJ put it, the claim was that by permitting some cases to be heard in private it infringed the principle of legality (which imports the need for a primary statute to be interpreted

73 *R v Bow County Court ex p Pelling*, 26 January 2000.

74 *R (on the application of Pelling) v Bow County Court* QBD (Admin) 19 October 2000.

in accord with fundamental rights).[75] Buxton LJ held that, because Part 39 requires the court to do justice and merely permitted private hearings in some limited types of case, it did not infringe the principle as he formulated it.

Dr Pelling was more successful in yet another attack, this time on the practice of family courts to sit in private and give judgment in private, unless they decide otherwise. He lost on this issue both in London and at Strasbourg.[76] But that was before the HRA had come into force. The Court of Appeal held[77] that the current practice is convention compliant but so also would an alternative: the new Family Justice Council should consider the issue.[78]

The general question came to a head in *Department of Economics, Policy and Development of the City of Moscow v Bankers Trust*.[79] It is commonly remarked that the main advantages of arbitration, as perceived by the parties, are speed, informality, and finality, as well as privacy and confidentiality.[80] In *Associated Electric and Gas Insurance Service v European Reinsurance of Zürich*,[81] Lord Hobhouse considered the purpose of arbitration and in particular the rationale for the duty of confidentiality. It was to determine disputes between parties to the arbitration in a manner that did not entail the actual or potential disclosure of information to persons with interests adverse to the parties. CPR Part 62.10(2) thus disapplies Part 39.2 in relation to the court's supervisory jurisdiction in 'arbitration claims', defined in Part 62.1. It says: '(1) the court may order that an arbitration claim be heard either in public or in private' and goes on to define what is to happen in the absence of any such order. Para. (3) (a) provides that generally the determination of points of law (either by way of a preliminary point or by way of an appeal will be heard in public, but para. (3) (b) says 'all other arbitration claims will be heard in private'.

In *the City of Moscow* there was such an 'arbitration claim' and the court duly sat in private. The judge gave a judgment that was not described, in the terms of para. 1.13 of the Practice Direction to Part 39, as being 'in private'. A brief summary was rapidly displayed in the LAWTEL website and, almost as rapidly, the judge ordered that it be withdrawn. Reversing the judge on this point because the information was in the public domain and because the LAWTEL summary was in any event harmless, the Court of Appeal took the opportunity to discuss the scope of

75 See per Lord Hoffman in *R v Secretary of State for the Home Department ex p Simms* [2000] 2 AC 115.

76 *Re P-B (a minor)* (child cases: hearings in open court) [1997] 1 All ER 58 and *B and P v UK*, 24 April 2001.

77 *Pelling v Bruce-Williams and Secretary of State for Constitutional Affairs* (Interested Party) [2004] EWCA Civ 845.

78 And see *Clibbery v Allen* [2002] EWCA Civ 45 per Thorpe LJ, [95] citing the LCD Consultation Paper, *Review of Access to and Reporting of Family Proceedings* (1993).

79 *Department of Economics, Policy and Development of the City of Moscow v Bankers Trust* [2004] EWCA CIV 314.

80 See Coleman J in *Hassneh Insurance v Mew* [1993] 2 Lloyd's REP 243.

81 *Associated Electric and Gas Insurance Service v European Reinsurance of Zürich* [2003] UKPC 11.

the modern exceptions to the principle of open justice. In effect, it put detail into the exceptions recognized by Lord Haldane in *Scott*.[82] Mance LJ spoke[83] of a number of statutes protecting the privacy of proceedings in a number of disparate cases, e.g. those:

- regulating the reporting of evidence in certain matrimonial cases;
- the hearing of evidence of sexual capacity in nullity proceedings;
- hearings relating to minors, those under the Children Act 1989;
- hearings under the Mental Health Acts;
- where the court sits in private for reasons of national security; and,
- hearings where information relating to a secret process, discovery or invention is in issue.[84]

He adopted the view of Butler-Sloss P in *Clibbery v Allan* as to the significance of an 'in chambers' hearing:[85]

> She advanced a three-fold distinction between cases 'heard in open court, those heard in private and those heard in secret where the information disclosed to the court and the proceedings remain confidential'. She went on ... to affirm that a hearing in the intermediate category ('in private' in her terminology) does not, of itself, prohibit the publication of information about the proceedings or given in the proceedings ... and to consider the scope of the implied duty of confidentiality arising in respect of documents disclosed in civil litigation.

Mance LJ said she had concluded that it is necessary to hold some proceedings in private and quoted her as saying:[86]

> There should be protection against publication of some of those proceedings. Such protection must be proportionate to the requirements of the administration of justice. It might be thought to be inconvenient and time-consuming to have to look at this problem in individual cases heard in private. There are groups of cases in which the answer is obvious and, in my view, there will only be a small number of cases ... where the advocates and the court may have to consider the point.

He then reviewed the Strasbourg jurisprudence and himself concluded:[87]

---

82 Above p. 60.

83 At para. 15.

84 The Administration of Justice Act, 1960 s. 12 as amended.

85 At [24]-[25], *Clibbery v Allen* [2002] EWCA Civ 45.

86 At [80]. At [79] she cited Lord Edmund-Davies in *Attorney General v Leveller Magazine* [1979] AC 440, 465.

87 At [27]. He cited *Håkansson and Sturesson v Sweden*, 21 February 1990, [66]; *Werner v Austria*, 24 November 1997, [45]; *B and P v UK*, 24 April 2001, [39]; *Suovaniemi v Finland* 23 February 1999 (Admissibility Application); and, cf. domestically, in proceedings under s. 97 of the Children Act 1989, *P v BW* [2003] EWHC 1541 (Fam) (Bennett J).

> The exceptions formulated in article 6 (1) are permissive. However, in so far as they contemplate the possibility of private hearings to protect Convention rights, such as 'the private life of the parties' … they seem to require the Court … to consider whether the strictness of the rules in *Scott v Scott* require some qualification ... It is not surprising that principles now recognized in the Human Rights Convention, particularly those relating to privacy, should involve a somewhat expanded or developed view of such interests in certain contexts ... However, there is nothing in Strasbourg jurisprudence, any more than in *Scott v Scott*, to suggest that parties can by simple agreement insist on a court restricting publication.

Applying both this jurisprudence (and he could have added the ECtHR's consideration of the relation between Arts 6 and 8 we saw in *Z v Finland*)[88] and his account of the common law, he concluded the modern law takes 'a more relaxed view' of the need for openness. In the generality of claims, CPR Part 39 says the starting point is openness. But both *Scott v Scott*, as developed by statute, and the Strasbourg case law recognize that sometimes privacy (secrecy) is necessary. In arbitration claims, the starting point is in favour of secrecy. Mance LJ said it is:[89]

> A special case, in relation to which there has been very considerable development during recent years. An alternative and overlapping consideration is that parties may be deterred from arbitrating or at any rate from invoking the court's supervisory role in relation to arbitration if their understanding regarding arbitral confidentiality and privacy is ignored … a party could well be deterred from making an arbitration claim in court if there was a risk that by doing so really confidential matters might be disclosed ... What would render the administration of justice impracticable or would reasonably deter parties entitled to justice from seeking it at the hands of the court … are to some extent matters of judgment and may develop to meet new contexts as well as over time, as social perceptions of the need to protect personal privacy and confidential information change.

But, he went on:

> The consideration that parties have elected to arbitrate confidentially and privately cannot dictate the position in respect of arbitration claims brought to court under CPR 62.10. CPR 62.10 therefore only represents a starting point. Such proceedings are no longer consensual. The possibility of pursuing them exists in the public interest. The courts, when called upon to exercise the supervisory role assigned to them under the Arbitration Act 1996, are acting as a branch of the state, not as a mere extension of the consensual arbitral process. Nevertheless, they are acting in the public interest to facilitate the fairness and well-being of a consensual method of dispute resolution, and both the Rule Committee and the courts can still take into account the parties' expectations regarding privacy and confidentiality when agreeing to arbitrate.

---

88 *Z v Finland*, 25 February 1997, [95], [97], [99], above p. 61.

89 At [32]-[34]. And see *Associated Electric and Gas Insurance Service v European Reinsurance of Zürich* [2003] UKPC 11.

Mance LJ continued by discussing the extent of the duty to give judgment in public in such arbitration claims. It is convenient to examine what he said about this as we consider the duty to give reasons generally.

Overall the ECtHR has been kind to the UK. In *Campbell and Fell* it upheld the system of private disciplinary hearings against prisoners. It reasoned:[90]

> A Board's adjudications are, as befits the character of disciplinary proceedings of this kind, habitually held within the prison precincts and the difficulties over admitting the public to those precincts are obvious. If they were held outside, … problems would arise as regards the prisoner's transportation to and attendance at the hearing. To require that disciplinary proceedings concerning convicted prisoners should be held in public would impose a disproportionate burden on the authorities of the State.

So also, in *B and P v UK* the ECtHR held that:[91] 'the requirement to hold a public hearing is subject to exceptions.' That case concerned the presumption in favour of a private hearing in cases under the Children Act 1989. It said:[92]

> To enable the deciding judge to gain as full and accurate a picture as possible of the advantages and disadvantages of the various residence and contact options open to the child, it is essential that the parents and other witnesses feel able to express themselves candidly on highly personal issues without fear of public curiosity or comment … English procedural law can therefore be seen as a specific reflection of the general exceptions provided for in Article 6(1).

By contrast, in *Riepan v Austria* a convict was tried under the general criminal law for further offences. The trial took place inside a prison. The Court said:[93]

> It was undisputed in the present case that the publicity of the hearing was not formally excluded. However, hindrance in fact can contravene the Convention just like a legal impediment. The Court considers that the mere fact that the trial took place in the precincts of [a] Prison does not necessarily lead to the conclusion that it lacked publicity. Nor did the fact that any potential spectators would have had to undergo certain identity and possibly security checks in itself deprive the hearing of its public nature. Nevertheless, … the Convention is intended to guarantee not rights that are theoretical or illusory but rights that are practical and effective.

It went on to hold 'a trial complies with the requirement of publicity only if':[94]

---

90 *Campbell and Fell v UK*, 28 June 1984, [87]. It has been applied many times including *R (on the application of Bannatyne) v Secretary of State for the Home Department* [2004] EWHC 1921 (Admin) citing *inter alia*, *Ezeh and Connors v UK*, 9 October 2003 [GC].

91 *B and P v UK*, 24 April 2001.

92 At [38]-[39].

93 *Riepan v Austria*, 14 November 2000, [28]-[29].

94 It added, para. 29: 'In many cases these conditions will be fulfilled by the simple fact that a hearing is held in a regular courtroom large enough to accommodate spectators.'

(a) 'the public is able to obtain information about its date and place' and
(b) 'this place is easily accessible to the public'.

CPR Part 39.2(2) provides: 'The requirement for a hearing to be in public does not require the court to make special arrangements for accommodating members of the public.'[95] So also, the Practice Direction to Part 27 (small claims) says:[96]

> 4.1(3) A hearing or part of a hearing which takes place other than at the court, for example at the home or business premises of a party, will not be in public.
>
> 4.2 a hearing that takes place at the court will generally be in the judge's room but it may take place in a courtroom.

The question is does *Riepan* affect the legality of these provisions? In *R (on the application of Pelling) v Bow County Court*,[97] the claimant wanted access to a small claims court. Laws LJ held that such a court can sit behind a door locked for security reasons. Clearly, the courts cannot ignore security and in *Riepan* the ECtHR did not do so: spectators at trials can be subject to physical security checks. In *Pelling*, the publication by display on the Court's notice board of the small claims list satisfied the first of these *Riepan* conditions. The provision in Part 39.2 that no special arrangements are required and in the Practice Direction that private hearings can take place other than in court and that they can take place in the judge's room (most small claims do) probably do not satisfy the second. The provision in the Practice Direction that the parties can agree to a private hearing certainly is in conflict with *Riepan*. In *Scarth v UK*,[98] the ECtHR considered the small claims procedure which existed under the old rules. That procedure was then called arbitration. It was conducted in private, but by a judge. The court had no difficulty, but gave no reasons, for holding that it did not comply with Art. 6. The ECtHR mentioned the new CPR provisions but did not comment on them. This is a pity because it seems difficult to reconcile Art. 6 with the continued discretion for the judge to sit in private merely because the parties agree.

---

95 This provision almost certainly is a result of the decision in *Forbes v Smith* [1998] 1 All ER 973 (approved in *Hodgson v Imperial Tobacco* [1998] 1 WLR 1056) that chambers proceedings are open to the public. In *Hodgson* there was some discussion of these practical questions.

96 The Practice Direction adds:

1.14 References to hearings being in public or private or in a judge's room contained in the Civil Procedure Rules (including the Rules of the Supreme Court and the County Court Rules scheduled to Part 50) and the practice directions which supplement them do not restrict any existing rights of audience or confer any new rights of audience in respect of applications or proceedings which under the rules previously in force would have been heard in court or in chambers respectively.

97 *R (on the application of Pelling) v Bow County Court* [2001] EWCA Civ 122.

98 *Scarth v UK*, 22 July 1999.

Waiver

Every legal system recognizes a power to waive rights, and most rights can be waived. In some other contexts it is called gift. The power extends even to the fundamental rights of the Convention.[99] But, as Mance LJ indicated in the *City of Moscow*, the public's interest in the functioning of the State's courts goes beyond the parties.[100] Our concern is with the balance between the parties and the public.

Of course, parties can agree (before or after a dispute arises) to have their rights settled in private.[101] Indeed, the Convention itself recognizes this possibility. Under the title *Examination of the case and friendly settlement proceedings* Article 38 says:

> 1. If the Court declares the application admissible, it shall ...
>
> (b) place itself at the disposal of the parties concerned with a view to securing a friendly settlement of the matter on the basis of respect for human rights as defined in the Convention and the protocols thereto.
>
> 2. Proceedings conducted under paragraph 1.b shall be confidential.[102]

And Rule 62 of its Rules of Court provide:

> 1. Once an application has been declared admissible, the Registrar ... shall enter into contact with the parties with a view to securing a friendly settlement of the matter in accordance with Article 38(1)(b) of the Convention. The Chamber shall take any steps that appear appropriate to facilitate such a settlement.
>
> 2. In accordance with Article 38(2) of the Convention, the friendly-settlement negotiations shall be confidential and without prejudice to the parties' arguments in the contentious proceedings. No written or oral communication and no offer or concession made in the framework of the attempt to secure a friendly settlement may be referred to or relied on in the contentious proceedings.

---

99 Morris, 'Fundamental Rights: Exclusion by Agreement', 2001 30 ILJ, 49, discussed the waiver of Convention rights in the context of labour law. And see de Schutter, 'Waiver of Rights and State Paternalism under the European Convention on Human Rights', 2000 NILQ 481.

100 Para. 20, citing Lord Woolf in *R v Legal Aid Board, ex p Kaim Todner* [1999] QB 966.

101 See *City of Moscow*, [2]. Mance LJ cited the Departmental Advisory Committee Report on the Arbitration Bill, February 1996 (chaired by Lord Saville) paras. 10–17: 'there is ... no doubt whatever that users of commercial arbitration in England place much importance' on privacy and confidentiality 'as essential features'. For a recent application, see *Stretford v Football Association* [2006] EWHC 479 (Ch).

102 Article 39, entitled *Finding of a friendly settlement*, goes on 'If a friendly settlement is effected [it shall issue a decision] which shall be confined to a brief statement of the facts and of the solution reached'.

3. If the Chamber is informed by the Registrar that the parties have agreed to a friendly settlement, it shall, after verifying that the settlement has been reached on the basis of respect for human rights as defined in the Convention and the Protocols thereto, strike the case out of the Court's list.

Perhaps, to English lawyers, the most familiar example of such a settlement is *Harman v UK* which led to changes in the law of contempt of court and the rules of court.

The CPR, themselves, make similar but narrower provision.[103] Thus, Part 23.8 says:

The court may deal with an application without a hearing if – (a) the parties agree as to the terms of the order sought;

(b) the parties agree that the court should dispose of the application without a hearing, or

(c) the court does not consider that a hearing would be appropriate.

Its Practice Direction adds:

8. The procedural judge should keep, either by way of a note or a tape recording, brief details of all proceedings before him, including the dates of the proceedings and a short statement of the decision taken at each hearing.

10.1. Rule 40.6 sets out the circumstances where an agreed judgment or order may be entered and sealed.[104]

Outside such procedures, settlement may be achieved, on the one side, by a State determination or, on the other, by negotiation or ADR. Indeed, any outcome of ADR (including arbitration) does not so much 'determine' rights as re-define them. The results of such processes take effect as contract.[105] ADR, like arbitration, is a private matter. Private litigants can agree to private settlement or a procedure for private settlement before or after a dispute has arisen and they can agree whether or not the consequences are binding. The courts, including the ECtHR,[106] recognize the

103 The provision is narrower because under the Convention the court is 'at the disposal of the parties' whereas under the CPR and any British court sponsored ADR scheme, ADR is at arm's length from the court. One example of such a scheme is at the Central London County Court under CPR Part 26 Practice Direction B, discussed below at p. 96.

104 CPR Part 40.6 says: '(1) This rule applies where all the parties agree the terms in which a judgment should be given or an order should be made. (2) A court officer may enter and seal an agreed judgment or order if – ... (b) none of the parties is a litigant in person ...'

105 See, for example: *Bremer Oeltransport v Drewry* [1933] 1 KB 753, 760; *Haines v Carter* [2002] UKPC 49.

106 *Stran Greek Refineries and Stratis Andreadis v Greece*, 9 December 1994.

validity of such agreements.[107] They have nothing to do with the judicial organs of the State.

It is these last that need to be public and for the benefit of the public as a whole. The contrary would render considerable parts of our civil process anomalous. The courts' coercive powers in relation to case management and the duties of disclosure imposed by rule and common law would make little sense. Nor does the distinction between the determination of rights and the declaration of status (as is recognized in some patent cases[108] where confidentiality agreements are sometimes upheld after consideration of particular facts) justify any idea that the parties can agree to use the power of the State in private.

All this is so before the advent of the CPR. But in those days civil procedure was based on the principle of what Sir Jack Jacob liked to call 'party control'.[109] In the courts that has now gone and there is even less cause today to say that the parties can simply agree to waive the publicity requirements that apply to the State's legal system. Subject to its limited exceptions and to a margin of appreciation, as we saw in *Sutter* and in *Axen*, Art. 6 requires the public determination of rights.[110] *Sutter* and *Axen* went further than a literal reading of Art. 6. That says 'everyone is entitled' and no doubt anyone can waive an entitlement. But according to these cases, Art. 6 is not merely for the benefit of the parties. Public proceedings are for the common benefit. *Scott v Scott* is part of the Strasbourg jurisprudence.

The ECHR institutions have considered the question of waiver specifically in arbitration. In *Bramelid and Malsmtröm v Sweden*, the Commission said:[111]

> Article 6(1) … does not prevent a decision of this kind being taken in the first instance by an organ which is not in the nature of a court, provided that the matter can thereafter be brought within a reasonable time before a court with jurisdiction to decide the matter both as to law and to fact … the Convention does not prevent a person from waiving the rights guaranteed by Article 6(1) of the Convention, when civil rights and obligations are in issue, provided that this waiver is not made under duress.

In *Jon Axelsson v Sweden* it was more expansive:[112]

> The Commission notes that in so far as arbitration is based on agreements between the parties to the dispute, it is a natural consequence of their right to regulate their mutual relations as they see fit. From a more general perspective, arbitration procedures can also be said to pursue the legitimate aim of encouraging non-judicial settlements and of relieving the courts of an excessive burden of cases ... By not requesting a hearing … the Commission finds that the applicants must be considered to have unequivocally waived their right under Art. 6 of the Convention to a public hearing before the Court of Appeal.

---

107 *Cable and Wireless v IBM United Kingdom* [2002] EWHC 2059 (Comm).

108 E.g. *Lilly Icos v Pfizer* (No.2) [2002] EWCA Civ No. 2.

109 E.g. Sir Jack Jacob, *The Fabric of Civil Justice*, 1987, pp. 11 et seq.

110 *Sutter v Switzerland*, 22 February 1984, [26], p. 59 above.

111 *Bramelid and Malsmtröm v Sweden*, 12 October 1982.

112 *Jon Axelsson v Sweden*, 13 July 1990, ECommHR.

> The Commission furthermore finds no indication that the litigation involved any issues of public interest which could have rendered a public hearing necessary irrespective of the applicants' request.

So also, in *Nordström-Janzon and Nordström-Lehtinen v Netherlands* it said:[113]

> The arbitration was thus based on a voluntary agreement according to which disputes between the parties should not be settled by the ordinary courts but under a special arbitration system. Consequently, there was a renunciation by the parties of a procedure before the ordinary courts satisfying all the guarantees of Art. 6 of the Convention ... In some respects – in particular as regards publicity – it is clear that arbitral proceedings are often not even intended to be in conformity with Art. 6, and the arbitration agreement entails a renunciation of the full application of that Article ... each Contracting State may in principle decide itself on which grounds an arbitral award should be quashed ... the Commission observes that the applicant's argument that the mere appearance of a lack of independence or impartiality should lead to a quashing of the arbitral award has no basis in Dutch law ... It finds it reasonable that in this respect Dutch law requires strong reasons for quashing an already rendered award, since the quashing will often mean that a long and costly arbitral procedure will become useless and that considerable work and expense must be invested in new proceedings.

As we shall see, this decision is difficult to reconcile with the case law on judicial bias where appearances have indeed been held to be important. The decision that apparent bias discovered only after the arbitration award rarely affects an award is unsustainable.[114] In principle, and apart from this case, the Court has never said otherwise.[115] There can be no true agreement unless a party has full knowledge. Consent requires knowledge. The reliance on Dutch law is irrelevant: to repeat the point, the European human rights machinery is not an appeal from national systems; it is supervisory of them.[116]

On a number of occasions the ECtHR has discussed the possibility of a waiver of Convention rights outside arbitration. In many of these cases, it does not mention the *Sutter/Axen* dimension to the State's judicial decision making.

Deweer v Belgium concerned a composition of prospective criminal proceedings. The court said:[117]

---

113 *Nordström-Janzon and Nordström-Lehtinen v Netherlands*, 27 November 1996, *Ecommhr, London and Amsterdam Properties v Waterman Partnership* [2003] EWHC 3059 (TCC).

114 It is, of course, different if the bias is or should have been known beforehand, *Thyssen Canada v Mariana Maritime* [2005] EWHC 219 (Comm). See Batchelor, 'Assessing arbitrator bias', (2004) NLJ Vol.154, 1902.

115 *Oberschlick v Austria* (No.1), 23 May 1991.

116 But, cf. *Roche v UK*, 19 October 2005, p. 15 above.

117 *Deweer v Belgium*, 27 February 1980, [49] et seq. And see: *Thompson v UK*, 15 June 2004, one of several cases where military law has been considered; and *Yavuz v Austria*, 27 May 2004, citing *Colozza v Italy*, 12 February 1985, [27]; and, *T v Italy*, 12 October 1992,

> The 'right to a court', which is a constituent element of the right to a fair trial, is no more absolute in criminal than in civil matters. It is subject to implied limitations ... By paying the BF 10 000 ... by way of settlement ... Mr Deweer waived his right to have his case dealt with by a tribunal. In the Contracting States' domestic legal systems a waiver of this kind is frequently encountered both in civil matters, notably in the shape of arbitration clauses in contracts, and in criminal matters in the shape, *inter alia*, of fines paid by way of composition. The waiver, which has undeniable advantages for the individual concerned as well as for the administration of justice, does not in principle offend against the Convention ... Nevertheless, in a democratic society too great an importance attaches to the 'right to a court' ... for its benefit to be forfeited solely by reason of the fact that an individual is a party to a settlement reached in the course of a procedure ancillary to court proceedings. In an area concerning the public order (ordre public) of the member States of the Council of Europe, any measure or decision alleged to be in breach of Art. 6 calls for particularly careful review ... Absence of constraint is at all events one of the conditions to be satisfied; this much is dictated by an international instrument founded on freedom and the rule of law.[118]

The issue did not arise, and the court did not discuss, what other conditions must be satisfied. We shall come to what these might be. In *Neumeister v Austria* it was concerned with the mechanism of waiver:[119] 'particularly in the specific field covered by the Convention, the waiver of a right, even the mere right to a sum of money, must result from unequivocal statements or documents.'

Meanwhile, in *Le Compte, Van Leuven and De Meyere v Belgium* the court dealt with professional disciplinary proceedings against some doctors. It said:[120]

> Demands of flexibility and efficiency, which are fully compatible with the protection of human rights, may justify the prior intervention of administrative or professional bodies ... which do not satisfy the ... requirements in every respect; the legal tradition of many member States of the Council of Europe may be invoked in support of such a system ... conducting disciplinary proceedings of this kind in private does not contravene the Convention, provided that the person concerned consents.

It thus, and by a side wind and in a way that was unnecessary for its decision, slipped the idea of a general possibility of waiver into its jurisprudence. Nevertheless, in *Albert and Le Compte* it seemed to accept that the possibility had been established:[121]

---

[26], Cf. Parker, 'Restorative Justice in Business Regulation? *The Australian Competition and Consumer Commission's Use of Enforceable Undertakings*', (2004) 67 MLR 209.

118 In *H v a Firm*, 24 May 2004, unreported, QBD, it was held that the usual pressure of commercial negotiation was not economic duress. In *DSNB Subsea v Petroleum Geo-services ASA* [2000] BLR 530, [131] Dyson J said: 'The ingredients of actionable duress are that there must be pressure, (a) whose practical effect is that there is compulsion on, or a lack of practical choice for, the victim, (b) which is illegitimate, and (c) which is a significant cause inducing the claimant to enter into the contract.'

119 *Neumeister v Austria*, 7 May 1974, [36].

120 *Le Compte, Van Leuven and De Meyere v Belgium*, 23 June 1981, [51] and [59].

121 *Albert and Le Compte*, 10 February 1983, [35].

> The nature of some of the rights safeguarded by the Convention is such as to exclude a waiver of the entitlement to exercise them, but the same cannot be said of certain other rights. Thus, neither the letter nor the spirit of Article 6(1) would prevent a medical practitioner from waiving, of his own free will and in an unequivocal manner the entitlement to have his case heard in public.[122]

So also, in *H v Belgium*, a case concerning practice at the bar, it said:[123]

> The rule requiring a public hearing … may also yield in certain circumstances to the will of the person concerned. Admittedly, the nature of some of the rights safeguarded by the Convention is such as to exclude a waiver of the entitlement to exercise them, but the same cannot be said of certain other rights. Thus, neither the letter nor the spirit of Article 6(1) prevents an avocat from waiving, of his own free will and in an unequivocal manner, the entitlement to have his case heard in public; conducting disciplinary proceedings of this kind in private does not contravene the Convention. The evidence adduced does not establish that H intended to waive his right to a public hearing. He cannot be blamed for not having demanded to exercise a right which was not afforded him by the practice of the Belgian bars and that he had little prospect of securing.

Håkansson and Sturesson v Sweden was again concerned with waiver on the part of the litigants of a right to publicity, the terms in which that was admissible, and the effect on the Article 6 right[124] repeating what it said in *H v Belgium* the Court combined its views in *Neumeister* and *Le Compte, Van Leuven and De Meyere*.

Håkansson and Sturesson itself was decided in the context of Swedish agricultural law, and its provisions for licensing and compulsory purchase. The court considered that there was a waiver of the right to a public hearing because the applicants had not asked for one. It is not usually suggested that the public character of a trial is solely or mainly for the benefit of either party.[125] The court is under a duty to sit in public even if a party waives his right, and even if an applicant might be estopped from complaining. It may be that the explanation is that the national law in *Håkansson and Sturesson* was concerned with review of administrative proceedings and the court thought the proceedings were more administrative than judicial or it was a matter of

---

122 It cited *Neumeister*, 27 June 1968, [36] and *Le Compte, Van Leuven and de Meyere*, para. 59. It added [39]: 'the principles set out in paragraph 2 and in the provisions of paragraph 3 … are applicable, mutatis mutandis, to disciplinary proceedings subject to paragraph 1 in the same way as in the case of a person charged with a criminal offence.'

123 *H v Belgium*, 30 November 1987, [54].

124 *Håkansson and Sturesson v Sweden*, 21 February 1990, [66]. It cited among other cases, *Pauger v Austria*, 28 May 1997, [60] (there is no prevailing public interest because the case concerns only the interpretation of transitional provisions relating to widowers' pensions).

125 In *Re Trusts of X Charity; Y v Attorney General* [2003] EWHC 1462 (Ch), Sir Andrew Morritt V-C said that, if it is right, it is an implied restriction contrary to the decision in *Sutter v Switzerland* and to undermine the policy both domestic and European which requires hearings to be held in public.

public law to which Art. 6 did not apply.[126] However that may be, in *Gustafson*[127] it again repeated its view that a claimant under the Swedish Administrative procedure law was entitled to a hearing and entitled to waive that right. It held that Art. 6 was engaged. In *Göç v Turkey*, it said:[128] 'Article 6(1) entails an entitlement to an "oral hearing" unless there are exceptional circumstances.' The Court did not define what these may be. Or it may simply be that in *Håkansson and Sturesson* and similar cases, it was wrong to forget that a public hearing is a public right. Indeed, in *Gustafson*, in his Concurring Opinion, Judge Walsh said:

> A public hearing was not refused as it was never asked for. In fact every oral hearing is in practice a public hearing. The applicant had waived an oral hearing in addition to not asking for a public hearing. In my view he had in effect waived a public hearing. Additionally, it is to be noted that under Swedish law all such case files and the decisions thereon are available to the public.

In *Oberschlick v Austria* (No. 1) the Court said:[129] 'According to the Court's case-law, waiver of a right guaranteed by the Convention – in so far as it is permissible – must be established in an unequivocal manner'. And in *Pfeifer and Plankl v Austria* it added:[130] 'In the case of procedural rights a waiver, in order to be effective for Convention purposes, requires minimum guarantees commensurate to its importance.'

Nevertheless, in *Suovaniemi v Finland* the Court said:[131]

> There is no doubt that a voluntary waiver of court proceedings in favour of arbitration is in principle acceptable from the point of view of Article 6 ... Even so, such a waiver should not necessarily be considered to amount to a waiver of all the rights under Article 6 ... [and even] an unequivocal waiver ... valid only in so far as such waiver is 'permissible'. Waiver may be permissible with regard to certain rights but not with regard to certain others. A distinction may have to be made even between different rights guaranteed by Article 6. Thus, in the light of the case-law it is clear that the right to a public hearing can be validly waived even in court proceedings. The same applies, a fortiori, to arbitration proceedings, one of the very purposes of which is often to avoid publicity. On the other hand, the question whether the fundamental right to an impartial judge can be waived at all, was left open in the *Pfeifer and Plankl v Austria*, as in any case in the circumstances of that case there was no unequivocal waiver.[132]

---

126 See above p. 18.

127 *Gustafson v Sweden*, 1 July 1997, [47].

128 *Göç v Turkey*, 11 July 2002, [47].

129 *Oberschlick v Austria* (No. 1), 23 May 1991, [51].

130 *Pfeifer and Plankl v Austria*, 25 February 1992, [37].

131 *Suovaniemi v Finland*, 23 February 1999.

132 It repeated what the Commission had said in *Nordström-Janzon and Nordström-Lehtinen* that 'long and costly arbitral procedure will become useless and that considerable work and expense must be invested in new proceedings'.

And it noted, 'throughout the arbitration the applicants were represented by counsel, the waiver was accompanied by sufficient guarantees commensurate to its importance'. Once again, the Court did not mention the principle laid down in *Sutter* and repeated in *Axen*.

Zuckerman has suggested that the requirement for openness has two aspects, one litigant related and the other public. I am arguing that it is wrong in Art. 6 to equate the right to a fair trial with that for a public hearing. The former is for the benefit of the parties and can, with knowledge, be waived.[133] There is no doubt that apparent or actual bias in a judge can be cured by disclosure and an offer to recuse which is unambiguously rejected by the parties. So also, the choice of how to present a case and the evidence to lead is directly or indirectly for the parties. They cannot later complain about the choices they have made.

The latter, the public aspect of a trial, has implications beyond the parties and neither their consent nor convenience can displace the public's right to know how the State's judiciary behave.[134] If the parties can waive publicity a right to a public trial is, as Zuckerman said,[135] a private right. That is precisely what *Scott v Scott* denied and for which there is little authority in the British courts or at Strasbourg. *The Trustor AB v Smallbone* litigation was complex. Suffice it to say, at one point the claimants gave an undertaking not to reveal the written evidence given by the defendants. The court held that publication of the full judgment would undermine that undertaking and acceded to an application that it should not be.[136] Zuckerman, rightly, suggested that the principle of publicity was not borne in mind.

It is difficult at face value to accept the Strasbourg cases which seem to acknowledge a right to waive a public hearing. Indeed, in many of them,[137] the court discussed a possibility of a public hearing on both facts and law at some point in the total adjudication process: for example, an appeal process that satisfies these criteria can remedy a previous defect. This discussion would be otiose if there were a general right to avoid a public trial. And, these cases were about processes outside ordinary courts. It is a big jump to ignore what the court has said about these conditions

133 See *Ruddy v Procurator Fiscal, Perth* [2006] UKPC D2 and the discussion of partiality as a procedural irregularity, below p. 201 et seq.

134 In a criminal case, the accused failed to surrender to his bail and his trial proceeded without him. A majority of the House of Lords, *R v Jones* (Anthony) [2002] UKHL 5, held that he had waived his right to a fair trial. *Jones v UK*, 9 September 2003, differs because the ECtHR took the view the English position was uncertain. For our purposes, what is important is that the trial itself was public; the only question is, was it fair? There is a distinction between a public trial and a fair one.

135 Zuckerman, *Civil Procedure*, 2003, 2.85, p. 85.

136 *Truster AB* v *Smallbone* (No.1) [2000] 1 All ER 811, affirmed 9 September 1999. All ER (D) 624.

137 The most important of these are *Le Compte, Van Leuven and De Meyere*, and *Albert and Le Compte*. It is significant that these are the cases from which the right to waive a hearing is derived.

and conclude there is general right of waiver of publicity in litigation in the State's courts.[138]

It may be that *Suovaniemi* can be explained by the court's statement:

> In deciding this question the Court limits itself to the particular circumstances of the present case, which concerned arbitral proceedings. In doing this it takes account also of the applicable legislative framework for arbitration proceedings and the control exercised by the domestic courts within that framework. Without having to decide whether a similar waiver would be valid in the context of purely judicial proceedings the Court comes to the conclusion that in the circumstances of the present case concerning arbitral proceedings the applicants' waiver of their right to an impartial judge should be regarded as effective for Convention purposes.

Of course, if a court has sat in private and the parties have not objected there may be an issue under Art. 35 about whether they can later complain. Nevertheless, as we have seen, the duties under the Convention are owed to other member states of the Council of Europe and not to private litigants. It is the duty of the State to prevent its courts adjudicating in private and s. 6 of the requires British courts to comply with the Convention, if need be against the express agreement of the parties.

Public Access to Documents

The modern trend to use writing, for example in witness statements, the preparation of skeleton arguments and opening speeches cuts down the scope of members of the public who listen to trials to understand what is going on. As early as 1983, the development worried Lord Scarman. He said:[139]

> The evidence and argument should be publicly known, so that society may judge for itself the quality of justice administered in its name, and whether the law requires modification. When public policy in the administration of justice is considered, public knowledge of the evidence and arguments of the parties is certainly as important as expedition: and, if the price of expedition is to be the silent reading by the judge before or at trial of relevant documents, it is arguable that expedition will not always be consistent with justice being seen to be done.

It is conflict which is not easy to resolve. Specifically, the problem arises in two ways: first, what can a judge read before trial and secondly, what documents can the public (or an interested non-party) have.

---

138 This is, of course, a lawyer's argument. However, the public trial is based also on other reasons, the freedom of expression, see above p. 48 et seq. It is a specific example of the need for lawyers to know about more than law, see above p. 39.

139 *Home Office v Harman* [1983] 1 AC 280, 316 D.

Pre-reading

In *Barings v Coopers Lybrand*,[140] Longmore LJ said, 'what the judge decides to pre-read in a case before trial is a matter for the judge's discretion, not a matter of principle'. But Potter LJ had misgivings:

> So to hold, is not in my view to accept that the developing powers of case management encouraged by the recent civil justice reforms are capable of turning inadmissible evidence into admissible evidence, but merely that some compromise between principle and practice is both necessary and desirable when complicated litigation takes place over previously well-trodden ground.

However, he went on:

> In a system where the judge also performs the function of a jury, he should, as a measure of self protection against unconscious influence, as well as for the avoidance of disquiet on the part of the objecting party, exercise caution before reaching a decision which will involve him in reading a body of inadmissible evidence which that party fears may adversely affect the outcome of the case ... In days when pre-reading is not merely permitted as a practice, but is regarded as necessary for the proper despatch of judicial business, no other approach is practicable. This approach, and the need to trust the judge to exclude inadmissible matters from his mind when coming to his decision, is an inevitable incident of disputes over admissibility. It does not amount to admitting as evidence that which is inadmissible; it simply requires the judge to prepare himself in advance while leaving over questions of admissibility for decision if and when they arise in the course of the hearing.

Potter LJ was right on both counts: it is necessary and inevitable for the judge to trespass on the inadmissible. It is necessary for the efficient dispatch of business. It is inevitable for two reasons. A determination of admissibility can (generally)[141] only be made after the material has been seen. Secondly, even the CPR rules on disclosure applied to documents that may contain material inadmissible as evidence. But Potter LJ was also right to express the 'disquiet' that must be felt.

Trial Documents

In 1999, Potter LJ held that, even under the old rules, there was an inherent jurisdiction to give access to a member of the public access to material privately read by the

140 *Barings v Coopers Lybrand* [2000] 3 All ER 910, CA.

141 But see the brief discussion of *Balfour v Foreign Commonwealth Office* [1994] 1 WLR 681 below.

judge and used by him for his decision.[142] Colman J said in *Law Debenture Trust (Channel Islands) v Lexington Insurance*:[143]

> The essential purpose of granting access to such documents is to provide open justice, that is to say to facilitate maintenance of the quality of the judicial process in all its dimensions, so that the public may he satisfied that the courts are acting justly and fairly and the judges in accordance with their judicial oath. That, however, does not involve merely the perceived quality of final judgments with reference to the evidence, the submissions and the law, but the quality of judicial control of the trial on a day to day basis.

S.32 of the Freedom of Information Act 2000 exempts all documents filed at a court from its disclosure provisions. Maybe this is because this aspect of the inherent jurisdiction is now reflected in the CPR as regards witness statements[144] and the use of disclosed documents.[145] For example, CPR R. 32.13 provides:

> (2) Any person may ask for a direction that a witness statement is not open to inspection.
>
> (3) The court will not make a direction under paragraph (2) unless it is satisfied that a witness statement should not be open to inspection because of –
>
> (a) the interests of justice;
>
> (b) the public interest;
>
> (c) the nature of any expert medical evidence in the statement;
>
> (d) the nature of any confidential information (including information relating to personal financial matters) in the statement; or
>
> (e) the need to protect the interests of any child or patient.

The jurisdiction can apply after the end of a trial. Bingham LCJ explained in *Smithkline Beecham Biologics v Connaught Laboratories*:[146]

> For reasons which are very familiar, it is no longer the practice for counsel to read documents aloud in open court or to lead the judge, document by document, through the evidence. The practice is, instead, to invite the judge to familiarise himself with material

142 *GIO Personal Investment Services v Liverpool and London Steamship Protection and Indemnity Association* (FAI General Insurance intervening) [1999] 1 WLR 984. And see *Dian AO v Davis Frankel and Mead (a firm)* [2004] EWHC 2662 (Comm) (a party to separate but associated litigation) and *Chan U Seek v Alvis Vehicles* [2004] EWHC 3092 (the press).

143 *Law Debenture Trust (Channel Islands) v Lexington Insurance* [2003] EWHC 2297 (Comm).

144 CPR Parts 32.13, 22.

145 CPR Parts 5.4, 5. This rule has been amended several times.

146 *Smithkline Beecham Biologics v Connaught Laboratories* [1999] 4 All ER 498.

> out of court to which, in open court, economical reference, falling far short of verbatim citation, is made. In this new context, the important private rights of the litigant must command continuing respect. But so too must the no less important value that justice is administered in public and is the subject of proper public scrutiny.

To which Lord Woolf added in *Barings v Coopers Lybrand*:[147]

> When documents are put before the court for the purpose of being read in evidence ... the onus is no longer on the person contending they have entered the public domain to show this has happened. The onus is on the person contesting this is the position to show that they did not enter the public domain because, for example, the judge did not in fact read them or because of the need to protect the ability of the court to do justice in a particular case. This is the only practical solution. The judge cannot be cross-examined as to what he has or has not read.

In *Lilly Icos v Pfizer* (No. 2) Buxton LJ put it this way:[148]

> Not everything that is disclosed or copied in court bundles falls under this rule: [it] is restricted to documents to which the judge has been specifically alerted, ... [and], since the ... approach is based upon the assumed orality of a trial, documents, however much pre-read by the judge, remain confidential if no trial takes place, but the application is, for instance, dismissed by consent, albeit by a decision announced in open court.

And:[149]

> The central theme of these rules is the importance of the principle that justice is to be done in public, and within that principle the importance of those attending a public court understanding the case. They cannot do that if the contents of documents used in that process are concealed from them: hence the release of confidence once the document has been read or used in court.

Nevertheless, written opening speeches are excluded.

In *Cox v Jones Mann* J emphasized that the rules speak of refusing inspection 'in the interests of justice' but went on to distinguish the interests of the parties from those of third party witnesses.[150] Most of his order was impeccable, in particular the willingness to allow inspection of witness statements which relate to withdrawn allegations. The order did however require redaction of the names of third parties against whom allegations were made. No doubt he was following CPR 39.2 (4) which permitted the court to 'order that the identity of any party or witness must not be disclosed if it considers non-disclosure necessary in order to protect the interests of that party or witness'. It is unclear why this is in the interests of justice. Mann J

---

147 *Barings v Coopers Lybrand* [2000] 3 All ER 910, [43], [53].

148 *Lilly Icos v Pfizer* [2002] EWCA Civ 2.

149 *Lilly Icos v Pfizer* [2002] EWCA Civ 2, [9].

150 *Cox v Jones* [2004] EWHC 1006 (Ch).

asked whether 'the cat is now out of the bag and cannot be stuffed back in it?' and answered that part of the cat could be.[151]

It is important to stress that these rights to inspect documents are a response by the courts acting under the inherent jurisdiction, and the rules, to replicate the older oral procedures. Information which would have been available under the old ways is still available, that which was not is still not.

These rules do not apply to transcripts of any hearing. These are generally available for payment without an order, Practice Direction to CPR 39, para. 6.3.

The Giving of Reasons for Decisions

As early as 1932, in its discussion of what has become known as administrative law, the Donoughmore-Scott Committee remarked:[152] 'It may well be argued that there is a third principle of natural justice, namely, that a party is entitled to know the reason for the decision, be it judicial or *quasi*-judicial.' They were ahead of their times. It is clear that the judicial duty is relatively novel,[153] but in Britain predates any direct influence of the Strasbourg jurisprudence. But in 2002 in *English v Emery Reimbold and Strick* Lord Phillips said that, although it was not universally mandatory, 'There is a general recognition in the common law jurisdictions that it is desirable for judges to give reasons for their decisions'.[154] These reasons must relate to the determination of factual matters as well as law.[155] In *Sahota v Sohi* Park J said:[156]

> I am writing this judgment on the basis that the persons who will be most concerned with it know what the case was about, and that I do not need to rehearse the underlying facts in any detail. For any reader who is unfamiliar with the background I will describe

151 In *Glidepath BV v Thompson* [2005] EWHC 818 (Comm) it was held that the right of non-parties to inspect documents may not apply to those forming part of an application to stay an arbitration.

152 Donoughmore-Scott Committee, Sect. III para. 3p. 80. And at Sect. III para. 14 pp 100 et seq. They cited *ex p Arlidge* as regards right to see inspectors' reports. And see *West Midlands Joint Electricity Authority v Pitt* [1932] 2 KB 1 as regards the right to know the case to be met.

153 See: Montrose, 'Reasoned Judgments', (1958) 21 MLR 80; and, Ho, 'The duty to give reasons', (2000) LS 42–65.

154 *English v Emery Reimbold and Strick, DJ and C Withers (Farms) v Ambic Equipment; Verrechia (trading as Freightmaster Commercials) v Commissioner of Police of the Metropolis* [2002] EWCA Civ 605, [15]. He cited the New Zealand *Lewis v Wilson and Horton* [2000] 3 NZLR 546 at 565 (Para. 75) per Elias CJ.

155 In *Comfort v Lord Chancellor's Department* [2004] EWCA Civ 349, [32] Peter Gibson LJ said: failure to give reasons on an 'important a matter in controversy constitutes … an error of law'. And see *Redman v Royal Berkshire Fire Authority* EAT All ER (D) 09 (Mar) 5 January 2004.

156 *Sahota v Sohi* [2006] EWHC 344 (Ch), [5].

some aspects of the facts and the underlying issues from time to time as this judgment progresses.

He was mindful of his obligation to give reasons. Reading the judgment, however, I am left also with the impression that he was also aware that more detail might intensify the already bad relations between the parties, and thus add to the costs.

In Chapter 1, I suggested that the giving of reasons is part of the general process of democratization. I could add it was also part of the levelling (up or down, I do not mind) of society. In more legal terms, we may also hazard the guess that it is in part a consequence of the decline of the jury. This is because as the judges have moved from being umpires to being adjudicators, the role of the appellate court correspondingly has shifted toward the more classic public law control of what the courts once called inferior tribunals but which now includes all decision makers lower in even the judicial hierarchy.

The duty to give reasons is also associated with the moves away from orality that date from the mid-1950s in the Court of Appeal[157] and the 1970s at trial. The new duty has spawned a series of appeals as to the adequacy of the reasoning of trial courts and tribunals[158] and as to its application to decision-makers who are not themselves determining rights or obligations between parties.[159] Later I shall suggest that this increased demand for reasons is associated with an expansion of the rules against bias. They certainly take place in the same period and quite probably out of the same cause. Both help ensure that the parties know that they have been fairly

157 And more directly because an appeal is in general a review of the decision of the lower court, cf. *Assicurazioni Generali SpA v Arab Insurance Group* [2002] EWCA Civ 1642. The appeal court does not normally hear evidence afresh, but considers the appeal on the basis of the record of the evidence given in the court below, *Lewis v Secretary of State of Trade* [2001] 2 BCLC 597.

158 See for example: *Heffer v Tiffin Green (a firm)* CA (Civil Division), *The Times*, 28 December 1998, where the court said: 'First, as he was not generally making findings of fact as he went, the judge's reading of the evidence was accompanied by a series of stream-of-consciousness comments that generally fell some way short of being findings of fact.' And see: *Sandry v Jones* CA (Civ) Transcript, 6 July 2000; *Nash v Chelsea College of Art and Design* [2001] EWHC Admin 538, [34]; *Al Fayed* v *Metropolitan Police Commissioner* [2004] EWCA Civ 1579; *Bahl v The Law Society* [2004] EWCA Civ 1070; *Gupta v General Medical Council* [2001] UKPC 61; *R (on the application of Luthra) v General Medical Council* [2004] EWHC 458; *Threlfall v General Optical Council* [2004] EWHC 2683 (Admin); *Baird v Thurrock Borough Council* [2005] All ER (D) 81 (Nov); *Ryell v Health Professions Council* [2005] EWHC 2797 (Admin); *Tariquez-Zaman v University of London (London Deanery of Postgraduate Medical and Dental Education)* [2005] All ER (D) 414 (Nov); and, *Adami v Ethical Standards Board for England* [2005] All ER (D) 266 (Nov) (CA).

159 *In The Matter of the Trusts of the X Charity sub nom Y v HM Attorney* [2003] EWHC 1462 (Ch). The main judgment was given in private because it was not possible to either try the application for directions or give the judgment publicly because publicity would prejudice the interests of justice. Sir Andrew Morritt V-C gave a public judgment for so holding.

heard and both are designed to enhance public confidence in the administration of justice.

In general, although much has changed, the guidance given by Griffths LJ in Eagil Trust is still good law:[160]

> In the case of discretionary exercise, as in other decisions on facts or law, the judge should set out his reasons, but the particularity with which he is required to set them out must depend on the circumstances of the case before him and the nature of the decision he is giving.

In *Hyams v Plender*[161] the Court of Appeal held that where a judge has refused permission to appeal, reasons, brief, but sufficient to be explanatory, must to given. It also said that the Court may certify that the cost of providing a transcript of the judgment of the lower court should be at the public expense if it would be excessive for a particular litigant and that the cost of a transcript of the evidence should also be borne by the public if there are reasonable grounds for an appeal.[162]

The UK courts have faced a different question. In *The Antaios*[163] it was held that in granting or refusing permission to appeal under the predecessor provision to s. 69 of the Arbitration Act 1979 the court should follow the practice of the House of Lords (and endorsed by the ECtHR in *Nerva v UK*)[164] and say no more than that permission is granted or refused. The position was similar to House of Lords practice of which Lord Diplock explained:[165]

> Refusal of leave to appeal does not imply approval by this House of a judgment sought to be appealed against. That judgment carries the same authority as any other unappealed judgment of the Court of Appeal – neither more nor less.

In a lecture in 1987,[166] Bingham LJ said he personally regretted that commercial judges (to whom all applications for permission to appeal (as we now say) to the High Court are initially assigned) should be enjoined in *The Antaios* against giving reasons in this way. Nevertheless, in 2002 in *Mousaka v Golden Seagull Maritime*,

160 *Eagil Trust v Piggott-Brown* [1985] 3 All ER 119. And see *Threlfall v General Optical Council* [2004] EWHC 2683 (Admin); *Allport v Wilbraham* [2004] EWCA Civ 1668

161 *Hyams v Plender* [2001] EWCA Civ 2078. It also noted that any appeal does not automatically stay the execution of a judgment and that a strike out does not automatically follow a failure by a litigant in person to comply with an undertaking that a skeleton argument will be supplied a statement. See also *Perotti v Collyer-Bristow (a firm)* [2004] EWCA Civ 639.

162 Following paras. 5.17–18 of the Practice Direction to CPR Part 52.

163 *Antaios Cia Naviera SA* v *Salen Rederierna AB, The Antaios* [1985] AC 191.

164 *Nerva v UK*, 11 July 2000, Admissibility Decision, [1].

165 *Gilbert-Ash (Northern) v Modern Engineering (Bristol)* [1974] AC 689.

166 Sir T. Bingham, 'Reasons and Reasons for Reasons: Differences Between a Court Judgment and an Arbitration Award', (1988) 4 Arb Int 141.

David Steel J abandoned his practice of giving reasons for the grant or refusal of permission in such cases:[167]

> The provision of reasons might satisfy some degree of curiosity but in fact would be completely worthless. It might also be subversive of the arbitral process if the judge's reasons were expressed in different terms or at least with a different emphasis to those of the arbitrators.

But in the same year in *North Range Shipping* the Court of Appeal was asked whether *The Antaios* guidance still held good. Tuckey LJ said:[168]

> At the very least we think an unsuccessful applicant for leave should be told why he has failed ... But any further reasons need only be brief so as to show the losing party why he has lost. Such reasons will, of course be given against a background of a full hearing, a reasoned award and detailed submissions as to why leave to appeal should be granted. In other words, the judge's brief reasons are directed to a fully informed applicant ... The arbitral process with its commercial advantages of privacy and finality does not involve [court] hearings but that is what the parties have chosen. In any event … we do not accept that the giving of reasons is pointless. It may be the end of the road for the applicant but he is entitled to know shortly why he has reached it. We do not think that this subverts the arbitral process; rather it might be said to strengthen it, particularly if the judge adopts the reasons of the arbitrators ... The message in short must be that reluctance to honour an award should not be allowed to masquerade as a request for further reasons.

A number of explanations for requiring reasons have been given. In *Suominen v Finland* the ECtHR offered three. It said:[169]

- It demonstrates to the partics that they have been heard.
- It 'affords a party the possibility to appeal against it, as well as the possibility of having the decision reviewed by an appellate body', and
- Only with 'a reasoned decision that there can be public scrutiny of the administration of justice'.

This second function is most commonly advanced. Thus, Griffiths *LJ in Eagil Trust v Pigott-Brown*:[170]

---

167 *Mousaka* v *Golden Seagull Maritime* [2002] 1 WLR 395.

168 *North Range Shipping v Seatrans Shipping* [2002] EWCA Civ 405, [27]-[29]. In *BLCT* (13 096) v *J Sainsbury* [2003] EWCA Civ 884, the Court of Appeal added that where leave to appeal without an oral hearing was refused under s. 69 Arbitration Act 1996, the applicant was not entitled to an oral hearing under Art. 6 unless there are exceptional circumstances.

169 *Suominen v Finland*, 1 July 2003, [37].

170 *Eagil Trust v Pigott-Brown* [1985] 3 All ER 119, 122. And see: *Threlfall v General Optical Council* [2004] EWHC 2683; *Allport v Wilbraham* [2004] EWCA Civ 1668.

> I cannot stress too strongly that there is no duty on a judge, in giving his reasons, to deal with every argument presented by counsel in support of his case. It is sufficient if what he says shows the parties, and if need be, the Court of Appeal the basis on which he has acted.[171]

In *Hiro Balani v Spain*, the ECtHR said in very similar terms:[172]

> The Court reiterates that Article 6(1) obliges the courts to give reasons for their judgments, but cannot be understood as requiring a detailed answer to every argument. The extent to which this duty to give reasons applies may vary according to the nature of the decision. It is moreover necessary to take into account, *inter alia*, the diversity of the submissions that a litigant may bring before the courts and the differences existing in the Contracting States with regard to statutory provisions, customary rules, legal opinion and the presentation and drafting of judgments. That is why the question whether a court has failed to fulfil the obligation to state reasons, deriving from Article 6 of the Convention, can only be determined in the light of the circumstances of the case.

So also, in *Hirvisaari v Finland* it said:[173]

> The Court reiterates that … reflecting a principle linked to the proper administration of justice, judgments of courts and tribunals should adequately state the reasons on which they are based. The extent to which this duty to give reasons applies may vary according to the nature of the decision and must be determined in the light of the circumstances of the case ... Thus, in dismissing an appeal, an appellate court may, in principle, simply endorse the reasons for the lower court's decision. A lower court or authority in turn must give such reasons as to enable the parties to make effective use of any existing right of appeal.

Thus, in that case, where the grounds of appeal were the inadequate reasons of the trial court, the ECtHR held that it was insufficient for the appeal court merely to repeat what the lower court said. And, in *Escolano v Spain*,[174] it held that duty to give reasons included a duty to communicate them in sufficient time for the parties to consider whether to lodge an appeal within any prescribed time limit.

Two points can be made. The construction of articulated reasons probably improves the quality of decision making but it also increases the cost of doing so. Secondly, most judgments are constructed with the losing party in mind.

---

171 Sachs LJ in *Knight v Clifton* [1971] Ch 700, 721.

172 *Hiro Balani v Spain*, 9 December 1994 (a trade mark case) [27]. Cited by Tuckey LJ in *North Range Shipping v Seatrans Shipping* [2002] EWCA Civ 405.

173 *Hirvisaari v Finland*, 27 September 2001, [30].

174 *Escolano v Spain*, 25 January 2000, [36]-[37]; *Brualla Gómez de la Torre v Spain*, 19 December 1997, [31], and *Edificaciones March Gallego SA*, [33].

In *English v Emery Reimbold and Strick* Lord Phillips concluded that the duty to give reasons is generally less in civilian jurisdictions than in the common law, and that the ECHR has not extended the duty in England:[175]

> It does not seem to us that the Strasbourg jurisprudence goes further and requires a judgment to explain why one contention, or piece of evidence, has been preferred to another. The common law countries have developed a tradition of delivering judgments that detail the evidence and explain the findings in much greater detail than is to be found in the judgments of most civil law jurisdictions.

We can leave aside the questions whether Lord Phillips was right in his conclusions regarding the Strasbourg requirements for reasons and whether, if so, differences between civilian and common law judgments are explained by the historical considerations sketched above.[176] We need not ask whether the formulation is merely a modern, inclusive way of asserting the superiority and anti-authoritarian basis of the common law.[177] Certainly, *Suominen*, and *Hiro Balani* sits uneasily with the conclusion.[178]

More importantly, Lord Phillips also discussed other functions (in addition to aiding a possible appellate court) of the giving of reasons. He said it had been said they are also desirable because:

2. justice must not only be done but be seen to be done.
3. they make decisions acceptable to the parties, particularly the losing party,[179] and to members of the public.
4. the requirement concentrates the mind of the judge. 'if it is fulfilled, the resulting decision is much more likely to be soundly based on the evidence than if it is not'.[180] We may add, this consideration brings the review of judicial discretion in line with modern public law approaches to the review of

---

175 *English v Emery Reimbold and Strick* [2002] EWCA Civ 605, [12]. At [8]-[14], Lord Phillips cited: *Torija v Spain*, 9 December 1994, [29]; *Ruiz v Spain*, 21 January 1999; *Van de Hurk v The Netherlands*, 19 April 1994, [59]; *Hiro Balani v Spain*, 9 December 1994; *Helle v Finland*, 19 December 1997, para. 60; *X v Federal Republic of Germany* (1982) 4 EHRR 398; *Webb v UK*, 2 July 1997, ECommHR. Beyond these cases in the ECtHR Lord Phillips cited no civilian authority.

176 At p. 40.

177 see p. 42 above.

178 So also, Lord Phillips did not seek a historical explanation of the duty. In a way the duty is surprising. The common law was founded on juries giving answers to general or specific issues raised at trials. The jury operated within the direction given by the judge. In much of the common law world the jury has been replaced by the judge and the reasons have replaced the direction.

179 *Flannery v Halifax Estate Agencies* [2000] 1 WLR 377.

180 *English v Emery Reimbold and Strick*. Lord Phillips cited Henry LJ in *Flannery v Halifax Estate Agencies* [2000] 1 WLR 377, 381.

discretion outside the courts.

5. they serve a vital function in constraining the judiciary's exercise of power.[181]
6. under the common law, they are necessary in setting precedents for the future.

In *Werner v Austria*, the ECtHR added a seventh reason:[182] the public delivery of judgments[183] has the same purpose as a public hearing, 'namely a fair trial, the guarantee of which is one of the fundamental principles of any democratic society, within the meaning of the Convention'. All this is different, the Court said, from its decision in *Håkansson and Sturesson v Sweden*[184] where, we have supposed, because the basic decision was administrative or a matter of public law a party could waive his right to a public hearing. As we have seen, without reasons, any right of appeal is illusory.[185]

Of these justifications, only the first (to make real any right of appeal) and part of the third refer to the interests of the parties. Each of the others is part of the contribution to open justice and freedom of expression of the court processes.

The court has also held that, although sometimes judgments need not be delivered in public, there is almost always a duty to ensure that they are published.[186] To put it another way: given that there is freedom of expression, is there a corresponding right of access to information or even correlative duties to tell or receive? The ECtHR has set out limits to the freedom. In *Guerra v Italy*, it said:[187]

> The court reiterates that freedom to receive information, referred to in paragraph 2 of Article 10 of the Convention, 'basically prohibits a government from restricting a person from receiving information that others wish or may be willing to impart to him'. That freedom cannot be construed as imposing on a State, in circumstances such as those of the present case, positive obligations to collect and disseminate information of its own motion.

181 *English v Emery Reimbold and Strick*, Lord Phillips cited Shapiro, 'In Defence of Judicial Candor' (1987) 100 Harv. L Rev 731 at 737.

182 *Werner v Austria*, 24 November 1997, [54].

183 It cited *Pretto*, [21].

184 *Håkansson and Sturesson v Sweden*, 21 February 1990, [67]. And so also, *Schuler-Zgraggen v Switzerland* (discussed above p. 141, *Zumtobel v Austria*, and *Pauger v Austria* discussed above p. 9n.124.

185 *Threlfall v General Optical Council* [2004] EWHC 2683 (Admin) and *Stefan v GMC* [1999] 1 WLR 1293.

186 *Szücs v Austria*, 24 November 1997, [43] the same passage appears in *Werner v Austria*, 24 November 1997 [55]. It cited: *Pretto*, [26]-[27]; *Axen v Germany*, 8 December 1983, [32]; and, *Sutter v Switzerland*, [34]. There is not always a duty to actually pronounce them publicly, *B and P. v UK*, 24 April 2001.

187 *Guerra v Italy*, 19 February 1998, [53].

This was different from the absence of a duty on the State to 'collect and disseminate information' generally.

It is in this context that we can ask whether the English practice of the private publication of law reports is compatible with Art. 6. Many such reports are available in libraries to which there may or may not be free public access or for a fee or subscription from sources as the Incorporated Council of Law Reporting, the All England Law Reports, lexis/nexis, WestLaw, Casetrack and others.[188] On the other hand, the principle of legality requires that information relating to what the law is shall be 'adequately accessible'. Thus, the question is open as to whether the requirement for payment satisfies the obligation that the courts give judgment in public.[189] It is not the same as that faced in *A v B*[190] where the question was the balance between Art. 10 rights to expression and Art. 8 rights to privacy. No doubt Art. 1 of the first Protocol protects the private publishers' copyright in added value matter such as headnotes. In any case, I am not suggesting that the publishers are in some way in breach of Art. 6. I am saying that the Article requires the State to make its courts' judgments publicly available.[191] I am also saying that the provisions we have looked at regarding public access to documents do not meet the point. Fundamentally, the public character of open justice is to keep watch on the judges. We have seen that most, if not all, applications under those rules are made either by the media writing about the litigants or by third parties hoping to find something to launch their own litigation. They are not made to watch the judges. That can only be done if there is systemic general reporting of what they do.

---

188 This private system, based in ownership of copyright, despite some publicity (and a degree of advertising licence) is the reason that not all judgments are reported and no one series, printed or electronic, covers all those that are. Arilidge, Eady, and Smith, *Contempt*, 2nd edn, 1999 say p. viii: 'It is difficult to see why such faith should a placed with judgment of non-specialist editors, often no doubt governed by commercial aor financial constraints, as to what may or may not be worth reporting.' I add that the situation is not helped by the inconsistent use of neutral citations.

189 See Sir H Brooke, 'Publishing the Courts: Judgments and Public Information on the Internet', An Address at the Commonwealth Law Conference, Melbourne, 15 April 2003, at www.dca.gov.uk/judicial/speeches/ljb150403.htm#part5.

190 *A v B (a company)* [2002] EWCA Civ 337, [11(xii)] per Simon Brown LJ citing *Reynolds v Times Newspapers* [2001] 2 AC 127, 207; *Al-Fagih v H.H. Saudi Research and Marketing (UK)* [2002] EMLR 215, [26]; and, *Loutchansky v Times Newspapers* (*Nos.2-5*) [2002] QB 783, [22].

191 Her Majesty's Courts Service website says: 'Only judgments selected by the judge concerned appear in our database'.

The (Apparent) Ignoring of the Principle

The giving of reasons for decisions is as much a part of the openness of justice as is an open trial. Nevertheless, in *English v Emery Reimbold and Strick* Lord Phillips seemed to adopt Mahoney JA's view in *Soulemezis v Dudley (Holdings) Pty*:[192]

> The court's order is a public act. The judgment given for it is a professional document, directed to the parties and to their professional advisers. It may, in a particular instance, delineate, develop or even decorate the law but that is peripheral and not essential to its nature.

There are difficulties with each of the elements of this statement. A court order is different from its reasons, its judgment. A court order, particularly affecting non-parties, is one thing: the reasons justifying it are another.[193] A court order is obviously primarily for the parties, the reasons, if published, may develop the law. The problem with Mahoney JA's formulation is that it excluded the sentiments of the House of Lords in *Scott v Scott*. The ability of the public to scrutinize reasons, and, more importantly, as has been emphasized time and time again, for judges to sense that they are being watched, is not to see decorations of the law: it is to keep watch on judicial decision-making. Mahoney JA's view is an understandable but professionally centred view. Even decisions and the reasons for them which do not add to the law still need publicity so the public or even legal academics can know how far the courts lean towards consistency.

Lord Woolf CJ, among others, has been rightly concerned with the growth of law reports and their over-citation in forensic argument.[194] There is a line of authorities, both judicial and statutory, which seek to limit the numbers of cases cited.[195] Thus, in *A v B* (a company), he suggested that where an area of law is settled, fewer authorities

---

192 *English v Emery Reimbold and Strick DJ and C Withers (Farms) v Ambic Equipment*; *Verrechia (trading as Freightmaster Commercials) v Commissioner of Police of the Metropolis* [2002] EWCA Civ 605, Lord Phillips quoted *Soulemezis v Dudley (Holdings) Pty* (1987) 10 NSWLR 247, 273.

193 It is comparatively rare for orders to affect non-parties. One example was an injunction preventing the publication of information in which the public may be interested, *Spycatcher*.

194 In a later case he was similarly concerned with disproportionate citation and sought to give a direction limiting the number of cases that can be cited, *Anufrijeva v Southwark LBC*; *R (on the application of N) v Secretary of State for the Home Department*; *R (on the application of M) v Secretary of State for the Home Department* [2003] EWCA Civ 1406.

195 See Zuckerman at 25. Usefully, he pointed to a number of practical difficulties in using sanctions to enforce the rule. The point, however, is that advocacy is the attempt to persuade. That which is not persuasive should not form part of the advocate's arsenal. Judges at all levels should, and are required by the Overriding Objective, to indicate arguments that will not persuade them.

should be used or accepted by judges.[196] He went further, and made a similar error to Mahoney JA in the Practice Note issued by in 2001. It said:[197]

> A judgment falling into one of the categories [defined in the next paragraph] may not in future be cited before any court unless it clearly indicates that it purports to establish a new principle or to extend the present law. In respect of judgments delivered after the date of this Direction, that indication must take the form of an express statement to that effect.

To limit the citation of authorities to those which the advocate says have utility is one thing;[198] to extend the prohibition to anything not authorized by the giver of the judgment is quite another. That, of course, mistakes the fundamental nature of the common law, one that also distinguishes it from civilian systems. A judge in giving reasons for his decision is making a statement for the benefit of the parties. It is public for the benefit of legal commentators and the common good. Within our precedent system, it is later judges (and commentators) who, out of that material, find the 'reason' for the decision. A judge giving a decision can no more determine its reasons than can one Parliament bind its successors, and on similar grounds. The later judge can always re-interpret, or the later Parliament, ignore, that which has gone before. Under our system, finding the reason is necessarily an act of *interpretation* and not *declaration* or, as we saw earlier (as we discussed the fallacy in *Osman*), *determination.* This means that the true meaning of a decision is never and can never be fixed or certain.[199] Leaving an assessment of its wider importance to a giver of the reason is to maim the common law. The Practice Note feeds on a 'theory' of law that is vastly less predictable than either the traditional common law or any civilian system. The consequence of the Practice Note is that decisions falling within its prohibitions are not reported and because they are not, the judges involved are under no effective public scrutiny.

Nelson J undid some of the damage in *Lewis v Eliades* (No.9) holding:[200]

> The Practice Direction is aimed at preventing the courts being burdened with a weight of inappropriate and unnecessary authorities which, because of their nature may be limited in their value. Where however an eminent textbook upon a subject sets out a proposition and cites an authority for it, it is perfectly proper for such an authority to be bought to the

---

196 *A v B* (a company) [2002] EWCA Civ 337, [8]. And see The Practice Direction to CPR Part 52 (appeals) 5. (3)–(5).

197 Practice Note (Citation of Authorities) [2001] 1 WLR 1001, 6.1. In *Mohammed v Secretary of State for the Home Department* [2002] EWHC Admin 57 Turner J described *Clark v University of Lincolnshire* [2000] 3 All ER 752, 762 as the 'spur' for this extraordinary and little known (among academic lawyers) direction.

198 Andrews at 14.35, p. 372, suggested that greater selectivity should be shown by law reporters and counsel. Zuckerman at 1.57, p. 25, offered an uncritical discussion of the Practice Direction.

199 See Llewellyn, *The Bramble Bush: on Our Law and Its Study*, 1929.

200 *Lewis v Eliades* (No.9) [2005] EWHC 2966 (QB), [32].

> attention of the court even though it may fall foul, on its face, of the Practice Direction. I have taken into account the fact that the [otherwise unreportable] decision was an application with only one party present, that arguments and the law were not therefore fully developed and it accordingly suffers from these limitations.

The damage was, however, only limited by finding a way of ignoring the Practice Direction.

Compulsory or Semi-Compulsory ADR

Throughout the CPR, but most particularly in the Overriding Objective (which informs the interpretation of the rest and is a guide to the use of every discretion), there is an emphasis on the need for the parties and their lawyers to co-operate in the settlement of disputes. In *McMillan Williams v Range* Ward LJ described one consequence of this approach:[201]

> The parties launched into argumentative correspondence, standing on their heads as they each inconsistently proclaimed their total willingness to be reasonable, flexible, commercially realistic and so forth and so on but then adamantly stating that in the light of the strength of their case and the weakness of the other side's case they were not prepared to compromise beyond a certain point. Between the bottom lines of each side was the inevitable yawning chasm … I do not intend to review this tedious correspondence, some of the letters being pages long, in any detail. My attitude is best summed up as 'a plague on both your houses' ... In my judgment this is a case where we should condemn the posturing and jockeying for position taken by each side of this dispute and thus direct that each side pay its own costs of their frolic in the Court of Appeal. I would allow the appeal with no order for costs.

The burden of this chapter has been that courts of justice provided by a State must be open and public. The principle is based on a culture and a particular theory of democracy shared as part of their common tradition of all the members of the Council of Europe, what the Charter of Fundamental Rights of the European Union calls its 'spiritual and moral heritage'. As we noted earlier, *Scott v Scott* was not based in arguments about law or convenience. And it is a principal at least as much part of the common law as it is of the jurisprudence of the Convention.

However, in Chapter 1, I suggested there was a contrast between the static objective idea of a fair and public trial in Art. 6 and the modern ideas of consumerism, management and efficiency, including co-operation, contained in the CPR.[202] Nowhere does this contrast come into sharper focus than the courts' attitude to

201 *McMillan Williams v Range* [2004] EWCA Civ 294, [29]-[30].

202 See further Pavlich, *Justice fragmented: mediating community disputes under post-modern conditions*, Routledge, 1996.

ADR.[203] As Ward LJ put it:[204] 'mediation [has an] established importance as a track to a just result running parallel with that of the court system. Both have a proper part to play in the administration of justice.' And, writing outside the court, Lightman J has argued:[205]

> Litigation is a high-risk gamble-and the risks and burden of costs today are so substantial that for any well-advised client, litigation must be the course of last resort if any reasonable alternative is available ... In litigation there is only one winner-and that is generally the lawyer.

In *Roberts v Williams* Rix LJ said:[206]

> Litigation of this kind is very damaging to the parties' health, to their peace of mind and to their pockets. For them it is no doubt a matter of high emotion and principle. If they saw, as in these courts very unfortunately we repeatedly see, how ruinous such neighbour disputes are to the parties, they would shrink from drawing any nearer to the precipice ... a skilled mediator would assist the parties in one day to find a solution to their dispute which both parties will be able to live with. I would urge them both to think very deeply about mediation. Their refusal to undertake it might affect their right to costs hereafter.

Both in Britain and at Strasbourg the courts have been anxious to respect agreements between parties to settle disputes in private. For example, Admiralty and Commercial Court Guide says:[207]

> G1.2 Whilst the Commercial Court remains an entirely appropriate forum for resolving most of the disputes which are entered in the Commercial List, the view of the Commercial Court is that the settlement of disputes by means of ADR:
>
> (i) significantly helps parties to save costs;
>
> (ii) saves parties the delay of litigation in reaching finality in their disputes;

---

203 Ingleby, 'Court Sponsored Mediation: the Case Against Mandatory Participation', (1993) 56 MLR 441, reviewed the then literature. His conclusion that 'if it really is the case that "there's no point in looking for justice, you should just settle for what's on offer", then why have courts at all?' is a valid today as it is when he wrote. See also: Underhill, 'The English courts and ADR – policy and practice since April 1999', Part 1, EBLR 2003, 14(3), 259, Part 2, EBLR 2005, 16(1), 183 which provided a useful, review of the cases but does not provide a consideration of Art. 6; and, Jackson J (Technology and Construction Court) Address to TECBAR, TeCSA and SCL (2005) Cons LJ Vol.21, 265 which again did not discuss the ECHR.

204 *Burchell v Bullard* [2005] EWCA Civ 358, [43].

205 Sir G Lightman, 'Litigation: the last resort', (2004) NLJ Vol.154, 185.

206 *Roberts v Williams* [2005] EWCA Civ 1086.

207 And see the Chancery Guide (Paras. 17.1 and 17.3), the Queen's Bench Guide (Para. 6.6), the Admiralty and Commercial Court Guide (Paras. D8.8 and G1 and 2) and the Technology and Construction Court Guide (Para. 6.4).

(iii) enables parties to achieve settlement of their disputes while preserving their existing commercial relationships and market reputation;

(iv) provides parties with a wider range of solutions than those offered by litigation; and

(v) is likely to make a substantial contribution to the more efficient use of judicial resources.

G1.4 Legal representatives in all cases should consider with their clients and the other parties concerned the possibility of attempting to resolve the dispute or particular issues by ADR and should ensure that their clients are fully informed as to the most cost effective means of resolving their dispute.

In *Cable and Wireless v IBM United Kingdom* Coleman J said:[208]

> The English courts should nowadays not be astute to accentuate uncertainty (and therefore unenforceability) in the field of dispute resolution references. There is now available a clearly recognised and well-developed process of dispute resolution involving sophisticated mediation techniques provided by trained mediators in accordance with procedures designed to achieve settlement by the means most suitable for the dispute in question.

And, he added:[209]

> The reference to ADR is analogous to an agreement to arbitrate. As such, it represents a free-standing agreement ancillary to the main contract and capable of being enforced by a stay of the proceedings or by injunction absent any pending proceedings.

So also, in *Royal Bank of Canada Trust v Secretary of State for Defence (Costs),*[210] the court took seriously and applied a 'formal pledge' issued on behalf of the government that 'Alternative dispute resolution will be considered and used in all suitable cases wherever the other party accepts it'.

---

208 *Cable and Wireless v IBM United Kingdom* [2002] EWHC 2059 (Comm), [25].

209 Ibid. [34]. The mere fact that negotiations are in progress is not sufficient to found a stay, *Assiouti v Hosseini* 26 November 1999 (CA) (Transcript: Smith Bernal).

210 *Royal Bank of Canada Trust v Secretary of State for Defence (Costs)* [2003] EWHC 1841 (Ch). Lord Chancellor's Department, *Press Notice* 23 March 2001. Underhill, *op. cit.*, noted that the issue was concerned with the meaning of law. He rightly questioned whether such can ever be suitable for ADR. He cited *Farah v British Airways*, *The Times* 26 January 2001 CA – strike out should not be used in an area of developing jurisprudence. Jackson J, *op. cit.*, however, reported: 'Subsequent monitoring shows that this pledge has been honoured. In the financial year 2002-03 there was a massive increase in the use of ADR in disputes involving government bodies. It has been estimated that this saved the public purse over £6 million in costs.'

ADR, and negotiation and mediation in particular, has at least two advantages. First, it is likely to be conducted in private.[211] Secondly, it is commonly far less elaborate than a trial.[212] What may take a court (or arbitrator) days or weeks may be disposed of in hours. The process (apart from Early Neutral Evaluation, ENE, and even that is less elaborate than at trial) is far less dependent on evidence and the costs of presenting it may be significantly reduced or avoided altogether.

Dispute settlement is often more than the readjustment of money. Sometimes an apology will do. Sometimes, however, public vindication is the only cure. The courts are now fairly unanimous in praising ADR. As Dyson LJ put it in *Halsey*:[213]

> As was explained in Lord Woolf's Final Report on Access to Justice (p.11), for some time before the Civil Procedure Rules ('CPR') came into force, resort by parties involved in litigation to ADR had been encouraged by the courts in various ways. The CPR, practice directions and pre-action protocols have built on these early developments. It is unnecessary to make extensive reference to demonstrate this.[214]

In *Al-Khatib v Masry*, Thorpe LJ went so far as to say:[215] 'there is no case, however conflicted, which is not potentially open to successful mediation, even if mediation has not been attempted or has failed during the trial process'.

Litigation is thus now conducted under the shadow of ADR. The issue is: what powers the courts have to compel or induce the parties to settle, if need be by third party intervention, what teeth do the courts have? Four powers are possible. The court can order it, or stay the proceedings until it has been attempted, or the parties have explained themselves, or punish any unreasonable refusal to use it. Our problem is how far do these devices comply with Art. 6?

In *Anufrijeva v Southwark LBC*, the court was concerned with claims for damages under the HRA itself. Lord Woolf noted that such claims: 'if pursued in court by adversarial proceedings, is likely to cost substantially more to try than the amount of any damages that are likely to be awarded.' He held that the preferred method of bringing such a claim is judicial review where permission is required before an application can be made at all. He said:[216]

---

211 In an appropriate case an injunction lies to enforce the confidence, *Venture Investment Placement v Hall* [2005] EWHC 1227.

212 Braithwaite, 'Reasonable Alternative,' 148 SJ 29, 23 July 2004, 858, emphasized that mediation is not the only, or even the most common form of ADR. That is still the round table discussion. *Haines v Carter* [2002] UKPC 49 nevertheless illustrates why it is important that all settlements, including those reached through mediation, should be drawn with clarity.

213 *Halsey v Milton Keynes General NHS Trust et al.* [2004] EWCA (Civ) 576, [4].

214 At [6], he cited Genn, 'Court-based ADR initiatives for non-family civil disputes: the Commercial Court and the Court of Appeal' (March 2002), at pp. 58 et seq.

215 *Al-Khatib v Masry* [2004] EWCA Civ 1353.

216 *Anufrijeva v Southwark LBC*; *R (on the application of N) v Secretary of State for the Home Department*; *R (on the application of M) v Secretary of State for the Home Department* [2003] EWCA Civ 1406, [80]-[81]. He used similar language earlier in *R (on the application*

> Before giving permission to apply for judicial review, the ... judge should require the claimant to explain why it would not be more appropriate to use any available internal complaint procedure or proceed by making a claim to the PCA or LGO at least in the first instance ... and ... consideration given to deferring permission for the damages claim, adjourning or staying that claim until use has been made of ADR.

Unless a party is prepared to use ADR, it could not have access to the courts at all.

The experimental Practice Direction B to CPR Part 26 relates to the Central London County Court.[217] Having imposed requirements that the parties and the court shall consider ADR, it provides that:

> 4.1 If one or more of the parties states in his reply that he objects to mediation, the case will be referred to a district judge who may –
>
> (1) direct the case to be listed for a hearing of the objections to mediation;
>
> (2) direct that a mediation appointment should proceed;
>
> (3) order the parties to file and serve completed allocation questionnaires; or
>
> (4) give such directions as to the management of the case as he considers appropriate.

So also, the Admiralty and Commercial Court Guide says:

> G1.6 At the case management conference if it should appear to the judge that the case before him or any of the issues arising in it are particularly appropriate for an attempt at

---

of Cowl) v Plymouth CC; also known as: *Cowl v Plymouth CC*; *Re Cowl* (Practice Note) [2001] EWCA Civ 1935.

Lord Woolf's view on damages is not self-evident. It is true that the HRA exceptionally requires (S. 8(4)) the court to apply the Strasbourg principles and that that Court regularly gives damages small by reference to the same criteria. In that court, this is acceptable because it also makes a declaration that the State's conduct is unlawful. The official declaration can be cathartic. Even after a domestic court's judgment, that may be less than at Strasbourg. Vindication will obviously be far less after ADR than with a public pronouncement.

On damages see, e.g. Law Commission Discussion Paper: Monetary Remedies in Public Law. 11 October 2004; and, The Law Commission and the Scottish Law Commission (law com No. 266 (Scot law com No. 180) *Damages under The Human Rights Act 1998*, Cm 4853, SE/2000/182, www.lawcom.gov.uk. And see: *R (on the application of Greenfield) v Secretary of State for the Home Department* [2005] UKHL 14; Chakrabarti, Stephens and Gallagher, 'Whose cost the public interest?', [2003] PL 697–715, Clayton, Ruck Keene and Dunlop, 'Key Human Rights Act Cases in the Last 12 Months', [2004] EHRLR, 614; Hartshorne, 'The Human Rights Act 1998 and Damages for Non-Pecuniary Loss', EHRLR [2004] 660; and, Clayton, 'Damage limitation: the courts and the Human Rights Act damages', PL [2005] 429.

217 It says it is to apply between 1 April 2004–31 March 2005. It is apparently still in force.

> settlement by means of ADR but that the parties have not previously attempted settlement by such means, he may invite the parties to use ADR.
>
> G1.7 The judge may, if he considers it appropriate, adjourn the case for a specified period of time to encourage and enable the parties to use ADR. He may for this purpose extend the time for compliance by the parties or any of them with any requirement under the rules, the Guide or any order of the Court.
>
> G1.8 The Judge may further consider in an appropriate case making an ADR Order in the terms set out in Appendix 7.

Such an order includes the clause: 'The parties shall take such serious steps as they may be advised to resolve their disputes by ADR procedures before the neutral individual or panel so chosen by no later than' a named date.

These provisions supplement the CPR. As Dyson LJ put it in *Halsey*:

> CPR 1.4 (1) obliges the court to further the overriding objective of enabling the court to deal with cases justly by actively managing cases, and Rule 1.4 (2) (e) defines 'active case management' as including 'encouraging the parties to use an alternative dispute resolution procedure if the court considers that appropriate and facilitating the use of such procedure'. Rule 26.4 (1) provides that 'a party may, when filing the completed allocation questionnaire, make a written request for the proceedings to be stayed while the parties try to settle the case by alternative dispute resolution or other means'.

He could also have added that the *Court's duty to manage cases*, includes in CPR Part 1.4(2)(f) 'helping the parties to settle the whole or part of the case' and that the *General powers of management*, include in Part 3.1(2)(f) the power to 'stay the whole or part of any proceedings or judgment either generally or until a specified date or event'. CPR Part 26 says:

> (2) Where … (b) the court, of its own initiative, considers that such a stay would be appropriate, the court will direct that the proceedings be stayed for 1 month.
>
> (3) The court may extend the stay until such date or for such specified period as it considers appropriate.

In *Guinle v Kirreh*,[218] under these powers of case management, Arden J ordered the appointment of a mediator. She made no mention of Art. 6. Her order included: 'The parties shall take such serious steps as they may be advised to resolve their disputes by ADR procedures before the independent mediator'.

In *Muman v Nagasena*, Mummery LJ imposed a stay in charity proceedings,[219] 'until after an attempt has been made by both parties to resolve this dispute by mediation'. He added:

---

218 *Guinle v Kirreh*: *Kinstreet v Balmargo* [2000] CP Rep 62.

219 *Muman v Nagasena* [2000] 1 WLR 299 CA.

> In this case very substantial sums of money have been spent on litigation without achieving a resolution. The spending of money on this kind of litigation does not promote the religious purposes of this charity. It is time for mediation. No more money should be spent from the assets of this charity until … all efforts have been made to secure a mediation of this dispute.

Again, he made no mention of Art. 6.

Blackburne J, acting under his powers in CPR Part 1, made an order for mediation in *Shirayama Shokusan v Danovo*.[220] Many of the items of claim were trivial and the parties would remain in a commercial relationship whatever the outcome of the dispute.[221] He added: 'Nor do I consider that any Human Rights Act issue is engaged by the order that I am making.'

This power to order ADR has, however, not been universally accepted. In *Jewo Ferrous BV v Lewis Moore* (A Firm) Peter Gibson LJ said:[222] 'this court recognises that not every case is appropriate for ADR ... ADR is still voluntary. It requires the consent of both parties'.

So also, in *Halsey*, Dyson LJ pointed out that the Commercial Court's ADR order[223] 'stops short of actually compelling the parties to undertake an ADR'. He added:[224]

> It is one thing to encourage the parties to agree to mediation, even to encourage them in the strongest terms. It is another to order them to do so. It seems to us that to oblige truly unwilling parties to refer their disputes to mediation would be to impose an unacceptable obstruction on their right of access to the court. The court in Strasbourg has said … that the right of access to a court may be waived, for example by means of an arbitration agreement, but such waiver should be subjected to 'particularly careful review' to ensure that the claimant is not subject to 'constraint'. If that is the approach of the ECtHR to an *agreement* to arbitrate, it seems to us likely that *compulsion* of ADR would be regarded as an unacceptable constraint on the right of access to the court and, therefore, a violation of article 6. Even if (contrary to our view) the court does have jurisdiction to order unwilling

---

220 *Shirayama Shokusan v Danovo* Ch D [2003] All ER (D) 114 (Dec), 5 December 2003, unreported. ADR was also ordered in: *Hayes t/a Tudor Rose Windows v Stewart* [2002] EWCA Civ 513; *Buxton Building Contractors v Durand Primary School Governors* [2004] EWHC 733 (TCC) and *C v RHL* [2005] EWHC 873 (Comm).

221 *Shirayama Shokusan v Danovo Ch.D* [2004] All ER (D) 442 (February), 26 February 2004, unreported. At a subsequent hearing, he exempted a non-party from the scope of the order, *Shirayama Shokusan v Danovo Ch.D* [2003] All ER (D) 114 (December), 5 December 2003, unreported, [36].

222 *Jewo Ferrous BV v Lewis Moore* (A Firm) [2000] CP Rep 57 (CA).

223 At [30]. And at [11] he said 'we reiterate that the court's role is to encourage, not to compel. The form of encouragement may be robust'.

224 *Halsey*, [9]-[10]. And see also *Re Northampton Ice Cream* [2005] All ER (D) 101 (Nov) where Lindsay J held the court had no jurisdiction to compel mediation.

> parties to refer their disputes to mediation, we find it difficult to conceive of circumstances in which it would be appropriate to exercise it.[225]
>
> If the court were to compel parties to enter into a mediation to which they objected, that would achieve nothing except to add to the costs to be borne by the parties, possibly postpone the time when the court determines the dispute and damage the perceived effectiveness of the ADR process. If a judge takes the view that the case is suitable for ADR, then he or she is not, of course, obliged to take at face value the expressed opposition of the parties. In such a case, the judge should explore the reasons for any resistance to ADR. But if the parties (or at least one of them) remain intransigently opposed to ADR, then it would be wrong for the court to compel them to embrace it.

Despite the line of cases against *Halsey* (and the Practice Direction to Part 26 providing for the experiment in the Central London County Court, and which Dyson LJ did not discuss), it is difficult to disagree. Whatever its merits, whatever sanction is imposed whether it be for contempt or a strike out of the whole or part of a case or in costs or interest, any such order must have the effect of keeping a litigant out of court. The ECtHR has never allowed this. In *Göç v Turkey* it was argued that the exclusion of oral proceedings was:[226]

> intended to provide a speedy means for dealing with compensation claims without the expense and delay of an oral hearing. The legislative scheme was thus consistent with the trend in European countries towards arbitration and mediation in the context of minor disputes and the move away from oral hearings.

Nevertheless, the ECtHR held that orality was required at some stage in the proceedings and by implication that efficiency alone was not a sufficient reason for excluding publicity.

If, then, the court has no power to order ADR, does it have power to coerce it by for example imposing a stay until one or other lay party has attended the court to explain its position. Tuckey LJ answered the question in *Tarajan Overseas v Kaye*:[227]

> There is no doubt that the court, in exercising its case management powers, can order the attendance of a party: CPR Part 3,1.2(c). One good reason why this may be appropriate is to facilitate settlement if the court takes the view that the case before it is one which the parties should strive to settle. There would be nothing wrong either in requiring the attendance of a party with a view to making an ADR order which, of course, is not coercive but simply suspends the proceedings to enable the parties to explore (if they agree) the prospect of settlement with the assistance of an experienced mediator. Such an order is one which could be made however, and usually is made, without the attendance of any party. What would be objectionable, however, is to make an order that a party should

225 He adopted what the editors of Volume 1 of the White Book (2003) said at para. 1.4.11.

226 *Göç v Turkey*, 11 July 2002, [44].

227 *Tarajan Overseas v Kaye* [2001] EWCA Civ 1859, [11]-[14].

attend with a view to putting pressure on the party concerned to drop the proceedings altogether.

But as the court indicated in *Halsey*, delay for mediation may also take more than a reasonable time. In *SITA v Watson Wyatt and Maxwell Batley* (Pt 20 defendant)[228] mediation was proposed too late to affect the costs. So also in *The Wethered Estate v Davis* the claimant was found to be reasonable in refusing mediation until a trespass had been ended and the issues clarified.[229]

Granted that the court has this much power, does it have any additional power to coerce it by, for example, penalities in costs, and does it matter whether it is the court or another party which suggested it? In *Halsey* the court explained:[230]

> CPR 44.3 (2) provides that 'if the court decides to make an order about costs (a) the general rule is that the unsuccessful party will be ordered to pay the cost of the successful party; but (b) the court may make a different order'. CPR 44.3 (4) provides that 'in deciding what order (if any) to make about costs, the court must have regard to all the circumstances, including – (a) the conduct of the parties'. Rule 44.3 (5) provides that the conduct of the parties includes '(a) conduct before, as well as during, the proceedings and in particular the extent to which the parties followed any relevant pre-action protocol'.

It went on:[231]

> In deciding whether to deprive a successful party of some or all of his costs on the grounds that he has refused to agree to ADR, it must be borne in mind that such an order is an exception to the general rule that costs should follow the event. In our view, the burden is on the unsuccessful party to show why there should be a departure from the general rule … factors which may be relevant to the question whether a party has unreasonably refused ADR will include (but are not limited to) the following:[232]
>
> (a) the nature of the dispute;
>
> (b) the merits of the case;

---

228 *Société Internationale de Telecommunications Aeronotiques v Wyatt* [2002] EWHC 2401 (Ch).

229 *The Wethered Estate v Davis* [2005] EWHC 1903.

230 At [12]. One of the earliest cases was *Paul Thomas Construction v Hyland* (2002) 18 Const LJ 345 where pre-issue refusal to contemplate ADR led to an order for costs on an indemnity basis. So also in *Malkins Nominees v Société Financière Mirelis* [2002] EWHC 1221 (Ch); the refusal or ignoring an offer of ADR led to costs penalties.

231 *Halsey*, [13], [16].

232 Layout adjusted. At [17]-[26] the court expanded on the meaning of these factors. And see: Sheppard, 'We must strike a balance between ADR and the courts', *The Times*, 12 October 2004. He said the mood of clients changed between the 1980s and 1990s. And see Dodd and Rees, 'The cost of refusing to mediate' (2004) NLJ Vol.154. The authorities and practice are reviewed by Cooksley, 'Mediation – needed in PI?', [2004] *Journal of Personal Injury Law* 225. And see *Re Midland Linen Services, re*, Also known as: *Chaudhry v Yap* [2005] EWHC 3380.

(c) the extent to which other settlement methods have been attempted;

(d) whether the costs of the ADR would be disproportionately high;

(e) whether any delay in setting up and attending the ADR would have been prejudicial; and

(f) whether the ADR had a reasonable prospect of success.

In *Painting v Oxford University* Longmore LJ said:[233]

> [the claimant] herself made no attempt to negotiate, made no offer of her own and made no response to the offers of the University. That would not have mattered in pre-CPR days but, to my mind, that now matters very much. Negotiation is supposed to be a two-way street, and a claimant who makes no attempt to negotiate can expect, and should expect, the courts to take that into account when making the appropriate order as to costs.

In *Dunnett v Railtrack* (in railway administration) the successful respondent was denied its costs because it had refused an offer to use the Court of Appeal's own mediation service, Brooke LJ noted that 'the parties themselves have a duty to further the overriding objective'. He said:[234]

> Skilled mediators are now able to achieve results satisfactory to both parties in many cases which are quite beyond the power of lawyers and courts to achieve. This court has knowledge of cases where intense feelings have arisen, for instance in relation to clinical negligence claims. But when the parties are brought together on neutral soil with a skilled mediator to help them resolve their differences, it may very well be that the mediator is able to achieve a result by which the parties shake hands at the end and feel that they have gone away having settled the dispute on terms with which they are happy to live.

And, in an important passage, he went on:[235]

---

233 *Painting v Oxford University* [2005] EWCA Civ 161, [27].

234 *Dunnett v Railtrack* (in railway administration) [2002] EWCA Civ 303, [14]. And see *R (on the application of Cowl) v Plymouth CC*; also known as: *Cowl v Plymouth CC*; *Re Cowl* (Practice Note) [2001] EWCA Civ 1935; *Neal v Jones* (*t/a* Jones Motors) [2002] EWCA Civ 1731; *Malkins Nominees v Societe Finance Mirelis* [2002] EWHC 1221 (Ch); and *Yorkshire Bank v RDM Asset Finance* (QBD (Merc)) 30 June 2004. These cases are different from *Lawal v Northern Spirit (Costs)* [2004] EWCA Civ 208 because in them the issue had been the refusal of mediation. In this (the sequel to main *Lawal* litigation) the claimant had simply been offensive. In *Re Midland Linen Services, sub nom Chaudry v Yap* Ch 28th October 2004 (Leslie Kosmin QC) the principle was applied to a Part 36 offer.

235 Elsewhere, *Civil Litigation: Practice and Procedure in a Shifting Culture*, 2001, on the basis of the National Consumers' Council report that most litigants want an apology, an assurance that it will not happen to someone else or an inquiry, I suggested that the scope of injunctive relief is broad enough to encompass them if claimants would but ask. And see Davies Report, *Hospital Complaint Procedures*, 1973.

A mediator may be able to provide solutions which are beyond the powers of the court to provide. Occasions are known to the court in claims against the police, which can give rise to as much passion as a claim of this kind where a claimant's precious horses are killed on a railway line, by which an apology from a very senior police officer is all that the claimant is really seeking and the money side of the matter falls away.

As Jack J said:[236]

Mediation … involves the services of a skilled mediator. The process may take up time and can be expensive. In cases of difficulty, by reason of the ability of a mediator to oil the wheels of settlement in various ways, it is more likely to be effective than the simpler process of negotiation by discussion and offer and counter-offer. I suppose that the main task of a mediator is commonly to lower the proper expectations of the parties to a point where agreement is possible. As the process of settlement by negotiation is less time-consuming and cheaper than mediation, it may be suggested that parties should have the less reluctance to enter into it.

But in *Daniels v Metropolitan Police Commissioner* Dyson LJ said:[237]

If defendants, who routinely face what they consider to be unfounded claims, wish to take a stand and contest them rather than make payments (even nuisance value payments) to buy them off, then the court should be slow to characterise such conduct as unreasonable so as to deprive defendants of their costs, if they are ultimately successful.

Two cases have concerned the reasonableness of legal advisers in refusing ADR in defending actions impugning their professional competence. In *Hurst v Leeming* Lightman J said:[238]

Mediation is not in law compulsory ... But alternative dispute resolution is at the heart of today's civil justice system, and any unjustified failure to give proper attention to the opportunities afforded by mediation, and in particular in any case where mediation affords a realistic prospect of resolution of dispute, there must be anticipated as a real possibility that adverse consequences may be attracted ... The fact that a party believes that he has a watertight case again is no justification for refusing mediation.[239] That is the frame of mind of so many litigants ... The critical factor … is whether, objectively viewed, a mediation had any real prospect of success. If mediation can have no real prospect of success, a party may, with impunity, refuse to proceed to mediation on this ground. But refusal is a high risk course to take, for if the Court finds that there was a real prospect, the party refusing to proceed to mediation may … be severely penalized. Further, the hurdle in the way of a party refusing to proceed to mediation on this ground is high, for in making this objective

---

236 *Hickman v Blake Lapthorn* [2006] EWHC 12 (QB), [24].

237 *Daniels v Metropolitan Police Commissioner* [2005] EWCA Civ 1312, [31].

238 *Hurst v Leeming* [2001] EWHC 1051 (Ch). Underhill, op. cit., constructed out of this passage a test related to CPR 24 so that in any case where there is an objective reasonable prospect of success in the ADR it ought to be used.

239 In *Halsey* the court qualified this to refer only to reasonable belief and excludes unreasonable, [19], and see [23]-[26].

> assessment of the prospects of mediation, the starting point must surely be the fact that the mediation process itself can and often does bring about a more sensible and more conciliatory attitude on the part of the parties than might otherwise be expected to prevail before the mediation, and may produce a recognition of the strengths and weaknesses by each party of his own case and of that of his opponent, and a willingness to accept the give and take essential to a successful mediation. What appears to be incapable of mediation before the mediation process begins often proves capable of satisfactory resolution later.

So also, in *Jewo Ferrous BV v Lewis Moore* (A Firm) Peter Gibson LJ said:[240]

> It cannot be said … that Mr Moore is to be criticised or held to have been acting unreasonably in taking the view that this is simply not an appropriate case in which he should incur the trouble and expense of ADR with its uncertain outcome. It would be quite wrong for this court to encourage appellants seeking an excuse for avoiding or reducing the security, which otherwise would inevitably be ordered, to adopt the opportunistic ploy of asking for ADR, regardless of whether the appeal is truly an appropriate one for ADR.

In *Leicester Circuits v Coats Brothers*, the court explained:[241]

> [Counsel] described this mediation as a form of negotiation which came to nothing. With respect to that argument, we do not agree. The whole point of having mediation, and once you have agreed to it, proceeding with it, is that the most difficult of problems can sometimes, indeed often are, resolved … we take the view that having agreed to mediation it hardly lies in the mouths of those who agree to it to assert that there was no realistic prospect of success ... It seems to us that the unexplained withdrawal from an agreed mediation process was of significance to the continuation of this litigation. We do not for one moment assume that the mediation process would have succeeded, but certainly there is a prospect that it would have done if it had been allowed to proceed. That therefore bears on the issue of costs.

And in *Corenso (UK) v Burnden Group*, the court added:[242]

> The requirement on parties is to attempt to resolve their differences without resorting to court by alternative dispute resolution. In some cases the only available way may be mediation. In other cases, it may well be that negotiation, or attempts to use an honest broker, may be equally appropriate. So long as parties are showing a genuine and constructive willingness to resolve the issues between them, it does not seem to me that a party will be automatically penalised because that party has not gone along with a particular form of alternative dispute resolution proposed by the other side.

In *Burchell v Bullard* Ward LJ said:[243] 'it seems to me, first, that a small building dispute is par excellence the kind of dispute which … lends itself to ADR ... The defendants cannot rely on their own obstinacy to assert that mediation had no

---

240 *Jewo Ferrous BV v Lewis Moore* (A Firm) [2000] CP Rep 57 (CA).

241 *Leicester Circuits v Coats Brothers* [2003] EWCA Civ 290, [16], [18], and [27].

242 *Corenso (UK) v Burnden Group* [2003] EWHC QB 1805, Judge Reid QC, [60].

243 *Burchell v Bullard* [2005] EWCA Civ 358, [41].

reasonable prospect of success'. In *Hickman v Blake Lapthorn* Jack J thought the test for refusal to negotiate is the same as for refusal to enter ADR, whether it is unreasonable.

In all these cases, except *Halsey*, there was no discussion of Art. 6, and there the court seemed to think the article was only engaged if the court ordered rather than coerced ADR. But, on its face, that distinction is difficult to maintain. Compliance with an order and compliance under coercion are both to act contrary to an original intention.[244] As with orders for ADR, in the ordinary case there must be doubt whether costs sanctions for those who refuse are compliant with the requirements for a fair and public trial.[245]

A way out of the dilemma implicit in *Halsey* was provided by the subsequent decision of the Court of Appeal in *Reed Executive v Reed Business*.[246] There, the court applied the rule in *Walker v Wilsher*.[247] Negotiations (including ADR) can be 'open' or 'without prejudice save as to costs'[248] or completely 'without prejudice'. In *Reed*, they were of this last type. The court refused to allow the content of such communications to be used in determining whether or not a party was reasonable in refusing ADR. The effect is that if the parties do not chose to use this form of negotiation, that is, do not use the full 'without prejudice' umbrella, they can be taken to have agreed to their discussions being open at least as to costs. They are not coerced into paying a penalty for not using ADR. They have agreed to a regime which includes it. Without discussing the Convention, the Court of Appeal made *Halsey* Art. 6 compliant.[249]

---

244 Cf. Shaw, *St Joan*, 'Light your fire: do you think I dread it as much as the life of a rat in a hole?'.

245 See to the contrary Fielding, 'Mediation post-Halsey', (2004) NLJ Vol.154, 1394. He added, somewhat mysteriously, 'There is also a view that the Art 6 human rights objection is weak because over three-quarters of the cases ordered to mediation settle'.

246 *Reed Executive v Reed Business* [2004] EWCA Civ 887.

247 *Walker v Wilsher* (1889) 23 QBD 335. Concessions made under the rubric 'without prejudice' generally cannot be referred to in court for any purpose. There are exceptions. If they lead to a settlement, they are admissible as to its terms. See generally, e.g. *Rush and Tompkins v Greater London Council* [1989] AC 1280; *Unilever v Procter and Gamble* [2000] 1 WLR 2436 (CA); and, *Gnitrow v Cape* [2000] 1 WLR 2327.

248 *Calderbank v Calderbank* [1976] Fam 93 and *Cutts v Head* [1984] L.R.Ch. 290.

249 In *Hall v Pertemps Group* [2005] All ER (D) 15 (Nov) Lewison J held where alleged threats made in the course of the mediation give rise to satellite litigation and are averred in the pleadings in respect of that litigation, there was a waiver of the 'without prejudice' principle only in respect of that discrete matter.

Chapter 3

Equality of Arms and Related Doctrines

The related doctrines of equality of arms, the right of access to the court, and the right to be heard (together with the requirement for an impartial tribunal, which we shall come to in Chapter 5) stand alongside open justice as the pillars of the ECtHR's conception of a fair trial.[1] They are also part of our procedural code: the first is assumed by the system, the second, as we shall see, is expressly mentioned in the CPR and the third is one of the most pervasive principles of the common law.

Put briefly, equality of arms requires that one side to litigation shall have no advantage over the other by way, for example, of being able to provide the tribunal with evidence or comments not available to the other side. The doctrine does not apply, at any rate with the same force, to the resources that a party can devote to either the collection of that material or its presentation. This chapter considers the doctrine in general terms, leaving more detailed consideration of the presentation of facts to the next.

It may seem strange that the right of access has caused as much trouble as we shall see it has. As regards access to the court itself, the issue has arisen in relation to fees payable on the issue of proceedings, and the ability of prisoners to consult lawyers, on some occasions even before that. Again, the right of access is not absolute. Much of the CPR is devoted to setting out the court's powers to manage litigation. Included in these are powers to strike out a case or part of a case for a number of disparate reasons, for example: because it is not arguable; because there has been an abuse of court or its processes in one way or another; or, because the case is stale or has dragged on too long. We shall look at these.

Conceptually, the right to be heard has links to both equality of arms and the right of access. It is helpful, however, to consider it under a separate head. I shall argue that it is additional to equality of arms and the right of access. Once more it is not absolute. The court must be careful in making orders in the absence of one party but it can do so. The right to be heard does not apply where justice could not be done because, for example, evidence might be destroyed or assets dissipated. Necessarily, but with enhanced force under the CPR, the court is reluctant to lose a fixed date for a trial or to grant adjournments. This chapter looks at the kind of criteria the courts use. So also the right does not necessarily mean that there is a right to oral

1 See: *Delcourt v Belgium*, 17 January 1970, [28]: 'The principle of equality of arms does not exhaust the contents of art.6(1); it is only one feature of the wider concept of fair trial by an independent and impartial tribunal'; and see, *Monnell and Morris v UK*, 2 March 1987, [62].

proceedings although often it does. Much of the litigation has concerned the review of decisions of disciplinary tribunals. We shall see that, in general, there must be orality at some point before a final decision is made.

Equality of Arms

The expression 'equality of arms' is civilian rather than one familiar to the common law.[2] The idea of arms, associated with a fight, is also out of tune with the enforced co-operation required of modern litigation. Much of the meaning, however, is, unsurprisingly, fundamental to any legal system. Such differences as there are between the common law and the civilian worlds are a result of the greater role of the judge in the civilian trial and the assumption in the common law (once almost amounting to a rule of law) that all advocates are equal. In *Fretté v France* the ECtHR explained:[3]

> The principle of equality of arms – one of the elements of the broader concept of fair trial – requires each party to be given a reasonable opportunity to present his case under conditions that do not place him at a substantial disadvantage *vis-à-vis* his opponent. It also implies in principle the opportunity for the parties to a trial to have knowledge of and discuss all evidence adduced or observations filed, even by an independent member of the national legal service, with a view to influencing the court's decision.

It followed that the applicant could not be expected to pay regular visits to the registry of the *Conseil d'État* to check whether his case had been listed on the notice boards on which it was legally required to be displayed 4 days at least before a sitting. The Court added: 'such a requirement would not have been compatible with the "diligence" which the Contracting States must exercise to ensure that the rights guaranteed by Article 6 are enjoyed in an effective manner.'

So also, in *Stran Greek Refineries*[4] the issue that eventually the court had to decide concerned legislative intervention in pending litigation between the applicant and the State. The ECtHR ruled there had been a violation of Art. 6.

In Re C (a child) (contact: conduct of hearing) the judge refused to allow evidence and argument on a patently arguable issue. She went too far. Wilson LJ said:[5] 'Judges exercising jurisdiction in relation to children have … a broader discretion in the mode of their conduct of the hearing than do judges in the exercise of a conventional civil jurisdiction,' but as Laws LJ put it:

---

2 Lexis reports the earliest case in which the phrase is used is March 1994, *R v Secretary of State for the Home Department ex p Abdi*, *The Times* 10 March 1994 by Sedley J.

3 *Fretté v France*, 26 February 2002, [47] and [49].

4 *Stran Greek Refineries and Stratis Andreadis v Greece*, 9 December 1994, [46]. And see *Walston (No 1) v Norway*, 3 June 2003, [56].

5 *Re C (a child)* (contact: conduct of hearing) [2006] EWCA Civ 144.

> In our system, which remains adversarial, it is an elementary duty of the judge to ensure a fair hearing, as much in family cases as in any other. That is entirely consistent with the broader procedural discretions enjoyed by family judges, as Wilson LJ has described them.

So also, where a court is to be guided by either experts or assessors, it should do so openly in circumstances in which the parties have an opportunity to make submissions on that guidance before any decision is made.[6]

Generally, the resolution of conflicts of evidence or opinion between two people generally requires that both sides be given equal opportunities to put their side of the story[7] and to challenge evidence led by the other side.[8] There is an obligation[9] 'to conduct a proper examination of the submissions, arguments and evidence'. A court cannot comply with Art. 6 if it merely defers to a decision of an administrative body on a fact which is crucial for the determination of the case.[10] In private law litigation, the principle has often arisen as regards the giving of evidence. In *Van de Hurk v The Netherlands* the ECtHR said:[11]

> The effect of art.6(1) is, *inter alia*, to place the 'tribunal' under a duty to conduct a proper examination of the submissions, arguments and evidence adduced by the parties, without prejudice to its assessment of whether they are relevant to its decision.

In *Ankerl v Switzerland*, it added:[12] 'the issue of compliance with the principle of equality of arms had to be looked at in the context of the fairness of the hearing as a whole.' Here, although the applicant's wife had not, by operation of law, been able to give sworn evidence, what she had to say had been heard and was taken into account in the national court. Ankerl lost because the evidence he led was not good enough. By contrast, in *Dombo Beheer v Netherlands* a former Dutch law prevented a director of a company, in effect a party to the litigation, from giving evidence. The ECtHR said:[13]

> In the instant case, it was incumbent upon the applicant company to prove that there was an oral agreement between it and the Bank to extend certain credit facilities. Only two persons had been present at the meeting at which this agreement had allegedly been reached [one] representing the applicant company and [one] representing the Bank. Yet

---

6 *Watson v General Medical Council* [2005] EWHC 1896.

7 *Ruiz-Mateos v Spain*, 23 June 1993, [63]. For one recent British example, see *R (on the application of Anglian Water Services) v The Environment Agency* [2003] EWHC 1506 (Admin).

8 *Mild and Virtanan v Finland*, 26 July 2005.

9 *Buzescu v Romania*, 24 August 2005, [63]; *Buxton Building Contractors v Durand Primary School Governors* [2004] EWHC 733 (TCC).

10 *ID v Bulgaria*, 28 July 2005.

11 *Van de Hurk v The Netherlands*, 19 April 1994, [59].

12 *Ankerl v Switzerland*, 23 October 1996, [36].

13 *Dombo Beheer v Netherlands* 27 October 1993, [34].

> only one of these two key persons was permitted to be heard, namely the person who had represented the Bank. The applicant company was denied the possibility of calling the person who had represented it, because the Court of Appeal identified him with the applicant company itself.

The general principle was re-affirmed in *Steck-Risch v Liechtenstein*:[14] 'The concept of a fair trial, of which equality of arms is one aspect, implies the right for the parties to have knowledge of and to comment on all evidence adduced or observations filed'. So also in *Parsil v Turkey* where neither the applicant nor his lawyer was informed of submissions to the Court of Cassation:[15]

> To require an applicant's lawyer to take the initiative and inform himself periodically on whether any new elements have been included in the case file would amount to imposing a disproportionate burden on her or him and would not necessarily have guaranteed a real opportunity to comment on the opinion.

There is an obligation on the court to ensure that an appellant has copies of the written observations made by the other side even where the court does not rely on them.[16] We may suspect that this can be satisfied by rules requiring each side to serve the other with documents it files.

In *Neumeister v Austria*,[17] the ECtHR held that the principle only applies where there ought to be a public hearing. In *Werner v Austria*, the court told us that:[18] 'requirements resulting from the right to adversarial proceedings are in principle the same in both civil and criminal cases;' and,[19] and, in *Walston v Norway* (No 1), it clarified this, saying:[20] 'the existence of a violation is conceivable even in the absence of prejudice. It is for the applicants to judge whether or not a document calls for their comments.' By contrast, in *Brandstetter v Austria*,[21] the court, having held that a court appointed expert was not biased, went on to say that equality did not require the appointment of further experts at the request of a party.

I have suggested that any differences between the common law and civilian application of the principle is largely due to the differing roles of the advocate and the judge in the two systems. The corollary is also true. As the assumption about

14 *Steck-Risch v Liechtenstein*, 19 May 2005, [55].

15 *Parsil v Turkey*, 26 July 2005, [29].

16 *Milatova and others v Czech Republic*, 21 September 2005.

17 *Neumeister v Austria*, 27 June 1968.

18 *Werner v Austria*, 24 November 1997, [66] and see [65].

19 At [65].

20 See: *Walston* (No 1) v *Norway*, 3 June 2003, [58]; *Fortum v Finland*, 15 July 2003, [39]. This last related to a decision of the Supreme Administrative Court in a competition case where a rival firm had submitted documentation which the applicants were not allowed to see.

21 *Brandstetter v Austria*, 28 August 1991.

the equality of advocates has weakened,[22] and the judge has assumed a greater and more positive role in the trial, so the scope for the principle to be expressly applied in the English common law has increased. There is thus no surprise that the principle is directly reflected in the CPR. The overriding objective includes, 'so far as is practicable – (a) ensuring that the parties are on an equal footing'.

There are exceptions to the general rule. In England, it is possible,[23] and apparently quite common,[24] for redactions to be made on grounds of relevance. There are numerous other occasions when either a rule requires or the court can order the disclosure or non-disclosure of documents or information or evidence. Substantive law protects legal professional privilege.[25] Rules of court, often giving the court discretion, include those that facilitate pre-reading of trial bundles, disclosure on assessment, as well as public interest immunity in criminal and civil cases. There are in addition powers to restrict evidence both of fact and from an expert. Each of these can, at least potentially, engage Art. 6 either because equality of arms is threatened or because the public character of the proceedings is at risk.

The Right of Access to the Court

Court Fees

In two fairly recent cases, the question of access has been raised in relation to court fees. The impact of fees is one thing, the funding of the system another. We come to the macro funding question in Chapter 5. At the micro level, in *ex p Witham* Laws J took the opportunity to discuss the nature of a constitutional right:[26]

> The common law does not generally speak in the language of constitutional rights, for the good reason that in the absence of any sovereign text, a written constitution which is logically and legally prior to the power of legislature, executive and judiciary alike, there is on the face of it no hierarchy of rights such that any one of them is more entrenched by the law than any other. And if the concept of a constitutional right is to have any meaning, it must surely sound in the protection which the law affords to it.

22 Following *Arthur J.S. Hall v Simons* [2002] 1 AC 615 where it was acknowledged that a barrister could be liable in negligence, it became necessary to have regard to the competence of individual advocates. See also, e.g. *Moy v Pettman Smith* [2005] UKHL 7. So also, the wasted costs jurisdiction again directs attention to the performance of the individual lawyer.

23 *GE Capital v Bankers Trust* [1995] 1 WLR 172.

24 *Three Rivers DC. v Bank of England* (No.6) [2004] EWCA Civ 218.

25 *Carlson v Townsend* [2001] EWCA Civ 511.

26 *R v Lord Chancellor, ex p Witham* [1998] QB 575. In *Watkins v Secretary of State for the Home Department* [2006] UKHL 17 it was held that the idea of a constitutional right was not broad enough to modify the rule, even when there was malicious infringement of the right of access, that is that there is no cause of action without proof of special damage. We return to the relation between of a constitutional right and the HRA in Chapter 6.

He concluded: 'the right to a fair trial, which of necessity imports the right of access to the court, is as near to an absolute right as any which I can envisage.' He added:

> As regards the 1950 convention jurisprudence I will say only that, as it seems to me, the common law provides no lesser protection of the right of access to the Queen's courts than might be vindicated in Strasbourg.

Witham was concerned with court fees and whether it was lawful to set them in such a way that those on income support cannot afford to sue. The answer was that it was not. Laws J also distinguished court fees from legal aid.

In *ex parte Lightfoot* he returned to the issue. A further distinction had to be made. Rules set the fee required for an individual to petition for his or her own bankruptcy at such a level that they excluded many for whom it was the only way out of poverty. Laws J continued the tone of his judgment in *Witham*. He said:[27]

> Access to justice is a fundamental requirement of the rule of law. Its imperative rests upon the need for objective and independent adjudication of disputes between man and man, and between man and state … A sound principle may be undermined, even destroyed, if it is pressed into service in areas to which it does not necessarily belong. All the more so where the principle in question belongs to the special category of constitutional rights in a common law system which lacks a sovereign text. This is a category of rights which has not been consistently recognised in the common law's long history; though its seeds and sometimes its maturity have always been somewhere to be found.

And, went on:

> The law should be astute to confine the concept of constitutional right to that special class of rights which, in truth, everyone living in a democracy under the rule of law ought to enjoy. Access to justice is one. Freedom of the person, of speech, thought, and religion are others. They are largely articulated in the principal provisions of the European Convention on Human Rights ... If the courts were to hold that more marginal claims of right should enjoy the protection of a rigorous rule of statutory construction not applied in contexts save that of the protection of fundamental rights and freedoms, they would impermissibly confine the powers of the elected legislature.

The rule, having been made by Parliament and under powers granted by Parliament, was lawful.

Lightfoot went on appeal. Like Laws J, Simon Brown LJ distinguished:

> this case from *Ex p Witham* on the ground that the mandatory deposit is not for access to the court but rather towards the costs of services being provided by others for the petitioner's benefit ... There must come a point at which a constitutional right of the character identified in *Ex p Witham* shades into no more than a highly desirable social interest.

---

27 *R v Lord Chancellor, ex p Lightfoot* [2000] QB 597.

He said: 'Article 6(1) accordingly appears to me to have no application to the bankruptcy process sought to be instigated, as here, at the suit of a debtor.' There was, he said, no determination of any civil right and there was no dispute, indeed there was no other party. However that may be, in England then, access to the court is a constitutional right, but it is a right which should not be given too wide a scope.

We can note that Art. 6(1) does not mention the word *dispute*: it confines itself to the determination of civil rights and obligations.[28] In effect, Simon Brown LJ drew a distinction between a civil right and a civil status. It is a distinction without a difference: once a bankruptcy has been determined, civil rights are affected. In *Bock v Germany* the ECtHR referred to[29] 'the particular diligence required in cases concerning civil status and capacity' and in *Capital Bank AD v Bulgaria* it said 'the applicability of Article 6(1) to bankruptcy proceedings is beyond doubt'.[30] Long ago England abolished physical imprisonment *for* debt. *Lightfoot* preserves social incarceration *by* debt. Even if it was correct when decided in 2000, it is dubious whether it can live with this 2006 decision in *Capital Bank AD*.

Other Aspects of the Right of Access

Many of the English cases have been concerned with convicted prisoners' access to lawyers and to the courts. Typical and important among these is *Raymond v Honey*.[31] A prison governor opened a letter addressed to a solicitor. He then refused to pass on papers by which a prisoner sought to commit him for contempt. Lord Bridge said:

> First, any act done which is calculated to obstruct or interfere with the due course of justice, or the lawful process of the courts, is a contempt of court; secondly … a convicted prisoner, in spite of his imprisonment, retains all civil rights which are not taken away expressly or by necessary implication. To these I would add a third principle, equally basic, that a citizen's right to unimpeded access to the courts can only be taken away by express enactment.[32]

This confirmed the ECtHR's view in *Golder* that:[33] 'Hindrance in fact can contravene the Convention just like a legal impediment'. But the right is not absolute. The ECtHR argued:[34]

---

28 But see *Gustafson v Sweden*, 1 July 1997, [38], discussed below.

29 *Bock v Germany*, 29 March 1989, [49]. It was a divorce action.

30 *Capital Bank AD v Bulgaria*, 24 February 2006, 86. Earlier, in *M v UK*, 4 May 1987, the Commission held that bankruptcy was a fiscal matter and outside Art. 6. But that decision related to the activities of the trustee in bankruptcy and not the actual status.

31 *Raymond v Honey* [1983] AC 1.

32 He cited: *Chester v Bateson* [1920] 1 KB 829; and, *R* and *W Paul v The Wheat Commission* [1937] AC 139.

33 *Golder v UK*, 21 February 1975, [26].

34 At [38] and [39].

> As this is a right which the Convention sets forth … without, in the narrower sense of the term, defining, there is room, apart from the bounds delimiting the very content of any right, for limitations permitted by implication ... The Government and the Commission have cited examples of regulations, and especially of limitations, which are to be found in the national law of states in matters of access to the courts, for instance regulations relating to minors and persons of unsound mind.

As we have seen it added in *Ashingdane v UK*:[35] 'the limitations applied must not restrict or reduce the access left to the individual in such a way or to such an extent that the very essence of the right is impaired'. Nevertheless, the Commission explained:[36]

> In the majority of the Contracting States, the right of access to courts is restricted or subject to special conditions in respect of minors, vexatious litigants, persons of unsound mind, persons declared bankrupts and … persons who are bound by an arbitration agreement. Such regulations are not in principle contrary to Art. 6 of the Convention, where the aim pursued is legitimate and the means employed to achieve the aim is proportionate.

Clayton and Tomlinson have collected a range of occasions where, they say, permission is required before proceedings can be brought at all.[37] These include mental patients, minors, prisoners and bankrupts. In English proceedings this rather misstates the position. Mental patients and minors can generally only sue and be sued by a litigation friend and, although permission is common for such a role, it is not an absolute requirement. Permission is required in respect of certain types of complaint about conduct relating to the Mental Health Act whether or not it is brought by the patient him or herself. Apart from this, it is not a question of permission but of some other procedural hurdle. Nevertheless, they are right that each of these instances is a departure from the general rule of unrestricted access. In each case, the ECtHR has posed the question: is the procedural requirement justified by some other purpose and proportionate to it.

In *Polanski v Condé Nast Publications* the House of Lords had to consider a different aspect of the scope of the right of access. The claimant had been convicted in California in 1978 but fleed to his native France before sentence. He was a fugitive from justice. The English proceedings were a libel claim. He wanted permission

---

35 *Ashingdane v UK*, 28 May 1985, [57]. It was followed in, among other cases: *Lithgow v UK*, 8 July 1986, [194]; *Bellet v France*, 4 December 1995; and *Fayed v UK*, 21 September 1994, [65]; and also by the Court of Appeal in *J and PM Dockeray (a firm) v Secretary of State for the Environment, Food and Rural Affairs* [2002] EWHC 420 (Admin) (14 days was sufficient in which to lodge an appeal against a valuation of cattle culled in a foot and mouth outbreak).

36 *Jon Axelsson v Sweden*, 13 July 1990, ECommHR.

37 Clayton and Tomlinson *The Law of Human Rights*, vol 1, para. 11.22 and para. 11.191. They cite: mental patients, *Ashingdane v UK*, 28 May 1985; minors, *Golder v UK*, 21 February 1975; vexatious litigants *H v UK*, 1985 ECommHR; prisoners, *Campbell and Fell v UK*, 28 June 1984; and bankrupts, *M v UK*, 4 May 1987, ECommHR.

to give his evidence by video link (under a video conferencing, VCF, order under Annex 3 to Practice Direction to CPR 32). He feared he would be extradited if he came to give it in person. The Court of Appeal unanimously refused because the general policy of the court should be to discourage litigants from escaping the normal processes of the law rather than facilitating it. The House of Lords by a bare majority of 3 to 2 granted the permission. Lord Nicholls argued:[38]

> It may seem unattractive that a person can, at one and the same time, evade justice in respect of his criminal conduct and yet seek the assistance of the courts in protection of his own civil rights. But the contrary approach, adopted in the name of the public interest, would lead to wholly unacceptable results in practice. It would mean that for so long as a fugitive remained 'on the run' from the criminal law, his property and other rights could be breached with impunity. That could not be right. Such harshness has no place in our law. Mr Polanski is not a present-day outlaw. Our law knows no principle of fugitive disentitlement ... in the situation under consideration a VCF order will not assist the fugitive's evasion of justice. Whether a VCF order is made or not, the fugitive will not come to this country.

It was a close decision. In the minority, Lord Slynn thought that the action could be brought in France. To which Baroness Hale replied that because the alleged libel was in English it should be tried in an English language court. The point, particularly in her hands, does not seem relevant. The alleged wrong took place in every jurisdiction where the defendants published their magazine. The action could properly be tried anywhere. The consideration only becomes relevant if there is some other reason why England presented difficulties. Also in the minority, Lord Carswell said he would not support a rule that effectively led to a recognition of outlawry.[39] Yet, he was prepared to prevent any fugitive from giving evidence by video link. It is difficult to see in what way he was not denying effective access to the court to that whole class of potential litigants. He cited cases from the ECtHR[40] to the effect that access to court is not absolute. That was not in question. What was proposed here was a device that effectively kept a class of litigant out of the court. As Lord Nicholls suggested that was not proportionate or even relevant to the purpose of maintaining the efficacy of the British criminal process, assuming that even that was relevant to a civil action.

Summary judgment

Strictly speaking, the term *summary judgment* only applies to proceedings under CPR Part 24. However, in so many other places the court is given power to make orders that inevitably lead to a result which is identical in substance to those under Part 24. It would be confusing and indeed perverse not to consider them together.

---

38 *Polanski v Condé Nast Publications* [2005] UKHL 10, [26], [28]. Apparently, USA law does recognize a principle of fugitive disentitlement. *Polanski* was applied to a witness in *Bank of Credit and Commerce International v Rahim*, Ch D 11 November 2005 unreported.

39 At [90].

40 *A v UK*, 17 December 2002; *Eliazer v Netherlands*, 16 October 2001; and, *McElhinney v Ireland*, 21 November 2001.

The problem with any summary procedure is that full safeguards are omitted. Those missing may include: to know in advance that there is a case to be answered or what it is or the inability in law, or in practice, to produce and test evidence. If the procedure is supplementary to some other proceeding, it may involve a judge who has already taken a view on the conduct of a party (or even a non-party) appearing to try an issue under the influence of bias.

In *Gustafson v Sweden* the ECtHR told us:[41]

> The applicability of Article 6(1) under its 'civil head' requires the existence of a 'dispute' over a 'right' which can be said, at least on arguable grounds, to be recognized under domestic law. That dispute must be genuine and serious; it may relate not only to the existence of a right but also to its scope and to the manner of its exercise. Furthermore the outcome of the proceedings must be directly decisive for the right in question.

In principle, proceedings (for example, case management) that do not satisfy this test do not engage Art. 6.[42] The rule was applied in *APIS v Slovakia*.[43] It is difficult, on its facts, to see how the court arrived at this conclusion. The complaint was against the grant of an interim injunction that prevented the use of property until trial. Elsewhere the court has held that the temporary deprivation of a right can engage Art. 6.[44] Leaving this anomaly aside, we are thus left to consider decisions that do determine rights.

CPR Part 24(2) says the court may give 'summary judgment … on the whole of a claim or on a particular issue if it considers that there is no real prospect of succeeding' and there is no other compelling reason why it should be disposed of at a trial. In parenthesis the rule itself adds: 'Rule 3.4 makes provision for the court to strike out a statement of case or part of a statement of case if it appears that it discloses no reasonable grounds for bringing or defending a claim.' So also, as one shall see, there are powers to strike out claims or defences where these is a breach of a rule or order of the court. The disciplinary powers of the court go beyond striking out. There is a whole range. They include: requiring steps to be taken within a certain period; granting a permission to continue subject to a condition (which may be a substantial payment in to court); making orders as to costs (including security for costs); requiring the attendance of a party or a legal representative; and, making special provision for a rate of interest on any award.

---

41 *Gustafson v Sweden*, 1 July 1997, [38].

42 *Österreichische et al. v Austria*, 2 December 1991 and *Ewing v UK*, 6 May 1989, ECommHR.

43 *APIS v Slovakia*, 13 January 2000.

44 *Le Compte, Van Leuven and De Meyere v Belgium*. On the general question, see: *Markass Car Hire v Cyprus*, 6 November 2002; and, also *R (on the application of M) v Secretary of State for Constitutional Affairs*; also known as: *R (on the application of M) v Lord Chancellor* [2004] EWCA Civ 312 where an interim and without notice Anti-Social Behaviour Order was held to be lawful. Plainly, there must be times, where to justice at all, there must be power to issue temporary orders affecting property on without notice applications.

More importantly, if a defendant does not make an acknowledgement of service or file a defence, the claimant is entitled to make a request or apply for a default judgment, CPR Part 12.[45] The rules specify which is appropriate. The difference is that a judgment made on request is an executive act: it does not require a judge. Judges respond to applications. Strange as it might seem, the majority of claims end in a judgment by request, that is, without a judge being involved. The claimant is not so much seeking a court order but rather access to the enforcement machinery of the State. No doubt as a system it makes some kind of theoretical sense. There are two main difficulties. First, claimants are frequently careless in defining their claims. We shall consider that aspect later as we consider the funding of the court system in Chapter 5. Secondly, there may be Convention implications of making an enforceable judgment without a trial unless there are safeguards.

When I discussed compulsory or coerced ADR, I suggested there is a difference between the static objective ideas in Art. 6 and modern ideas of efficiency. The whole of this jurisdiction provides another example of this contrast. However, in relation to that jurisdiction efficiency might lead to a litigant being shut out of the court. Here, that is not so. Most directly under Parts 3, 12 and 24, a party against whom an order is made is entitled to apply to have it set aside. He or she is not shut out or subjected to a penalty unrelated to the controversy. The opposing side, on the other hand, can rest in the knowledge that the court system will not be frustrated. The court, and indeed the State itself, does not suffer the indignity of having its orders flouted. I am not concerned with the dignity of the court as such. But, there is a Convention obligation, in part derived from Art. 6, to provide a working legal system. As the ECtHR put it:[46]

> The right of access to a court includes not only the right to institute proceedings but also the right to obtain a 'determination' of the dispute by a court. It would be illusory if a Contracting State's domestic legal system allowed an individual to bring a civil action before a court without ensuring that the case would be determined by a final decision in the judicial proceedings.

A system that can be avoided by those who not want orders made against them would scarcely satisfy that obligation. The whole point of having a legal system is that it is the coercive arm of the State. As between the parties, the Convention is a two-way street. Both sides cannot always have what the text seems to give them: balances must be struck and justice must be attempted. That is what courts do. Within the CPR, not least in relation to the court's disciplinary powers, there is ample scope for discretion to be exercised with this in mind. It is the apparent lack of detailed guidance on the use of discretion in the Convention, and thus from the Court, that has led some to the conclusion that the Convention is largely irrelevant to English civil procedure. To take one example, in *Stock v Stock*, the Court of Appeal

---

45 It would seem that the procedure is a successor to an older method of commencing an action, the physical arrest of the defendant.

46 *Sukhorubchenko v Russia*, 10 February 2005.

held, on the basis of the Overriding Objective, that a judgment entered in default of a defendant's appearance should be set aside where new admissible evidence became available giving an explanation for the non-attendance. Latham LJ remarked:[47] 'It does not seem to me that Article 6 … adds anything in the circumstances of this case to the requirement of this court to have regard to the overriding objective in the way that I have indicated.' The fact that it does not add anything does not say that the Convention is irrelevant. I shall argue that it re-enforces the Overriding Objective.

Strike out and relief from sanctions

The principal means provided by the CPR for the striking out of a claim or defence, or any part of either, are contained in Parts 3 and 24. In *S v Gloucestershire CC* the court discussed the relationship between them. May LJ said:[48]

> The power to strike out a statement of case under CPR r.3.4(2)(a) is where it appears to the court that it discloses no reasonable grounds for bringing the claim. The power to give summary judgment against a claimant under CPR r.24.2 is where the court considers that the claimant has no real prospect of succeeding on the claim and that there is no other reason why the case should be disposed of at a trial. These provisions mean what they say and do not require judicial interpretation ... For a summary judgment application to succeed … where a strike out application would not succeed, the court will first need to be satisfied that all substantial facts relevant to the allegations … are before the court; that these facts are undisputed or that there is no real prospect of successfully disputing them; and that there is no real prospect of oral evidence affecting the court's assessment of the facts ... Secondly, the court will need to be satisfied that, upon these facts, there is no real prospect of the claim … succeeding and that there is no other reason why the case should be disposed of at a trial. If by this process the court does so conclude and gives summary judgment, there will, in my view, have been proper judicial scrutiny of the detailed facts of the particular case such as to constitute a fair hearing in accordance with art.6 of the Convention.

CPR Part 3.4 is thus concerned with claims that are bad in law. The court assumes that the allegations are true. Under CPR Part 24 witness statements maybe appropriate. We have seen that in *Osman*[49] the ECtHR itself misunderstood the power to strike out in what is now CPR Part 3. More helpfully in *TP and KM v UK* it said:[50]

> The decision of the House of Lords did end the case, without the factual matters being determined on the evidence. However, if as a matter of law, there was no basis for the claim, the hearing of evidence would have been an expensive and time-consuming process which would not have provided the applicants with any remedy at its conclusion.

47 *Stock v Stock*, 17 October 2000 (Transcript).

48 S. *v Gloucestershire CC*; *L v Tower Hamlets LBC* [2001] 2 WLR 909. In *Taylor v Midland Bank Trust* [1999] CA it was held that applications under CPR Part 3 can also be treated as being under Part 24. For a useful review of the cases, see Gerlis, 'Summary confusion', (2003) LSG Vol.100 37, 24 July 2003.

49 Above p. 16, n. 44.

50 *TP and KM v UK*, 10 May 2001, [102].

> There is no reason to consider the striking out procedure which rules on the existence of sustainable causes of action as *per se* offending the principle of access to court. In such a procedure, the plaintiff is generally able to submit to the court the arguments supporting his or her claims on the law and the court will rule on those issues at the conclusion of an adversarial procedure.

As Lord Woolf put it:[51] 'Although a strike out may appear to be a summary remedy, it is in fact indistinguishable from deciding a case on a preliminary point of law.'

Applications can be, and commonly are, made under both CPR Part 3 and Part 24 at one hearing. In either case, it is important that the court must be certain that the claim will fail. In *Barrett v Enfield LBC* Lord Browne-Wilkinson said:[52]

> [I]n an area of the law which was uncertain and developing … it is not normally appropriate to strike out. In my judgment it is of great importance that such development should be on the basis of actual facts found at trial not on hypothetical facts assumed (possibly wrongly) to be true for the purpose of the strike out.

The court also has power to strike out a claim or defence because it is an abuse of process, that is, an abuse of the access to State power. In *Reckitt Benkiser (UK) v Home Pairfum* Laddie J held that the power extended to striking out a valid cause of action.[53] But he limited this by citing Simon Brown LJ in *Broxton v McClelland* saying:[54]

> The fact that a party who asserts a legal right is activated by feelings of personal animosity, vindictiveness or general antagonism towards his opponent is nothing to the point ... an action is only [an abuse] if the Court's processes are being misused to achieve something not properly available to the plaintiff in the course of properly conducted proceedings.

Nevertheless, in *Reckitt Benkiser* Laddie J went on to say:

> The court's powers under the CPR are wide. They should be tailored to meet the circumstances of the case ... it does not follow that in all cases of abuse the correct response is to strike out the claim. The striking out of a valid claim should be the last option. If the abuse can be addressed by a less draconian course, it should be.

Thus, the court could hold in *Arrow Nominees v Blackledge*[55] that whatever used to be, the rule now is that:

---

51 *Kent v Griffiths* [2001] QB 36.

52 *Barrett v Enfield LBC* [2001] 2 AC 550, 557, followed in *Hughes v Richards* (*t/a* Colin Richards) [2004] EWCA Civ 266.

53 *Reckitt Benkiser (UK) v Home Pairfum* [2004] EWHC 302.

54 *Broxton v McClelland* [1995] EMLR 485, 497–498. In *Grovit v Doctor* [1997] 1 WLR 640 HL, to commence and continue proceedings with no intention of bringing them to trial was held to be an abuse of process.

55 *Arrow Nominees v Blackledge* [2000] 2 BCLC 167, per Chadwick LJ approving, a passage of Millett J in *Logicrose v Southend United Football Club Times*, 5 March 1988.

> it is not a proper exercise of the court's power under the rules or its inherent power to strike out a claimant's case where the claimant has been found to be in contumacious breach of the rules or an order of the court or even is guilty of conduct amounting to a fraud on the court and so a gross contempt, if it can be shown that notwithstanding the claimant's conduct there is no substantial risk that a fair trial of his claim cannot follow.

It maybe that an order for the deposit of security for costs is appropriate.[56]

Part 3.9 of the CPR gives the court power to grant relief from sanctions imposed under the rules and it provides a checklist of the circumstances the court should consider. In *CIBC Mellon Trust v Stolzenberg Etherton* J explained:[57]

> The Court, in such a case, must consider each of the nine items listed in r.3.9(1) which are relevant to the case, carrying out the necessary balancing exercise methodically, and explaining how the ultimate decision has been reached ... The Court must bear in mind that, where the effect of the sanction is to preclude a trial on the merits, the effect is to deprive the applicant of access to the Court, a concept which now has a particular resonance under article 6 ...

The Court of Appeal has considered this checklist on numerous occasions. For instance in *Price v Price*, it said that a failure to comply can lead to relief being granted on conditions. In that case it held that it would only be granted in respect of those issues which could still be the subject of a fair trial and that other claims which the defendant would have difficulty in defending because of the lateness should be excluded. Brooke LJ said:[58]

> if this court considers that a refusal of an extension of time in this case would be a proportionate response to the claimant's failure to state clearly what he is claiming and the reasons underlying his claim, despite so many requests by the defendant's insurers, his convention rights would not thereby be imperilled because the concept of a fair trial betokens fairness to both sides.

In *Hackney LBC v Driscoll*[59] the Court of Appeal held that once a defendant knows about the proceedings and has participated in them, the court had the necessary jurisdiction to make an order affecting him and the judge was bound to take into account all the criteria set out in the CPR Part 39.3(5) even where he (the defendant) had not been given notice of the trial date. No HRA point was taken although Brooke LJ mentioned it. So too, in *Richardson v Langtree Group*, where again the HRA was not mentioned, the respondent failed to comply with an order requiring service of a disclosure list or the action would be struck out (an 'unless order'). Nevertheless, the

---

56 *Shaw v Palmer* [2004] EWHC 388 (QB), *CIBC Mellon Trust v Mora Hotel* [2002] EWCA Civ 1688.

57 *CIBC Mellon Trust v Stolzenberg* [2003] EWHC 13 affirmed [2004] EWCA Civ 827, [44], citing *Woodhouse v Consignia* [2002] EWCA Civ 275.

58 *Price v Price (trading as Poppyland Headware)* [2003] EWCA Civ 888, [35].

59 *Hackney LBC* v *Driscoll* [2003] EWCA Civ 1037.

appellant continued with the action and appeared at the trial. The Court of Appeal held that the claim was rightly allowed to continue.[60]

Time factors

We have seen that Art. 6 says 'In the determination of his civil rights and obligations … everyone is entitled to a … hearing within a reasonable time'. In *Attorney-General's Reference* (No. 2 of 2001) Lord Bingham said:[61]

> In its application to civil proceedings, the rationale of the reasonable time requirement is not in doubt. The state should not subject claimants to prolonged delay in pursuing their claims, whatever the outcome, nor defendants to prolonged uncertainty and anxiety in learning whether their opponents' claims will be established or not. The ill consequences of delay in civil litigation … need no elaboration. In domestic law, a battery of statutory limitations, procedural rules and equitable doctrines address the problem. Article 6(1) gives a further remedy to those prejudiced, at the hands of the state, by this pernicious evil.

In *Havlickova v Czech Republic* the ECtHR reiterated the general criteria:[62]

> The reasonableness of the length of proceedings must be assessed in the light of the circumstances of the case and with reference to the following criteria: the complexity of the case, the conduct of the applicant and the relevant authorities and what was at stake for the applicant in the dispute.

But:

> While it is true that that the conduct of the parties contributed to some extent to the length of the proceedings, … even in legal systems applying the principle that the procedural initiative lies with the parties, the latter's attitude does not absolve the courts from the obligation to ensure the expeditious determination, required by Article 6(1).

The reasonable time requirement was a threshold not an ideal.[63]

The obligation applies to the whole of the proceedings. Thus, in *Nosal v Ukraine*, the ECtHR said:[64]

---

60 *Richardson v Langtree Group* [2004] EWCA Civ 1447. See also *Jeffrey v Jeffrey* [2005] EWHC 1697 (Ch).

61 *Attorney-General's Reference* (No. 2 of 2001) [2003] UKHL 68, [16], [21].

62 *Havlickova v Czech Republic*, 14 February 2006, [25], [27]. And see *RW v Poland*, 15 July 2003, [40], divorce proceedings took over 20 years and included a period with a lost court file. The same passage appears in *Sitarek v Poland*, 16 July 2003, [59]. And see: *Frydlender v France*, 27 June 2000, [43] (9 years 8 months in an employment dispute); *Sienkiewicz v Poland*, 30 September 2003, [35] (10 years 5 months was unreasonable even though each domestic court had not been guilty of undue delay); *Papachelas v Greece*, 25 March 1999, and, *Sikó v Hungary*, 4 November 2003.

63 *Farrell v HM Advocate* [2005] HCJAC 58.

64 *Nosal v Ukraine*, 29 November 2005, [40].

> The Court reiterates that the State's positive obligation, under Article 6(1) of the Convention, is to organize a system for the enforcement of judgments which is effective in both law and practice, and to ensure their execution without undue delay.

In *Price and Lowe v UK* it held:[65]

> A principle of domestic law or practice that the parties to civil proceedings are required to take the initiative with regard to the progress of the proceedings, does not dispense the State from complying with the requirement to deal with cases in a reasonable time. The manner in which a State provides for mechanisms to comply with this requirement – whether by way of increasing the numbers of judges, or by automatic time-limits and directions, or by some other method – is for the State to decide. If a State lets proceedings continue beyond the 'reasonable time' prescribed by Article 6 of the Convention without doing anything to advance them, it will be responsible for the resultant delay.

In *Co-Operative Retail Services v Guardian Assurance*[66] the action was struck out where the delay meant that a trial would take longer because it would have been an attempted reconstruction of events based on documentary evidence alone (because oral evidence was either not available because witnesses could not be found or was unreliable because memories must have faded). So also, in *Adoko v Jemal*, an ill-prepared case came to the Court of Appeal 'in complete disarray'. May LJ said:[67]

> Modern litigation culture, both before and since the advent of the civil procedure rules, requires a number of things. One of these is that parties to litigation should co-operate with the court to ensure that litigation is conducted justly and economically. One consideration to be found in r.1, which sets out the overriding objective, is that the court must, so far as is practicable, allot to individual cases an appropriate share of the court's resources while taking account of the need to allot resources to other cases.

And Laws LJ added: 'The proper and proportionate use of court resources is now to be considered part of substantive justice itself.' He probably meant *real justice* or *justice* with no adjective. The matters he referred to have nothing to do with the more usual distinction between substantive and procedural rules.

The ECHR was cited in neither case. Nevertheless, the obligation on the court and the parties to keep litigation moving is one attempt by the rules of court (i.e. by the State) to comply with the reasonable time requirement. There is nothing in the Convention that requires, or permits, the State to let the parties agree to extend time

---

65 *Price and Lowe v UK*, 29 July 2003, [23]. The proceedings lasted over 12 years. It can be noted that they all took place before the CPR came into force. And see: *Mitchell and Holloway v UK*, 17 December 2002; and, *Eastaway v UK*, 20 July 2004, where blaming the complainant for much of the delay, the Strasbourg court was less critical than the English, *Re Blackspur Group; Secretary of State for Trade and Industry v Eastaway* [2001] 1 BCLC 653.

66 *Co-Operative Retail Services v Guardian Assurance* 28 July 1999.

67 *Adoko v Jemal*, *The Times*, 8 July 1999, CA.

limits laid down by the rules or by court order. On occasions, however, the ECtHR has given a greater indulgence for the delays caused by the parties.[68]

In *Less v Benedict* there was a 3-year delay in bringing detailed costs assessment proceedings.[69] Warren J held that there was no infringement of Art. 6 because the rules made provision for either side to apply for a hearing. The court was not responsible for the delay:

> [it] does not become involved at all in a costs assessment until a hearing date is requested ... The court ... does not even know of, any delay on the part of the litigants who, for all the court knows, have dealt with the quantum of costs without the need for assessment (as happens in many, if not most, cases) ... the court ... would not, until the request for a hearing, have known that any issue remained between the parties.

In any event, he said in effect, it was unclear which side's Art. 6 rights were at issue. His plea that 'It should be remembered that the CPR were drafted with the ECHR in the background and were clearly intended to be compliant with it' is beside the point. Merely because the CPR are intended to comply does not mean that they do. He did not cite *Robins v UK* where the ECtHR found that the reasonable time requirement includes the determination of costs[70] nor the cases we come to in the next section. The fact that the court does not know whether there has been a settlement is irrelevant to whether Art. 6 requires the State to make rules requiring the parties to notify the court.

Be that as it may, as Mummery LJ said in *Bangs v Connex South Eastern*, where there is undue delay in giving its determination after a hearing by an employment tribunal, it:[71]

> may result in a breach of art 6 and possibly give rise to state liability to pay compensation to the victim of the delay, but it does not in itself give rise to a question of law, which would found an appeal challenging the correctness of the delayed decision.

Delay after issue There is no doubt that delay after the issue of proceedings can engage Art. 6. Thus, in *Frydlender v France*, the ECtHR said:[72]

---

68 *Ciborek v Poland*, 4 November 2003 (the State was not responsible for delays caused by a claimant). In *Papachelas v Greece*, 25 March 1999, [40] it said 'The Court reiterates that only delays for which the State can be held responsible may justify a finding that a "reasonable time" has been exceeded'. But a legal system which permits delay may be the responsibility of the State.

69 *Less v Benedict* [2005] EWHC 1643 (Ch). And see *Botham and Lamb v Imran Khan* [2004] EWHC 2602 (QB) where no Art. 6 point was taken.

70 *Robins v UK*, 23 September 1997.

71 *Bangs v Connex South-Eastern* [2005] EWCA Civ 14.

72 *Frydlender v France*, 27 June 2000, [45].

> It is for the Contracting States to organize their legal systems in such a way that their courts can guarantee to everyone the right to a final decision within a reasonable time in the determination of his civil rights and obligations.

So also, in *Doran v Ireland*, it said:[73]

> As to the conduct of the competent authorities, the Court recalls that, whether or not a system allows a party to apply to expedite proceedings, the courts are not exempted from ensuring that the reasonable time requirement of Article 6 is complied with, as the duty to administer justice expeditiously is incumbent in the first place on the relevant authorities.

And in *Pizzati v Italy* it added:[74]

> Where the judicial system is deficient in this respect, a remedy designed to expedite the proceedings in order to prevent them from becoming excessively lengthy is the most effective solution Such a remedy offers an undeniable advantage over a remedy affording only compensation since it also prevents a finding of successive violations in respect of the same set of proceedings and does not merely repair the breach a posteriori, as does a compensatory remedy of the type provided for under Italian law for example.

And went on:[75]

> The Court finds it reasonable that in this type of proceedings where the State, on account of the poor organisation of its judicial system, forces litigants – to some extent – to have recourse to a compensatory remedy, the rules regarding legal costs may be different and thus avoid placing an excessive burden on litigants where their action is justified. It might appear paradoxical that, by imposing various taxes – payable prior to the lodging of an application or after the decision – the State takes away with one hand what it has awarded with the other to repair a breach of the Convention. Nor should the costs be excessive and constitute an unreasonable restriction on the right to lodge such an application and thus an infringement of the right of access to a tribunal.

In other cases the court has begun to be more specific. Thus, in *Beumer v Netherlands*[76] the ECtHR held that, having regard to the number of adjournments sought by the authorities (mainly because the relevant law was too complex) and what was at stake for the applicant, a time of almost 5 years to determine an entitlement to social security benefits exceeded what was reasonable.

---

73 *Doran v Ireland*, 31 July 2003, [47]. The proceedings, which concerned an action for negligence in sale of land, lasted 8 years and 5 months. And see *Ciborek v Poland*, 4 November 2003.

74 *Pizzati v Italy* 29 March 2006 [GC], [73].

75 *Pizzati v Italy* 29 March 2006 [GC], [91].

76 *Beumer v Netherlands* 29 July 2003.

And so also in England. In *Wakefield v Channel Four Television* the claim was for libel.[77] The claimant applied for a stay until the outcome of disciplinary proceedings in the GMC largely arising out of the same facts. Eady J said that:

> It is ... important, especially perhaps [because of Art. 6] to have regard to the interests and rights of the Defendants ... There is also a public dimension to be considered, and which has been brought into sharper focus following the implementation of the CPR regime.

There was, he said, power to stay having regard to parallel proceedings but here the claim was an attempted 'gagging writ' whose purpose was to silence critics not to vindicate a reputation.

In Scotland, in a curiously opposite case, where an essential step is erroneously omitted but both parties continued to prepare for trial Art. 6 was not engaged.[78]

In *Pizzati v Italy* the Grand Chamber expressed its frustration. It said it:[79]

> feels it important to point out that the reason why it has been led to rule on so many length-of-proceedings cases is because certain Contracting Parties have for years failed to comply with the 'reasonable-time' requirement under Article 6(1) and have not provided for a domestic remedy for this type of complaint. The situation has worsened on account of the large number of cases coming from certain countries, of which Italy is one. The Court has already had occasion to stress the serious difficulties it has had as a result of Italy's inability to resolve the situation ... the Court, like the Commission, after years of examining the reasons for the delays attributable to the parties under the Italian procedural rules, has had to resolve to standardize its judgments and decisions. This has allowed it to adopt more than 1,000 judgments against Italy since 1999 in civil length-of-proceedings cases.

Delay – statutes of limitation, delay before issue In relation to delay after the issue of proceedings, the State's duty is clear, and the case management powers of the CPR further reinforce the UK's compliance. The more difficult questions are whether either statutes of limitation, which prevent older claims being heard, or delay before the issue of proceedings engage Art. 6. Or, by contrast, is there a positive obligation under the article for the State to provide some sort of limitation act so as to prevent defendants being harried by stale claims?

As regards this last, to take one fairly recent example in domestic law, in *Rowe v Kingston upon Hull CC*[80] it was held that the statute required a claim to be made within 3 years of the date at which the claimant has knowledge of the injury, not within 3 years of the date that there is knowledge of the right to bring an action. The statute, the court said, pursued a legitimate aim. The defendants would have faced great difficulties in tracing witnesses and it was irrelevant to the exercise of the

77 *Wakefield v Channel Four Television* [2005] EWHC 2410.

78 *Will v Argyll and Clyde Acute Hospitals NHS Trust* Outer House, 2004 SCLR 642.

79 *Pizzati v Italy* 29 March 2006 [GC], [64]-[66].

80 *Rowe v Kingston upon Hull CC* [2003] EWCA Civ 1281. But see *Das v Ganju*, 31 March 1999.

discretion to disallow the time limits that they would have faced those difficulties if the action had been brought within the primary limitation period.

In Europe, until recently the leading decision was *Stubbings v UK*.[81] It was and is unsatisfactory. At its broadest the decision answered one question: a statute of limitation can be Convention compliant. As the court said:[82]

> It is noteworthy that limitation periods in personal injury cases are a common feature of the domestic legal systems of the Contracting States. They serve several important purposes, namely to ensure legal certainty and finality, protect potential defendants from stale claims which might be difficult to counter and prevent the injustice which might arise if courts were required to decide upon events which took place in the distant past on the basis of evidence which might have become unreliable and incomplete because of the passage of time.

In *Stubbings* a 6 year period had been held by the House of Lords to be absolute although it was accepted that the claimant could not have known of the injury at that time.[83] The ECtHR held this was Convention compliant. The case in that court is unsatisfactory for the reasons given in the two dissenting judgments. The majority said that because the criminal prosecution could be brought or a compensation order made did the limitation not impair the very essence of the applicants' right of access to a court. As the dissents argued, the continuing possibility of criminal prosecution did little or nothing for the determination of a claimant's particular civil rights. The availability of criminal proceedings did not assert or deny a claimant's rights. The court was looking not at the claimant's rights (which the article is concerned with) but at the defendant's liability (which it is not).[84] Judge MacDonald put it this way:[85]

> It is clear from the jurisprudence of the Court that limitations on the right of access to national courts 'must not restrict or reduce the access left to the individual in such a way or to such an extent that the very essence of the right is impaired.' The Convention 'is intended to guarantee not rights that are theoretical or illusory but rights that are practical and effective.' In the present case, the … harm suffered by the applicants caused them to be unable to bring proceedings within the statutory time period. When they did become aware of the link between their present psychological conditions and the earlier abuse, they found that the 'very essence' of their right of access to court had not only been restricted or reduced but had indeed become illusory.

Fortunately, the ECtHR decision in *Stubbings* is almost certainly inconsistent with its more recent and more realistic decision in *Shofman v Russia*. There the applicant

81 *Stubbings v UK*, 22 October 1996. It cited, among other authorities, the English Law Reform Committee, Limitation of Actions in Personal Injury Claims, May 1974.

82 *Stubbings v UK*, 22 October 1996, [51].

83 *Stubbings v Webb* [1993] AC 498.

84 Cf. *Polanski v Condé Nast Publications* [2003] EWCA Civ 1573, where the CA fell into a similar error in refusing leave for the claimant to use video evidence because of factors outside his claim.

85 *Stubbings v UK*, 22 October 1996, dissent by Judge MacDonald, [3].

brought paternity proceedings as soon as he discovered that he might not be the relevant child's father, but those proceedings were time barred under legislation where the limitation period ran without exception from the date of registration of the birth. The court said:[86]

> The Government did not give any reasons why it should have been 'necessary in a democratic society' to establish an inflexible time-limit with time running irrespective of the putative father's awareness ... and not to make any exceptions to the application of that time-limit ... According to the Court's case-law, the situation in which a legal presumption is allowed to prevail over biological and social reality, without regard to both established facts and the wishes of those concerned and without actually benefiting anyone, is not compatible, even having regard to the margin of appreciation left to the State, with the obligation to secure effective 'respect' for private and family life.

In ways that were unimagined when the Limitation Acts were consolidated, the CPR now provide case sensitive opportunities for the court to respond to the issues identified in *Stubbings*. The new powers are contained in the application of the pre-action protocols, in the rules relating to case management (including the powers to strike out), and in the rules relating to costs. I have previously argued that the legislative intent of limitation periods is actually achieved by the CPR and the statute is now otiose.[87] It suffices here make two points: cases have been struck out for delay within a limitation period;[88] and, modifying an earlier view I had taken, there may be good reason for statute to provide closure on possible business to business disputes thus providing a bar to claims regardless of whether a fair trial is possible.[89]

Vexatious litigants

S.42 of the 1981 Senior Courts Act (as it is renamed)[90] authorizes the court to restrict the right of access of a litigant who is constantly vexatious.[91] Lord Bingham CJ explained in *Attorney-General v Barker*:[92]

> The hallmark of a vexatious proceeding is in my judgment that it has little or no basis in law (or at least no discernible basis); that whatever the intention of the proceeding may be, its effect is to subject the defendant to inconvenience, harassment and expense out of all proportion to any gain likely to accrue to the claimant; and that it involves an abuse of the

86 *Shofman v Russia*, 24 November 2005, [43], [44].

87 Jacob, *Civil Litigation: practice and procedure in a shifting culture*, 2001, at p. 59 et seq., esp. p. 63.

88 E.g. *Arbuthnot Latham Bank v Trafalgar Holdings* [1998] 1 WLR 1426.

89 And see James, 'The Law Commission Report on the Limitation of Actions', (2003) 22 CJQ 41-64, discussing Law Com No. 270, 9 July 2001.

90 The Supreme Court Act, 1981 is renamed by the Constitutional Reform Act 2005 sched. 11, Part 1 para. 1, and see s. 59.

91 There is also a power to order that any further step in an action cannot be taken without a further order, *Grepe v Loam* (1887) 37 Ch D 168.

92 *Attorney General v Barker* [2000] 1 FLR 759 [19].

> process of the court, meaning by that a use of the court process for a purpose or in a way which is significantly different from the ordinary and proper use of the court process.

In *H v UK*, the Commission said:[93]

> The vexatious litigant order ... did not limit the applicant's access to court completely, but provided for a review by a senior judge ... of any case the applicant wished to bring. The Commission considers that such a review is not such as to deny the essence of the right of access to court; indeed, some form of regulation of access to court is necessary in the interests of the proper administration of justice and must therefore be regarded as a legitimate aim.

Following the restrictions on appeals and the increase in paper only decisions introduced by the Access to Justice Act 1999[94] (as explained in *Tanfern*), there has been a substantial increase in the administrative work load of the Court of Appeal Office and of the members of court. In *Bhamjee v Forsdick* (No.2) Lord Phillips MR reflecting new managerial concerns remarked:[95] 'In recent years the courts have become more conscious of the extent to which vexatious litigation represents a drain on the resources of the court itself, which of necessity are not infinite'. Earlier, in the permission hearing, *Bhamjee v Forsdick* (No.1), Brooke LJ explained the size of the problem.[96] But as Laws LJ said in *Attorney-General v Ebert*[97] 'a s.42 order is draconian': it might be disproportionate to the mischief. A graded series of orders taking account of the amount of vexation has been created.[98] In *Bhamjee v Forsdick* (No.2) the Court of Appeal discussed them. It was careful to ensure they were within the Strasbourg jurisprudence. Lord Phillips MR argued:[99]

---

93 *H v UK*, 1985 ECommHR, cited in *Ebert v Official Receiver* [2002] 1 WLR 320, and see [9].

94 And see Lord Slynn in *Piglowska* (above) discussing the Act while it is still a Bill.

95 *Bhamjee v Forsdick* (No.2) [2003] EWCA Civ 1113, [8].

96 *Bhamjee v Forsdick* (No.1) [2003] EWCA Civ 799. He authorized the permissions only appeal for the precedent to have value under Practice Note (Citation of Authorities) discussed above.

97 *Attorney General v Ebert* [2001] EWHC Admin 695.

98 At [53]. The guidance is codified in CPR 3.11 and Practice Direction 3C. There is flexible jurisdiction. In *Perotti v Collyer-Bristow (a firm)* [2004] EWCA Civ 639 the court imposed an order that any further application to the Appeal Court should be on paper: 'the nuisance posed by Mr Perotti's litigious activities is now so extreme that the court would be entitled to take this unusual step to protect its own processes and the interests of other litigants.' In *Attorney General v Ebert* [2005] EWHC 1254 an order was made enjoining the defendant from 'corresponding or in any way communicating with any judge or officer of the Court Service in an insulting or abusive manner' and from seeking to reopen statute barred matters. In *Attorney General v Chitolie* [2004] EWHC 1943 (Admin) the order prohibited the respondent from acting as a litigation friend or a McKenzie friend or otherwise assisting any third party in the conduct of civil proceedings without the leave of the High Court.

99 *Bhamjee v Forsdick* (No.2) [2003] EWCA Civ 1113, [16]-[17], [49]-[50].

> This court … like any court, has an inherent jurisdiction to protect its processes ... The Strasbourg jurisprudence … proclaim the message that the right of access to the courts may be subject to limitations in the form of regulation by the state, so long as two conditions are satisfied:
>
> (i) the limitations applied do not restrict or reduce the access left to the individual in such a way or to such an extent that the very essence of the right is impaired;
>
> (ii) a restriction must pursue a legitimate aim and there must be a reasonable relationship of proportionality between the means employed and the aim sought to be achieved.

Murdie has suggested that this sort of litigant, rather than being merely troublesome or eccentric, may be suffering from a psychiatric condition known as de Clerembault's syndrome. He argued that:[100]

> widely recognized in European psychiatry, the litigious form of the condition (which has been termed 'querulant delusions') is little known in the UK. The syndrome is named after a French psychiatrist, Gaëtan Gatian de Clerambault who described three categories of the condition as 'erotomania, litigious behaviour and morbid jealousy'.[101] Anglo-Saxon perceptions of the syndrome have concentrated on the 'erotomaniac' aspect, which in the English-speaking world was initially considered as being confined to women.

It is a delusional (paranoid) disorder.[102] *Attorney-General v Douglas* may be typical. Brooke LJ described the background in this way:[103]

> This is a sad case ... There is no family history of psychiatric disorder nor any previous psychiatric history on her part. In 1997 she gave a psychotherapist a history of good adjustment within the family, school and with friends and peers. After returning from Jamaica she continued her education, culminating in an Access course and eventually went to Lancaster University where she gained an Honours degree in law. Since then she went to the College of Law … in a classroom teaching situation shortly after she joined the College she was the only student present from an ethnic minority and the tutor made a comment about a 'nigger in the wood pile'. In a subsequent report from the same psychotherapist, written in February 2000, the view is expressed that she developed a significant psychological problem as a result of the difficulties on her course.

---

100 Murdie, 'Vexatious litigants and de Clerambault syndrome', (2002) NLJ Vol.152, 61.

101 He cited: Baruk, 'Les délires passionels' in (1959) 1 *Trait de Psychiatrie* p. 532 reproduced in *Themes and Variations in European Psychiatry* (1974) (Hirsch and Shepherd, EDS). He also cited: Goldstein in 'More forensic romances: De Clerambault's syndrome in Men', (1987) 15 (3) *Journal of the American Academy of Psychiatric and Law*, p. 267; and, Leong in 'De Clerambault Syndrome (Erotomania) in the Criminal Justice System: Another look at this recurring problem', (1994) 39 (2) *Journal of Forensic Sciences*, p. 378.

102 Delusional disorders are a form of psychosis in which a person has paranoid delusions which are often long-lasting, and do not have an obvious physical or medical causes (e.g. head injuries).

103 *Attorney General v Douglas* [2001] EWHC Admin 610, [2], [3].

In the result the Court simply adjourned the proceedings and refused to accept an undertaking she was prepared to give to abandon her litigation. It also declined to make a time-limited order.

If Murdie is right, although Lord Phillips in *Bhamjee v Forsdick* (No.2) was careful to ensure the new orders complied with Art. 6, there has to be some doubt whether they engage Art. 14.[104] The discrimination is based on a medical condition, but given the graduated terms of the guidance, which itself introduces procedures short of the statutory power, it can be said with confidence that the new powers are a proportionate response. Thus, Keene LJ was too robust in *Attorney-General v Wheen*[105] in saying: 'It is ... wholly unarguable that [the jurisdiction] conflicts' with the Convention. On the contrary, the imposition of a requirement for permission before the commencement of proceedings in respect of a limited class of potential litigants, more particularly if that class is suffering from a known mental illness, does engage Art. 14. However, there is compliance provided the measured proportionality of Lord Phillips' approach is applied.

Security for costs

The right to legal representation may be infringed in other situations. Thus, it has been held in England that an impecunious litigant should not be ordered give security for costs of a trial more than he was likely to be able to raise, *Chapple v Williams*,[106] and similarly in the ECtHR that a security which is disproportionate to income was not compatible with Art. 6.[107] This did not necessarily apply to the security of costs of an appeal where the other side had already obtained a judgment, *Tolstoy Miloslavsky v UK*.[108] The ECtHR pointed out that Art. 6 does not require any right of appeal. But that where such a right exists, the safeguards of Art. 6 apply.[109] The court held the costs order in that case pursued the legitimate aims of protecting a party from being faced with an irrecoverable bill for legal costs and, because it has regard to the prospect of success, the interests of the fair administration of justice. But it might have been different if the potential appellant could not afford the security.[110] On the other hand, an adjournment may be appropriate where a respondent to committal

---

104 The leading English authority on the scope of Art. 14 is Laws LJ in *Carson v Secretary of State for Work and Pensions* [2003] EWCA Civ 797, [35].

105 *Attorney General v Wheen* [2001] IRLR 91 7 December 2000. He was considering s. 33(1) of the Employment Tribunals Act, 1996 which is in similar terms to s. 42 of the Senior Courts Act.

106 *Chapple v Williams*, 8 December 1999 [1999] CPLR 731. And see *Abraham v Thompson* [1997] EWCA Civ 2179, discussing the then RSC Order 23, now CPR Part 25 II, rr.14 et seq.

107 *Aït-Mouhoub v France*, 28 October 1998, [52].

108 *Tolstoy Miloslavsky v UK*, 13 July 1995, distinguished in *Nasser v United Bank of Kuwait* [2002] 1 WLR 1868.

109 *Tolstoy Miloslavsky v UK*, 13 July 1995.

110 *Garcia Manibardo v Spain*, 15 February 2000 and *Kreuz v Poland*, 19 June 2001.

proceedings has applied for legal aid and is awaiting a decision of the Legal Services Commission.[111]

International law

State immunity The doctrine of state immunity is part of international law accepted by the United Kingdom and the other States of the Council of Europe. Together with the associated doctrine of sovereign immunity, it provides an immunity, which can be waived, from being sued in domestic courts. It is a general exception to Art. 6 of the Human Rights Convention. In *McElhinney v Ireland*[112] the ECtHR said: 'States enjoy a certain margin of appreciation, although the final decision as to the observance of the Convention's requirements rests with the Court.' Accordingly:

> The Court must ... examine whether the limitation pursued a legitimate aim ... The Court considers that the grant of sovereign immunity to a State in civil proceedings pursues the legitimate aim of complying with international law to promote comity and good relations between States through the respect of another State's sovereignty.

And, as it added in *Al-Adsani v UK*:[113]

> Just as the right of access to a court is an inherent part of the fair trial guarantee in that Article, so some restrictions on access must likewise be regarded as inherent, an example being those limitations generally accepted by the community of nations as part of the doctrine of State immunity.

In England the matter is governed by the State Immunity Act 1978. In *Al-Adsani* itself by a bare majority of 9 to 8, the ECtHR upheld a recognition of a claim for immunity in a civil action for torture alleged to have been committed by Kuwait. However, in Britain, apparently in the face of the HRA, the scope of the doctrine is reduced. As we have seen in *Harb v His Majesty King Fahd Bin Abdul Aziz* the Court of Appeal held that a claim for immunity was a public matter and the court should sit in public. More importantly, on facts very similar to *Al-Adsani*, in *Jones v Saudi Arabia*,[114] the Count of Appeal held that the doctrine which protects the State does not necessarily protect its officials where torture was alleged. So also the immunity can be waived. In *Aziz v Embassy of Republic of Yemen*[115] the court held that there was a real issue as to whether immunity had been waived and the evidence of the ambassador was important but not necessarily conclusive.

---

111 *Berry Trade v Moussavi* [2002] EWCA Civ 477. And see *Croissant v Germany*, 25 September 1992, [27], upholding the power of a German criminal court to appoint a lawyer for the defence.

112 *McElhinney v Ireland*, 21 November 2001, [34]-[35].

113 *Al-Adsani v UK*, 21 November 2001, [54] and [56].

114 *Jones v Saudi Arabia*, Also known as: *Jones v Minister of the Interior Al-Mamlaka Al-Arabiya AS Saudiya* [2004] EWCA Civ 1394.

115 *Aziz v Embassy of the Republic of Yemen* [2005] EWCA Civ 745.

Enemy aliens Lawrence Collins J helpfully set out the modern law in *Amin v Brown*.[116] The claimant was an Iraqi resident in Iraq. The claim related to the management of a flat in London. Having set out the authorities, the judge said:

> an enemy national resident in the enemy state has no right of access to an English court during the war as a claimant or other actor in any proceedings, except by licence of the Crown ... The basis of the rule is that the enemy subject in this country cannot come to sue in the courts any more than could an outlaw, and that the courts will give no assistance to proceedings which, if successful would lead to the enrichment of an alien enemy, and therefore would tend to provide his country with the sinews of war.

However:

> An English court faced with the decision whether or not a state of war existed to which the United Kingdom was a party would have to approach the question by ascertaining whether a state of war had broken out, and if so, whether it had yet been terminated. Those were issues essentially in the last resort for the executive.

He considered modern state practice and a number of statements by ministers and concluded that he was 'satisfied that HMG's position is that there is not, and has not been, a state of war between the United Kingdom and the Republic of Iraq'. Mere armed conflict is not war.[117] He concluded he was 'satisfied that … there is no warrant for extending [disability of alien enemies] to modern armed conflict not involving war in the technical sense'. It is a pity that Lawrence Collins J did not discuss whether Art. 6 was engaged. In principle, any rule that excludes a right of access to the court engages the Article. However, the English rule is part of International Law and can safely be read into the Convention. Moreover, the finding that the 'traditional concept of war has virtually disappeared from state practice' preserves the right of access.

The Right to be Heard

The right to be heard is fundamental to any adversarial proceedings, civil or criminal,[118] (we discuss later in this section whether the right also implies an oral hearing). It does not apply to other proceedings even where they must be in public, for example, those under the Inquiries Act 2005 or an inquest. In such proceedings

116 *Amin v Brown* [2005] EWHC, 1670.

117 The humanitarian Geneva Conventions of 1949 apply to 'declared war or any other armed conflict'.

118 But the proceedings must be adversarial. Thus, there is no right to be heard when an authority is considering whether to apply for Anti-Social Behaviour Order, *Wareham v Purbeck DC* [2005] EWHC 358 (Admin), a decision that is at one with *Miailhe v France* (No.2), 26 September 1996 and *National Panasonics v The Commission, European Court of Justice*, Case 136/79, 26 June 1980.

there may not be a right to cross-examine.[119] The right to be heard, it is important to note, is additional to equality of arms. That can be satisfied even if both parties have been denied the opportunity to give oral or indeed any presentation of their cases. A right to be heard may not be[120] because, as the court put it, and as we have seen:[121]

> the concept of fair trial also implies in principle the right for the parties to a trial to have knowledge of and comment on all evidence adduced or observations filed with a view to influencing the court's decision.

In *Colozza v Italy* there were difficulties in serving notice of a trial and it went ahead without the accused. There is no great surprise that the ECtHR discovered a right to heard:[122]

> Although this is not expressly mentioned in paragraph 1 [of Art. 6] … the object and purpose of the Article taken as a whole show that a person 'charged with a criminal offence' is entitled to take part in the hearing.

There is no surprise because it is difficult to see how there can be 'a fair and public hearing' of either a criminal or civil trial if a party is not told in advance about it.[123]

Again, the right is not absolute. It may not, for instance, apply or apply only in a modified form to permission-to-appeal proceedings[124] or proceedings involving only questions of law. There is no doubt that it is a right that is capable of being waived. For example, CPR Part 32.2(1) says at every hearing other than a trial, 'any fact which needs to be proved … is to be proved by … evidence in writing'.

Without Notice Hearings

The idea that balances must be struck is illustrated by the requirements imposed when an applicant seeks an order in the absence of the other side. Balcombe LJ explained in *Brink's Mat v Elcombe*:[125]

> The courts today are frequently asked to grant *ex parte* [the old name for *without notice*] injunctions, either because the matter is too urgent to await a hearing on notice or because

---

119 *R (on the application of D) v Secretary of State for the Home Department* (Inquest intervening) [2006] EWCA Civ 143.

120 *Ekbatani v Sweden*, 26 May 1988, [30].

121 *MS v Finland*, 22 March 2005, [32]. And see also references at n. 20 p. 109 above.

122 *Colozza v Italy*, 12 February 1985, [27]. And *See Sejdovic v Italy*, 1 March 2006.

123 But note *Hackney LBC v Driscoll* [2003] EWCA Civ 1037 above.

124 *Porter v UK*, 9 November 1987 EcommHR. 'Civil rights and obligations' were not being determined. In *Miller v Sweden*, 8 February 2005, less technically, it referred to a 'a less strict standard' applying to applications for leave to appeal.

125 *Brink's Mat v Elcombe* [1988] 1 WLR 1350. And see: *Memory Corporation v Sidhu*, unreported, 21 January 2000; and, *Gadget Shop v Bug. Com*, *The Times* 28 March 2000 (Transcript).

> the very fact of giving notice may precipitate the action which the application is designed to prevent.

As the court said in *Ansah v Ansah*:[126]

> Orders made *ex parte* are anomalies in our system of justice which generally demands service or notice of the proposed proceedings on the opposite party. Nonetheless, the power of the court to intervene immediately and without notice in proper cases is essential to the administration of justice.

The most common examples are search orders and freezing injunctions, interim injunctions for alleged defamation, breach of confidence and copyright, and non-molestation orders in family proceedings.[127] Of course, whether an order should be made is a matter for the judge. Frequently, however, it is questioned only after the defendant has been served with it. *Brink's Mat* itself was such a case. Ralph Gibson LJ set out the relevant principles:[128]

> (i) The duty of the applicant is to make 'a full and fair disclosure of all the material facts'.
>
> (ii) The material facts are those which it is material for the judge to know in dealing with the application as made: materiality is to be decided by the court and not by the assessment of the applicant or his legal advisers.
>
> (iii) The applicant must make proper inquiries before making the application. The duty of disclosure therefore applies not only to material facts known to the applicant but also to any additional facts which he would have known if he had made such inquiries.
>
> (iv) The extent of the inquiries which will be held to be proper, and therefore necessary, must depend on all the circumstances of the case including:
>
> (a) the nature of the case which the applicant is making when he makes the application;
>
> (b) the order for which application is made and the probable effect of the order on the defendant; and
>
> (c) the degree of legitimate urgency and the time available for the making of inquiries.

---

126 *Ansah v Ansah* [1977] Fam 138.

127 See generally CPR Part 25. As regards injunctions generally and search and freezing orders in particular, see the Practice Direction to Part 25. As regards interim injunctions, both with and without notice, see *American Cyanamid v Ethicon* [1975] AC 396. As regards defamation, see HRA s. 12(3) and ECHR Art. 10, on this last see *Imutran v Uncaged Campaigns* [2001] 2 All ER 385. *The University of Oxford v Broughton* [2004] EWHC 2543 is an unusual case. An interim injunction was granted against 'persons unknown'.

128 *Brink's Mat v Elcombe* [1988] 1 WLR 1350. Layout adjusted.

(v) … the court will be astute to ensure that a plaintiff who obtains an *ex parte* injunction without full disclosure is deprived of any advantage he may have derived by that breach of duty.

(vi) … The answer to the question whether the non-disclosure was innocent, in the sense that the fact was not known to the applicant or that its relevance was not perceived, is an important consideration but not decisive by reason of the duty on the applicant to make all proper inquiries and to give careful consideration to the case being presented.

(vii) Finally … the court has a discretion, notwithstanding proof of material non-disclosure which justifies or requires the immediate discharge of the *ex parte* order, nevertheless to continue the order, or to make a new order on terms.

Slade LJ sounded a note of caution:

the nature of the principle … is essentially penal and in its application the practical realities of any case before the court cannot be overlooked. By their very nature, *ex parte* applications usually necessitate the giving and taking of instructions and the preparation of the requisite drafts in some haste. Particularly in heavy commercial cases, the borderline between material facts and non-material facts may be a somewhat uncertain one. While in no way discounting the heavy duty of candour and care which falls on persons *making ex parte* applications, I do not think the application of the principle should be carried to extreme lengths.

And, Balcombe LJ justified the rule:

The rule that an *ex parte* injunction will be discharged if it was obtained without full disclosure has a twofold purpose. It will deprive the wrongdoer of an advantage improperly obtained. But it also serves as a deterrent to ensure that persons who make *ex parte* applications realise that they have this duty of disclosure and of the consequences (which may include a liability in costs) if they fail in that duty. Nevertheless, this judge-made rule cannot be allowed itself to become an instrument of injustice. It is for this reason that there must be a discretion in the court to continue the injunction, or to grant a fresh injunction in its place, notwithstanding that there may have been non-disclosure when the original *ex parte* injunction was obtained.

More recently, the Court of Appeal reminded us that, particularly where an injunction is sought with incomplete evidence, there is a basic requirement that there is a real urgency and all the more so where an early effective hearing date is available.[129] So also, it is important to have regard to its scope and the effect on the defendant.[130] None of this is informed by the Convention but it is clearly an attempt by the courts to achieve fairness between the parties.

It is a separate question whether Art. 6 is engaged. Some doubt on this is cast in *R (On the application of M)*. There, interim an anti-social behaviour order was sought.

129 *Mayne Pharma (USA) v TEVA UK* [2005] EWCA Civ 137.

130 *Moat Housing Group – South v Harris* [2005] EWCA Civ 287 (anti social behaviour injunction).

In what appears to be a non-sequitor, giving the judgment of the court, Kennedy LJ said:[131]

> Because an application for an interim order without notice can only be made when the justices' clerk is satisfied that it is necessary for the application to be made without notice, and because the order can only be made for a limited period, when the court considers that it is just to make it, and in circumstances where it can be reviewed or discharged … it seems to us to be impossible to say that it determines civil rights.

It suffices here to say: (1) the ECtHR, in a decision not cited in *M*, has held that without notice hearings can be Art. 6 compliant;[132] (2) at least one of the cases on which it did rely, *Schuler-Zgraggen*,[133] is, as we have seen, of dubious authority; and, (3) it may be that *M* is confined to anti-social behaviour orders because there is a Convention obligation to prevent such conduct.[134]

Adjournments

The right to be heard is often in issue where one party asks for an adjournment on the grounds either of ill-health or a difficulty with legal representation or, more simply, does not appear. There is nothing in the rules relating to a party's non-appearance which requires a court to decide against him or her: if the court has all the information it needs, there is no reason why it cannot get on with its substantive task[135] and, where appropriate, decide in favour of an absent party. CPR Part 39.3 makes provision for such situations. On its face, the rule deals only with non-appearance and not an application to postpone. It allows the court to proceed but gives it power to restore the case.[136] CPR Part 39.3(5) provides:

> Where an application is made … by a party who failed to attend the trial, the court may grant the application only if the applicant – (a) acted promptly when he found out that the court had exercised its power to strike out or to enter judgment or make an order against him;
>
> (b) had a good reason for not attending the trial; and
>
> (c) has a reasonable prospect of success at the trial.

---

131 *R (on the application of M) v (1) Secretary of State for Constitutional Affairs and Lord Chancellor (First Defendant) (2) Leeds Magistrates' Court (Second Defendant) and Leeds CC (Interested Party)* [2004] EWCA Civ 312, [39].

132 *Chappell v UK*, 30 March 1989

133 *Schuler-Zgraggen*, see p. 141 above.

134 *Moreno Gomez v Spain*, 16 November 2004.

135 *British Mensa v Gallant* (Transcript), CA, 30 June 1999.

136 Such a procedure is acceptable to the Strasbourg court, *Sukhorubchenko v Russia*, 10 February 2005.

The Practice Direction adds that an applicant must state, 'when the applicant found out about the order against him'. The Practice Direction to CPR Part 29 provides:

> (6) Litigants and lawyers must be in no doubt that the court will regard the postponement of a trial as an order of last resort ...
>
> (7) The court will not postpone any other hearing without a very good reason ...

Each case must, of course, be judged on its on facts. In *Republic of Iraq v Al-Kobayci Lindsay* J appeared not to mind whether the factors in para. 3(5) are a rule or matters to influence the use of a discretion.[137] Mummery LJ explained in *Brazil v Brazil*:[138]

> An over analytical approach to the issue is not appropriate, bearing in mind the duty of the court, when interpreting the rules and exercising any power given to it by the rules, to give effect to the overriding objective of enabling it to deal with cases justly. The perfectly ordinary English phrase 'good reason' … is a sufficiently clear expression of the standard of acceptability to be applied to enable a court to determine whether or not there is a good reason for non-attendance.

A date set for a trial or an appeal is important. In *Cook v Bates* there was a series of delays. Eventually, an appeal was fixed to be by video conference. Still, the appellant did not appear. The appeal was dismissed without recourse to the merits. Munby J said:[139] 'Enough is enough. There has been more than enough delay in this litigation. I am satisfied that further delay will cause [the respondent] serious prejudice'. On the other hand, in *Rotherham MBC* v *Jones* a key witness was prevented from attending and 'the risk of injustice [outweighed] the need for an early hearing'.[140]

The court uses similar criteria to Part 39.3(5) where there is a request for an adjournment rather than a mere no show. In *Eastwood v Winckworth Sherwood* the EAT applied the same principles on the grounds of the impossibility of a proper and just presentation of a case.[141] In *Teinaz* Peter Gibson LJ said:[142]

> A litigant whose presence is needed for the fair trial of a case, but who is unable to be present through no fault of his own, will usually have to be granted an adjournment, however inconvenient it may be to the tribunal or court and to the other parties. That litigant's right to a fair trial under Article 6 of the European Convention on Human Rights demands nothing less. But the tribunal or court is entitled to be satisfied that the inability of the litigant to be present is genuine, and the onus is on the applicant for an adjournment to prove the need for such an adjournment.

137 *Iraq v Al-Kobayci* [2006] All ER (D) 55 (Apr). There is no full report.
138 *Brazil v Brazil* [2002] EWCA Civ 1135, [12].
139 *Cook v Bates* [2005] EWCA Civ 205, [13].
140 *Rotherham MBC v Jones* [2004] EAT 30 September 2004, unreported.
141 *Eastwood v Winckworth Sherwood* [2006] All ER (D) 174 (Feb) EAT.
142 *Teinaz v Wandsworth LBC* [2002] EWCA Civ 1040.

This formulation has the benefit of defining some possible but ultimately irrelevant factors. But it is, however, clear that the powers of an appeal court are limited. In *Teinaz* the court emphasized that the decision is for a lower court and an appeal court can only intervene on the usual grounds that relevant factors are not been taken into account or irrelevant ones are. So also, as Arden LJ said in *Andreou v LCD*:[143]

> The decision in *Teinaz* stressed that there is a high hurdle which an appellant has to overcome in order to succeed in a complaint that the exercise of discretion by the tribunal was improper and should be set aside.

As importantly, but half hidden in Peter Gibson LJ's formulation, is the requirement that 'the inability of the litigant to be present is genuine'. For example, a doctor's letter stating that the litigant is unfit for work, even because of a stress related illness, may not be sufficient. The incapacity should be stated to be such as to prevent the litigant from taking part.[144] The appeal court has however accepted fresh evidence justifying an adjournment where the court below has refused it.[145]

In *Ahmed v Butt* a litigant in person applied for an adjournment based on his sore throat and inability to speak. After the adjournment was refused, the judge repeatedly made it clear that he could not hear what was being said.[146] The hearing should have been postponed.

One factor that does weigh heavily is the prospect of success.[147] This is odd because by definition the judge cannot at that stage have had all the relevant material. In some sense, it looks as if practice and the rule require a case to be prejudged. Nevertheless, so long as the criteria of *Teinaz* are applied it is probably acceptable.

In *Great Future International v Sealand Housing Corp* (No.4) Neuberger J suggested a set of criteria more applicable where an adjournment is sought because of difficulties in obtaining representation. These were:[148]

- the importance of the proceedings and their likely adverse consequences to the party seeking the adjournment;
- the risk of the party being prejudiced in the conduct of the proceedings if the application is refused;
- the risk of prejudice or other disadvantage to the other party if the adjournment

---

143 *Andreou v LCD* [2002] EWCA Civ 1192.

144 *Blunkett v Quinn* [2004] EWHC 2816.

145 *Skipsey v O'Rourke* [2005] EWCA Civ 912.

146 *Ahmed v Butt* [2005] EWCA Civ 1448. But note *Stanford v UK*, 23 February 1994, trial not unfair where the accused could not hear but his lawyers made no complaint.

147 *Fox v Graham Group Times*, 3 August 2001; *St Ermin's Property v Draper* [2004] EWHC 697 (Ch); *Pritchard Englefield (a Firm)* v *Steinberg* [2005] EWCA Civ 288.

148 *Great Future International v Sealand Housing Corporation* (No.4) (Ch D) 8 June 2001 (unreported). My formulation is taken from Gerlis, 'How to tackle courts when unfit for duty', (2005) LSG Vol.102 p. 32. At common law a party cannot demand an adjournment as of right to obtain legal advice, *R v Lipscombe, ex p Biggins* (1862) 26 JP 244.

is granted;
- and, the extent to which the party applying for the adjournment has been responsible for creating the difficulty that led to the application.

Where the legal representatives though no fault of their own or their client had only a small opportunity to master a large case file, an adjournment ought to have granted.[149] So also, it should where a case raised complex issues and the appellants did not expect them to be determined at that hearing.[150] Similarly, when there was an outstanding application for legal aid, an adjournment might have been appropriate.[151] It might also have been appropriate where one party had fallen out with his or her solicitors and materials such as witness statements had not been served.[152] The case was stronger where it was based on contested oral evidence and not only was there an outstanding application for legal assistance but also one or both sides had limited English or knowledge of the legal system.[153] It may be otherwise where the delays were a party's own fault and justice demanded an early determination.[154] But often prejudice to the innocent party could be cured by a costs order.[155]

The right to be heard arises in other contexts. A court ought not to have proceeded with a hearing of an application to commit where it knew that the alleged contemnor was ill[156] or wished to be heard in person but was prevented from being present by matters over which he had no control[157] or where a judge had not heard potentially relevant evidence in mitigation because of the absence.[158] Nor should a court have enforced an arbital award where the defendant had not been told of the claim before the arbitration.[159]

There is another set of considerations. There is a widespread practice of judges, before or during a hearing, indicating to one or both parties their preliminary thoughts.[160] There is, no doubt, a line between case management and a useful

---

149 *Re C–B (a child)* (care proceedings: human rights claim) [2004] EWCA Civ 1517.

150 *Henry Butcher International v KG Engineering* (*a* partnership); *Henry Butcher International v Gyte* [2004] All ER (D) 330 (Oct) CA.

151 *Berry Trade v Moussavi* [2002] EWCA Civ 477.

152 *Primus Telecommunications Netherlands v Pan European* [2005] EWCA Civ 273.

153 *Islam v Meah* [2005] EWCA Civ 1485.

154 *Warne v Little* [2004] EWCA Civ 1025; *Law Debenture Trust v Elektrim Finance* [2005] EWCA Civ 1354.

155 *Primus Telecommunications Netherlands v Pan European* [2005] EWCA Civ 273.

156 *Tankaria v Morgan* [2005] EWHC 3282.

157 *Raja (Claimant) v Van Hoogstraten (Defendant) and Tombstone* (Proposed Intervenor) [2004] EWCA Civ 968.

158 *Symes v Phillips* [2005] EWCA Civ 533.

159 *Kanoria v Guinness* [2006] EWCA Civ 222.

160 *Hart v Relentless Records* [2002] EWHC 1984 (Ch), [37]-[38]. And see: Sir G Lightman, Speech to the London Solicitors' Litigation Association, 'The Case for Judicial Intervention', 9 November 1999, on the Senior Judges website; but note the doubts in David Burrows, 'Judicial indications: how far can you go?', (2005) Fam LJ No. 35 Jan 58.

indication with a view to saving time and costs on the one side and a demonstration of bias on the other. The first is appropriate, the second, not. We come to the general issue of judicial bias in Chapter 5.

In general, the court has power to limit evidence[161] or to receive it by written witness statements alone. Nevertheless, the greater the importance of a point to the litigation, the greater the obligation to satisfy all parties that they have been heard on it.[162] The power to limit evidence must be exercised with that in mind. There is, however, no obligation to admit irrelevant evidence.[163]

The position is similar to where a judge wishes to cite an authority in his or her judgment that was not mentioned in argument. The Court of Appeal has said that where such an authority is relevant, significant and material the court:[164]

> should refer that authority to the parties and invite their submissions before concluding its decision. This is more than mere good practice. Failure to do so may amount to a breach of natural justice and of the right to a fair hearing … the authority must alter or affect the way the issues have been addressed to a significant extent. Beyond that, however, the interests of justice do not demand that any shortcomings in a litigant in person's presentation of his or her case should be overcome by affording the litigant the indulgence of the chance to do better second time round.

In a succession of cases, the ECtHR has held that the right to a trial is meaningless unless it includes matters arising beforehand. Nevertheless, in *Kent Pharmaceuticals* the Court of Appeal held that because the applicant was able to challenge the use of documents disclosed by the Serious Fraud Office to the Department of Health in separate proceedings the Department brought, it could not succeed in an independent action to recover them. The Court left open whether Art. 6 was engaged.[165]

We shall discuss another aspect of the right to be heard as we consider the right, particularly of the Crown, to withhold documents and evidence on the grounds that a wider public interest may be damaged, the so-called public interest immunity.

Paper Decisions

Paper decisions, that is, where a court makes a decision without the parties making oral submissions, raise particular issues concerning the right to be heard. As Lord

161 CPR Part 32. In *Re M (a Child)* [2004] EWCA Civ 1621, [20], Thorpe LJ called it 'extraordinarily wide'.

162 *Cleaver v HPL Universal Services Handling* (In Liquidation) EAT 29 September 2004 (unreported).

163 *X v Germany*, 6 March 1964, ECommHR.

164 *Sheridan v Stanley Cole* (Wainfleet) [2003] EWCA Civ 1046, [30] et seq. It adopted the test applied by Judge Serota in *Albion Hotel (Freshwater) v Maia E Silva* [2002] IRLR 200, [35].

165 *R (on the application of Kent Pharmaceuticals) v Director of the Serious Fraud Office* [2004] EWCA Civ 1494.

Hope has pointed out:[166] 'It is, of course, more costly and time-consuming to deal with cases by means of oral hearings. Arrangements have to be made to ensure that they are conducted fairly.' The English courts have refined the idea that justice cannot be done on paper alone. They have discussed the issue in a series of cases dealing with a variety of decision-making bodies.[167] Clarke LJ defined the issue:[168]

> The key point as a matter of principle is that the question whether the procedure satisfies article 6 (1), where there is a determination of civil rights and obligations, must be answered by reference to the whole process. The question in each case is whether the process involves a court or courts having 'full jurisdiction to deal with the case as the nature of the decision requires'. There may be cases in which a public and oral hearing is required at first instance and other cases where it is not, just as there may be cases in which the potential availability of judicial review will not be sufficient to avoid a breach of article 6 (1).

The overall test was satisfied 'when the process is considered as a whole there has been a fair and public hearing'. The whole process includes all the proceedings from the time when an application is made to the final decision including any appellate stage. As Dyson LJ put it:[169] 'A combination of the authority's decision-making process and judicial review by the High Court is sufficient to ensure compliance with article 6.'

In *Tehrani*, Lord Mackay summarized the position in relation to disciplinary tribunals:[170]

> As far such tribunals are concerned, no breach of the Convention arises if the tribunal is subject to control by a court that has full jurisdiction and itself complies with the requirements of Article 6(1). In other words, when dealing with a disciplinary tribunal, such as the PCC, a right of appeal to a court of full jurisdiction does not Purge a breach of the Convention. It prevents such a breach from occurring in the first place.

Nevertheless, in *P (a barrister)*, an argument that a later appellate court could correct any defect was described as: fundamentally flawed [and] would involve the

166 *R (on the application of Smith) v Parole Board*: *R (on the application of West) v Parole Board* [2005] UKHL 1, Lord Hope. [64], and see Lord Slynn, [48].

167 They were discussed in *R (on the application of Thompson) v The Law Society* [2004] EWCA Civ 167. The bodies include: planning authorities, the Parole Board (*Smith v The Parole Board* [2003] EWCA Civ 1269), and a series of professional disciplinary bodies, The Law Society (Thompson), the bar, the GMC, the Nursing Council (*Tehrani v United Kingdom Central Council for Nursing Midwifery and Health Visiting* [2001] IRLR 208).

168 *Thompson v The Law Society*, per Clarke LJ, [69].

169 *R (Adlard) v The Secretary of State for the Environment, Transport and the Regions* [2002] EWCA Civ 735, [46].

170 *Tehrani v United Kingdom Central Council for Nursing Midwifery and Health Visiting* [2001] IRLR 208, [55].

risk of a profligate waste of time and money for all parties which could be wholly avoided.[171]

As Lord Mustill warned in *ex p Doody*:[172]

> that it is not enough to persuade the court that some procedure other than the one adopted by the decision-maker would be better or more fair. Rather, they must show that the procedure is unfair. The court must constantly bear in mind that it is to the decision maker, not the court, that Parliament had entrusted not only the making of the decision but also the choice as to how the decision is made.

Sullivan J explained:[173]

> A 'fair' hearing does not necessarily require an oral hearing, much less does it require that there should be an opportunity to cross-examine. Whether a particular procedure is 'fair' will depend upon all the circumstances, including the nature of the claimant's interest, the seriousness of the matter for him and the nature of any matters in dispute.

In *West v Parole Board*[174] Lord Bingham cited Mason J as saying:[175]

> the expression 'procedural fairness' more aptly conveys the notion of a flexible obligation to adopt fair procedures which are appropriate and adapted to the circumstances of the particular case. The statutory power must be exercised fairly, that is, in accordance with procedures that are fair to the individual considered in the light of the statutory requirements, the interests of the individual and the interests and purposes, whether public or private, which the statute seeks to advance or protect or permits to be taken into account as legitimate considerations.

And, Lord Bingham went on:

> While an oral hearing is most obviously necessary to achieve a just decision in a case where facts are in issue which may affect the outcome, there are other cases in which an oral hearing may well contribute to achieving a just decision.

He cited Brennan J in the United States Supreme Court:[176]

---

171 *P (a barrister) v General Council of the Bar Visitors* (Inns of Ct) 24 January 2005.

172 *R v Secretary of State for the Home Department ex p Doody* [1994] 1 AC 531, 560D-561A

173 *R (Vetterlein) v Hampshire CC* [2001] EWHC Admin 1736, approved in *R (Adlard) v The Secretary of State for the Environment, Transport and the Regions* [2002] EWCA Civ 735.

174 *R (on the application of Smith) v Parole Board*: *R (on the application of West) v Parole Board* [2005] UKHL 1, [28].

175 *Kioa v West* (1985) 159 CLR 550, 572; *sub nom Kioa v Minister for Immigration and Ethnic Affairs* (1985) 62 ALR 321, 347.

176 Lord Bingham [31]. *Goldberg v Kelly* (1970) 397 US 254, 269.

> written submissions do not afford the flexibility of oral presentations; they do not permit the recipient to mold his argument to the issues the decision maker appears to regard as important. Particularly where credibility and veracity are at issue ... written submissions are a wholly unsatisfactory basis for decision.

Subject to the important exception relating to permission, the ECtHR has held that justice cannot be done on paper alone. In *Göç v Turkey* it was argued that the exclusion of oral proceedings was:[177]

> intended to provide a speedy means for dealing with compensation claims without the expense and delay of an oral hearing. The legislative scheme was thus consistent with the trend in European countries towards arbitration and mediation in the context of minor disputes and the move away from oral hearings.

Nevertheless, the ECtHR held that orality was required at some stage in the proceedings and by implication that efficiency alone is not a sufficient reason for excluding publicity.[178] It said, in terms which are no more than a specific instance of the ideas advanced in *West v Parole Board*, that this is especially true where the applicant is denied the opportunity to[179] 'explain orally ... the moral damage [in his claim] which ... entailed for him in terms of distress and anxiety'.

The court took the opposite view in a rather unsatisfactory decision. In *Schuler-Zgraggen v Switzerland*, it held the applicant could have asked for a public hearing but had waived her right to do so. We have already seen that some parts of the line of authority purporting to establish a right to waive is dubious. The court then held that since the subject-matter was her medical history she would not have wanted the public to be the present. It would seem that that is a matter for the applicant and not the court. Lastly, it held:[180]

> it is understandable that in this sphere the national authorities should have regard to the demands of efficiency and economy. Systematically holding hearings could be an obstacle to 'the particular diligence required in social-security cases' and could ultimately prevent compliance with the 'reasonable time' requirement of Article 6(1).[181]

It may be that *Schuler-Zgraggen* can be confined to social security claims.[182] More generally, the ECtHR has held that there must an opportunity for an oral hearing at some stage unless there is something to show that 'the subject matter of the dispute

177 *Göç v Turkey*, 11 July 2002, [44].

178 See: *Fejde v Sweden*, 29 October 1991; and, *Ekbatani v Sweden*, 26 May 1988. See further, disclosure p. 156 below.

179 *Göç v Turkey*, [51].

180 *Schuler-Zgraggen v Switzerland*, 24 June 1993, [58].

181 Strangely, it cited *Boddaert v Belgium*, 12 October 1992, [39]. That was concerned with the judicial investigation of a series of possibly related murders.

182 HHJ Bowsher QC in *Austin Hall Building v Buckland Securities* [2001] Build LR 272, 80 ConLR 115 applied it in upholding the validity of s. 108 of the Housing Grants, Construction and Regeneration Act 1996.

was of such a nature that it was better dealt with in written proceedings'.[183] In *Brugger v Austria* the proceedings concerned compliance of a tool shed with planning laws. The ECtHR re-affirmed that, unless there are exceptional circumstances, orality is generally required. It added, citing among other cases *Schuler-Zgraggen*:[184]

> The Court has accepted such exceptional circumstances in cases where proceedings concerned exclusively legal or highly technical questions ... In particular, the Court had regard to the rather technical nature of disputes over benefits under social-security schemes and has repeatedly held that in this sphere the national authorities, having regard to the demands of efficiency and economy, could abstain from holding a hearing if the case could be adequately resolved on the basis of the case-file and the parties' written observations.

Beyond that, *Schuler-Zgraggen* cannot be taken as authority for absolving contracting States from their obligations to provide a legal system, and the resources, that deliver the promises in Article 6(1). In a recent decision, *Miller v Sweden*, and one that was not clouded by suggestion of waiver, the Court again re-affirmed the importance of an oral (and public) hearing.[185]

I have already criticised the small claims in the CPR provisions which seem to allow the parties to agree that the proceedings be held in private. The considerations in *Göç* and *Schuler-Zgraggen* concerning paper decisions raise doubts as to whether the Practice Direction to Part 27.10 (relating also to small claims)[186] is Convention compliant.

This much applies to a substantive hearing. The position is different where permission to appeal is required against the decision of a lower court. The issues arise both of how much a losing applicant should be told and how far the permission process itself can be on paper without any (substantial) oral hearing. Hewson argued:[187]

> The paper process is problematic, because it lacks transparency. It is inconsistent with the constitutional principle that justice must be open. It may not be clear what papers the judge has actually read; how much time he has spent on the case; how much he has understood, and to what extent his paper reasons reflect the input of a novice lawyer acting as judicial assistant. Even assuming the judge is conscientious and puts a lot of time into his paper decision, he may still be wrong, or change his mind later.

Whatever the merits of what she said, it is against the tide. The ECtHR has accepted the paper process as convention compliant. For example, in *Monnell v UK* that court

183 *Birnleitner v Austria*, 24 February 2005.

184 *Brugger v Austria*, 26 January 2006, [22].

185 *Miller v Sweden*, 8 February 2005.

186 It said: 'The court may, if all parties agree, deal with the claim without a hearing'. And see CPR Part 23.8, its Practice Direction paras. 8, 10, and 11, and CPR Part 40.6. See above at p. 71.

187 Hewson, (2003) NLJ Vol.153, p. 97.

considered the Court of Appeal, Criminal Division's procedure for dealing with applications for permission to appeal. It said:[188]

> The issue for decision in such proceedings is whether the applicant has demonstrated the existence of arguable grounds which would justify hearing an appeal ... The limited nature of the subsequent issue of the grant or refusal of leave to appeal did not in itself call for oral argument at a public hearing.

On the civil side, applications are made initially to the trial court. If permission is refused there, a written application can be made. If permission is refused the applicant has a right to an oral hearing, CPR Part 52.3(4). The Rules go on to say:

> (6) Permission to appeal will only be given where –
>
> (a) the court considers that the appeal would have a real prospect of success; or
>
> (b) there is some other compelling reason why the appeal should be heard.

In *Tanfern*[189] the Court of Appeal was at pains to explain the effect of the new appeals regime in relation to both first and second appeals. The emphasis was on the trial judge's initial decision and in part (especially in relation to the Court of Appeal) the restrictions are driven by questions of resources and costs. No doubt, in our modern age these are important issues. But there are others. We have noted that one feature of the contemporary idea of fairness is that the parties, the consumers, come away satisfied. It is, no doubt, with this in mind that Neuberger LJ told us:[190]

> The mere fact that an applicant for permission to appeal feels very strongly about the injustice of the result he is seeking to challenge is plainly not, of itself, enough to justify the grant of permission to appeal. However, where the strong feelings are at least arguably objectively justified, that is, in my view, a fact which this court can, even should, take into account when deciding whether to give permission to appeal.

The satisfaction of the consumers can be given a higher priority than efficiency.

---

188 *Monnell and Morris v UK*, 2 March 1987, [56]-[58]. So also, in *Axen v Germany*, 8 December 1983, the ECtHR held that where the appeal court is minded to refuse permission to appeal no oral hearing was necessary.

189 *Tanfern v Cameron-Macdonald* [2000] 1 WLR 1311.

190 *Malcolm v Mackenzie* (Application for Permission to Appeal) [2004] EWCA Civ 584, [4].

The Right to Representation

What, we may ask, do lawyers do that clients cannot do for themselves?[191] To take an analogy, it is after all easy to see that surgery requires somebody else, someone to wield the scalpel. But why does truth telling require a third party? The answer is, of course, that legal argument is often more than truth telling. As Kennedy LJ once explained:[192]

> the taking of a statement from a lay witness dealing with facts possibly some time ago and covering a substantial period of time is a skilled art, so is the eliciting of evidence on the basis of such a statement, and in each case it is a lawyer's art.

But, even apart from art, there is skill. To generalize, clients know, or think they know, the merits of their case. And, merits are always important but usually in an inchoate way. What are at issue are not merits but their translation into legal form.[193] That process requires knowledge of law and the rules by which a case may be established in a court, that is, familiarity with the rules of procedure and evidence. It is a process which is conditioned by, but which goes beyond, the relevant. Overarching these considerations, just as doctors and patients have different understandings of an illness, so lawyers and clients understand a legal wrong in different ways. I have discussed this aspect of professional knowledge elsewhere and it is unnecessary to elaborate on it here.[194] It suffices to say that there is a difference between subjective and objective knowledge.[195] It is vastly more difficult for litigants in person to display the required objectivity.

There is a surprising lack of case law at Strasbourg concerning the general right to representation. One reason may be that in the Convention the right is express only as regards criminal proceedings.[196] The ECtHR has confirmed that 'where

---

191 See Lord Simon in *Waugh v British Railways Board* [1980] AC 521, 535 quoting Sir Thomas More, Utopia, 1516, tr. Robinson, 1551, Bk. 2 [Chapter 7]: 'euery man shuld pleade his owne matter, and tell the same tale before the iudge, that he would tel to his man of lawe. So shall there be lesse circumstaunce of wordes, and the trwth shal soner cum to light; whiles the iudge with a discrete judgement doth waye the wordes of hym whom no lawier hath instruct with deceit' and Boswell, *Life of Johnson*, ed. Birkbeck Hill (1950), vol. v, 26: 'As it rarely happens that a man is fit to plead his own cause, lawyers are a class of the community, who, by study and experience, have acquired the art and power of arranging evidence, and of applying to the points at issue what the law has settled. A lawyer is to do for his client all that his client might fairly do for himself, if he could.'

192 *Ex p Wagstaff* [2001] 1 WLR 292. And see: *R (on the application of Khan) v Secretary of State for Health* [2003] EWCA Civ 1129, above p. 58 n.55.

193 Cf. Cain, 'The general practice lawyer and the client', in Dingwall and Lewis, EDS, *The Sociology of the Professions: Lawyers, Doctors and Others* (1983) London: Macmillan Publishing.

194 *Doctors and Rules, A Sociology of Professional Practice*, 1989, 1998.

195 The ECtHR referred to this aspect in *Airey v Ireland*, 9 October 1979, [24].

196 See: *Thompson v UK*, 15 June 2004; *Artico v Italy*, 13 May 1980.

deprivation of liberty is at stake, the interests of justice in principle call for legal representation ... and for that legal representative to be duly heard'.[197] The ECtHR has considered the issue in relation to legal aid and in relation to prisoners' attempted contacts with their lawyers. We shall come to legal aid – much of what it has said there assumes the right and seeks to make it into a reality. In relation to prisoners in *Golder*, as we have seen, the Court relied on Art. 6 but in a series of other cases, it applied Art. 8.[198] Beyond this, it has set out the basic position. In *Matos E Silva* it said:[199]

> In the Court's view, no question of hindering access to a tribunal arises where a litigant, represented by a lawyer, freely brings proceedings in a court, makes his submissions to it and lodges such appeals against its decisions as he considers appropriate.

In England, the right has been considered in a variety of contexts. In *Steel and Morris* the ECtHR suggested that the right of access to the court can be achieved by a simplification of procedure.[200] The CPR have thus gone some way to making the right more effective. Reflecting the modern emphasis on consumers, the CPR seek to minimize, or even obliterate, the distinction between the subjective knowledge of the client and objective understanding of the lawyer. The rules are in plain English. There is a glossary. There are copious cross-references. Each of these devices is intended to make it easier for non-lawyers to represent themselves.[201] The CPR permit a company to be represented by a non-lawyer employee.[202]

So also, as we have seen, in Part 1.1(2) they require the court to ensure 'so far as is practicable ... that the parties are on an equal footing'. The day after the commencement of the CPR an application was made to prevent one side being represented by more senior counsel than the other. In a decision that must be read subject to what the ECtHR now says about legal aid and related matters Neuberger J said:[203]

> it has always been a fundamental right of every citizen to be represented by advocate and/or solicitors of his or her choice. That right is not of course absolute; circumstances may cut it down. Thus a person's chosen lawyer may be ill or engaged elsewhere or conflicted out. A legally aided party may find that the Legal Aid Board is not prepared to fund his

---

197 *Hooper v UK*, 16 November 2004, [20].

198 *Silver and others v UK*, 25 March 1983, [83]-[105]; *Campbell v UK*, 25 March 1992, [32]-[54]; and, most recently, *Jankauskas v Lithuania*, 24 February 2005.

199 *Matos E Silva v Portugal*, 16 September 1996, [64].

200 *Steel and Morris*, 15 February 2005, [60].

201 See Moorhead and Sefton, 'Litigants in person, Unrepresented litigants in first instance proceedings', DCA Research Series 2/05, March 2005, summarized by Moorhead, 'Litigants in person: ghosts in the machine', *Legal Action* (2005) 8–9 November.

202 CPR. Part 39.6. It has been held that such an employee must be able to understand the disclosure rules, *Tracto Teknik v LKL International* [2003] EWHC 1563 (Ch).

203 *Maltez v Lewis*, 16 Const LJ 65, 27 April 1999. Approved in *Sarwar v Alam* [2001] EWCA Civ 1401 and applied in *R v Legal Aid Board, ex p Duncan*, 16 February 2000.

or her particular selection of legal representative. Further, it is clear that no party has the right to expect a hearing date to be fixed on the basis of the availability of his or her choice of advocate or solicitor. Subject to that type of consideration, it seems to me that there is a fundamental right to a choice of legal representative; indeed, I would go so far as to say it is an important feature of any free society.

But, he went on: 'The court is quite able to ensure compliance with the overriding objective … where the parties' respective legal representatives could be said to be unequal, or where one party's legal representative could be said to be inappropriate.' Neuberger J mentioned orders for costs and the possibility for extra sympathy for the poorer party in relation to disclosure, and went on: 'The court is well used to dealing with cases where, for one reason or another, it appears that one side is more competently or expertly represented than the other.'

The remarks are only partly correct. In the English system, costs generally follow the event: a winner is entitled to recover what has been reasonably spent. This provides an important source of qualification to Neuberger J's dicta. In a series of cases, where the winners were represented their costs have been challenged on the basis that the normal rates charged by the solicitors were too high. Often these cases involve the instruction of London solicitors when more local and less expensive firms might have sufficed. Among the relevant factors are:[204]

i) The importance of the matter to the litigant;
ii) The legal and factual complexities, in so far as the relevant litigant might reasonably be expected to understand them; and,
iii) The location of the litigant's home, place of work, and the location of the court in which the relevant proceedings (if any) had been commenced.

Thus, although Neuberger J is right in general there may nevertheless be consequences beyond the trial and caused by the quality of the representation.

In *Re O (children)* Wall LJ said:[205]

Every judge who has heard cases conducted by litigants in person, whether at first instance or on appeal, knows only too well that they are an extremely diverse cross-section of the population. But two obvious points must be made. The first is that litigants in person are as entitled to a fair hearing as any other litigant. The second is that they are as entitled as everybody else to be treated with courtesy. There is never any excuse for judicial discourtesy ... Our joint experience [it was a two judge court], both at first instance and in this court, is that we have only rarely found litigants in person to be discourteous. We have, of course, experienced anger and abuse by litigants in person (notably at the conclusion of judgment), but more commonly litigants in person are nervous, anxious or

---

204 *Wraith v Sheffield Forgemasters* [1998] 1 WLR 132. Kennedy LJ offered a review of the authorities. It was applied in among other cases *Gazley v Wade* [2004] EWHC 2675 QBD.

205 *Re O (children)*: *Re* W-*R (a child)*: *Re W (children)* [2005] EWCA Civ 759, [54], [55].

> upset. Sometimes, as a consequence, they are less coherent and less self-controlled than they would be in other circumstances. The corollary to this, in our view, is that any judge hearing a litigant in person is under a particular obligation to remain courteous and to ensure that the litigant in person has a full and fair hearing.

And:

> we are … critical of those members of the legal profession who do not obey the rules when dealing with litigants in person, and who do not extend to them the normal courtesies they extend to professional opponents.

Nevertheless, it is wrong to give an impression that the courts, perhaps especially the Court of Appeal, have always been happy with litigants in person. Thus, on one occasion, Brooke LJ lamented:[206]

> What happened before the Recorder is an illustration of the difficulties facing courts today when cases are conducted by litigants in person. Very often such persons do not have English as their first language (though both [parties], I hasten to add, have addressed us perfectly clearly today), and such persons very often have no legal training or legal knowledge whatsoever.

Sometimes, indeed, substantive and procedural law, not to speak of facts, can be complex. It is all very well to say the court can sort it out. The difficulties are threefold.[207] First, the judge has no chance to assess the case on the basis of the client's inner thoughts as can a lawyer under the cloak of legal professional privilege. Assembling the relevant evidence has to be done before trial and often before a court touches the case. Where the litigant in person has an arguable case it is not efficient or even always accurate to let the judge articulate it for him or her. The difficulty is to determine beforehand what is an arguable case.

Secondly judges, even at the lowest level in the hierarchy, are typically more expensive than legal aid lawyers. It is true that legal aid and judges' salaries come out of different budgets. But both are publicly funded, subject to the dubious legality of requiring litigants to provide the entire cost of civil justice, which we discuss in Chapter 5. Apart from this policy, it costs the public purse more per hour not to provide legal aid and even if a judge spends less time than would a lawyer, quite possibly more in total.[208] It will be noted that the ECtHR has never held in relation to

---

206 *Assiouti v Hosseini*, 26 November 1999.

207 See Burger, 'A better route to redress? Possible changes to personal injury litigation within the small claims court', [2005] *Journal of Personal Injury Law* 283, discussing the proposal of Better Regulation Task Force, 'Better Routes to Redress', May 2004. He argued that litigants in person have difficulties in identifying the correct defendant, the duties of care, breach, value of claims (especially in face of insurance companies) getting and interpreting medical reports.

208 The CAB office at the Royal Courts of Justice does valuable work, but it is a sticking plaster approach to justice.

those systems where the court or the State can impose a lawyer that it is in conflict with Art. 6. Indeed, in *Airey v Ireland* it appeared to say that such systems are Convention compliant. In *Artico v Italy*, the court recognized that so long as the lawyer was active neither the State nor its courts could supervise what was done: it was otherwise if a nominated lawyer refused to do anything.[209]

Thirdly, there are many occasions where the court relies on the integrity of those appearing before it. In the usual case, this reliance is based on the unwritten as well as written lawyers' codes of professional behaviour, the consequent disciplinary control and the existence of professional insurance. A barrister cannot make an allegation of fraud unless it is within the facts contained in the instructions. The operation of the disclosure scheme (and the consequential document destruction rules) is based in part on solicitors' understandings and the duty to make clients aware of them. Companies can now be represented by their employees but only so long as they can convince the court that they are aware of the disclosure rules:[210] there is no such obligation on the litigant in person. Elsewhere, for example in some actions involving confidential information (perhaps commercial secrets or involving health records), the information can be made available only to the lawyers. In a without notice application (perhaps for an interim injunction), there is a duty to say all that is known in support of the other side's case. It is a duty easier to discharge (or at least to be seen to discharge), if a lawyer does it. Indeed, in the special case of a search order, although an application can be made by a litigant in person, it must be executed by a solicitor. So also, it is useful to note, for example, that the Chancery Guide says:[211] 'The provisions of this Guide in general apply to litigants in person' but 'Where a litigant in person is the applicant, the court may ask one of the represented parties to open the matter briefly and impartially, and to summarise the issues.' Again, at the expense of that represented party.

It is trite law that, on occasions, someone who is not a qualified lawyer, a McKenzie friend, can assist a litigant in person.[212] This can only be done with the

---

209 *Artico v Italy*, 13 May 1980.

210 Practice Direction paras. 5.2 to 5.6 amplifying CPR 39.6.

211 Chapter 15, 1 and 5.

212 *McKenzie v McKenzie* [1971] p. 33, CA, following *Collier v Hicks* (1831) 2 B and Ad 663, 109 ER 1290. The Queen's Bench Guide says: '2.4.1 A party who is acting in person may be assisted at any hearing by another person (often referred to as a McKenzie friend) subject to the discretion of the Court. The McKenzie friend is allowed to help by taking notes, quietly prompting the litigant and offering advice and suggestions. The litigant however, must conduct his own case; the McKenzie friend may not represent him and may only in very exceptional circumstances be allowed to address the court on behalf of the litigant under s. 27(2)(c) of the Courts and Legal Services Act 1990.'

And see Moorhead, 'Access or Aggravation, Mackenzie Friends and Lay Representation', (2003) 22 CJQ 133.

permission of the court.[213] It should be refused only in exceptional cases.[214] It is basic that such a person should not have interests which are contrary to those of the litigant in question.[215] In *ex p Pelling* (No.1),[216] the separate question arose as to whether such a person had rights to speak for a 'client'. The court stressed that they do not: the rights in issue were those of the litigant.

The right to legal representation arises in other contexts. A trial is not necessarily unfair merely because a party fails to obtain legal representation.[217] On the other hand, where an application is made for committal for contempt (a criminal matter within Art. 6.3) the respondent is generally entitled to be represented and the court should not proceed unless the right to representation is waived.[218] It is, however, clear that the right is not infringed where the lack of representation is due to a party's own fault.[219]

The right to representation also arises in the jurisdiction to make wasted costs orders against lawyers themselves. It is a power designed to prevent lawyers doing unnecessary work beyond their instructions and is only to be used in clear cases. Thus, if an opposing party makes an application, the client's legal professional privilege remains untouched. So also, as Lord Hobhouse put it in *Medcalf v Mardell*:[220]

> Unpopular and seemingly unmeritorious litigants must be capable of being represented without the advocate being penalized or harassed whether by the executive, the judiciary

---

213 *Re O (children): Re W-R (a child): Re W (children)* [2005] EWCA Civ 759.

214 *Re D (a child)* CA (Civ Div.) [2005] All ER (D) 324 (Mar) where the suggested friend was a struck off solicitor. And see also Sir Stephen Brown P *Re Pelling* (Rights of Audience) [1997] 2 FLR 458 [1997] Fam Law 655 quoting Neill LJ in *C v C* (unreported) 26 October 1994 and Lord Woolf MR in *D v S* (Rights of Audience) [1997] 1 FLR 724. Most recently, see *M v Singer* [2004] EWHC 793 (QB) where Newman J said of Dr Pelling 'he should not act as an advocate for the Claimant in this case again, and where in any other case in any other court he applies to be an advocate for another or to act as a McKenzie Friend, he should draw the court's attention to this judgment'. A similar order preventing the respondent from acting as a McKenzie Friend was made in *Attorney General v Chitolie* [2004] EWHC 1943 (Admin). See: *D v S* (Rights of Audience) [1997] 1 FLR 724; *Noueiri v Paragon Finance* (No.2) Also known as: *Paragon Finance v Noueiri* (Practice Note) [2001] EWCA Civ 1402.

215 *Hodson v Hodson* [2006] All ER (D) 318 (Feb).

216 *R v Bow County Court ex p Pelling* (No.1) [1999] 1 WLR 1807 (CA). Later, in *FM (A Child by AM his litigation friend) v Singer* [2004] EWCA 793 (QB), the court took a less indulgent view of Dr Pelling's conduct.

217 *Warne v Little* [2004] EWCA Civ 1025; *R (on the application of Elliot) v Solicitors Disciplinary Tribunal* [2004] EWHC 1176 (Admin).

218 *Re K (Children)* [2002] EWCA Civ 1559, applying *Benham v UK*, 10 June 1996 and followed in *Begum v Anam* [2004] EWCA Civ 578. And see *Perks v UK*, 12 October 1999; and, now *Lloyd v UK*, 1 March 2005; *Beet and others v UK*, 1 March 2005.

219 *Jahree v The State* [2005] UKPC 7 (Mauritius); *Law Debenture Trust v Elektrim Finance* [2005] EWCA Civ 1354.

220 *Medcalf v Mardell* (Wasted Costs Order) (2002) UKHL 27, [52]-[53].

> or by anyone else ... It may require more courage to represent a client in the face of a hostile court but the advocate must still be prepared to act fearlessly.

Beyond all this, there is one issue that has troubled the courts. In a variety of situations there is power to order that all the assets of an individual be frozen so that no dealings can be made without the permission of the court. In civil proceedings, such orders are common where a claimant has established that there was a genuine fear that the defendant would dispose of his or her funds so as to prevent the claimant getting the fruits of any victory. Here, they are known as freezing or seizure injunctions. Similar orders are also available under the Drug Trafficking Act 1994 and the Proceeds of Crime Act 2002 where again there is fear that assets will be disposed of, frustrating any eventual judgment. Each of these orders is draconian and the severity is only partly mitigated by the possible allowance of a fixed but reasonable amount for living expenses.[221] We are interested in whether the court has power, and if so on what terms, to allow a defendant the funds for any legal representation whether in an action challenging the order or for other purposes. In a rather unconvincing decision under the Proceeds of Crime Act, *Customs and Excise Commissioners v S*, the Court of Appeal held that, not only was there no power to allow a potential defendant the funds for a defence or even a challenge to the order, but that this did not engage Art. 6.[222] On the facts of the case, the outcome is understandable but as a matter of principle a court order which prevents an effective challenge to its legality seems to be one of the things Article 6 is intended to prevent. Scott Baker LJ reasoned that such an order was civil and not criminal. He cited, for instance, *Perotti v Collyer-Bristow* where Chadwick LJ said the test is:[223]

> Whether a court is put in a position that it really cannot do justice in the case because it has no confidence in its ability to grasp the facts and principles of the matter on which it has to decide.

This dictum itself is too indulgent. By analogy with rules on bias that we shall come to, the correct test is not whether the court has confidence, but whether the reasonable observer knowing the facts (probably that the defendant rather than the court knows) would have that confidence. He said, citing *Raimondo v Italy*:[224]

> there is a distinction between depriving a person of his possessions and temporary measures to prevent him from using them. A restraint order constitutes a control in the use of property which will be lawful if, as in the present case, it serves a legitimate aim, namely the preservation of property believed to be the proceeds of crime for confiscation, so as to deprive offenders of their benefit from crime.

---

221 In *Compagnie Noga d'Importation et d'Exportation v Australian and New Zealand Banking Group* [2006] EWHC 602 (Comm) it was held that it is not appropriate to vary an order to allow the defendant to put up a bail bond on behalf of his business partner's brother.

222 *Customs and Excise Commissioners v S* [2004] EWCA Crim 2374

223 *Perotti v Collyer-Bristow (a firm)* [2003] EWCA Civ 1521.

224 *Raimondo v Italy*, 22 February 1994.

This, however, is to merge the two issues of the compliance of restraint orders with Article 1 of the First Protocol and their use to prevent a challenge to them. No doubt, restraint orders are generally compliant with the First Protocol, and for the reasons Scott Baker LJ gave. But that does not make it necessary to agree that an order that effectively removes the right to representation is also compliant with the right to a fair trial or is a proportionate restriction on the right to property. Where the applicant wishes to use funds to challenge the order it is difficult to see how this can be said to be a benefit from the supposed crime. Representation does not confer a benefit: it may alleviate a burden.

As regards freezing injunctions, it is common to include in the order that money may be spent on representation. That does not end the difficulties. Where the anticipated costs amount, for example, almost to the same as the known assets of the defendant there is a sense in which the defence is to be paid for out of the claimant's own money. The court is faced with a balancing exercise. The headnote to *PCW (Underwriting Agencies) v Dixon* says:[225]

> The sole purpose of a [freezing injunction] injunction was to prevent a [claimant] being cheated out of the proceeds of an action, should it be successful, by a defendant transferring his assets abroad or dissipating his assets within the jurisdiction. The remedy was not intended to give a [claimant] priority over those assets, or to prevent a defendant from paying his debts as they fell due, or to punish him for his alleged misdeeds, or to enable a plaintiff to exert pressure on him to settle an action.

Lloyd J remarked:

> I say nothing about the cost of defending himself in these proceedings. The [freezing injunction] jurisdiction was never intended to prevent expenditure such as this ... In my view justice and convenience require in the present case that the first defendant should be allowed the means of defending himself, even if it could be said that the [claimants] had laid claim to the whole of his assets as a trust fund. Similarly justice and convenience require that he should be able to pay his ordinary bills and continue to live as he has been accustomed to live heretofore.

Ferris J added in *Cala Cristal v Emran Al-Borno*:[226]

> *prima facie*, the defendant ought to be allowed to choose the legal representatives he thinks best qualified to present his case and to pay to those legal representatives such charges as may properly be payable as a matter of contract between himself and those representatives. It does not, it seems to me, lie in the mouth of a [claimant] to say that the defendant ought to have gone to a cheaper firm of solicitors, or one which would have spent fewer hours on his case, or to have conducted his case in some other way. At any

225 *PCW (Underwriting Agencies) v Dixon* [1983] 2 All ER 158. And see: *Finers (a firm) v Miro* [1991] 1 WLR 35.

226 *Cala Cristal v Emran Al-Borno*, *The Times*, 6 May 1994. The dictum should now be read with *Cantor Index v Lister* [2002] CP Rep 25.

> rate, in my view, the [claimant] ought not to be allowed to maintain that except possibly in the most extreme and extravagant circumstances.

In *Sundt Wrigley v Wrigley* Bingham MR recognized that the balancing act might involve ordering a defendant to find extra money by the sale of assets.[227] So also, more technically, if the claim alleges breach of trust, the defendant might well be required to defend, or defend first, out of non-trust funds.

The Provision of Legal Assistance

In *Airey v Ireland*, the ECtHR considered the kind of help English courts often give to litigants in person, the kind that Neuberger J referred to when a litigant is not, or is badly, represented. The ECtHR said:[228]

> it is not realistic, in the Court's opinion, to suppose that, in litigation of this nature [proceedings for judicial separation], the applicant could effectively conduct her own case, despite the assistance which, as was stressed by the Government, the judge affords to parties acting in person.

And in *Steel and Morris*, MacDonalds, the burger manufacturer, successfully sued two distributors of a defamatory pamphlet. The ECtHR was impressed by the complexity of the issues both of fact and law and by the unequal economic strength of the parties leading to the non-representation of the defendants. It held that legal aid ought to have been available. Defending the action in the ECtHR the government also relied on 'the considerable latitude afforded to the applicants by the judges', but:[229]

> in an action of this complexity, neither the sporadic help given by the volunteer lawyers nor the extensive judicial assistance and latitude granted to the applicants as litigants in person, was any substitute for competent and sustained representation by an experienced lawyer familiar with the case and with the law of libel.

But, the court went on in *Airey*: 'this does not therefore imply that the State must provide free legal aid for every dispute relating to a "civil right"':

> To hold that so far-reaching an obligation exists would, the Court agrees, sit ill with the fact that the Convention contains no provision on legal aid for [civil] disputes ... However ... art.6(1) may sometimes compel the State to provide for the assistance of a lawyer when such assistance proves indispensable for an effective access to court either because legal representation is rendered compulsory, as is done by the domestic law of certain Contracting States for various types of litigation, or by reason of the complexity of the procedure or of the case.

---

227 *Sundt Wrigley v Wrigley* 23 June 1993 CA unreported.

228 *Airey v Ireland*, 9 October 1979, [24].

229 *Steel and Morris v UK*, 15 February 2005, 69. See Hudson, 'Free speech and equality of arms – the decision in *Steel and Morris v United Kingdom*' [2005] EHRLR 301.

In *McVicar v UK*, the Court clarified this, saying:[230]

> Article 6(1) leaves to the State a free choice of the means to be used in guaranteeing litigants a right of effective access to a court. The question whether or not that Article requires the provision of legal representation to an individual litigant will depend upon the specific circumstances of the case and, in particular, upon whether the individual would be able to present his case properly and satisfactorily without the assistance of a lawyer.

So also, as we have seen, in *Steel and Morris* it suggested that the right of access sometimes can be achieved by an alternative strategy, the simplification of procedure.

However that may be, in other cases the ECtHR has added the extra qualification that the consequences to the individual should also be taken into account[231] including most particularly whether the individual is liable to a term of imprisonment (or extra imprisonment). Of course, this most often applies in criminal proceedings but it arises also in civil matters where punishments, including imprisonment for contempt, are considered.

In *A v UK*,[232] the ECtHR began the task of answering whether the relatively new English conditional fee arrangements satisfy the *Airey* test. Combined with the 'Green Form' scheme, which allows 2 hours free advice, it thought it would. The Court did not consider any of the difficulties of the cfa such as whether the different financial interests of the client and lawyer under such an arrangement made any difference. It may be that this financial wedge removes effective representation.

On one occasion, the Court introduced an unhelpful note into its case law. In *Aerts v Belgium*, it held that:[233]

> It was not for the Legal Aid Board to assess the proposed appeal's prospects of success; it was for the Court of Cassation to determine the issue. By refusing the application on the ground that the appeal did not at that time appear to be well-founded, the Legal Aid Board impaired the very essence of [the] right to a tribunal.

If this is the case, every litigant, with however hopeless a case, would be entitled to be heard by a full court. Decisions that a case is not arguable and indeed how it should be argued are of necessity made before any hearing. The point of having legal representation is in part that a litigant's case be argued as effectively as possible. But it is also that professional objectivity can filter the bad points that a litigant's subjective view might wish to be taken. And in *Steel and Morris* the Court confirmed that 'the prospects of success' can be relevant.[234]

---

230 *McVicar v UK*, 7 May 2002, [48].

231 *Benham v UK*, 10 June 1996; *Aerts v Belgium*, 30 July 1998; *Lloyd and 35 others v UK*, 1 March 2005. And note *Edwards and others v UK*, 16 November 2004.

232 *A v UK*, 17 December 2002, [96].

233 *Aerts v Belgium*, 30 July 1998, [60].

234 *Steel and Morris v UK*, 15 February 2005, [62].

Faced with this jurisprudence the English courts have said that it is only in exceptional cases where the withholding of legal aid would make the assertion of a civil claim practically impossible, or where it would lead to an obvious unfair unfairness of the proceedings that the mere lack of means to employ a lawyer, or the failure of the State to fund one, infringes Art. 6.[235] The test is 'whether the individual would be able to present his case properly and satisfactorily without the assistance of a lawyer'. As Chadwick LJ put it:[236]

> This court, and other courts, have ample experience of cases in which the material is not presented in an ideal form; and have not found it impossible to reach just decisions in such cases. The test under art 6(1) … is whether a court is put in a position that it really cannot do justice in the case because it has no confidence in its ability to grasp the facts and principles of the matter on which it has to decide … it is the task of courts to struggle with difficult and ill-prepared cases; and courts do so every day.

The problem though is not whether the courts cope with ill-prepared cases, it is whether, for example, bad preparation prevents cases reaching the court at all perhaps by way of inadequate knowledge of a cause of action or appropriate damages.

---

235 e.g. *Holder v Law Society* [2003] EWCA Civ 39, [24] per Carnwath LJ and *Customs and Excise Commissioners v S*, [54]; *Pine v Law Society* (No.1) [2001] EWCA Civ 1574; *R v Legal Services Commission, ex p Jarrett* [2001] EWHC Admin 389.

236 *Perotti v Collyer-Bristow (a firm)* [2003] EWCA Civ 1521, [32].

Chapter 4

Disclosure and Restrictions on Evidence

In Chapter 2, I suggested that unless there is open and honest evidence it is difficult to see how justice can be achieved. I added that it is more important than all other requirements. Chapter 3 discussed equality of arms in general terms, leaving more detailed consideration of the production of facts to this. Strictly, the rules on disclosure are not about the giving of evidence to the court. They apply to a wider range of materials and are intended to facilitate the *preparation* rather than *presentation* of each side's case. It is, however, convenient to outline them here. It is unnecessary to offer an extended discussion: this book is about the impact of the human rights regime on our system of civil litigation not the whole process. Legal professional privilege, the rule against self-incrimination and the doctrine of public interest immunity are however more important for our purposes. They are exceptions to the rules on disclosure but, because they operate on evidence as well, it is convenient to discuss them under separate heads.

Legal professional privilege is a device designed to enhance candour between the lay client and the lawyer. Where it applies both the other side and the court are denied access to relevant materials. It is necessary to consider the court's response to legislative action against money-laundering and similar devices. Much of this is beyond our concerns. However, the provisions make such serious inroads into the scope of this privilege that we cannot ignore them. The privilege is intended to support the rule of law by encouraging lay clients to act fully informed as to their rights. These provisions limit that policy.

The doctrine of public interest immunity excludes material from disclosure and its use as evidence. It is based on the idea that there may a greater public interest in keeping particular information secret than the proper administration of justice. Logic suggests that it should be considered with the other devices that require or permit material to excluded from disclosure and the court. Convenience demands that we take it as the last heading in this Chapter.

In the civil process the rule against self-incrimination is largely anomalous. It excludes evidence that might lead to criminal proceedings. It represents a clash between the purposes of the civil and criminal processes. As such it throws the functions of civil litigation into relief.

It is appropriate in this Chapter to say something of the law of evidence and how the courts respond to material obtained surreptitiously. They are useful illustrations of the ECtHR's application of the margin of appreciation and, domestically, of the extent of the new powers of case management.

Disclosure

The common law is unusual in providing a separate stage of compulsory disclosure (and inspection) of documents before trial, CPR Part 31. It arises, in part, out the separation of our system of distinguishing pre-trial from trial stages, itself a feature of our absent jury. Nevertheless, it is within the margin of appreciation permitted to States. What is required under Art. 6 is that the rules apply equally to all parties, and Part 31 does so.

In general, disclosure applies after the issue of the claim and indeed after the service of the statements of case. It used to be called discovery but the CPR have modified it so the new name is helpful.

Subject now to questions of proportionality it applies to all[1] 'documents on which each party relies; the documents which adversely affect his own case; adversely affect another party's case; or, support another party's case'. There are exceptions, the most important of which are documents covered by legal professional privilege, by the rule against self-incrimination and those that are protected by public interest immunity. In some cases, statute and the CPR make provision for pre-action disclosure[2] and disclosure by non-parties.[3] So also, under the rule in *Norwich Pharmacal*, disclosure can be ordered against innocent third parties.[4]

It is significant that in each of these situations, one of the factors the court will take into account is whether the order is proportionate. As Rix LJ put it in *Black v Sumitomo Corporation*:[5]

> In appropriate circumstances, where the jurisdictional thresholds have been crossed, the court might be entitled to take the view that transparency was what the interests of justice and proportionality most required. The more diffuse the allegations, however, and the

1 CPR Part 31.6.

2 Senior Courts Act 1981, s. 33, as amended; CPR Part 31.16. It is also required, at various points by the Pre-Action Protocols, *Bermuda International Securities v KPMG (a firm)* [2001] EWCA Civ 269. An order will be refused if it appears that the disclosure would have been given without it, *Merpo Group v Dynamic Processing Solutions* [2003] EWHC 119 (Ch), but it will be granted where it might help to prevent a claim being issued, *Moresfield v Banners (a firm)* [2003] EWHC 1602 (Ch). The jurisdiction was discussed in *Black v Sumitomo Corporation* [2001] EWCA Civ 1819, applied in *Snowstar Shipping v Graig Shipping* [2003] EWHC 1367 (Comm).

3 Senior Courts Act 1981, s. 34, CPR Part 31.17. See *Frankson v Home Office*; *Johns v Home Office* (*Rowe v Fryers*) [2003] EWCA Civ 655; *Black v Sumitomo Corporation* [2001] EWCA Civ 1819.

4 *Norwich Pharmacal v Customs and Excise Commissioners* [1974] AC 133. Now see *Ashworth Security HA v MGN* [2002] UKHL 29; *Mersey Care NHS Trust v Ackroyd* [2003] EWCA Civ 663 (where the *Norwich* order could have resulted in the disclosure of the name of a journalist who might have a defence under the Contempt of Court Act and Art.10 of the ECHR). And now see *Mersey Care NHS Trust v Ackroyd* (No.2) [2006] EWHC 107.

5 *Black v Sumitomo Corporation* [2001] EWCA Civ 1819.

wider the disclosure sought, the more sceptical the court is entitled to be about the merit of the exercise.

We return in a moment to proportionality.

The Relevance of Confidence

Lord Keith in *Home Office v Harman* said:[6]

> [Disclosure as we now call it] constitutes a very serious invasion of the privacy and confidentiality of a litigant's affairs. It forms part of English legal procedure because the public interest in securing that justice is done between parties is considered to outweigh the private and public interest in the maintenance of confidentiality. But the process should not be allowed to place upon the litigant any harsher or more oppressive burden than is strictly required for the purpose of securing that justice is done.

Art.6 guarantees the right to a public trial. Confidential information is in general protected by Art. 8(1) which says: 'Everyone has the right to respect for his private and family life, his home and his correspondence.' There are, however, numerous occasions where a rule requires or court orders a breach of confidence. The issue is, are these permitted by Art. 8(2) which says:

> there shall be no interference by a public authority with the exercise of this right except such as is in accordance with the law and is necessary in a democratic society in the interests of national security, public safety or the economic well-being of the country, for the prevention of disorder or crime, for the protection of health or morals, or for the protection of the rights and freedoms of others.

Ackner LJ explained:[7]

> The fact that information has been communicated by one person to another in confidence is not, of itself, a sufficient ground for protection from disclosure in a court of law of either the nature of the information or the identity of the informant if either of those matters would assist the court to ascertain facts which are relevant to an issue on which it is adjudicating ... The private promise of confidentiality must yield to the general public interest, that in the administration of justice truth will out, unless by reason of the character of the information or the relationship of the recipient of the information, a more important public interest is served by protecting the information or the identity of the informant from disclosure in a court of law.

Disclosure will not, of course, be ordered where one of the exceptions applies.

Ackner LJ's position itself is modified by the CPR because now disclosure will also not be ordered if[8] 'it would be disproportionate to the issues in the case to permit

6 *Home Office v Harman* [1983] 1 AC 280, 308.

7 *Campbell v Tameside MBC* [1982] QB 1065.

8 CPR Part 31.3(2).

inspection of documents within a category or class of document'. In *Catt v Church of Scientology*,[9] Bell J thought that 'the question of disclosure being offensive to the disclosing party [cannot] bear on the question of proportionality'. But in *Simba-Tola v Trustees of Elizabeth Fry Hostel*[10] the staff records of a probation and bail hostel were protected partly because they were confidential and partly because they were of marginal relevance to the claim.

In *McPhilemy*,[11] which was directly concerned with whether amendments should be allowed to the statements of case with consequential effects on what should be disclosed, the Court of Appeal held that both the amendments and the disclosure should only be allowed if they were proportionate to the disposal of the main issue between the parties. So also, in *Three Rivers DC v Bank of England* (No.6), Tomlinson J held (in a decision that must now be read subject to the speeches of the House of Lords), on the authority of *Science Research Council v Nasse*[12] and *Wallace Smith Trust v Deloitte Haskins Sells*[13] (both pre-HRA decisions), that:[14]

> If the disclosure of the documents in question is shown to be necessary in the interests of the litigation, then that need overrides confidentiality ... However, in such a case, the court will be concerned to see whether the needs of the litigation can otherwise be satisfied, e.g. by considering redactions, disclosure from other sources or other appropriate means.

All this is convention compliant. Within the UK's margin of appreciation, it mirrors the balance of openness and privacy required by Arts 6 and 8 that we saw described by the ECtHR in *Z v Finland.*[15]

These rules describe the duty to disclose documents to the other side. There is also a consequential duty. Although the secrecy of material is broken by disclosure, it does not become public. CPR Part 31.22 says:

> (1) A party to whom a document has been disclosed may use the document only for the purpose of the proceedings in which it is disclosed, except where:
>
> > (a) the document has been read to or by the court, or referred to, at a hearing which has been held in public;
> >
> > (b) the court gives permission; or
> >
> > (c) the party who disclosed the document and the person to whom the document belongs agree.

9 *Catt v Church of Scientology Religious Education College* [2001] C.P. Rep. 41.

10 *Simba-Tola v Trustees of Elizabeth Fry Hostel* [2001] EWCA Civ 1371.

11 *McPhilemy v Times Newspapers* [1999] EMLR 751.

12 *Science Research Council v Nasse* [1980] AC 1028.

13 *Wallace Smith Trust (in liquidation) v Deloitte Haskins and Sells* [1997] 1 WLR 257.

14 *Three Rivers DC v Bank of England* (No.6) [2002] All ER (D) 130. The exceptions to public trials set out in CPR Part 39.2(3) do not apply.

15 *Z v Finland*, 25 February 1997. Above p. 61, discussing open justice.

> (2) The court may make an order restricting or prohibiting the use of a document which has been disclosed, even where the document has been read to or by the court, or referred to, at a hearing which has been held in public.

The public, interested non-parties, and indeed the court are not entitled to see material that is disclosed but not put in evidence. Hobhouse J in *Prudential Assurance v Fountain Page* explained:[16]

> It may be thought desirable to express the duty as an implied undertaking to the court. But, whether it is so expressed or not, it is in my judgment a duty that is owed to the court and which can be enforced by the court ... Breach of the duty amounts to a contempt of court, which may be trivial or serious depending upon the circumstances. The court has the power wholly or partially to release the recipient from the duty, or undertaking, and to permit use to be made of the documents nevertheless.

CPR Part 31.22 was also considered in *Lilly Icos v Pfizer* (No.2) where the Court of Appeal said:[17]

> (i) The court should start from the principle that very good reasons are required for departing from the normal rule of publicity ...
>
> (ii) ... the court should take into account the role that the document has played or will play in the trial ... The court should start from the assumption that all documents in the case are necessary and relevant for that purpose, and should not accede to general arguments that it would be possible, or substantially possible, to understand the trial and judge without access to a particular document.
>
> (iii) In dealing with issues of confidentiality between the parties, the court must have in mind any 'chilling' effect of an order upon the interests of third parties ...
>
> (iv) Simple assertions of confidentiality and of the damage that will be done by publication, even if supported by both parties, should not prevail. The court will require specific reasons why a party would be damaged by the publication of a document ...
>
> (v) It is highly desirable, both in the general public interest and for simple convenience, to avoid the holding of trials in private, or partially in private ...
>
> (vi) Patent cases are subject to the same general rules as any other cases, but they do present some particular problems and are subject to some particular considerations.

---

16 *Prudential Assurance v Fountain Page* [1991] 1 WLR 756, 774–775, quoted in *Clibbery v Allen* [2002] EWCA Civ 45 by Thorpe LJ, [105].

17 *Lilly Icos v Pfizer* (No.2) [2002] EWCA Civ 2, [25].

It is easier to obtain protection in interim proceedings than at trial.[18]

Legal Professional Privilege

Legal professional privilege is of two kinds.[19] Both prevent documents and other material from disclosure to a court. *Litigation privilege* covers all documents brought into being for the purposes of litigation. It thus embraces material created by parties, their lawyers and potential witnesses. *Legal advice privilege* covers communications between lawyers and their clients whereby legal advice is sought or given. It is confined to information given to lawyers and generated by them but can apply even where litigation is not contemplated. It applies to all such information, however important and however trivial. In the *Three Rivers* litigation the Court of Appeal and House of Lords differed as to scope of the meaning of legal advice. Broadly, the Court of Appeal sought to confine it to advice as to rights and obligations.[20] The House of Lords expanded it to include any advice in a legal context.

Where it applies, as Lord Nicholls once pointed out,[21] the court may be denied access to important, relevant and probative material. It prioritizes the integrity of the lawyer-client relationship over the fairness of a public trial.

There are two difficulties and maybe a third. First, the privilege is in contrast to the more limited value accorded by the English courts to all other professional and non-professional confidential communications. There, as we have seen, confidence is important but it can be overridden where the interests of justice require. Secondly, where either form of the privilege applies, it is absolute. In England, there is no higher public interest that can 'trump' it. It belongs to the client, and only the client (or statute) can permit it to be breached. Thirdly, litigation privilege is confined to adversarial proceedings.

To take these in turn. In contrast to the respect accorded to all other professional and non-professional confidential communications those with lawyers are absolutely protected. In these other cases, as we have seen, confidence is important: it can be overridden where the interests of justice require. In *Niemietz v Germany*, the applicant happened to be a lawyer but the ECtHR was primarily concerned with whether professional or business activities in general are protected by Art. 8. But, it added,[22] 'where a lawyer is involved, an encroachment on professional secrecy may have repercussions on the proper administration of justice and hence on the rights guaranteed by Article 6'.

18 *HRH Prince of Wales v Associated Newspapers* [2006] EWHC 11 (Ch).

19 *Three Rivers DC v Bank of England* (No.5) [2004] UKHL 48, per Lord Scott [10]. The cases establishing the privilege were collected by Lord Taylor in *R v Derby Magistrates' Court ex p B* [1996] AC 487.

20 *Three Rivers DC v Bank of England* (No.6) [2004] EWCA Civ 218.

21 *R v Derby Magistrates Court, ex p B* [1996] AC 487, 510.

22 *Niemietz v Germany*, 16 December 1992, [37].

In *Three Rivers* Lord Scott asked:[23] 'Why is it that the law has afforded this special privilege to communications between lawyers and their clients that it has denied to all other confidential communications?' The answer of each of the members of the House was clothed in the language of case law but amount to the assertion that confidentiality must be guaranteed in order that lawyers can do their jobs so that, among other things, the law can be properly applied. Advocate-General Slynn put it in *A M* and *S Europe v European Commission*:[24]

> [The privilege] springs essentially from the basic need of a man in a civilized society to be able to turn to his lawyer for advice and help, and if proceedings begin, for representation; it springs no less from the advantages to a society which evolves complex law reaching into all the business affairs of persons, real and legal, that they should be able to know what they can do under the law, what is forbidden, where they must tread circumspectly, where they run risks.

As Lord Scott said:[25]

> the idea that it is necessary in our society, a society in which the restraining and controlling framework is built upon a belief in the rule of law, that communications between clients and lawyers, whereby the clients are hoping for the assistance of the lawyers' legal skills in the management of their (the clients') affairs, should be secure against the possibility of any scrutiny from others, whether the police, the executive, business competitors, inquisitive busy-bodies or anyone else.

To repeat the point, where the privilege applies, the court can be denied access to relevant, probative material. Seen in this light, it is not so obvious that the privilege achieves its purpose. I have stressed the importance the common law and the Convention place on a public trial. The trial is diminished if it does not have access to all the relevant material.

The second difficulty is the absolute nature of the privilege. In *Morgan Grenfell*, Lord Hoffmann[26] pointed out that the ECtHR held the privilege to be part of the right of privacy guaranteed by Art. 8 and that it has been recognized as part of Community law. This much is true but those institutions do not follow the English courts in holding that legal professional privilege is absolute. On the contrary, the language used in *Niemietz* (which he did not cite) and in *Foxley* (which he did) is of proportionality. And of course this is what Art. 8(2) directs the court's attention to. In this respect English law still has to absorb the ideas of balance and proportionality, essential to the philosophy of the Convention.

---

23 At [28].

24 *A. M* and *S Europe v European Commission* [1983] QB 878, 913.

25 *Three Rivers DC v Bank of England* (No.5) [2004] UKHL 48, [34]. He cited Zuckerman, *Civil Procedure*, paras. 15.8 to 15.10.

26 *R (on the application of Morgan Grenfell) v Special Commissioner of Income Tax* [2002] UKHL 21, citing: *Campbell v UK*, 25 March 1992; *Foxley v UK*, 20 June 2000; and, *AM and S Europe v EC Commission* (Case 155/79) [1983] QB 878 [1982] ECR 1575.

Doctors, priests, journalists and others along with lawyers need to be able to promise confidentiality in order to do their jobs. All are protected, but except lawyers, only to a point. The court can order the breach of their promise of confidence. The interests of each of these confidants are not the same but each provides a contribution to civilized society. The doctor needs to know the full history of his patient in order to provide the right and not the wrong treatment. The priest cannot provide guidance or absolution with half a confession. On occasion, a journalist cannot broadcast a public wrong without giving a private promise. Civilized society demands that each of these be respected. There can be few (who are not lawyers) who can believe that lawyers or the rule of law itself, make a contribution to our way life more important than these others. Each makes a unique and important contribution. One of the lessons of the modern world is the necessity for professional modesty. The failure by lawyers or judges to recognize this brings law into disrepute.

This book would not be written unless I too accepted the importance of the rule of law. That is not in dispute. I depart from the House of Lords in their prioritizing that concept over all other values of civilized society. The privilege has been described by Lindsay J 'as a towering public interest'.[27] It is not the only tower. Perhaps the suggestion of Lord Phillips that the proposal of the Law Reform Committee on Privilege in Civil Proceedings of 1967 should be revisited should be taken up but with a wider investigation.[28]

The third difficulty is that litigation privilege (where even information created by potential witnesses is protected) is confined to adversarial proceedings. *In re L*[29] the House of Lords ordered the disclosure to the police (who were not parties) of an expert's report commissioned by a mother in proceedings relating to the custody of her child. The majority held that the proceedings were not adversarial and so outside the scope of the privilege. The difficulty is that it leaves doubts as to what is adversarial. In *Three Rivers* there were suggestions that it might be arguable that much litigation under the CPR is no longer adversarial. There seems little reason to think this so. The apparent problem is that as Lord Nicholls said in *Re L*:

> The expression adversarial carries with it a connotation of confrontation and conflict. Ideally, these characteristics have no place in family proceedings. In family proceedings all parties should be working together to assist the court in finding the answer which will best promote the welfare of the child.

There is much truth in the idea that the CPR have imported into general litigation an emphasis on co-operation first applied in family proceedings in particular by the 1989 Children Act. If this is so, and family proceedings are not adversarial, logic might suggest that no proceedings are adversarial. While it is, of course, true that

27 *Saunders v Punch* [1998] 1 WLR 986.

28 *Three Rivers DC v Bank of England* (No.6) [2004] EWCA Civ 218. Law Reform Committee on Privilege in Civil Proceedings, 16th Report (Cmnd 3472), paras. 17–19.

29 *Re L (a minor)* (Police Investigation: Privilege) [1997] AC 16.

modern litigation is not conducted with the same antagonism as previously there are still opposing parties. Again, as Lord Nicholls said:

> The contrast between inquisitorial and adversarial needs handling with care, for at least two reasons. First, the contrast suggests that proceedings are either wholly adversarial or wholly inquisitorial. They partake wholly of the one character or wholly of the other. This is not always so. Proceedings may possess some adversarial features and some inquisitorial features.

Antagonistic, antipathetic and adversarial need not be synonyms. There are grades. At one end of the range there is a full-blooded contest. At the other, there is an investigation. Between these there are contentious proceedings, non-contentious proceedings (which, curiously, includes arbitration), and a variety of inquiries where blame will or might be allocated. Whatever the scope of Art. 6, it is clear that it bites some way along this scale. As we have seen the ECtHR insists that Art. 6 is concerned with 'adversarial' proceedings.[30] This very English discussion is a leftover from the old days when our judges placed the liberty of England and its adversarial, jury-based trial in contrast to the supposed lack of freedom elsewhere in Europe.

There is a further point. If the effect of the CPR is to abolish litigation privilege, they are to that extent void. The Civil Procedure Act 1997 under which they are made does not permit the Rules Committee to affect substantive law.

Disclosure on Assessment

It was assumed in *Bailey v Ibc Vehicles*,[31] that the legal professional privilege veil can be lifted by a costs judge. This was clarified in *South Coast Shipping v Havant BC*[32] where it was held that if the costs judge considered the documents to be of sufficient importance, the receiving party should be put to an election of (a) waiving the privilege for the purposes of the assessment or (b) of adducing secondary evidence about the contents of the documents or (c) of not relying on them. Disclosure in those circumstances, the court said, does not entail a requiring waiver of privilege in breach of the Human Rights Act 1998.

It is, of course, true that a party is always entitled to use his own privileged documents.

Protection against Money-laundering and Similar Devices

Both Community and UK domestic law make provision for the compulsory disclosure of material that might disclose illegal activity to enforcement agencies of information (most often in England Serious Organised Crime Agency, SOCA,

---

30 Above p. 41 and see *Werner v Austria*, 24 November 1997, [66].

31 *Bailey v IBC Vehicles* [1998] 3 All ER 570.

32 *South Coast Shipping v Havant BC* [2002] 3 All ER 779.

the successor to the National Criminal Intelligence Service, NCIS).[33] This might relate to the transfer into legal enterprises of money obtained through defined crimes or might be the result of possible tax evasion or anti-competitive conduct. We are not concerned with much of this. On some occasions, however, the obligation to disclose is imposed on professional advisers and it can be accompanied by a prohibition on disclosure to anybody, even the client, of information which is likely to prejudice an investigation or proposed investigation. At both these points, it can impinge on ordinary civil processes. For example, in *C v S*[34] in litigation involving an innocent bank there was a conflict between the general rule relating to disclosure and the then statutory money-laundering scheme. Under this last, and still, there were obligations to inform the NCIS of suspicions formed by the adviser and also not to tell the client. Orders were made and an appeal heard largely in the absence of the claimant. Zuckerman has rightly criticized the procedure.[35] It is difficult, he said, to see how the court can protect the interests of an excluded party when the only source of information is the applicant. Moreover, he went on, the procedure was not 'proportionate' to its purpose because a client who learnt his bank account has been frozen in secret proceeding could infer that he or she was the subject of an investigation.

There are however two points. This is far from being the only example of the court acting on information from only one side. Others include the grant of some interim remedies and acceding to claims for public interest immunity. In those there are safeguards. The difficulty here is that there are no developed protections. Secondly, although Zuckerman spoke of 'proportionality', the criticism is more of effectiveness.

Nevertheless, the thrust of Zuckerman's objection was accepted by the Court of Appeal in *Bank of Scotland v A*.[36] There, we were told, the proper course for a bank was to seek agreement from the NICS or other authority as to what can be disclosed and failing that agreement to seek a declaration with the police joined as respondent. This would have the advantage that there would be a real contest for the court to adjudicate upon. But still the procedure involves the court in making a secret order and may cause the judge who made it to be involved in later proceedings to which the client is actually a party. As the court put it without any more explanation:

33 For example, Council Directive of 4 December 2001 (2001/97/EEC) and Part 7 of the Proceeds of Crime Act 2002. And see Webster, 'Seriously re-organised money laundering,' (2005) NLJ Vol.155 No. 7181 p. 930, describing the effects of the Serious Organised Crime and Police Act 2005. As to the future see: Delahunty, 'Three is one too many', (2005) LSG Vol.102 No. 24, 15; Webster, 'Seriously re-organised money laundering', (2005) NLJ 155 930; and, Young, 'Money laundering – the third European Directive', (2005) NLJ 155, 1128.

34 *C v S* (Money Laundering: Discovery of Documents) (Practice Note) [1999] 1 WLR 1551.

35 Zuckerman, 2.151.

36 *Bank of Scotland v A* [2001] EWCA Civ 52.

> It is obviously undesirable that a judge should be aware of information which is not known to a party appearing before the judge. Despite this concern there can be circumstances where in the public interest this course is necessary.

We were not told anything about the circumstances in which that which is 'undesirable' can be in the public interest.

Bank of Scotland v A was considered in *Tayeb v HSBC Bank*.[37] There, a local branch, in the event wrongly, became suspicious about a large transfer into the claimant's account. It first froze the account and then re-transferred the money to the originating bank. It did so, however, without reference to either the court or the NCIS. It was held that the bank was liable for the whole sum.

In *Morgan Grenfell* in 2002 a unanimous House of Lords reversed an equally united Court of Appeal. Restating the importance of legal professional privilege as a fundamental human right, Lord Hoffmann said:[38]

> the courts will ordinarily construe general words in a statute, although literally capable of having some startling or unreasonable consequence, such as overriding fundamental human rights, as not having been intended to do so. An intention to override such rights must be expressly stated or appear by necessary implication.

Later he explained 'A necessary implication is a matter of express language and logic not interpretation'. The issue in *Morgan Grenfell* was less clear cut than cases involving suspected money laundering. The question was the extent of the Revenue's powers to compel the disclosure of information: the House was at pains to say there was no suggestion of any illegal activity. Nevertheless, the statement was unqualified. Indeed, Lord Hoffmann quoted himself in *ex p Simms*:[39]

> In the absence of express language or necessary implication to the contrary, the courts … presume that even the most general words were intended to be subject to the basic rights of the individual. In this way the courts of the United Kingdom, though acknowledging the sovereignty of Parliament, apply principles of constitutionality little different from those which exist in countries where the power of the legislature is expressly limited by a constitutional document.

All this is peripheral to our concerns. In 2005, they became central. An earlier decision, *P v P* (Ancillary Relief: Proceeds of Crime)[40] held that there is no legal professional privilege exemption for the obligations to avoid tipping-off and to report. However, in *Bowman v Fels*[41] there was routine matrimonial litigation over the beneficial interest in a property. The claimant's solicitors, following advice from

37 *Tayeb v HSBC Bank* [2004] EWHC 1529.

38 *R (Morgan Grenfell) v Special Commissioner for Income Tax* [2002] UKHL 21.

39 *R v Secretary of State for the Home Department, ex p Simms* [2000] 2 AC 115, 144.

40 *P v P* (Ancillary Relief: Proceeds of Crime) [2003] EWHC 2260 (Fam).

41 *Bowman v Fels* [2005] EWCA Civ 226. The Law Society, Bar Council and NCIS intervened.

the Law Society, notified the NCIS of their suspicion that the defendant had included the cost of the work he carried out at the property within his business accounts even though those works were unconnected with his business. That is, they suspected a tax fraud but one which was irrelevant to the litigation. They made a without notice application to a judge for an order vacating the trial date because they were told that it was unlikely that consent from the NCIS would be obtained before the trial started. The judge granted that application. Another judge on the application of the defendant's solicitors set that order aside. The Court of Appeal thus faced the question whether the solicitors were in fact aiding a transaction concerning property obtained through crime. The Court was robust:[42]

> The function of litigation – to resolve rights and duties according to law – and the public scrutiny to which it is subject, together with the presence and role of the judge … distinguish legal proceedings from any 'transaction' that the European legislator can have had in mind, as well as offering safeguards against misconduct.

The Court pointed out:[43]

> So far as UK domestic law is concerned, it is elementary that when a lawyer is advising a client or acting for him in litigation, he may not disclose to a third party any information about his client's affairs without his express or implied consent.

It discussed the law of the European Union and concluded:[44]

> In relation to both access to justice through legal proceedings on the one hand and legal professional privilege on the other, the driving principles behind European Community law, ECHR law and UK domestic law are … virtually identical ... In summary, legal proceedings are a state-provided mechanism for the resolution of issues according to law. Everyone has the right to a fair and public trial in the determination of his civil rights and duties which is secured by article 6 of the European Convention on Human Rights.

And so:

> Parliament cannot have intended that proceedings or steps taken by lawyers in order to determine or secure legal rights and remedies for their clients should involve them in 'becoming concerned in an arrangement which … facilitates the acquisition, retention, use or control of criminal property', even if they suspected that the outcome of such proceedings might have such an effect.

But it went on:[45]

42 At [62].
43 At [78].
44 At [82] and [84].
45 At [88].

> There is another very important principle underlying the proper administration of justice that would be jettisoned if a wide meaning were given to [the section]. In so far as a lawyer gains information from documents disclosed by another party to adversarial litigation and not read in open court, he will be committing a contempt of court if he discloses them to a third party without the express or implied permission of the court or express, clear, Parliamentary sanction.

So also:[46]

> The need to encourage co-operation and the value of consensual settlement have been underlined both nationally, by the Woolf Reforms in particular, and internationally, e.g. in the acquis[47] of the Council of Europe and the developed practices of courts in countries such as the USA and Canada. Consensual settlement gives effect to the parties' perception of the strengths and weaknesses of their respective positions, which would otherwise have to be determined by litigation to judgment. Any consensual agreement can in abstract dictionary terms be called an arrangement. But we do not consider that it can have been contemplated that taking such a step in the context of civil litigation would amount to 'becoming concerned in an arrangement which … facilitates the acquisition, retention, use or control of criminal property' within the meaning of [the section]. Rather it is another ordinary feature of the conduct of civil litigation, facilitating the resolution of a legal dispute and of the parties' legal rights and duties according to law in a manner which is a valuable alternative to the court-imposed solution of litigation to judgment.

It added:

> We appreciate that this means that there is a distinction between consensual steps (including a settlement) taken in an ordinary litigious context and consensual arrangements independent of litigation.

Bowman v Fels marked a turning point.[48] It gave priority to the normal conduct of litigation over State interests in law enforcement. Further, although it is dubious that litigation privilege can apply to settlements (the better word is agreements) where there has not been a threat of litigation, *Bowman v Fels* seems to say that the retention of information is not an offence, at least so long as there is the possibility of a dispute if the parties adopted a less co-operative attitude. The Court thus essentially overruled *P v P*. Transaction lawyers (i.e. those who advise on transactions rather than disputes) may be in a different position but given the breadth of the decision in *Three Rivers* even they may now be relieved.[49]

Does all this show a growing impatience with the lawmakers? Is the resurrection of the rule of law in *Three Rivers* related to the attacks on it by the conspiracy of

46 At [100], [101].

47 A French term usually referring to the total body of European Union law accumulated so far.

48 See The Law Society guidance at its website:… BowmanvFelsGuidance0905.pdf.

49 See now, *Law Society Guidance: Anti-Money Laundering Guidance for Solicitors Conducting Private Client Work*, 23 February 2006.

the executive, including the EU Commission, and the Parliaments in London and Strasbourg in their palpably unwinnable 'wars' on crime, drugs, terrorism, tobacco and whatever else? The language of war in each of these policy areas is used to justify restrictions on normal liberty. Sometimes the UK courts' response is recourse to the ECHR. At other times, they use the law-finding techniques of the common law *(Three Rivers)* or their powers of interpretation of statute (*Bowman v Fels*). Rightly, the courts are becoming irritated with policy based on exaggeration bloated by feeding on hyperbole. Whatever the utility of such language in developing legislation, it does not make doing justice in individual cases easy, and, of course, that is where courts have to do their business.

The Privilege against Self-incrimination

In 1982, Lord Wilberforce told us the privilege against self-incrimination[50] 'has been too long established in our law as a basic liberty of the subject (in other countries it has constitutional status) to be denied'. In context it is unclear whether that is his view or a paraphrase of counsel's argument. Perhaps this does not matter: subsequent cases attribute it to him. *In re Arrows* (No.4) Lord Browne-Wilkinson described the privilege in a modern context:[51]

> One of the basic freedoms secured by English law is that (subject to any statutory provisions to the contrary) no one can be forced to answer questions or produce documents which may incriminate him in subsequent criminal proceedings. The principle evolved from the abhorrence felt for the procedures of the Star Chamber under which the prisoner was forced, by the use of torture, to answer self-incriminating questions on the basis of which he was subsequently convicted. Although physical torture is a thing of the past, the principle remains firmly embedded in our law: a witness can refuse to answer self-incriminating questions without punishment and a judge in civil proceedings customarily warns a witness that he need not answer such questions. Similarly, the privilege entitles a party to civil litigation to refuse to give disclosure of documents which may incriminate him.

Elsewhere, other courts attribute the privilege to the need, in a criminal trial, for the prosecution to prove its case. Whatever the accuracy of the privilege evolving from the procedures of an ancient court,[52] Lord Browne-Wilkinson's description of its scope in the civil process was undoubtedly right. The privilege extends to all

50 *Rank Film Distributors v Video Information Centre* [1982] AC 380.

51 *Re Arrows* (No 4), *Hamilton v Naviede* [1995] 2 AC 75.

52 It is dubious whether Star Chamber was the only court that used torture in the sixteenth and seventeenth centuries. One objection to torture is that its results are unreliable. Star Chamber has received its obloquy not for this but because it was not a common law court. Lord Browne-Wilkinson was repeating the victor's slogans of the constitutional struggles of the seventeenth century. In *Smith v Director of Serious Fraud Office* [1993] AC 1, Lord Mustill also referred to the reaction against 'Star Chamber and the Council'.

material which may lead to a chain of inquiry and it extends not only to material which may incriminate but also to that which may lead to a penalty.[53] It does not apply to investigations under statutory powers.[54] As with legal professional privilege, where the self-incrimination privilege applies, the court is denied access to relevant, probative material.[55] And as with legal professional privilege, it can be waived.[56]

There is a clash of cultures. On the one side the civil process requires justice to be done between the parties and to that end requires all relevant material to be available to each of them and to the court. It is a principle which is enhanced by the CPR. Before their advent the main method by which it was advanced was by discovery (now modified and renamed disclosure), a process with equitable and inquisitorial roots. On its other side, the criminal process is unhappy with convictions based on compulsory confessions.

The results of this culture clash is, as Lord Wilberforce put it,[57] 'a strange paradox': 'the worse, i.e. the more criminal ... activities can be made to appear, the less effective is the civil remedy that can be granted'.

Various devices have been suggested, and rejected, to avoid the rigour of the rule in civil cases. Among them is the idea that the civil court should sit in secret. Of this Lord Fraser remarked:[58]

> Such procedure would raise considerable practical difficulties and it would also be objectionable on principle. There are cases where in order that justice may be done the court has to sit in camera ... but it is important that such cases should be limited to those where proceedings in private are absolutely necessary in the interests of justice.

Zuckerman has suggested that the reason why the privilege applies to disclosure of pre-existing documents is that technically disclosure is made by giving evidence. He also said that the application is 'anachronistic'. As Lord Templeman said in *Istel v Tully*:[59]

> The privilege can only be justified on two grounds, first that it discourages the ill-treatment of a suspect and secondly that it discourages the production of dubious confessions ... It is difficult to see any reason why in civil proceedings the privilege against self-incrimination should be exercisable so as to enable a litigant to refuse relevant and even vital documents which are in his possession or power and which speak for themselves ... I regard the privilege against self-incrimination exercisable in civil proceedings as an archaic and

53 Ward and Gardner, 'The Privilege Against Self-Incrimination-In Search of Legal Certainty', [2003] EHRLR 388, discussed the privilege, and how the Strasbourg court has implied it into Art. 6. And see *Kansal v UK*, 27 April 2004.

54 *R v Hertfordshire County Council, ex p Green Environmental Industries* [2000] 2 AC 412.

55 *Re Arrows* (No 4), *Hamilton v Naviede* [1995] 2 AC 75

56 In *Re L (a minor)* (Police Investigation: Privilege) [1997] AC 16.

57 *Rank Film Distributors v Video Information Centre (a firm)* [1982] AC 380.

58 *Rank Film Distributors v Video Information Centre* (*a firm*) [1982] AC 380.

59 *AT and T Istel v Tully* [1993] AC 45.

> unjustifiable survival from the past when the court directs the production of relevant documents and requires the defendant to specify his dealings with the plaintiff's property or money.

Zuckerman argued further that the application of the privilege in civil search orders is 'absurd' because in many cases the potential criminal proceedings can be aided by a criminal search order.

Evidence

This book is not the place to indulge in any extended discussion of the law and practice of evidence or expert evidence. One good reason is that the ECtHR scarcely gets involved. In *Pélissier and Sassi v France* the Grand Chamber emphasized:[60]

> The Convention does not lay down rules on evidence as such. It cannot therefore exclude as a matter of principle and in the abstract that evidence obtained in breach of provisions of domestic law may be admitted. It is for the national courts to assess the evidence they have obtained and the relevance of any evidence that a party wishes to have produced. The Court has nevertheless to ascertain whether the proceedings considered as a whole, including the way in which the evidence was taken, were fair as required by Article 6(1).

The point is, as the court said *Miailhe v France* (No.2):[61]

> It must nevertheless satisfy itself that the proceedings as a whole were fair, having regard to any possible irregularities before the case was brought before the courts of trial and appeal and checking that those courts had been able to remedy them if there were any.

Or, to take two recent cases, in *Buzescu v Romania* it said:[62] 'Fairness must be assessed with regard to the proceedings as a whole.' And in *Turek v Slovakia* it added:[63]

> The Court will bear in mind that, according to Article 19 of the Convention, its duty is to ensure the observance of the undertakings of the Contracting States to the Convention. In particular, it is not its function to act as a court of appeal and to deal with errors of fact or of law allegedly committed by a national court unless and in so far as they may have infringed rights and freedoms protected by the Convention. Furthermore, as a general rule, it is for the national courts to assess the evidence before them as well as the relevance of the evidence which defendants seek to adduce.

The position in civil cases was clarified in *Suominen v Finland* where the ECtHR said:[64]

---

60 *Pélissier and Sassi v France*, 25 March 1999 [GC], [67].

61 *Miailhe v France* (No.2), 26 September 1996, [43]

62 *Buzescu v Romania*, 24 August 2005, [68].

63 *Turek v Slovakia*, 14 February 2006, [114].

64 *Suominen v Finland*, 1 July 2003, [33].

> The requirement of equality of arms applies in principle to civil cases as well as to criminal cases. As regards litigation involving opposing private interests, equality of arms implies that each party must be afforded a reasonable opportunity to present their case – including their evidence – under conditions that do not place them at a substantial disadvantage *vis-à-vis* their opponent. However, the requirements inherent in the concept of 'fair hearing' are not necessarily the same in cases concerning the determination of civil rights and obligations as they are in cases concerning the determination of a criminal charge.

Doubtless, however, the approach to evidence is the same as in civil litigation. Such differences there are between civil and criminal evidence are justified by the different purposes of each form of trial. The European case law is heavy with recognition of the fact that national courts must be allowed a margin of appreciation. In the same way, our appeal courts are very reluctant to interfere with a trial court's decisions on admitting evidence. Remote control or supervision on such matters is neither wise nor efficient. So, turning to England, CPR 32.1 says:

> (1) The court may control the evidence by giving directions as to –
>
> (a) the issues on which it requires evidence;
>
> (b) the nature of the evidence which it requires to decide those issues; and
>
> (c) the way in which the evidence is to be placed before the court.
>
> (2) The court may use its power under this rule to exclude evidence that would otherwise be admissible.
>
> (3) The court may limit cross-examination.

The discretions in Part 32 clearly engage Art. 6. The question is: do they, or the way they are applied, offend it? In *Mealey Horgan*,[65] the court held that it should use its powers to exclude a party from adducing evidence at trial only in extreme circumstances. So also in *Roberts v Williams* the new evidence which it was sought to adduce would have amplified the pleaded case rather than add a new one.[66] The application was made very late so as to affect the trial date. It was unsatisfactory for the trial judge to hear only part of the evidence that went to an important issue. Elsewhere, the court has reminded itself that appellate courts are reluctant to interfere with management decisions.[67] But, as Peter Gibson LJ put it in *Cobbold v Greenford LBC* the general principle is:[68]

65 *Mealey Horgan v Horgan*, *The Times*, 6 July 1999, QBD. The defendant served his witness statements 2 weeks late.

66 *Roberts v Williams* [2005] EWCA Civ 1086.

67 *Royal and Sun Alliance Insurers v T and N* [2002] EWCA Civ 1964, [37] and [38].

68 *Cobbold v Greenford LBC*, unreported, 9 August 1999.

> The overriding objective (of the CPR) is that the court should deal with cases justly. That includes, so far as practicable, ensuring that each case is dealt with not only expeditiously but also fairly. Amendments in general ought to be allowed so that the real dispute between the parties can be adjudicated upon provided that any prejudice to the other party or parties caused by the amendment can be compensated for in costs, and the public interest in the efficient administration of justice is not significantly harmed.

Thus, in *Hayes v Transco*,[69] probably out of a desire to adhere to the timetable for completing a trial, and, because it permitted the claimant to introduce new material, a restriction upon the defendant's cross-examination and the refusal of an application to admit previously excluded material were outside the acceptable range of responses at which the judge could legitimately arrive. The appeal court stressed:

> Nothing in this judgment is intended to fetter in any way the useful power which judges have to control cross-examination, which can often be unnecessarily prolix or even unnecessary altogether. All depends upon the facts of the particular case.

Even if, despite the management powers in CPR Part 32, secondary evidence is admitted, it does not follow that much weight ought to be attached to it. Thus, in *Post Office Counters v Mahida*,[70] the claimants sought reimbursement for discrepancies in the accounts of a sub-post mistress. The claimant prepared schedules setting out what they were, but was unable to produce the original dockets and foils. The court held that, by doing so, it denied the defendant the opportunity to verify those calculations.

Covert Surveillance

A special case arises where the evidence put in by one side has been obtained surreptitiously. In *Khan v UK*, the ECtHR held that:[71]

> While Article 6 guarantees the right to a fair hearing, it does not lay down any rules on the admissibility of evidence as such, which is therefore primarily a matter for regulation under national law. It is not the role of the Court to determine, as a matter of principle, whether particular types of evidence – for example, unlawfully obtained evidence – may be admissible or, indeed, whether the applicant was guilty or not. The question which must be answered is whether the proceedings as a whole, including the way in which the evidence was obtained, were fair.

Accordingly, material obtained in breach of Art. 8 (the right to privacy) can be admissible. Nevertheless, it has also said, *Glaser v UK*,[72]

---

69 *Hayes v Transco* [2003] EWCA Civ 1261.

70 *Post Office Counters v Mahida* [2003] EWCA Civ 1583.

71 *Khan v UK*, 12 May 2000, [34]. And see: *Chalkley v UK*, 12 June 2003; *Lewis v UK*, 25 November 2003.

72 *Glaser v UK*, 19 September 2000, [63].

> The essential object of Article 8 is to protect the individual against arbitrary interference by public authorities. There may however be positive obligations inherent in an effective 'respect' for family life ... In both the negative and positive contexts, regard must be had to the fair balance which has to be struck between the competing interests of the individual and the community, including other concerned third parties, and the State's margin of appreciation.

In the domestic context, this balance is applied. Thus, in *Rall v Hume*,[73] Potter LJ said:

> In principle ... the starting point on any application of this kind must be that, where video evidence is available which, according to the defendant, undermines the case of the claimant to an extent that would substantially reduce the award of damages to which she is entitled, it will usually be in the overall interests of justice to require that the defendant should be permitted to cross-examine the claimant and her medical advisers upon it.

In *Ford v GKR Construction*,[74] surreptitious video evidence was crucial in determining the level of damages. It was, however, made very late and although the eventual damages were less than the payment in, the defendants were sufficiently at fault to deprive them of the usual order in costs. So too, in *Jones v University of Warwick*[75] the deceitful way in which the video was made created a liability in costs. On the other hand, where the surreptitious evidence infringes legal professional privilege it is likely to be excluded.[76]

It is not clear that even this level of disapproval is sufficient. In *Martin v UK* there was a friendly settlement where a local authority placed a hidden video camera to watch for suspected nuisance.[77] No doubt, a court ought to have all relevant evidence. Nevertheless, if a party uses devious methods to obtain it, it can expect the court to provide some sort of punishment short of an actual striking out.

Public Interest Immunity

Public interest immunity (PII) is a device to prevent the use in legal proceedings of documents and other information where a public interest outside the court outweighs the public interest in the due administration of justice. Conveniently, Simon Brown LJ and the ECtHR have traced its development[78] and we need not follow the detail of their analysis. The law in this area can at best be described as a workable mess.

---

73 *Rall v Hume* [2001] 3 All ER 248 254.

74 *Ford v GKR Construction* 22 October 1999.

75 *Jones v University of Warwick* [2003] EWCA Civ 151.

76 *R v Grant* (Edward) [2005] EWCA Crim 1089.

77 *Martin v UK* (Admissibility), 19 February 2004. And see *Chalkley v UK*, 12 June 2003.

78 Sir Simon Brown, 'Public Interest Immunity' [1994] p. 579 and *Jasper v UK*, 16 February 2000, esp [36].

It is workable because, as we shall see, it is moving towards creating a case specific judicial discretion. It is a mess because it has come out of a range of unsatisfactory decisions of an earlier era. The rules in criminal and civil cases until recently have moved along separate but similar paths.[79] It is difficult, and unnecessary here, to attempt to sort out the differences. Such as they are, are mainly dependent on different values involved in civil and criminal trials, on different general obligations to give disclosure, on the different roles of trial and appellate courts and on the differences in procedure including most importantly the different role of the judge where there is a jury. There are two other differences. In *R v H*[80] the House of Lords pointed out first that: 'The duty of prosecuting counsel is not to obtain a conviction at all costs but to act as a minister of justice' and, secondly:

> The English law of crown privilege, later public interest immunity (or PII), was largely developed in civil cases. This was because … disclosure was left largely to the judgment of the prosecuting authorities and the prosecution and only exceptionally did the court make any ruling. Thus the defence were commonly unaware of what had not been disclosed and there was no judicial decision against which a defendant could appeal.

One reason for the similarity is that information which might be relevant to a subsequent civil action, for example, for false arrest or malicious prosecution might also be relevant to a prior criminal trial. But, as we shall see, it is a pity that in defining aspects of the new law of PII, the House wholly ignored the civil process. It raised a new range of questions, and did not stop to answer.

Origins in Crown Privilege: Inspection

The modern law began in *Duncan*[81] where the House of Lords held that a ministerial certificate that information should not be disclosed was conclusive.[82] The decision was widely criticized[83] and in *Conway*[84] the House took the opportunity to assert a right to inspect. This is wider than merely checking to see if a document properly matched the description in the certificate. That was always allowed. That is similar to inspection of a document for which legal professional privilege is claimed. The new inspection goes to the merits.

To this point, the law was called *Crown Privilege*, but in *Rodgers*[85] the House resiled from this, renaming it *public interest immunity*. Elsewhere, I have argued that

---

79 For a long time, it was assumed that the protection of informers was *sui generis* and not an aspect of PII.

80 *R v H* [2004] UKHL 3, [13] and [19].

81 *Duncan v Cammell Laird* [1942] AC 624.

82 Sir Simon Brown [1994] PL 579.

83 By, e.g. Devlin J in *Ellis v Home Office* [1953] 2 QB 135 and see Jacob, 'From Privileged Crown to Interested Public', [1993] PL 121.

84 *Conway v Rimmer* [1968] AC 910.

85 *Rogers v Home Secretary* [1973] AC 388.

this is because the law generally is becoming less deferential to the Crown.[86] The withholding is based on the balance of the public interest in the due administration of justice and some other important interest outside the court. So also, the withholding is not a privilege, but, because of that balance, was a duty whether or not the documents helped or hindered the Crown's case. Thus far, only the Crown could make the claim. However, in *D v NSPCC*,[87] the House held that a minister's certificate was not essential. What mattered was the balance: in an appropriate case, those outside government could make a claim. It follows from this, and earlier case law, that, in the balancing the public interest, the duty may be on the court itself to prevent the information from entering the public arena even if the parties do not make a claim. It is this that causes the Crown Proceedings Act 1947 to say:

> 28 (1) Subject to and in accordance with rules of court... : –
>
> (a) in any civil proceedings ... to which the Crown is a party, the Crown may be required by the court to make discovery of documents and produce documents for inspection; ...
>
> Provided that this section shall be without prejudice to any rule of law which authorises or requires the withholding of any document or the refusal to answer any question on the ground that the disclosure of the document or the answering of the question would be injurious to the public interest.
>
> (2) Without prejudice to the proviso to the preceding subsection, any rules made for the purposes of this section shall be such as to secure that the existence of a document will not be disclosed if, in the opinion of a Minister of the Crown, it would be injurious to the public interest to disclose the existence thereof.

CPR to refer to:[88]

> any rule of law which ... requires a document to be withheld from disclosure or inspection on the ground that its disclosure or inspection would damage the public interest.

It reflects the terms of the section. It will be noticed that the section refers to 'the opinion of a Minister of the Crown'. No doubt, when it was passed, such an opinion merely had to be stated. The impact of modem public law has changed this. Generally, public officials must now give reasons for their opinions. It is to these we now turn.

86 Jacob, 'From Privileged Crown to Interested Public', [1993] PL 121, and *The Republican Crown*, Dartmouth, 1996.

87 *D v National Society for the Prevention of Cruelty to Children* (NSPCC) [1978] AC 171.

88 CPR Part 31.19(8). It is unclear whether the proviso applies to PII in respect of non-governmental information (a situation not imagined in 1947). The proviso probably does not, but the CPR does.

Class Claims

Where the ministerial certificate was conclusive, it was easy to allow class claims to be made. Indeed, the issue was not important. It was much the same thing whether a document was in a class or was covered by a description. In a genuine class claim, protection is afforded to documents whose disclosure is harmless because they are part of a group, some of which need protection. The problem only became important when the court began to inspect under the power in *Conway*. It scarcely makes sense that a court can say 'we have inspected the documents and find that no damage will come from disclosure yet it must not be disclosed'. Greater detail has to be given of the prospective damage. A class is still capable of protection but it is a class defined by reference to the reasons for which it needs protection. To take two fairly recent cases, in *Wiley*,[89] the House of Lords held that there was no general class of public interest immunity for primary documents arising from an investigation, such as witness statements. On the other hand, in *Taylor v Anderton*,[90] it was held that 'class immunity' did apply to investigating officers' reports. There was a need for investigating officers to feel free to report on professional colleagues or members of the public without the apprehension that such persons might know their opinions, and that the prospect of disclosure in other than unusual circumstances would have an undesirable and inhibiting effect on their reports. At the end of day, it was, said the House, a matter for the trial judge.

In *McNally*[91] an application was made for PII on two broad and overlapping grounds, namely, the importance to the public interest of the protection afforded to informers, in particular as to their identity, and, the risk of undermining the effectiveness of the police in their reliance on informers. But Auld LJ said:

> The acceptance of the need to soften the rigidity ... so as to permit a balance of competing public interests in a case specific manner is part of a wider jurisprudential move away from near absolute protection of various categories of public interest in non-disclosure ... Now, with the advent of Human Rights to our law, this move has the force of European jurisprudence behind it.

He cited Lord Bingham in *Brown v Stott*:[92]

> The jurisprudence of the European Court very clearly establishes that while the overall fairness of a criminal trial cannot be compromised, the constituent rights comprised, whether expressly or implicitly, within Article 6 are not themselves absolute. Limited qualification of these rights is acceptable if reasonably directed by national authorities towards a clear and proper public objective and if representing no greater qualification than the situation calls for ... The case law shows that the court has paid very close attention

89 *R v Chief Constable of West Midlands Police, ex p Wiley* [1995] 1 AC 274.

90 *Taylor v Anderton and the Police Complaints Authority* [1995] 1 WLR 447.

91 *The Chief Constable of the Greater Manchester Police v McNally* [2002] EWCA Civ 14.

92 *Brown v Stott* [2003] 1 AC 681 (PC).

> to the facts of particular cases coming before it, giving effect to factual differences and recognising differences of degree. *Ex facto oritur jus*. The court has also recognised the need for a fair balance between the general interest of the community and the personal rights of the individual, the search for which balance has been described as inherent in the whole of the Convention … the law has moved on since *D v NSPCC* and has received a decisive impetus towards a more case specific approach with the advent of Human Rights to our law.

The nature of the outside interests which are protected have varied over time. In the new atmosphere of relative transparency in government, what was once protected may not now be. Probably, now the most common reason for the protection of information is the protection of police methods and informers, but other interests are also capable of protection. Indeed, it was held in *Balfour v Foreign Commonwealth Office*[93] that once there is an actual or potential risk to national security demonstrated by a minister's certificate, the court should not exercise its right to inspect the document. This assertion of judicial impotence was undermined by the decision in *R v C* where in the Court of Appeal Rose LJ (we shall come to the way the House of Lords handled the question) said:[94]

> In order to carry out the balancing exercise between competing interests which English domestic law requires, it is necessary for a trial judge to consider the material in relation to which PII is claimed by the prosecution, to hear prosecution submissions in relation to it, to hear such submissions as the defence are able to make and to know the issues raised by the defence, whether in police interview, statement or defence or otherwise.

It is not clear that *Balfour* is still good law. The more the outside interest to be protected is within the cognizance of the court, the more able the court is to refuse disclosure without further evidence. National security is something judges are not well equipped to determine, not because they must not judge but because in some circumstances they do not have the necessary experience. Nevertheless, judicial impotence is not a happy spectacle.

Inspection, Evidence and Representations: Special Counsel

Until recently, the advantage for the court in not inspecting the documents was that the judge's mind could not be influenced by material that should not be made public. Nevertheless, increasingly, inspection has been ordered in both civil and criminal cases. Finally, in *Davis*,[95] the Court of Appeal (Criminal Division) outlined three

93 *Balfour v Foreign Commonwealth Office* [1994] 1 WLR 681, applied in *R v Secretary of State for the Home Department ex p McQuillan* [1995] 4 All ER 400. As early as 1994, sir Simon Brown, 'Public Interest Immunity' [1994] PL 579, at 589, suggested that evidence is required as to the existence of national security.

94 *R v C* [2003] EWCA Crim 2847, [33 (v)].

95 *R v Davis, Johnson and Rowe* [1993] 1 WLR 613. The case went to the ECtHR as *Rowe and Davis v UK*, 16 February 2000.

different procedures to be adopted where the prosecution wanted to claim PII. Normally, notice should be given to the defence that an application is to be made and an indication given of at least the category of the material that is held. The defence then has the opportunity to make representations to the court. There are, however, cases where the disclosure of the category of the material in question in effect would reveal that which the prosecution contend should not be revealed. Here, the defence should still be notified that an application is to be made, but the category of the material need not be disclosed and the application should be without notice. Thirdly, and rarely, where to reveal even the fact that a without notice application is to be made in effect would be to reveal the nature of the evidence in question. In such cases the application should be without notice without the defence being told.[96]

In *Chahal v UK*[97] and *Tinnelly v UK* the ECtHR expressed concern, as the court put it in *Tinnelly*, that:[98]

> The right guaranteed to an applicant under Article 6(1) of the Convention to submit a dispute to a court or tribunal in order to have a determination of questions of both fact and law cannot be displaced by the *ipse dixit* of the executive.

It went on:

> The Court notes that in other contexts it has been found possible to modify judicial procedures in such a way as to safeguard national security concerns about the nature and sources of intelligence information and yet accord the individual a substantial degree of procedural justice ... The introduction of a procedure, regardless of the framework used, which would allow an adjudicator or tribunal fully satisfying the Article 6(1) requirements of independence and impartiality to examine in complete cognisance of all relevant evidence, documentary or other, the merits of the submissions of both sides, may indeed serve to enhance public confidence.

The blanket rule in *Balfour* that a ministerial certificate was conclusive infringed Art. 6. *Chahal* was concerned with the special problems of PII in immigration and *Tinnelly* with those in Northern Ireland. Legislation was passed to provide for the appointment of 'special counsel' in cases involving national security in immigration[99] and in Northern Ireland.[100] Under this, where it is necessary on national security grounds for the relevant tribunal or court to sit in camera, in the absence of the affected individual and his or her legal representatives, the Attorney General may appoint a special counsel to represent the interests of the individual in the proceedings. The legislation provides that the special counsel is not however 'responsible to the person whose interest he is appointed to represent', thus ensuring that the special counsel

---

96 Compare CPR Part 31.19(1).

97 *Chahal v UK*, 15 November 1996.

98 *Tinnelly v UK*, 10 July 1998, [72]-[79], esp. [78]. It followed this in *Devlin v UK*, 30 October 2001, [31], and again in *Devenney v UK*, 19 March 2002, [28].

99 Special Immigration Appeals Commission Act 1997.

100 Northern Ireland Act 1998.

is both entitled and obliged to keep confidential any information which should not be disclosed.

In a remarkably openly bad-tempered decision the House of Lords divided 3–2 on whether a Specially Appointed Advocate procedure can be used by the Parole Board. Lord Woolf suggested:[101] 'The use of an SAA is … never a panacea for the grave disadvantages of a person affected not being aware of the case against him. The use of an SAA can be, however, a way of mitigating those disadvantages.' By contrast, Lord Steyn said:[102] 'the special advocate procedure empties the prisoner's fundamental right to an oral hearing of all meaningful content'.

In a series of decisions the ECtHR has dealt with PII in more ordinary cases. In 2001,[103] it held that the disclosure of relevant evidence was not an absolute right because there may be competing interests, such as national security or the need to protect witnesses at risk of reprisals or keep secret police methods of criminal investigation, which must be weighed against the rights of the accused. Its own task is not to usurp the national court but to:

> ascertain whether the decision-making procedure applied in each case complied, as far as possible, with the requirements of adversarial proceedings and equality of arms and incorporated adequate safeguards to protect the interests of the accused.

In *Edwards and Lewis v UK*, it held:[104] 'any difficulties caused to the defence by a limitation on its rights must be sufficiently counterbalanced by the procedures followed by the judicial authorities.' We have seen that special counsel have been conceded by statute in the exceptional cases of immigration and Northern Ireland, but the court has used the same language in ordinary cases. The conclusion is that special counsel should be available there as well.

R v C began a retreat. The court said even taking into account the decision in *Edwards and Lewis v UK*[105] independent counsel to protect a defendant's interests should only be instructed in those rare cases where:[106]

> material is so sensitive that the defence cannot be informed that a PII hearing is to take place, or in which a judge in a PII hearing learns of material which is so highly prejudicial to a defendant that he ought not to make a ruling depending in whole or in part on that material without the benefit of further adversarial comment upon it.

---

101 *R (on the application of Roberts) v Parole Board* [2005] UKHL 45, [60]. The case is discussed by Metcalfe, 'Hear what?', (2005) SJ 149, 1004.

102 At [96].

103 *Atlan v UK*, 19 June 2001, [40]-[41], and *PG and JH v UK*, 25 September 2001, [68]-[69].

104 *Edwards and Lewis v UK*, 22 July 2003, [53].

105 *Edwards and Lewis v UK* 22 July 2003, following *Jasper v UK* [GC], 16 February 2000, [52].

106 *R v C* [2003] EWCA Crim 2847, [32(v)] and [35].

Rose LJ said:[107]

> It is a truism that both the English Common Law and Article 6 require a criminal trial to be fair. No one doubts that, since the coming into force of the Human Rights Act, common law principles in this respect have been refined and improved by reference to Convention principles, particularly in relation to equality of arms. But perhaps the time has come to recognise that, in an imperfect world, it is not always possible to achieve perfect fairness. The fairness of a particular trial has to be judged in isolation. But trials do not take place in isolation. They have to compete with each other for time and other resources, judicial, legal and financial, none of which are limitless.

On the appeal, perversely reported as *R v H*, the House of Lords said:[108]

> There is as yet little express sanction in domestic legislation or domestic legal authority for the appointment of a special advocate or special counsel to represent, as an advocate in PII matters, a defendant in an ordinary criminal trial ... But novelty is not of itself an objection, and cases will arise in which the appointment of an approved advocate as special counsel is necessary, in the interests of justice, to secure protection of a criminal defendant's right to a fair trial.

It pointed to difficulties:

> Such an appointment does however raise ethical problems, since a lawyer who cannot take full instructions from his client, nor report to his client, who is not responsible to his client and whose relationship with the client lacks the quality of confidence inherent in any ordinary lawyer-client relationship, is acting in a way hitherto unknown to the legal profession. While not insuperable, these problems should not be ignored, since neither the defendant nor the public will be fully aware of what is being done.

And:

> The appointment is also likely to cause practical problems: of delay, while the special counsel familiarizes himself with the detail of what is likely to be a complex case; of expense, since the introduction of an additional, high-quality advocate must add significantly to the cost of the case; and of continuing review, since it will not be easy for a special counsel to assist the court in its continuing duty to review disclosure, unless the special counsel is present throughout or is instructed from time to time when need arises

But:

> None of these problems should deter the court from appointing special counsel where the interests of justice are shown to require it. But the need must be shown. Such an appointment will always be exceptional, never automatic; a course of last and never first resort. It should not be ordered unless and until the trial judge is satisfied that no other course will adequately meet the overriding requirement of fairness to the defendant.

---

107 *R v C* [2003] EWCA Crim 2847, [29].
108 *R v H* [2004] UKHL 3, [22].

And, the House said 'When any issue of derogation from the golden rule of full disclosure comes before it, the court must address a series of questions':[109]

> (1) What is the material which the prosecution seek to withhold? This must be considered by the court in detail.
>
> (2) Is the material such as may weaken the prosecution case or strengthen that of the defence? If No, disclosure should not be ordered. If Yes, full disclosure should (subject to (3), (4) and (5) below) be ordered.
>
> (3) Is there a real risk of serious prejudice to an important public interest (and, if so, what) if full disclosure of the material is ordered? If No, full disclosure should be ordered.
>
> (4) If the answer to (2) and (3) is Yes, can the defendant's interest be protected without disclosure or disclosure be ordered to an extent or in a way which will give adequate protection to the public interest in question and also afford adequate protection to the interests of the defence? … In appropriate cases the appointment of special counsel may be a necessary step to ensure that the contentions of the prosecution are tested and the interests of the defendant protected.
>
> (5) Do the measures proposed in answer to (4) represent the minimum derogation necessary to protect the public interest in question? If No, the court should order such greater disclosure as will represent the minimum derogation from golden rule of full disclosure.
>
> (6) If limited disclosure is ordered pursuant to (4) or (5), may the effect be to render the trial process, viewed as a whole, unfair to the defendant? If Yes, then fuller disclosure should be ordered even if this leads or may lead the prosecution to discontinue the proceedings so as to avoid having to make disclosure.
>
> (7) If the answer to (6) when first given is No, does that remain the correct answer as the trial unfolds, evidence is adduced and the defence advanced?
>
> It is important that the answer to (6) should not be treated as a final, once-and-for-all, answer but as a provisional answer which the court must keep under review.

This is now the position for criminal proceedings. Our concerns are with civil litigation. The phrasing of the first question is not happy. Does it mean that the court should always inspect? In which case *Balfour* (that a court cannot go behind a ministerial certificate of national security) is indeed no longer good law. So also, does the requirement for consideration in detail mean the end of class claims? The probability is that the House meant neither of these things and if they did, they were probably obiter. The previous (but also relatively new) practice can be maintained. The court should give detailed consideration to the reasons claimed for the withholding. This might or might not involve inspection, but should be done before applying the procedures of question 4.

---

109 *R v H* [2004] UKHL 3, [36].

Caplan and Parkinson[110] have argued that the House also seemed to overthrow the previous ideas that the court must balance the public interest in the due administration of justice with the other public interests involved. They say the issue is now whether the trial can be fair. Again, this language is no doubt appropriate in criminal cases. It is far less clear that it is so in the civil process.

In *R v Greaves*,[111] Clarke LJ thought that the court, via its Registrar, should appoint special counsel but in *R v C*[112] Rose LJ said, in the absence of legislation, that it should be by the Attorney because no one else has the capacity to fund the scheme. In *R v H*, coming to the same conclusion, the House of Lords rejected this reason. It argued:[113]

> It is very well-established that when exercising a range of functions the Attorney General acts not as a minister of the Crown (although he is of course such) and not as the public officer with overall responsibility for the conduct of prosecutions, but as an independent, unpartisan guardian of the public interest in the administration of justice.[114] It is in that capacity alone that he approves the list of counsel judged suitable to act as special advocates or, now, special counsel, as when, at the invitation of a court, he appoints an *amicus curiae* ... no plausible alternative procedure was suggested. It would perhaps allay any conceivable ground of doubt, however ill-founded, if the Attorney General were to seek external approval of his list of eligible advocates by an appropriate professional body or bodies, but such approval is not in current circumstances essential to the acceptability of the procedure.

We can leave aside this maintenance of the Attorney's constitutional schizophrenia[115] and its relation to the real possibility of bias in the mind of a lay observer test the House itself laid down that we shall come to as we discuss *Porter v Magill*.[116] Our problem is how to apply this to the civil process. We have seen that PII can be sustained in claims not involving the Crown, *D v NSPCC*. It seems from the language of the House of Lords in *R v H* that even in such cases the court should, if the other conditions are satisfied, ask the Attorney in his capacity as the 'guardian of the public interest in the administration of justice' to appoint special counsel. The alternative, and perhaps easier, device would be to extend the terms of the Official Solicitor.[117] He is, at least, already an officer of the court. In either event, the question

---

110 Caplan and Parkinson, 'Testing the PII template', (2004) NLJ Vol.154, p. 238.

111 *R v Greaves* [2003] EWCA Crim 2353, 7 August 2003.

112 *R v C* [2003] EWCA Crim 2847, 16 October 2003.

113 *R v H* [2004] UKHL 3, [45]-[46].

114 It cited: *Halsbury's Laws of England*, 4th edn (1995), vol 44 (1), para. 1344; Edwards, The Law Officers of the Crown, 1964, pp. ix, 286, 301–302.

115 See Jacob, 'Some Reflections on Governmental Secrecy', [1974] PL 25 at n. 77. It is untouched by the Constitutional Reform Act 2005.

116 *Porter v Magill* [2001] UKHL 67, p.188 below.

117 Under s. 90 of the Senior Courts Act 1981. He has the advantage over the Attorney in that he expressly part of the machinery of the Court. The report of *R v H* does not make it clear

must arise who should pay for any special counsel. It seems hard on either of the parties to pay for a lawyer over whom they have no control.

The Contaminated Judge

In *Gaskin v Liverpool CC* Megaw LJ highlighted a difficulty:[118]

> Inspection of a document is a course which it is proper for a court to take in certain cases. It does, however, appear to me that it is a course which, while it can be taken, should not be undertaken lightly or ill-advisedly. It may put upon the court a burden which it is extremely difficult, perhaps in some circumstances impossible, to discharge fairly and satisfactorily. It leaves open at any rate the possibility of a feeling on the part of one of the parties to the proceedings that the judge or the members of the court, who has or have looked at these documents in private, may have done so without the opportunity of proper guidance as to their possible relevance or their context.

The problem of the judge contaminated by information in a PII decision is another example of a more general issue we shall look at as we consider judicial bias in the next chapter. We have seen that in *C v S*,[119] the Court of Appeal gave guidance as to how a conflict of private rights and a duty to give information to an investigating authority can be handled. In *Lamothe*[120] May LJ added:

> There is in my view a clear distinction between, on the one hand, a procedure such as that described in *C v S* for determining whether sensitive material need not be disclosed, and so would not become available for evidence, and, on the other hand, deciding a substantive issue in the proceedings upon evidence which is given and adduced in the absence of the claimants.

It is to be noted that both *C v S* were decided after the Human Rights Act repatriated the Convention.

In *Davis*,[121] the Court of Appeal said that although, PII applications limited the rights of the defence, in some cases the only alternative would be to require the prosecution to choose between following a 'with notice' procedure or declining to

---

whether the Official Solicitor was canvassed as a possibility for appointing special counsel in criminal cases.

118 *Gaskin v Liverpool CC* [1980] 1 WLR 1549 but see *Gaskin v UK*, 7 July 1989 on the merits.

119 Above p. 164, *C v S* (Money Laundering: Discovery of Documents) (Practice Note) [1999] 1 WLR 1551.

120 *Lamothe v Commissioner of Police of the Metropolis*, 25 October 1999, CA, approved in *R v H*.

121 *R v Davis, Johnson and Rowe* [1993] 1 WLR 613. See also *R (on the application of Director of Public Prosecutions) v Acton Youth Court*, 22 May 2001; *Gregory v UK*, No.22299/93, 25 February 1997, ECtHR.

prosecute.[122] It emphasized that it is for the trial judge to continue to monitor the position as the trial progresses. Issues might emerge during the trial that affected the balance and required disclosure 'in the interests of securing fairness to the defendant'. The question was thus, we can say, no different from any other case management decision.

Rose LJ said in *R v C*:[123] 'It has never, to our knowledge, been suggested that judges are incapable of ruling fairly … because they have heard inadmissible evidence.' And he went on:[124]

> we do not accept that a trial is necessarily unfair because a judge makes a decision or gives a ruling which might be affected because he had learnt of material unknown to the defence.

There are two obvious objections to this dictum. First, even given the flexibility of the fair minded judge that we shall see Laws LJ spoke about in *Sengupta v Holmes*,[125] people, and not only judges, rarely say they are so biased that they cannot make a fair decision. Secondly, the last sentence seems to say that, if only in such cases, judges can use inadmissible evidence rather than deliberately disregarding it.[126]

---

122 In *R v West* [2005] EWCA Crim 517 the Court of Appeal, having inspected the documents and heard counsel for Crown in the absence of the defence, held that the conviction was unsafe.

123 *R v C* [2003] EWCA Crim 2847, [17], but note Potter LJ's concerns in *Barings v Coopers and Lybrand* at p. 79.

124 *R v C* [2003] EWCA Crim 2847, [31].

125 *Sengupta v Holmes* [2002] EWCA Civ 1104, see below p. 209.

126 Cf. *R v Bromley Magistrates' Court, ex p Smith* [1995] 1 WLR 944; *R v Stipendiary Magistrate for Norfolk, ex p Taylor* (1997) 161 JP 773, *per Buxton J*. And note also the remarks of Potter LJ in *Barings v Coopers and Lybrand* [2000] 3 All ER 910, quoted at p. 79 above.

Chapter 5

Impartial and Independent Judges

Article 6(1) of the ECHR requires: 'an independent and impartial tribunal established by law'. It follows Art. 10 of the Universal Declaration of Human Rights:

> Everyone is entitled in full equality to a fair and public hearing by an independent and impartial tribunal, in the determination of his rights and obligations and of any criminal charge against him.

To take one of many cases, the ECtHR said in *Puolitaival v Finland* that there is a distinction between impartiality and 'independence proper'.[1] The court must be, and be seen to be, both impartial and independent. Partiality refers to factors affecting an individual judge. I shall argue that it is not an absolute. Later in this Chapter we come to judicial independence. It is concerned with constitutional and structural issues. I call it the constitutional dimension. Here too I shall argue that balance is required.

The Impartial Judge

Long ago Scrutton LJ told us:[2]

> A good legal system should have four – at least four – attributes. Its judges should be incorruptible and impartial ... The law they administer should be accurate, and founded on recognized principles ... Justice or judgments should be given quickly ... And justice should be accessible to citizens cheaply.

Although it says more, each of these is of course reflected in Art. 6. This chapter is concerned with the first of these attributes. Scrutton LJ continued 'it is sometimes difficult to be sure, hard as you have tried, that have put yourself in a perfectly impartial position between two litigants'. This chapter assesses some difficulties that the judges and the appeal courts that review their decisions have seen. The modern language often refers to *bias* but that is too stark a word to describe the subtleties of many of the problems. The word *bias* suggests there is no balance to be found. We shall see that time and time again the courts, including the House of Lords and

---

1 *Puolitaival v Finland*, 23 November 2004.

2 Sir TE Scrutton, 'The Work of the Commercial Courts', (1921) 1 CLJ 6.

the Court at Strasbourg, have held that decision-makers must achieve and be seen to achieve the required level of impartiality. There are degrees. It is not an absolute.

But first, importantly, Lord Devlin said:[3]

> The social service which the judge renders to the community is the removal of a sense of injustice. To perform this service the essential quality which he needs is impartiality, and next after that the appearance of impartiality. I put impartiality before the appearance of it simply because without the reality the appearance would not endure.

Elsewhere he combined ideas of openness with the separation of powers and the rules against (hidden) bias. How ever far we have moved in the third of a century since he wrote, these three principles are still a triumvirate challenged only occasionally but crucially by the upstart young ideas of expediency and efficiency. In a passage which shows how far our world has changed, he adopted the traditional view of the English that the jurisdictions of continental Europe cannot know a proper doctrine of the separation of powers. He argued:[4] 'the self-informed judge is a product of the inquisitorial and not the adversary system.' And:[5]

> To make a judge an expert on his own in any subject is to move the doing of justice from the court to the chamber and to draw the blinds. To give him a background understanding unshared with the Bar is to admit experts as well the parties to the chamber, but to leave the parties without effective counsel.

Lord Devlin said:[6] 'Everything that goes into the judge's mind on fact is seen to go in by way of evidence and during its passage it is subject to the advocate's comment.' While this view held sway there was little scope for challenges to the impartially of the courts. But what he said is no longer true and a whole line of cases has been spawned in the change.

In an important and powerful note Blom-Cooper argued:[7] 'The current law in the United Kingdom is wildly unhelpful and irrational. It should be reappraised and given a rational basis.' He said:

> Prejudice (or, if you like, preconceptions) and bias are not the same, either conceptually or in practice. Indeed, the case law is cluttered with expressions that demonstrate that the difference (not just in degree, but in essence) has been ignored or blurred by the judiciary.

He quoted Judge Frank in *Rt JP Linahan, Inc.*:[8]

---

3 Lord Devlin, 'The Judge as Lawmaker', (1976) MLR 1. And see him in *In re K* (Infants) [1965] AC 201, 237.

4 Lord Devlin, *The Judge*, 1979, p. 37.

5 At p. 46.

6 At p. 23.

7 Sir Louis Blom-Cooper, 'Bias on Appeal', [2005] PL, 225.

8 *Rt JP Linahan, Inc*, 1943, US Second Circuit Court of Appeals, 138 F.20.650.

> Democracy must, indeed, fail unless our courts try cases fairly, and there can be no fair trial before a judge lacking in impartiality and disinterestedness. If, however, 'bias' and 'partiality' be defined to mean the total absence of preconceptions in the mind of the judge, then no one has ever had a fair trial and no one ever will. The human mind, even at infancy, is no blank piece of paper. We are born with predispositions; and the process of education, formal and informal, creates attitudes which precede reasoning in particular instances and which, therefore, by definition, are pre-judices.

Blom-Cooper continued:

> Without acquired 'slants', pre-conceptions, life could not go on. Every habit constitutes a pre-judgment; were those pre-judgments which we call habits absent in any person, were he obliged to treat every event as an unprecedented crisis presenting a wholly new problem he would go mad. Interests, points of view, preferences, are the essence of living. Only death yields complete dispassionateness, for such dispassionateness signifies utter indifference.

Lucy, among others, has attempted a philosophical analysis. He argued:[9]

> For most ordinary human beings ... an impartial stance towards life and its constituents is both impossible and undesirable ... [But] impartiality is appropriate where there exists a conflict of interests between two or more parties, with a third party being involved to police the conflict or to resolve it ... It is no more possible for judges to divorce themselves from the commitments that give their lives meaning and value than for anyone else. Impartiality, however, only makes sense against a background of partiality.

Useful as such examinations are, they do not do much to give meaning in the real world. For that it is necessary to turn to the courts. They have tried on many occasions to articulate a test which would tell whether or not there is bias. In *De Cubber v Belgium*, the ECtHR recalled that a restrictive interpretation of Art. 6(1):[10]

> Notably in regard to observance of the fundamental principle of the impartiality of the courts – would not be consonant with the object and purpose of the provision, bearing in mind the prominent place which the right to a fair trial holds in a democratic society within the meaning of the Convention.

In *Piersack v Belgium* in a passage which it and other courts have quoted many times the ECtHR said:[11]

> While impartiality normally denotes absence of prejudice or bias, its existence or otherwise can, notably under Article 6(1) of the Convention, be tested in various ways. A distinction can be drawn in this context between a subjective approach, that is endeavouring to

9 Lucy, 'The Possibility of Impartiality', (2005) 25 OJLS 3.

10 *De Cubber v Belgium*, 26 October 1984, [30].

11 *Piersack v Belgium*, 1 October 1982, [30]. There is a strong but rebuttable presumption that there is no subjective bias, *Pullar v UK*, 10 June 1996. And see *Montgomery v HM Advocate* [2003] 1 AC 641; 2001 SC (PC) 1, per Lord Hope.

> ascertain the personal conviction of a given judge in a given case, and an objective approach, that is determining whether he offered guarantees sufficient to exclude any legitimate doubt in this respect.

Sir Richard Tucker suggested:[12]

> The position under art 6 is no different from that under the common-law rules under natural justice applicable to proceedings before domestic tribunals ... So far as art 6 is concerned, I consider that it adds nothing to the common-law requirements of natural justice.

In the ordinary case where partiality is alleged this may be true but, as we, shall see, Art. 6 also requires independence, and the appearance of independence, and as Ward and Demetriou have argued this is fundamentally new to domestic law.[13] So also, as the cases make clear, the common law has undoubtedly modified its approach, not in general, but in detail.

Faced with the jurisprudence from Strasbourg, in 1993 in *R v Gough*,[14] the House of Lords applied a test of whether there is 'real danger of bias'. In *Porter v Magill*,[15] it purported to accept the view of Lord Phillips MR *in re Medicaments and Related Classes of Goods* (No.2)[16] which he claimed it was in line with the Strasbourg jurisprudence. He called it 'a modest adjustment' of the test in *Gough*. The test he formulated was whether 'a fair-minded and informed observer [would] conclude that there was a real possibility, or a real danger, the two being the same, that the tribunal was biased'. However, in *Porter v Magill* the House rejected the use of the phrase 'real danger', so that we are now left with only 'a real possibility' of bias appearing in the mind of an observer. What might have been a modest adjustment has become much broader. The House adopted Kirby J's formulation in *Johnson v Johnson*[17] that 'a reasonable member of the public is neither complacent nor unduly sensitive or suspicious'. We shall come to what this member of the public may be supposed to know. In the meantime, what matters is not the formulation of these tests, nor whether one better or stricter than another nor whether they amount for the same thing. The question is always 'is this judge partial or impartial'? As we shall see the voluminous case law does not depart from this idea. Much depends on the facts, and merits, of each case. As Tuckey LJ remarked[18] 'Fairness is a "big picture" issue'.

---

12 *R (Nicolaides) v General Medical Council* [2001] EWHC Admin 625, [19], [28].

13 Ward and Demetriou, 'Human rights update', (2004) SJ Vol. 148 No. 5 p. 139.

14 *R v Gough* [1993] AC 646.

15 *Porter v Magill* [2001] UKHL 67.

16 *Re Medicaments and Related Classes of Goods* (No.2) [2001] 1 WLR 700.

17 *Johnson v Johnson* (2000) 200 CLR 488, [53] and, *Lawal v Northern Spirit* [2003] UKHL 35.

18 *Co-operative Group (CWS) v International Computers* [2003] EWCA Civ 1955.

The House of Lords itself has been unconvincing on a number of occasions. In *R v H* when discussing the similar absence of bias required of the Attorney-General it argued that: 'Counsel roundly acknowledged the complete integrity shown by successive holders of the office.' Complete integrity is not the issue. The question is what appears in the mind of the observer. Thus, even where in *Dimes v Proprietors of Grand Junction Canal*[19] Lord Cottenham LC was a shareholder in the defendant, the issue was not whether he was biased, but whether his holding could give rise to that impression, so also, in *Pinochet* (No.2)[20] the House was more concerned to be seen to be fair rather than to be fair, that is with appearances rather than reality: it seemed also to be unduly impressed by the magnitude of the substantive issues.

In *Locabail* the court said:[21]

> It would be dangerous and futile to attempt to define or list the factors which may or may not give rise to a real danger of bias. Everything will depend on the facts, which may include the nature of the issue to be decided. We cannot, however, conceive of circumstances in which an objection could be soundly based on the religion, ethnic or national origin, gender, age, class, means or sexual orientation of the judge. Nor, at any rate ordinarily, could an objection be soundly based on the judge's social or educational or service or employment background or history, nor that of any member of the judge's family; or previous political associations; or membership of social or sporting or charitable bodies; or Masonic associations; or previous judicial decisions; or extra-curricular utterances (whether in textbooks, lectures, speeches, articles, interviews, reports or responses to consultation papers); or previous receipt of instructions to act for or against any party, solicitor or advocate engaged in a case before him; or membership of the same Inn, circuit, local Law Society or chambers.

The approach of the ECtHR is different. Rarely does it decide cases with this kind of broad formulation. Its emphasis is on the particular facts to hand. Thus, in *Steck-Risch v Liechtenstein*, it was faced with a similar issue to that in *Locabail*. A judge was a member of the Constitutional Court, called upon to decide on the applicants' appeal against the Administrative Court's judgment in which his law-office colleague acted as presiding judge.[22] ECtHR held that there was no dual role because: (1) there was no overlapping sets of proceedings; (2) neither of the judges was a subordinate to the parties or to each other; (3) 'quashing of a lower court's decision by a supreme jurisdiction is a normal feature in any legal system, which does not cast doubt on the

---

19 *Dimes v Proprietors of Grand Junction Canal* (1852) 3 HL Cas 759, 10 ER 301.

20 *R v Bow Street Metropolitan Stipendiary Magistrate, ex p Pinochet Ugarte* (No.2) [2000] 1 AC 119. And note the rueful remark of Butler-Sloss P: it 'is obviously going to be cited to every court on almost every subject', *Re J (a minor)* (Transcript: Smith Bernal) 7 February 2000.

21 *Locabail (UK) v Bayfield Properties*; *Locabail (UK) v Waldorf Investment*; *Timmins v Gormley*; *Williams v HM Inspector of Taxes*; *R v Bristol Betting and Gaming Licensing Committee, ex p O'Callaghan* [2000] QB 451, [25].

22 *Steck-Risch v Liechtenstein*, 19 May 2005, [42] et seq.

competence of the judges who gave the decision'; and, (4) the two judges were not particularly close friends. There was no appearance of bias.

In one of his many challenges to the tolls on the Skye Bridge by Robbie the Pict (a name he adopted, no doubt to further his political claims), the fact that the judge and a number of those connected with the Bridge's construction were members of the Speculative Society (a debating club of former members of Edinburgh University) was sufficient to justify a recusal.[23]

Two recent cases have held that disqualification for apparent bias is not a discretionary matter. In *AWG Group (formerly Anglian Water) v Morrison* Mummery LJ said:

> In terms of time, cost and listing it might well be more efficient and convenient to proceed with the trial, but efficiency and convenience are not the determinative legal values: the paramount concern of the legal system is to administer justice, which must be, and must be seen by the litigants and fair-minded members of the public to be, fair and impartial. Anything less is not worth having.

But, then casting some doubt on whether efficiency and convenience are indeed irrelevant, he went on:

> Adjourning the trial now is bad enough for all concerned, but an even worse disaster, such as having to abort the trial several months into the hearing and to start all over again, may be waiting to happen. That would be inefficient, as well as unjust. It is a potential disaster that can be avoided. A decision must be made now one way or the other. By far the safer course is to remove all possibility of apparent bias by the recusal of the judge before the trial even begins. There will be other judges available to try this case and there will be other cases available for this judge to try.

More clearly, in *Gillies* the House of Lords held that the question whether a tribunal was properly constituted or was acting in breach of the principles of natural justice was essentially a question of law.[24]

Importantly, an impartial decision-maker is not always required. We have seen in the context of open proceedings that in *Campbell and Fell v UK*[25] prison discipline does not always engage Art. 6. So also, it does not, without more, necessarily prevent a governor from making decisions.[26] We have also seen that the ECHR is not concerned with administrative determinations so that such procedures are largely outside the scope of Art. 6.[27] Nevertheless, where a Chairman of the Planning Decision

---

23 *Robbie the Pict v Miller Buidheann*, 13 May 2005, unreported, transcript at http://www.scotcourts.gov.uk/opinions/A93_04.html.

24 *Gillies v Secretary of State for Work and Pensions* [2006] UKHL 2.

25 *Campbell and Fell v UK*, 28 June 1984, p. 68 above.

26 *R (on the application of Tangney) v Governor of Elmley Prison* [2005] EWCA Civ 1009.

27 *Bryan v UK*, 22 November 1995, above p. 18.

Committee expressed an inclination to follow an inspector's recommendation there was a real possibility of bias.[28]

The Judicial Oath

In another of Robbie the Pict's challenges, the court remarked:[29]

> Every judge is bound, both by his judicial oath and by the ethical obligation incumbent on anyone who exercises a judicial function, to behave honourably, sincerely and impartially towards litigants and those who represent them. These obligations are the cornerstones of judicial integrity. A litigant is entitled to expect integrity of the judge; but he in turn must give the judge his trust. That is the only basis on which litigation can be conducted in an atmosphere of confidence rather than suspicion.

Elsewhere, the Constitutional Court of South Africa put it this way:[30]

> The reasonableness of the apprehension must be assessed in the light of the oath of office taken by the judges to administer justice without fear or favour, and their ability to carry out that oath by reason of their training and experience. It must be assumed that they can disabuse their minds of any irrelevant personal beliefs or predispositions ... At the same time, it must never be forgotten that an impartial judge is a fundamental prerequisite for a fair trial.

So also in *Jones v DAS Legal Expenses Insurance*, speaking of the judge's problem the court said:[31]

> The first task is coolly to assess the circumstances. If the thought crosses the judge's mind that the conflict of interest could actually affect his mind, then he should recuse himself. More usually, the judge will know he is unaffected and he must then assess how strong the appearance of bias is. Sometimes he will be confident that the fair-minded observer in the back of his court would never object. Sometimes he may be quite unsure what the reaction will be and much may depend on the stance adopted by the parties. He must be sensitive to the need for justice to be seen to be done. But one can be sensitive while remaining thick-skinned. Judges must be robust and do what they are paid to do without fear as well as without favour, faithful to their judicial oaths.

This reliance on the judicial oath is no doubt correct. But it by no means follows that where there is such an oath that a judge is always loyal to it. Nevertheless, on some occasions both in Britain and at Strasbourg the reviewing courts have rejected

---

28 *Condron v National Assembly for Wales* [2005] EWHC 3007 QBD (Admin).

29 *Robbie the Pict, Petitioner*, SCCR 299, Appeal Court, High Court of Justiciary, 2003, [8].

30 *President of the Republic of South Africa v South African Rugby Football Union* 1999 (7) BCLR 725 (CC) 753.

31 *Jones v DAS Legal Expenses Insurance* [2003] EWCA Civ 1071.

allegations of partiality on the basis that the oath has been taken.[32] Thus, in *Salaman v UK* the Court said:[33]

> It is undisputed that the judge and the deceased whose will was being disputed in the proceedings were both freemasons ... There is no reason to doubt in particular that a judge would regard his oath on taking judicial office as taking precedence over any other social commitments or obligations.

Lord Reed considered the importance of the oath in *Starrs v Ruxton*, which concerned temporary sheriffs (We come to wider aspects of *Starrs* later). He said:[34]

> Before embarking on his duties the temporary sheriff took two oaths, namely the Oath of Allegiance and the Judicial Oath, before the Lord President ... I do not consider that the judicial oath is a sufficient guarantee to exclude all legitimate doubt. I accept that it is an important protection, both because of its innate gravity and the consequent weight of the obligation undertaken, and because any violation of the oath which was detected would be likely to be treated as a matter of the utmost seriousness ... In the case of full-time judges ... the avoidance of conflicts of interest arising from legal practice is guaranteed by more than the judicial oath alone. Why should the oath be regarded as a sufficient guarantee in respect of part-time judges?

As Lord Hope said in *Millar v Dickson*:[35]

> It is no answer for the judge to say that he is in fact impartial, that he abided by his judicial oath and there was a fair trial. The administration of justice must be preserved from any suspicion that a judge lacks independence or that he is not impartial. If there are grounds which would be sufficient to create in the mind of a reasonable man a doubt about the judge's impartiality, the inevitable result is that the judge is disqualified from taking any further part in the case.

Nevertheless, in *Kearney v Her Majesty*'s *Advocate* Lord Bingham again relied on the oath:[36]

> The fair-minded, informed observer would be aware of the proud spirit of independence which traditionally animates members of the Scots bar; of the judicial oath taken by temporary judges; of the limited role of the trial judge in criminal proceedings; and of the power of appellate courts to correct irregularities at trial.

32 *Taylor v Lawrence* [2002] EWCA Civ 90; *Attorney General v Covey, Attorney General v Matthews* [2001] EWCA Civ 254.

33 *Salaman v UK*, 15 June 2000.

34 *Starrs v Ruxton* 2000 JC 208, 11 November 1999.

35 *Millar v Dickson* [2001] UKPC D4, [65].

36 *Kearney v Her Majesty*'s *Advocate* [2006] UKPC D1, [8].

Real and Apparent Bias – Partiality for Interest

In *Dimes v Proprietors of Grand Junction Canal* Lord Campbell said:[37]

> No one can suppose that Lord Cottenham could be, in the remotest degree, influenced by the interest that he had in this concern; but ... it is of the last importance that the maxim that no man is to, be a judge in his own cause should be held sacred. And that is not to be confined to a cause in which he is a party, but applies to a cause in which he has an interest.

In that case the interest was a shareholding in the defendants. The House did not decide and was not asked to decide whether his holding as a trustee also disqualified. In *Pinochet* (No.2) Lord Browne-Wilkinson ignored the trustee issue and extended the idea of interest saying:

> In such a case, once it is shown that the judge is himself a party to the cause, or has a relevant interest in its subject matter, he is disqualified without any investigation into whether there was a likelihood or suspicion of bias. The mere fact of his interest is sufficient to disqualify him.

And he went on:

> There was no inquiry by the court as to whether a reasonable man would consider Lord Cottenham LC to be biased and no inquiry as to the circumstances which led to Lord Cottenham LC sitting.

The first part of this statement is accurate; the second is not. The report makes it clear that Lord Cottenham sat because under the then Chancery Rules a decision of the Vice-chancellor could not take effect unless it was 'enrolled' by the Lord Chancellor. He had a discretion whether to do so. It was the exercise of this discretion that was under challenge.

In *Pinochet* (No.2) Lord Hutton said:

> There could be cases where the interest of the judge in the subject matter of the proceedings arising from his strong commitment to some cause or belief or his association with a person or body involved in the proceedings could shake public confidence in the administration of justice as much as a shareholding (which might be small) in a public company involved in the litigation.

This, however, conflates two quite separate issues. Strong commitment to a belief is not the same as an interest: to be interested is not the same as to have an advantageous concern. There is a distinction between an association and an interest. Later we discuss the language permissible for the expression of commitment to a cause. It suffices here to note that no question of disqualification arose when, for example,

37 *Dimes v Proprietors of Grand Junction Canal* (1852) 3 HL Cas 759, HL (E).

Lord Brougham confessed in *Dimes* that he 'never from the beginning had the least doubt' about one of the questions submitted to the judges.

Lord Hoffmann's vice, if that was what it was, in *Pinochet* was not that he has a strong commitment. It was that he was associated with an intervening party. The problem was twofold. First, by concentrating on the link between Lord Hoffmann and an intervening party the House gave priority to form over substance. It equated an intervener with a party and an association with an interest. As Lord Hope (who had sat in *Pinochet* (No.2)) said in *Meerabux v Attorney General of Belize*:[38]

> The decision ... to apply the rule which automatically disqualifies a judge from sitting in a case in which he has an interest to the situation in which Lord Hoffmann found himself appears, in retrospect, to have been a highly technical one ... The extension of the rule was taken one step further when Lord Hoffmann was held to have been disqualified automatically by reason of his directorship of a charitable company. That company was not a party to the appeal, nor had it done anything to associate itself with those proceedings. But the company of which he was a director was controlled by ... a party. As Lord Steyn said in *Lawal v Northern Spirit*, public perception of the possibility of unconscious bias is the key.

He concluded:

> If the House of Lords had felt able to apply this test in the *Pinochet* (No.2) case, it is unlikely that it would have found it necessary to find a solution to the problem that it was presented with by applying the automatic disqualification rule.

The second problem is, as here, too often the courts allow litigation between real parties to be hijacked by a desire to consider wider questions of fact and law and thus allowing too many outside interests to be heard on matters that affect their concerns but not their civil rights or obligations.[39] While, no doubt, the old law made too much of it, it would be salutary if the judges were to remind themselves of the distinction between *ratio decidendi* and *obita dicta*.[40] The courts invite accusations of partiality whenever they are seen to be deciding policy issues beyond the interests of the parties. It is otherwise in the ECtHR where there is no doctrine of precedent.

---

38 *Meerabux v Attorney General of Belize* [2005] UKPC 12, [21].

39 Lord Phillips MR in *R (on the application of Burke) v General Medical Council* [2005] EWCA Civ 1003, [19], [21], added a further reason: he said it is:

> not the task of a judge when sitting judicially – even in the Administrative Court – to set out to write a text book or practice manual ... The court should not be used as a general advice centre. The danger is that the court will enunciate propositions of principle without full appreciation of the implications that these will have in practice, throwing into confusion those who feel obliged to attempt to apply those principles in practice.

And see p. 32, n. 119 above and *Wilson* (No.2). CPR Part 54 refers to 'directly affected'.

40 A failure to do so puts legal certainly in jeopardy and may itself breach Art. 6.

Its decisions and the reasons for them are guidance. Thus, in *Pizzati v Italy*[41] three further Governments intervened, not to affect the result between the parties but to obtain guidance as to how they should adjust their own legal systems.

Whatever the fate now of *Pinochet* (No.2), in *Locabail* the court attempted to explain the scope of the rule:

> It would be dangerous and futile to attempt to define or list the factors which may or may not give rise to a real danger of bias. Everything will depend on the facts, which may include the nature of the issue to be decided … a real danger of bias might well be thought to arise if there were personal friendship or animosity between the judge and any member of the public involved in the case; or if the judge were closely acquainted with any member of the public involved in the case, particularly if the credibility of that individual could be significant in the decision of the case; or if, in a case where the credibility of any individual were an issue to be decided by the judge, he had in a previous case rejected the evidence of that person in such outspoken terms as to throw doubt on his ability to approach such person's evidence with an open mind on any later occasion; or if on any question at issue in the proceedings before him the judge had expressed views, particularly in the course of the hearing, in such extreme and unbalanced terms as to throw doubt on his ability to try the issue with an objective judicial mind … or if, for any other reason, there were real ground for doubting the ability of the judge to ignore extraneous considerations, prejudices and predilections and bring an objective judgment to bear on the issues before him.

One proposition is perhaps clearer than most. In *Metropolitan Properties v Lannon* Lord Denning MR stated:[42]

> No man can be an advocate for or against a party in one proceeding, and at the same time sit as a judge of that party in another proceeding. Everyone would agree that a judge, or a barrister or solicitor (when he sits ad hoc as a member of a tribunal) should not sit on a case to which a near relative or close friend is a party. So also a barrister or solicitor should not sit on a case to which one of his clients is a party. Nor on a case where he is already acting against one of the parties. Inevitably people would think he would be biased.

Thus, where a barrister-arbitrator was instructed in another matter by one of the parties, he should not have sat.[43]

We can also add that recusal will normally be appropriate where the judge has relevant confidential information which is not known to one side.[44] On the other hand, experienced decision-makers can be expected to ignore prejudicial, irrelevant

---

41 *Pizzati v Italy* 29 March 2006 [GC]. The intervening Governments were those of The Czech Republic, Poland and Slovakia.

42 *Metropolitan Properties v Lannon* [1969] 1 QB 577, 600. In *Smith v Kvaerner Cementation Foundations* [2006] EWCA Civ 242 Lord Phillips MR said this 'has never been challenged'.

43 *ASM Shipping of India v TTMI of England* [2005] EWHC 2238 (Comm).

44 *Rustal Trading v Gill and Duffus* [2000] 1 Lloyd's Rep. 14 (QBD (Comm).

material in a newspaper[45] or even a witness statement. We come separately to the courts' discussions of recusal for matters that arise within a case.

Similar rules apply to expert witnesses. Under the CPR their duty is to the court and not the paying party. The mere fact of employment does not create partiality but other of their conduct or approach might. So also at Strasbourg, a trial may be unfair if an expert is allowed to be seen to be partisan, *Bonisch v Austria*.[46] But this does not mean that an expert who is or was employed by one side is necessarily disqualified.[47] There is an obligation on the court to ensure it is not seen (by the hypothetical neutral observer) to be partial, *Remli v France*.[48] This obligation is also not endless. A court is not partial merely because one party is unrepresented.[49]

Where all possible decision makers are equally partial, any of them is entitled to decide an issue.[50] As Parke B argued in *Dimes* 'this is a case of necessity, and where that occurs the objection of interest cannot prevail'.[51]

The Rule against Enquiries

There are three almost universal truths about litigation. First, the higher the stakes, the more inventive advocates will be. Secondly, issues raised often run in fashions. Thirdly, when all else seems lost, allegations of partiality against the decision-maker might be plausible: it is legal equivalent of sarcasm.

Pinochet (No.2) had such startling results that advocates began scouring the past careers and conduct of decision-makers: the privacy of members of the bench was put in jeopardy. *Locabail* tried to put an end to that. The court said candidly:[52]

---

45 *R (on the application of Mahfouz) v Professional Conduct Committee of the General Medical Council and The General Medical Council* (Third Party) [2004] EWCA CIV 233.

46 *Bonisch v Austria*, 6 May 1985.

47 *Brandstetter v Austria*, 28 August 1991; *Waller v Cornwall County Council* [2005] EWHC 1166.

48 *Remli v France*, 23 April 1996.

49 *Attorney General v Covey, Attorney General v Matthews* [2001] EWCA Civ 254. The court observed:

> In his application this morning, Mr Covey took the course of stripping off his clothes and throwing water at one member of the court ... He has not repeated his misconduct. He has made submissions which have no relevance whatsoever to the issues before the court.

50 *The King v The Justices of Essex*, 5 M. and S. 513, 105 ER 1139 (1816) per Lord Ellenborough CJ but this decision may have turned on particular statutory interpretation.

51 He cited Year Book, 8 Hen. 6, 19; 2 Roll. Abr. 93. There it was held that it was no objection to the jurisdiction of the Common Pleas that an action was brought against all its Judges, in a case which could only be brought in that court. The matter is not entirely clear, see per Holt CJ: 'The Mayor of Hereford was laid by the heels [we may suppose incapacitated], for sitting in judgment in a cause where he himself was lessor of the plaintiff in ejectment, though he by the charter was sole Judge of the Court', Anonymous, 1 Salkeld 396, 91 ER 343.

52 *Locabail (UK) v Bayfield Properties*; *Locabail (UK) v Waldorf Investment*; *Timmins v Gormley*; *Williams v HM Inspector of Taxes*; *R v Bristol Betting and Gaming Licensing*

> The proof of actual bias is very difficult, because the law does not countenance the questioning of a judge about extraneous influences affecting his mind; and the policy of the common law is to protect litigants who can discharge the lesser burden of showing a real danger of bias without requiring them to show that such bias actually exists.

Locabail itself, apart from some nuances, contains a useful but unremarkable exposition of the principles for assessing bias. Subject to one more recent decision,[53] when sitting judicially barristers are absolved of responsibility for the interests of other members of their chambers or former chambers. Solicitors maintain responsibility for acts of their partners and owe a duty to their firm's clients, even if they have not acted for them personally. But it is too inflexible to apply an analogy with the solicitors' professional rules. A nominal and indirect interest (arising from a directorship) which the judge does not know about does not disqualify. Nor does previous employment many years ago with one of the parties render a decision suspect.

Smith v Kvaerner Cementation Foundations and Bar Council (Intervener) is important both for it says about barristers sitting judicially and, we shall see, about waiver. As to the first point, Lord Phillips MR said:[54]

> Members of some chambers share expenses on the basis of contributing a percentage of earnings. In such circumstances, a ruling that reduced the earnings of counsel appearing before him could result in an increase of the contribution to expenses made by the Recorder ... we can see the force [in the] submission that changes in the way that some chambers fund their expenses and the fact that counsel can now act under a conditional fee agreement mean that, in some cases at least, there may be grounds for arguing that a Recorder should not sit in a case in which one or more of the advocates are members of his chambers. Indeed we understand that the Bar Council is currently considering the implications of conditional fee agreements in this context.

There is one decision that sits uneasily with these principles. In *Taylor v Lawrence* a firm of solicitors acting for one party in a neighbour's boundary dispute had charge of the judge's will. On the night before judgment he attended on the firm's probate department to execute a codicil. He was not invoiced for this service because, the report said, the amount would be nominal. The Court of Appeal held that none of this gave rise to a reasonable apprehension of bias. Lord Woolf said:[55]

> The manner in which the defendants learnt that the judge had not paid for the services provided ... is disgraceful. An inquiry agent telephoned [the firm], pretending to be the

---

Committee, ex p O'Callaghan [2000] QB 451, [3].

53 *Smith* (Appellant) *v Kvaerner Cementation Foundations* (Respondent) *and Bar Council* (Intervener) [2006] EWCA Civ 242.

54 *Smith* (Appellant) *v Kvaerner Cementation Foundations* (Respondent) *and Bar Council* (Intervener) [2006] EWCA Civ 242, [12] and [17].

55 *Taylor v Lawrence* [2002] EWCA Civ 90, [4].

judge's accountant, and elicited the information. This raises the question of whether this court ought to entertain an appeal based on material obtained in this way.

However that may be, the defendants did not know of the absence of an invoice until after the Court of Appeal's first decision. The case is not distinguishable from *Oberschlick v Austria* (No.1)[56] where it was 'not established that the applicant had waived his right to have his case determined by an "impartial" tribunal'.

The 'Fair-Minded and Informed' Observer

In *Taylor v Lawrence* we were also told:[57]

> The informed observer can be expected to be aware of the legal traditions and culture of this jurisdiction. [They] have played an important role in ensuring the high standards of integrity on the part of both the judiciary and the profession which happily still exist in this jurisdiction. Our experience over centuries is that this integrity is enhanced, not damaged, by the close relations that exist between the judiciary and the legal profession. Unlike some jurisdictions the judiciary here does not isolate itself from contact with the profession. Many examples of the traditionally close relationship can be given ...
>
> It is also accepted that barristers from the same chambers may appear before judges who were former members of their chambers or on opposite sides in the same case. This close relationship has not prejudiced but enhanced the administration of justice. The advantages in terms of improved professional standards which can flow from these practices have been recognised and admired in other jurisdictions.
>
> The informed observer will therefore be aware that in the ordinary way contacts between the judiciary and the profession should not be regarded as giving rise to a possibility of bias. On the contrary, they promote an atmosphere which is totally inimical to the existence of bias.

Whether any of this justifies the idea that solicitors should not charge for even nominal services to members of the judiciary must be uncertain. Lord Woolf's 'informed observer' is not an economist who often talks of the absence of 'a free lunch'.

Lord Hope explained in *Porter v Magill*:[58]

> Public perception of the possibility of unconscious bias is the key. It is unnecessary to delve into the characteristics to be attributed to the fair-minded and informed observer. What can confidently be said is that one is entitled to conclude that such an observer will adopt a balanced approach.

In *Lawal v Northern Spirit* Lord Steyn added:[59]

---

56 *Oberschlick v Austria* (No.), 23 May 1991.

57 *Taylor v Lawrence* [2002] EWCA Civ 90, [61]-[63].

58 *Porter v Magill* [2001] UKHL 67, [103].

59 *Lawal v Northern Spirit* [2003] UKHL 35, applied by Silber J in *R (on the application of PD) v West Midlands and North West Mental Health Review Tribunal* (Defendant) *and*

> What the public was content to accept many years ago is not necessarily acceptable in the world of today. The indispensable requirement of public confidence in the administration of justice requires higher standards today than was the case even a decade or two ago.

We may speculate that one reason why what was once acceptable is not now is that ours is a more venial age. Once we thought we could trust. Now we require clearer rules, preferably with no or limited discretion.[60] We have seen that there is an increased requirement that reasons be given for most types of decision. We noted that this increase took place at the same time as the courts redefined the meaning of the impartial judge. At that point we speculated that was is to increase the apparent fairness of a hearing. Now we can see it is also associated with this public confidence in the administration of justice.

Speaking of the modern informed observer, Lord Steyn continued, he 'may not be wholly uncritical of this culture. It is more likely ... he would be neither complacent nor unduly sensitive or suspicious'. As the ECtHR said in *Ferrantelli and Santangelo v Italy* and *Gautrin v France*:[61]

> When it is being decided whether in a given case there is a legitimate reason to fear that a particular body lacks impartiality, the standpoint of those claiming that it is not impartial is important but not decisive. What is decisive is whether the fear can be held to be objectively justified.

Even given the increased social and professional contacts that now take place between lawyers and with others, all this, of course, makes *Taylor v Lawrence* even less understandable.

More guidance on what the informed observer knows was given in *Gillies*. Lord Hope said:[62]

> The fair-minded and informed observer can be assumed to have access to all the facts that are capable of being known by members of the public generally, bearing in mind that it is the appearance that these facts give rise to that matters, not what is in the mind of the particular judge or tribunal member who is under scrutiny ... It is to be assumed too that he is able to distinguish between what is relevant and what is irrelevant, and that he is able when exercising his judgment to decide what weight should be given to the facts that are relevant.

In that case a tribunal member also worked for the Benefits Agency. Lord Hope continued:

Mersey Care NHS Trust (Interested Party) [2003] EWHC 2469, esp [16]. The House repeated this view of change in the idea of fairness in *R v H* [2004] UKHL 3, [11]. The quotation is from Kirby J in *Johnson v Johnson* (2000) 201 CLR 488, 509 (Para. 53).

60 Which explains why the House of Lords held in *Gillies v Secretary of State for Work and Pensions* [2006] UKHL 2 that bias is a question of law and not discretion.

61 *Ferrantelli and Santangelo v Italy*, 7 August 1996; *Gautrin v France*, 20 May 1998.

62 *Gillies v Secretary of State for Work and Pensions* [2006] UKHL 2, [6], [18]-[19].

> Her relationship with the Benefits Agency was as an independent expert adviser. Her advice was sought and given because of the skills that she was able to bring to bear on medical issues in the exercise of her professional judgment. A fair-minded observer who had considered the facts properly would appreciate that professional detachment and the ability to exercise her own independent judgment on medical issues lay at the heart of her relationship with the Agency. He would also appreciate that she was just as capable of exercising those qualities when sitting as the medical member of a disability appeal tribunal ... The fair-minded observer would understand that there is a crucial difference between approaching the issues which the tribunal had to decide with a predisposition in favour of the views of the [examining medical practitioner], and drawing upon her medical knowledge and experience when testing those views against the other evidence. He would appreciate, looking at the matter objectively, that her knowledge and experience could cut both ways as she would be just as well placed to spot weaknesses in these reports as to spot their strengths.

He concluded: 'The fact is that the bringing of experience to bear when examining evidence and reaching a decision upon it has nothing whatever to do with bias.' Baroness Hale added:

> [a] relevant fact of tribunal life is that professional people are often called upon to adjudicate upon disputes concerning exactly the same sort of decisions that they regularly make in their own professional practice.

She said:

> The 'fair minded and informed observer' is probably not an insider (i.e. another member of the same tribunal system). Otherwise she would run the risk of having the insider's blindness to the faults that outsiders can so easily see. But she is informed. She knows the relevant facts. And she is fair minded.

In *Sinclair Roche and Temperley v Heard the EAT* considered whether it should remit a case to the same or a different tribunal. It said:[63]

> The appellate tribunal will, in our view, ordinarily consider that, in the absence of clear indications to the contrary, it should be assumed that the tribunal below is capable of a professional approach to dealing with the matter on remission. By professionalism, we mean not only the general competence and integrity of the members as they go about their business, but also their experience and ability in doing that business in accordance with the statutory framework and the guidance of the higher courts.

More specific illustrations have been given in two cases. In *Diennet v France*, by a majority the ECtHR held that the Conseil d'Etat can remit a case to a tribunal which has previously heard it.[64] But in *P* (a barrister) *v General Council of the Bar Visitors* (Inns of Ct) a lay representative who was a member of the Professional Conduct

---

63 *Sinclair Roche and Temperley v Heard* [2004] IRLR 763, [46].

64 *Diennet v France*, 26 September 1995.

and Complaints Committee of the Bar Council sat as a panel member at a Visitors Tribunal hearing. The court said:[65]

> [The question] whether there is in this case a sufficient appearance of independence ... depends on the extent of the information which it may be assumed is in the possession of the outside observer and in particular whether it is to be assumed that he will be aware of the method of selection of members of the PCCC to serve on the visitors panel and of the infrequency of actual attendance at PCCC meetings by its lay members.

And later:

> [The *Locabail*] approach suggests that the observer is not to be assumed to have access to precisely the same scope of information as would be available to a court or tribunal seized of the issue whether an inference of actual bias should be drawn. The reason for the more limited scope of knowledge ... is that what matters is the public perspective and not the perspective of an investigative judge or tribunal which has gone behind the scenes to evaluate circumstances which would be invisible to the outside observer: see the closing words of the passage – 'there should be no risk that the courts will not ensure both that justice is done and that it is perceived by the public to be done'.

There is indeed a difficulty. If the informed observer knows all the background, there can never be a finding of objective, as opposed to subjective, bias. The state of mind of the observer is not what he or she would think if fully informed. Rather, it is what the observer would think assuming that he or she has, in Lord Hope's words 'access to all the facts that are capable of being known by members of the public generally' and in Lady Hale's phrase does not have 'the insider's blindness'.

Partiality as an Irregularity: Waiver

Judicial partiality is a species of procedural irregularity. As Parke B put it in *Dimes*:

> In answer to the ... question proposed by your Lordships, I have to state the unanimous opinion of the Judges, that ... the order or decree of the Lord Chancellor was not absolutely void, on account of his interest, but voidable only.

But as Lord Browne-Wilkinson said in *Pinochet* (No.2) where there is an interest impartiality cannot be presumed unless there is 'sufficient disclosure'. Thus, unlike other rights in Art. 6, a party can waive the right to an impartial tribunal. The position is similar to other types of unfairness. In *Stansbury v Datapulse*, where the fact (on the balance of probabilities) that one member of a judicial panel was drunk or asleep for part of a hearing and the civil proceedings were unfair. The Court of Appeal reasoned, although it may be desirable to do so:[66]

---

65 *P* (a barrister) *v General Council of the Bar Visitors (Inns of Ct)* 24 January 2005.

66 *Stansbury v Datapulse* [2003] EWCA Civ 1951, followed in *Fordyce v Hammersmith and Fulham Conservative Association* [2006] All ER (D) 10 (February). We may note that this provides a different test from the criminal law, where the issue for an appeal court is not

> It would be plainly unrealistic to on the grounds of practicality and sensibility to expect a complaint to made at the time of the alleged injustice. An applicant should not become have been to raise a grievance where in the circumstances it would have been unreasonable.

More generally, in cases of possible judicial partiality, practicality requires two things: first that the judge discloses matters which might indicate bias and, secondly, that to continue to litigate after knowledge has been acquired is to waive the objection.[67] The basic principle is that waiver requires that the person who is said to have waived[68] 'has acted freely and in full knowledge of the facts'. As Lord Bingham said in *Davidson v Scottish Ministers* (No.2):[69]

> It is not unusual for a judge, at the outset of a hearing, to mention a previous activity or association which could not, properly understood, form the basis of any reasonable apprehension of lack of impartiality. Provided it is not carried to excess, this practice is not to be discouraged, since it may obviate the risk of misunderstanding, misrepresentation or misreporting after the hearing. It is also routine for judges, before or at the outset of a hearing, to disclose a previous activity or association which would or might provide the basis for a reasonable apprehension of lack of impartiality. It is very important that proper disclosure should be made in such cases, first, because it gives the parties an opportunity to object and, secondly, because the judge shows, by disclosure, that he or she has nothing to hide and is fully conscious of the factors which might be apprehended to influence his or her judgment. When such disclosure is made, it is unusual for an objection to be taken ... There are of course a number of entirely honourable reasons why a judge may not make disclosure in a case which appears to call for it, among them forgetfulness, failure to recognize the relevance of the previous involvement to the current issue or failure to appreciate how the matter might appear to a fair-minded and informed observer who has considered the facts but lacks the detailed knowledge and self-knowledge of the judge.

---

whether a conviction is unfair, but whether it is safe. Thus, in *R v Moringiello* [1997] Crim. L.Rev. 902 the court said:

> If an allegation of this nature is to be made against a judge and it is a serious allegation to make, it must be raised at the time so that minds can be concentrated there and then on the accuracy or otherwise of the allegation. In addition the allegations must be specific, so it can be known what parts of the evidence it is said the judge failed to note, or failed to sum-up to the jury. Then it may be possible to discover whether in fact any prejudice was caused at all. Because it does not follow because a judge is asleep that prejudice has been caused at all. What is vital is that a judge should sum-up the case fairly to the jury and put the evidence in summary form comprehensively before them.

Everything depends on the circumstances. Thus, where a tribunal member dies (or, we can say, becomes incapacitated) during a hearing and much of the evidence is in writing, it may be possible to carry on, *R (on the application of Hitch) v Oliver QC* [2005] EWHC 291 (Admin).

67 *Times Newspapers v Singh* [1999] All ER (D) 1456; *Thyssen Canada v Mariana Maritime* [2005] EWHC 219 (Comm).

68 Lord Browne-Wilkinson in *R v Bow Street Magistrate, ex p Pinochet* (No.2) [2000] 1 AC 119, 137.

69 *Davidson v Scottish Ministers* (No. 2) [2004] UKHL 34, [19].

> However understandable the reasons for it, the fact of non-disclosure in a case which calls for it must inevitably colour the thinking of the observer.

Or as Lord Hope put it in the same case: 'Fairness requires that the quality of impartiality is there from the beginning, and a proper disclosure at the beginning is in itself a badge of impartiality.'

In *Locabail* the court said:[70]

> A party with an irresistible right to object to a judge hearing or continuing to hear a case may … waive his right to object. It is however clear that any waiver must be clear and unequivocal, and made with full knowledge of all the facts relevant to the decision whether to waive or not.

And in *Millar v Dickson* Lord Bingham observed:[71]

> In most litigious situations the expression 'waiver' is used to describe voluntary, informed and unequivocal election by a party not to claim a right or raise an objection which it is open to that party to claim or raise. In the context of entitlement to a fair hearing by an independent and impartial tribunal, such is in my opinion the meaning to be given to the expression.

In *Jones v DAS Legal Expenses Insurance* the court said:[72]

> we are a little uneasy about holding that Mr Jones was free to make his election when put to it on the first morning of the hearing. One cannot underestimate the daunting environment of the courtroom for litigants in person. Inevitably they are nervous. Their minds are bound to be totally focused upon that which they have rehearsed. The unexpected is difficult to deal with ... Given the way the matter was presented to him, he had little real choice. He had implicit faith in the tribunal, it never crossed his mind that they would not be impartial and we venture to think the overwhelming majority of those in his position would have succumbed as he did. We are left with the nagging doubt that Mr Jones was, and certainly feels that he was, hustled into acquiescing in the case continuing before that tribunal.

It went on:

> Waiver would never operate if 'full facts' meant each and every detail of factual information which diligent digging can produce. Full facts relevant to the decision to be taken must be confined to the essential facts. What is important is that the litigant should understand the nature of the case rather than the detail. It is sufficient if there is disclosed to him all he needs to know, which is invariably different from all he wants to know.

And:

---

70 *Locabail (UK) v Bayfield Properties* [2000] QB 431, 475.

71 *Millar v Dickson* [2001] UKPC D4.

72 *Jones v DAS Legal Expenses Insurance* [2003] EWCA Civ 1071.

> The courts must be assiduous in upholding the impartiality of its judges. Article 6 is a very powerful reinforcement of every litigant's ordinary expectation that in this country he will have a fair trial. Jealous as the court has to be to uphold that fundamental right, fairness to the other party demands that there has to be some end to ceaselessly searching for more and more information, sometimes only to fuel what has become or will become a litigant's obsession.

In *Smith v Kvaerner Cementation Foundations and Bar Council (Intervener)* the Recorder was head of the chambers of counsel both for the claimant and respondent. The Recorder was also quite often briefed by companies in the same group as the respondent. All this was declared at the outset of the hearing. The claimant's counsel advised his client that the apparent bias should be waived. The court said:[73]

> we do not think that it is part of counsel's duty or appropriate for counsel to seek to influence the decision to be taken by the lay client. The choice is the client's and, while it is proper for counsel to inform the client of the implications of the choice, it is not appropriate for counsel to urge the client to waive his right to object to the tribunal.

In *Ruddy v Procurator Fiscal*,[74] after the decision in *Starrs v Ruxton* in 1999, the applicants waited for that in *Millar v Dickson*, 2001. We come to both these decisions as we consider appointment and tenure. The appellants argued that, because the temporary sheriffs should not have sat, their sentences were void. Without citing *Dimes*, the Privy Council held that the sentences were voidable and that, because of the delay, they had acquiesced. As Lord Rodger said 'an effective remedy does not require to be kept open indefinitely'.

Nevertheless, in *Smith v Kvaerner Cementation* (in which *Ruddy* was not cited) the court said:[75]

> It is an important principle of the administration of justice that legal process should be finite. To reopen this case after a delay of four years plainly runs counter to that principle. But this is a case where Mr Smith has been denied the right to which Article 6 … entitled him – to a fair hearing before an independent and impartial tribunal. This, in our view, is the paramount consideration so far as the administration of justice is concerned … the Court of Appeal has far too many applications from litigants in person who pay no regard to advice from lawyers that their proposed appeals are wholly without merit. It should not be held against Mr Smith that, in the face of the discouragement that he received from all to whom he turned, he did not seek to pursue an appeal until, finally, he was advised that his case had merit.

---

73 *Smith* (Appellant) *v Kvaerner Cementation Foundations* (Respondent) *and Bar Council* (Intervener) [2006] EWCA Civ 242.

74 *Ruddy v Procurator Fiscal, Perth* [2006] UKPC D2.

75 *Smith* (Appellant) *v Kvaerner Cementation Foundations* (Respondent) *and Bar Council* (Intervener) [2006] EWCA Civ 242, [41], [48].

The Need for Temperate Language

Beyond partiality for interest, the most obvious example of partiality may be the expression of a prior view. We shall come to the constitutional question of what happens when a particular judge previously held executive or legislative office which affects a matter that later comes for his or her decision. Our concern here is with more mundane situations.

In Scotland in *Hoekstra v HM Advocate* (No.2) a judge wrote a flamboyant and negative newspaper article about the Human Rights Act itself. The court held he should not have sat on an appeal which involved the Convention:[76]

> In reaching this conclusion, we attach particular importance to the tone of the language and the impression which the author deliberately gives that his hostility to the operation of the Convention as part of our domestic law is both long-standing and deep-seated ... what judges cannot do with impunity is to publish either criticism or praise of such a nature or in such language as to give rise to a legitimate apprehension that, when called upon in the course of their judicial duties to apply that particular branch of the law, they will not be able to do so impartially.

In *Timmins v Gormley* the judge had criticised the CPR. The Court of Appeal said:[77]

> There is a long-established tradition that the writing of books and articles or the editing of legal textbooks is not incompatible with holding judicial office and the discharge of judicial functions ... It is the tone of ... opinions and the trenchancy with which they were expressed which is challenged here. Anyone writing in an area in which he sits judicially has to exercise considerable care not to express himself in terms which indicate that he has preconceived views which are so firmly held that it may not be possible for him to try a case with an open mind.

The kind of open mind required is exemplified by Megarry J in *Cordell v Second Clanfield Properties*:[78]

> Counsel cited a passage from the 3rd edition of Megarry and Wade's *Real Property*. It seems to me that words in a book written or subscribed to by an author who is or becomes a judge have the same value as words written by any other reputable author, neither more nor less. The process of authorship is entirely different from that of judicial decision. The author, no doubt, has the benefit of a broad and comprehensive survey of his chosen subject as a whole, together with a lengthy period of gestation, and intermittent opportunities for reconsideration. But he is exposed to the peril of yielding to preconceptions, and he lacks the advantage of that impact and sharpening of focus which the detailed facts of a particular case bring to the judge. Above all, he has to form his ideas without the aid of the purifying ordeal of skilled argument on the specific facts of a contested case. Argued law is tough law. This is as true today as it was in 1409 when Hankford J said: 'Home

76 *Hoekstra v HM Advocate* (No.2) 2000 SCCR 367, [23].

77 One of the appeals heard with *Locabail (UK) v Bayfield Properties* [2000] QB 451.

78 *Cordell v Second Clanfield Properties* [1969] 2 Ch 9.

> ne scaveroit de quel metal un campane fuit, si ceo ne fuit bien batu, quasi diceret, le ley per bon disputacion serra bien conus' (YB, 11 Hen 4, Mich, fo. 37).[79] I would, therefore, give credit to the words of any reputable author in book or article as expressing tenable and arguable ideas, as fertilisers of thought, and as conveniently expressing the fruits of research in print, often in apt and persuasive language. But I would do no more than that; and in particular I would expose those views to the testing and refining process of argument. Today, as of old, by good disputing shall the law be well known.

Nevertheless, even temperate but firm language may cause recusal.[80]

Recusal for Matters within the Case

It sometimes happens that a judge either at trial or on appeal learns some thing he or she should not know of, for example, the existence or size of a Part 36 offer (the former payment into court). In *Millensted v Grosvenor House (Park Lane)* the court said:[81]

> The purpose of the [rule] is obvious, it was made to prevent the premature disclosure of a fact which was not relevant to the issues to be tried, but the disclosure of which might prejudice one or more of the parties to the proceedings ... It is of course the duty of both judge and counsel to observe the rule, but what is to be done if the rule by inadvertence or otherwise is broken? In my judgment, this is in every case a matter for the trial judge to determine, having due regard to the object for which the rule was made.

Holding that this good law post-CPR, Dyson LJ said:[82] 'The problem of how a judge should deal with the improper disclosure of a Part 36 offer or payment is similar to that which arises where there has been an improper disclosure of without prejudice correspondence' and he cited Stanley Burnton J in *Berg v IML London* as saying:[83]

> The procedure of the court would be greatly hampered and the cost of litigation greatly increased if the court were too easily to come to the conclusion that the viewing of prejudicial irrelevant material necessarily disabled the court from continuing to hear the action.

If the judge is in doubt whether recusal is called for, one solution is to ask the parties. On the other hand, as the Court put it in *Taylor v Lawrence*:[84]

---

79 The Norman French translates as 'A man will not know of what metal a bell is made if it is not well rung, so, it is said, the law will be known through good argument'.

80 Lord Steyn did not sit in *A v Secretary of State for the Home Department* [2004] UKHL 56 because of objections based on previous writings. See his explanation, 'Deference: a tangled story', [2005] P.L 346, note 4.

81 *Millensted v Grosvenor House (Park Lane)* [1937] 1 KB 717.

82 *Garratt v Saxby* [2004] EWCA Civ 341, [19].

83 *Berg v IML London* [2002] 1 WLR 3271, 20.

84 *Taylor v Lawrence* [2002] EWCA Civ 90, [64].

Judges should be circumspect about declaring the existence of a relationship where there is no real possibility of it being regarded by a fair-minded and informed observer as raising a possibility of bias. If such a relationship is disclosed, it unnecessarily raises an implication that it could affect the judgment and approach of the judge. If this is not the position no purpose is served by mentioning the relationship.

In *Bahai v Rashidian* Donaldson MR said:[85]

The fact that a judge has determined the issues in an action and in so doing has expressed views on the conduct of the parties and of the witnesses, neither constitutes bias nor the appearance of bias in relation to subsequent applications in the action.

And Balcombe LJ added:

A judge properly exercising his judicial functions, e.g. by criticising the conduct of a party's solicitor in the course of his judgment on a matter which he considers relevant to his decision, cannot by that process be said to be biased. Bias is the antithesis of the proper exercise of a judicial function.

In *ex p Dallaglio* Bingham MR said:[86]

It not infrequently happens that judges find themselves called upon to criticise, sometimes in strong terms, parties or witnesses appearing before them. The subject of such criticisms are apt to complain that the judge was prejudiced or biased against them. But such criticisms will carry no weight for the appellate court provided the criticisms were based on material properly before the judge in that case and were not, in the light of that material, inappropriate. In such a case there is no element of extraneous prejudice or predilection and hence, in the eyes of the law, no question of bias.

More recently, in *Triodos Bank v Dobbs* Chadwick LJ said:[87]

It is always tempting for a judge against whom criticisms are made to say that he would prefer not to hear further proceedings in which the critic is involved. It is tempting to take that course because the judge will know that the critic is likely to go away with a sense of grievance if the decision goes against him. Rightly or wrongly, a litigant who does not have confidence in the judge who hears his case will feel that, if he loses, he has in some way been discriminated against. But it is important for a judge to resist the temptation to recuse himself simply because it would be more comfortable to do so. The reason is this. If judges were to recuse themselves whenever a litigant – whether it be a represented litigant or a litigant in person – criticised them (which sometimes happens not infrequently) we would soon reach the position in which litigants were able to select judges to hear their cases simply by criticising all the judges that they did not want to hear their cases.

---

85 *Bahai v Rashidian* [1985] 1 WLR 1337. And now see: *Amec Capital Projects v Whitefriars City Estates* [2004] EWCA Civ 1418; *Jones (T/A Shamrock Coaches) v Department of Transport Welsh Traffic Area* [2005] EWCA Civ 58.

86 *Re v Inner West London Coroner, ex p Dallaglio* [1994] 4 All ER 139.

87 *Triodos Bank v Dobbs* [2005] EWCA Civ 468, (Application for Stay of Appeal) [7].

Thus, in an *Australian* case, *Vakauta v Kelly*, in the course of a trial for personal injuries, the judge made intemperate remarks about the medical evidence. On appeal the court said:[88]

> It is inevitable that a judge who sits regularly to hear claims for damages for personal injury will form views about the reliability and impartiality of some medical experts who are frequently witnesses in his or her court. In some cases and notwithstanding the professional detachment of an experienced judge, it will be all but impossible to put such preconceived views entirely to one side in weighing the evidence of a particular medical expert. That does not, however, mean that the judge is disqualified from hearing the particular action or any other action involving that medical expert as a witness. The requirement of the reality and the appearance of impartial justice in the administration of the law by the courts is one which must be observed in the real world of actual litigation ... On the other hand, there is an ill-defined line beyond which the expression by a trial judge of preconceived views about the reliability of particular medical witnesses could threaten the appearance of impartial justice.

The *Phillips v Symes* litigation was tortuous and not always conducted with the co-operation required of modern litigants. In one of the reported cases the judge referred to two of the witnesses as 'rogues' and immediately withdrew the remark. On a complaint that he did not recuse himself, Waller LJ said:[89] 'Bias or apparent bias against a witness is as serious as bias or apparent bias against or in favour of a party' but these things must be taken in context. In another, an application was made for recusal because the judge was contemplating making a costs order against an expert witness whose evidence he had rejected. The application was refused.[90] Yet another was concerned an application to commit for contempt. Longmore LJ said:[91]

> It is occasionally necessary, after litigation against one defendant has begun, for proceedings to be brought against another defendant who has to be restrained from informing the first defendant of the existence of such second proceedings. If, in the course of such second proceedings, a judge learns something detrimental to the interests of the first defendant in his absence, it is (to say the least) a delicate question whether it can be appropriate for that same judge to continue hearing the first proceedings. This is a matter to which [the] claimants (who have instigated both sets of proceedings) and the judge must consider most carefully. There is no indication that the difficulty received the careful consideration which in this case it deserved.

It was an example of a very long standing problem of which Blackstone said is 'not agreeable to the genius of the common law'.[92]

88 *Vakauta v Kelly* (1989) 167 CLR 568.

89 *Phillips v Symes* [2003] EWCA Civ 1769, [75].

90 *Phillips v Symes* [2004] EWHC 2330 (Ch).

91 *Symes v Phillips* [2005] EWCA Civ 533, [61].

92 Blackstone, *Commentaries*, 16th edn (1825), Book IV, p. 287, cited by Lawton LJ in *Balogh v St. Albans Crown Court* [1975] QB 73.

Previous Litigation

Any problem of the judge being affected by previous litigation can arise either because he or she has made previous decisions or because he or she acted as counsel in some earlier stage of the same or one involving one or both of the same parties. In *Puolitaival v Finland* the court said:[93]

> Having regard in particular to the remoteness in time and subject matter of the first set of proceedings in relation to the second set and to the fact that [the judge's] functions as counsel and judge did not overlap in time, the Court finds that the applicants could not have entertained any objectively justified doubts as to [the judge's] impartiality.

On the other hand, in *Meznaric v Croatia* the judge (and later his daughter) acted at earlier stages in the same proceedings for the applicant's opponents.[94] The ECtHR held that the court did not have the appearance of impartiality.

A similar problem arises in relation to the Court of Appeal's Civil Division. There, applications for permission to appeal are first decided on the papers alone by a single Lord Justice. If permission is refused, the applicant has the right to an oral hearing. The question then arises, can the judge who refuses permission on paper sit either in the oral proceedings or, if permission is eventually granted, in the substantive appeal? In *Sengupta v Holmes Laws* LJ answered yes to both questions. He argued:[95]

> It is by no means infrequent that the first judge changes his mind on the renewed application, and sometimes where there is no new material; he is persuaded by the oral argument … [any reasonable and intelligent person possesses] a readiness to change one's mind upon some issue, whether upon new information or simply on further reflection, and to change it from a previously declared position … oral argument is perhaps the most powerful force there is, in our legal process, to promote a change of mind by a judge. That judges in fact change their minds under the influence of oral argument is not an arcane feature of the system; it is at the centre of it.

He made no mention of the Practice Direction to Part 52 which, in paragraph 4.13, expressly provides that the oral hearing may be before the same judge. Nor did he discuss s. 56(1) of the (renamed) Senior Courts Act 1981 which says:

> No judge shall sit as a member of the civil division of the Court of Appeal on the hearing of, or shall determine any application in proceedings incidental or preliminary to, an appeal from a judgment or order made in any case by himself or by any court of which he was a member.

---

93 *Puolitaival v Finland*, 23 November 2004.

94 *Meznaric v Croatia*, 15 July 2005.

95 *Sengupta v Holmes* [2002] EWCA Civ 1104, [29], [36], following *Khreino v Khreino* (No.1) (constitution of court) [2000] 1 FCR. And see *Umair v Umair* 2002 SC 153.

The section echoes *Oberschlick v Austria* (No.1).[96] It may be said that the refusal of permission is neither a judgment nor an order so the section does not apply. However, the provision is clearly aimed at apparent as well as actual bias. Even in the face of the Practice Direction, it is unlikely that the informed lay observer would appreciate that technical distinction.

More recently, the ECtHR said in *Indra v Slovakia*:[97]

> Regard must be had to the fact that both the original proceedings and the [subsequent] proceedings referred to the same set of facts. Furthermore, [they] ... could entail in some way reconsideration of the judicial decisions taken in the original proceedings ... It could, in the Court's opinion, have raised legitimate fears in the applicant that judge S would not approach his case with the requisite impartiality. In the Court's view, these circumstances serve objectively to justify the applicant's apprehension that judge S of the Supreme Court lacked the necessary impartiality.

Constitutional Dimensions – The Separation of Powers

There is one variety of partiality for interest that it is convenient to consider separately: we may call it constitutional partiality. Allegations sometimes arise out of either the manner of a judge's appointment or tenure or some prior legislative involvement. I shall argue that it also includes some administrative or organizational problems. It is rare indeed that the issue turns on actual bias or even a real possibility of bias. Constitutional partiality is about appearances. The ECtHR put it in *De Cubber v Belgium* and has repeated in many cases:[98]

> The personal impartiality of a judge is to be presumed until there is proof to the contrary ... However ... account must also be taken of considerations relating to the functions exercised and to internal organisation (the objective approach). In this regard, even appearances may be important; in the words of the English maxim quoted in, for example, *Delcourt*, 'justice must not only be done: it must also be seen to be done' ... What is at stake is the confidence which the courts in a democratic society must inspire in the public.

The considerations we have seen as regards partiality generally are applied in an exaggerated form and commonly with grand language. As early as 1984, in *Campbell and Fell v UK*, the Court said:[99]

96 *Oberschlick v Austria* (No.1), 23 May 1991.

97 *Indra v Slovakia*, 1 February 2005, [53]-[54].

98 *De Cubber v Belgium*, 26 October 1984, [25]-[26].

99 *Campbell and Fell v UK*, 28 June 1984, [78]. And see, e.g. *Findlay v UK*, 25 February 1997, [73], quoted by Lord Bingham in *R v Spear*; *R v Saunby* [2002] UKHL 31, [8]; and, *Morris v UK*, 26 February 2002.

> In determining whether a body can be considered to be 'independent' – notably of the executive and of the parties to the case the Court has had regard to the manner of appointment of its members and the duration of their term of office, the existence of guarantees against outside pressures and the question whether the body presents an appearance of independence.

And in *Belilos v Switzerland* it emphasized that[100] 'a number of considerations relating to the functions exercised and to internal organisation are relevant too; even appearances may be important'. In *Findlay v UK* it said:[101]

> The tribunal must ... be impartial from an objective viewpoint, that is, it must offer sufficient guarantees to exclude any legitimate doubt in this respect ... The concepts of independence and objective impartiality are closely linked.

Previous Legislative Involvement

Independence, and its appearance, is important to the modern law. As we have seen it is also novel. In *Gillies*, Baroness Hale said:

> Impartiality is not the same as independence, although the two are closely linked. Impartiality is the tribunal's approach to deciding the cases before it. Independence is the structural or institutional framework which secures this impartiality, not only in the minds of the tribunal members but also in the perception of the public.

It might have been thought that once a judge has satisfied the requirements as to appointment and tenure, it could be said that there is a sufficient guarantee of independence. So also, we have seen that a judge is entitled to express opinions either professionally or in articles or books on matters that he or she is called upon to adjudicate. As Lord Bingham explained in *Davidson v Scottish Ministers* (No.2):[102]

> Over time, of course, judges acquire a track record, and experienced advocates may be able to predict with more or less accuracy how a particular judge is likely to react to a given problem. Since judges are not automata this is inevitable, and presenting a case in the way most likely to appeal to a particular tribunal is a skill of the accomplished advocate. But adherence to an opinion expressed judicially in an earlier case does not of itself denote a lack of open-mindedness; and there are few experienced judges who have not, on fresh argument applied to new facts in a later case, revised an opinion expressed in an earlier. In practice, as the cases show, problems of apparent bias do not arise where a judge is invited to revisit a question on which he or she has expressed a previous judicial opinion, which must happen in any developed system.

---

100 *Belilos v Switzerland*, 29 April 1988, [66]-[67]. And see *Wettstein v Switzerland*, 21 December 2000, [44].

101 *Findlay v UK*, 25 February 1997, [73].

102 *Davidson v Scottish Ministers* (No.2) [2004] UKHL 34, [10].

It is then with some surprise that we find a line of cases both at Strasbourg and in Britain where challenges based on the previous legislative activity of a judge have been successful. Typical of the older thinking is the *Australian* case, *Kartinyeri v Commonwealth of Australia.* An unsuccessful application had been made for the judge to recuse himself because among other things he had, previously as a practising lawyer, given advice and assistance in connection with legislation the constitutionality of which he was called upon to determine. He concluded his decision with these words:[103]

> The most important factors are that there were no issues of fact or credibility involved in any advice that I gave, that the issues in this case are exclusively legal ones and, that I played no part at all in drafting, advocating or in any way implementing the legislation that the court has to consider.

The judge treated his advice on legislation as no different from any other advice given by a practising lawyer turned judge.

The watershed came in 1995 in *Procola v Luxembourg*. The ECtHR said:[104]

> The Court notes that four members of the *Conseil d'État* carried out both advisory and judicial functions in the same case. In the context of an institution such as Luxembourg's *Conseil d'État* the mere fact that certain persons successively performed these two types of function in respect of the same decisions is capable of casting doubt on the institution's structural impartiality.

In 2000, in *McGonnell v UK*,[105] there was a challenge to the Bailiff of Guernsey in a planning case where he had previously, as Deputy Bailiff, presided over the States of Deliberation at the adoption of a regulation he was required to interpret by way of adjudication. The Court reasoned:

> Neither Article 6 nor any other provision of the Convention requires States to comply with any theoretical constitutional concepts as such ... the Court is faced solely with the question whether the Bailiff had the required 'appearance' of independence, or the required 'objective' impartiality ... the Court considers that any direct involvement in the passage of legislation, or of executive rules, is likely to be sufficient to cast doubt on the judicial impartiality of a person subsequently called on to determine a dispute over whether reasons exist to permit a variation from the wording of the legislation or rules at issue.

McGonnell was most directly followed in *Thaler v Austria*, where the Court argued:[106]

---

103 *Kartinyeri v Commonwealth of Australia* (1998) 156 ADELAIDE LR 300 [38].

104 *Procola v Luxembourg*, 28 September 1995, [45].

105 *McGonnell v UK*, 8 February 2000, [51], [55].

106 *Thaler v Austria*, 3 February 2005, [33]. It followed the Commission in *Hortolomei v Austria*, 16 April 1998:

> Situations falling short of the direct involvement of a member of a tribunal in the subject matter to be decided may give rise to legitimate doubts as regards that tribunal's independence and impartiality.

McGonnell has had far reaching effects on the British legal system. The Lord Chancellor has not sat as a judge since the decision.[107] *McGonnell* was followed in *Davidson v Scottish Ministers* (No.2).[108] The Lord Advocate piloted the Scotland Bill in the House of Lords, advising the House on the effect of the Crown Proceedings Act 1947 on the remedies which might be available to the courts in Scotland against the Scottish Ministers. Later he became a judge in Scotland – a career pattern that used to be very common in England. He sat on an appeal involving those remedies. The passage from Lord Bingham in *Davidson* just given continues 'but problems are liable to arise where the exercise of judicial functions is preceded by the exercise of legislative functions'. Although he cited *Procola* and *McGonnell* there is little to explain this rider. In effect Blom-Cooper's complaint is about this 'but'. Lord Bingham later amplified it:

> A risk of apparent bias is liable to arise where a judge is called upon to rule judicially on the effect of legislation which he or she has drafted or promoted during the parliamentary process.

Lord Woolf said:

> The impartiality here could be said to have the 'structural' quality referred to in a different context in the judgment in *Procola* ... [But] If [he] was acting in a personal capacity or stating an opinion as to the desirability of the legislation and not as to its effect, the outcome could be different.

Lord Hope added:

> The word 'bias' is used as a convenient shorthand ... The essence of it is captured in the Convention concept of impartiality ... But the concept is wider than that. It includes an inclination or predisposition to decide the issue only one way, whatever the strength of the contrary argument. A doubt as to whether this is the case is enough, so long as it can be justified objectively.

---

where the assessors were nominated by and had close links with the bodies which had concluded the guidelines challenged in that case. It found that the applicant could legitimately fear that the assessors – notwithstanding their five year terms of office and formal independence of the executive – had a common interest contrary to his own and therefore that the balance of interests, inherent in the sending of representatives of the medical profession and the Health Insurance Boards in other cases, was liable to be upset in his case.

107 See *Hansard*, HL vol.610, WA 33, 23 February 2000; *Hansard*, HL vol.614, Col 419, 22 June 2000.

108 *Davidson v Scottish Ministers* (No.2) [2004] UKHL 34.

The decisions are not all one way. In 2006, in *Kearney v Her Majesty*'s *Advocate* no question of recusal arose. Lord Hope said:[109]

> It was not until ... I [became] Lord President that the necessary legislation to permit [temporary judges] was introduced. I have to confess that I bear much of the responsibility for the way the system was introduced and for the way in which, before the coming into force of the Scotland Act 1998, it was operated.

The Lord President is a judge not a minister. Lord Hope was referring not to policy decisions he made, but to negotiations he conducted. The difference is difficult to understand. Generally, the role of Law Officers in legislation (and much else) is not to promote policy. It is to advise government and parliament on the law. Policy is for ministers outside the Law Officers' Department. If both *Davidson* and *Kearney* are good law, prior activity mainly as an adviser creates a risk of apparent bias but bargaining over policy change does not. *Pinochet* (No.2) is indeed a fading memory.

We have seen that Lord Browne-Wilkinson was wrong in *Pinochet* (No.2) to say of *Dimes* that there was 'no inquiry as to the circumstances which led to Lord Cottenham LC sitting'. In fact, as the report makes clear, Lord Cottenham sat because a decision of the Vice-Chancellor could not take effect unless the Lord Chancellor decided to enrol it. A merely formal executive act would not have disqualified him. The distinction has been followed but not referred to in a number of cases. Thus, in *Panton v Minister of Finance* the Attorney General certified that there was no legal objection to the Governor-General assenting to an Act of the Jamaican Parliament. Later he became a judge and there was a challenge to the legislation he certified. On behalf of the Privy Council Lord Clyde explained:[110]

> The constitutionality of the legislation can hardly be described as a cause to which the judge was party. The certification falls far short of equating him with the second respondent so as to make him a champion of the constitutionality of the measure. He had no financial or proprietary interest in the outcome ...
>
> A judicial decision will also be focussed upon a particular issue and be reached after consideration of arguments presented for and against a particular proposition ... The certification by the Attorney General on the other hand ... is made without consideration being directed to any particular element of the legislation and on a pro forma which does not envisage reasoning or justification, although it will of course be made responsibly and honestly ... the independence of a judge is not to be affected by the fact that in a previous incarnation or even in his current capacity he has expressed a view on a point of law. It is not to be thought that a judge will have such mental allegiance to his earlier views or such lack of integrity as to be unable to approach the question with an open mind or to be embarrassed at the prospect of revising or rejecting the view which he had earlier expressed.

---

109 At [29]-[30].

110 *Panton v Minister of Finance* [2001] UKPC 33. It is notable that Lord Hoffmann was a member of the Board.

He concluded:

> It has also to be recognized that the purity of principle may require to give way to the exigencies and realities of life. In extreme cases the doctrine of necessity may require a judge to determine an issue even although he would otherwise be disqualified ... But at a less extreme level it is right that account should be taken in assessing the independence of a judge of the likely responsibilities and interests which he or she will invariably have had during the course of a professional career which has preceded a judicial appointment. In those countries where there is not an exclusively career judiciary judges are likely to have held offices or appointments in which they may have given public expression to particular points of view. This will necessarily be so where the career has involved an engagement in political life.

So also in *Pabla Ky v Finland*[111] an expert member of the Court of Appeal of Helsinki was concurrently a member of Parliament. The ECtHR said there was not 'any indication that [he] played any role in respect of the legislation which was in issue in the case':

> The only issue is whether due to his position as a member of the legislature his participation cast legitimate doubt on the objective or structural impartiality of the court which decided the applicant company's appeal … [He] had not exercised any prior legislative, executive or advisory function in respect of the subject matter or legal issues before the Court of Appeal.

By a majority the court concluded any fear as to lack of independence and impartiality could not be regarded as being objectively justified.

The decision in *Pabla Ky* was given after argument in *Davidson* but the House was able to consider it. Lord Hope said:

> Applied to our own constitutional arrangements, *Pabla Ky v Finland* teaches us that there is no fundamental objection to members of either House of Parliament serving, while still members of the House, as members of a court. Arguments based on the theory of the separation of powers alone will not suffice. It all depends on what they say and do in Parliament and how that relates to the issue which they have to decide as members of that tribunal.

In *Meerabux v Attorney General of Belize*[112] the appellant was former justice of the Supreme Court of Belize. He was removed from office by the Governor-General on the advice of the Belize Advisory Council following complaints of misbehaviour filed by the Bar Association of Belize and by an attorney in law. The Belize judge who heard the appeal was a member of the Bar Association because membership was compulsory. Lord Hope adopted a distinction between mere membership of

111 *Pabla Ky v Finland*, 22 June 2004.

112 *Meerabux v Attorney General of Belize* [2005] UKPC 12.

an association and active involvement drawn by Feldman.[113] The Belize judge was entitled to hear the case.

Much of this case law concerning both with appointment and tenure with and prior legislative involvement is startling. It sits uneasily with Lord Woolf's idea of the 'informed observer' who knows our legal culture. On the contrary, some of this case law has already changed the way we do things. Much goes further and provides challenges to some of our constitutional arrangements. More change may be required.

Independence

Independence of the judiciary is of course a commonplace demand of our constitutional arrangements. Like so much else its meaning is being transformed in the modern era. The questions are always how independent and independent of what. The remainder of this chapter explores issues relating to discussions among judges, appointment and tenure, listing and other administrative considerations, the funding of the system of civil justice and the making of rules for civil procedure.

Discussions

It is commonplace that benches of more than one judge often, probably usually, maybe virtually always, even where they are not reserved, discuss the decision before giving their judgments. What is less common is the kind of practice that Wall LJ described in *Re O (Children)*:[114]

> As it relates in part to the guidance issued by the Office of the President of the Family Division relating … we have taken the opportunity to show it in draft to the President, who has authorised us to say that in so far as it amplifies that guidance, he is in full agreement with it, and in particular with [124]-[138].

Also unusual is the kind of remark Lord Hope made in *Ruddy v Procurator Fiscal*:[115]

> The Board has had the advantage in this case of being able to draw not only upon Lord Rodgers long experience both as a Law Officer and as Lord Justice General but also upon the depth and quality of his legal scholarship. The benefits of our being able to conduct

---

113 Feldman, *English Public Law* (2004), para. 15.76, citing *Leeson v General Council of Medical Education and Registration* (1889) 43 Ch.D. 366 and *Allinson v General Council of Medical Education and Registration* [1894] 1 QB 750. He also cited Shetreet, *Judges on Trial* (1976), p. 310.

114 *Re O* (*children*): *Re* W-*R* (*a child*): *Re W* (*children*) [2005] EWCA Civ 759, 1. See Guidance issued by the Office of the President of the Family Division relating to McKenzie Friends [2005] Fam Law 405.

115 *Ruddy v Procurator Fiscal, Perth* [2006] UKPC D2, [5] and [6].

> this exercise under his guidance are plain to see ... Venturing into the areas of law that Lord Rodger has revealed to us is not an exercise for the uninitiated.

On one level, this is no more than generous and graceful. On another it sits uncomfortably with the discussion of the supposed fears of the fair-minded and informed observer in *Davidson v Scottish Ministers* (No.2). Maybe, as with *Starrs*, there is a retreat. Maybe, *Davidson* will come to be seen as having exaggerated the risk of bias.

In Canada, in *R v Beauregard Dickson* CJ noted that threats to individual independence can come from different sources:[116]

> The generally accepted core of the principle of judicial independence has been the complete liberty of individual judges to hear and decide the cases that come before them; no outsider – be it government, pressure group, individual or even another judge – should interfere in fact, or attempt to interfere, with the way a judge conducts his or her case and makes his or her decision.

So also in *Clancy v Caird* Lord Sutherland said:[117]

> It would, of course, be improper for any one member of the judiciary to attempt to influence another member of the judiciary as to the latter's decision-making process in any particular case.

It is doubtful if these statements should be taken literately. In all professional life, within and without the law, decisions have to be made and those charged with making them often consult their colleagues. It is unthinkable that it is improper to do so, or for those colleagues to offer advice. That advice may influence a decision. What may be improper is for the colleague to volunteer the advice, or to fail to recognize that the decision is for the decision-maker, or otherwise use pressure to influence what is decided. At least in the modern era, the kind of letter sent by Lord Simon LC to Lord Atkin before judgment in *Liversidge v Anderson* is unacceptable.[118] Having seen a draft of Lord Atkin's speech, he wrote:

> My eye catches your very amusing citation from Lewis Carol. Do you really, on final reflection, think this is necessary? I fear that it may be regarded as wounding to your colleagues who take the view you satirize, and I feel sure you would not willingly seek to hold them up to ridicule. I am all in favour of enlivening judgments with literary allusion but I would venture (greatly daring I know) to ask you whether the paragraph should be retained. Of course it is entirely for you. But I have gained so much from occasional suggestions of yours (mostly, it is true, in cases when we have been sitting together) and

116 *R v Beauregard* [1986] 2 SCR 56 (SCC), p. 69.

117 *Clancy v Caird*, 2000 SC 441, 2000 SCLR 526.

118 See Lewis, *Lord Atkin*, 1983, p. 139, and Jacob, 'I guidici inglesi', in *Magistrati e Potere nella Storia Europea*, Romanelli (ed.) ('The Modern British Judicial System in Historical Perspective', in *Magistrates and Power in Modern Europe*, Romanelli (ed.)), European University Institute, Florence, 1996.

> I trust you will forgive this query. I at any rate feel that neither the dignity of the House, nor the collaboration of colleagues, nor the force of your reasoning would suffer from the omission.

So also the approach by the Lord Chancellor, Lord Simonds. To Goddard LCJ and Lord Greene MR in 1953 concerning the application of Crown privilege (PII)[119] is surprising even for its time. The attempt was to persuade them to persuade the judges to modify their approach.[120]

It might be thought that these examples are from a different era. The third example where the Lord Chancellor may have sought to influence a judge is after the emergence of the cost consciousness of our own age. According to the press accounts,[121] the President of the Employment Appeals Tribunal, a High Court judge, was interpreting a rule on the basis that some people appealing against industrial tribunal decisions had a statutory right to argue their cases in person at preliminary hearings. To deny this would be unfair because many appeals were prepared without legal help. Lord Mackay LC, both in conversation and in correspondence, told him this was a waste of time and money, and that many appeals should be dismissed from written submissions only, as 'hopeless cases'. This was happening in Scotland. In consultation with his colleagues, the judge gave a reasoned response. The Lord Chancellor's reply included the following:[122]

> I ask you again for your immediate assurance … that preliminary hearings are not being used where no jurisdiction is shown in a notice of appeal.

He added: 'If you do not feel you can give me that assurance, I must ask you to consider your position.'

Three months later, the judge resigned, but we are told, not because of this dispute. In a debate in the House of Lords, Lord Mackay said[123] 'I utterly repudiate that I wrongfully interfered with the independence of the judiciary or misled your Lordships at any time'. But, he said: 'I am extremely sorry if I caused any offence whatsoever to [the judge]. If I could have used better language, with hindsight, I would have used it.' Lord Mackay maintained his view that 'the basic matter was one on which he was entitled to ask the judge for assurances that he was applying the rules as laid down by Parliament, in view of a two-year backlog of cases'.

These are all examples of the Lord Chancellor seeking to influence decisions in which he was not sitting. Indeed, they are each probably examples of attempted

---

119 See above p. 173 et seq.

120 PRO LCO2/3367, discussed in Jacob, 'From Privileged Crown to Interested Public', [1993] Public Law 121.

121 The most helpful is Purchas, 'Lord Mackay and the Judiciary', (1994) NLJ, Vol.144, 527.

122 Letter of 19 March 1993. See also *The Observer*, 6 March 1994. Much of what follows is taken from the ensuing debate in the House of Lords, *Hansard*, Off. Rep., 5th series, HL, 27 April 1994, cols.751–804.

123 *Hansard*, Off Rep, 5th series, HL, 27 April 1994, cols.791–804.

executive pressure on the judiciary. Of themselves they go some way to justify the decision in the Constitutional Reform Act to separate the judiciary from the Lord Chancellor. There is nothing in the Act, however, that makes it less likely that senior members of the judiciary may not lean on more junior colleagues.

Appointment and tenure

In *Starrs v Ruxton* the challenge was to the mode of appointment and tenure of temporary sheriffs in Scotland. The commission was for 1 year at a time and the executive had power of recall before then. The challenge was made before the conclusion of the trial. In *Millar v Dickson*[124] the legality of the system was again in issue. Here the challenge was made after the trial. The Privy Council took the opportunity to state or restate some basic propositions. Lord Bingham said: 'There are few, if any, Convention rights of more practical importance to the citizen than the right to a fair trial ... [It] should not ... be weakened or diluted, whatever the administrative consequences.' Lord Hope continued the theme:

> Central to the rule of law in a modern democratic society is the principle that the judiciary must be, and must be seen to be, independent of the executive ... [writing extra-judicially] Lord Fraser identified[125] security of tenure and immunity from suit as the two most important ways of ensuring that judges perform their duties impartially and without fear of the consequences. Of these, security of tenure is the more vulnerable to erosion at the hands of the executive.

Lord Clyde was only a little more measured:

> Judicial independence is of fundamental constitutional importance. It is an indispensable condition for the preservation of the rule of law. It is a principle which has been stoutly protected by the Scottish judges for centuries.[126] We are fortunate in this country that for a very considerable length of time this principle has never been lost, although through the annals of history there may have been times when its light burned less brightly. But the complaisance which such a situation can inspire should never allow it to be forgotten that the principle is not so robust that it can always withstand the pressures which some forms of government may impose upon it.

Crucially, the decision in *Starrs v Ruxton* was accepted by the prosecution and was not open to challenge before the House. Nevertheless, Lord Bingham quoted it extensively and with no sign of disapproval:

---

124 *Millar v Dickson* [2001] UKPC D4.

125 Title on Constitutional Law in The Laws of Scotland, *Stair Memorial Encyclopaedia*, vol.5 (1987), paras. 663–667.

126 He cited Mitchell, *Constitutional Law*, 2nd edn (1968), p. 261.

> The Lord Justice-Clerk drew attention in particular to the fact that temporary sheriffs were appointed for one year only and were subject to recall during that period at the instance of the Lord Advocate, perhaps without the possibility of challenge.

And quoting the Lord Justice-Clerk directly:

> Rather than a control over numbers, the use of the one-year term suggests a reservation of control over the tenure of office by the individual, enabling it to be brought to an end within a comparatively short period. This reinforces the impression that the tenure of office by the individual temporary sheriff is at the discretion of the Lord Advocate … I consider that there is a real risk that a well-informed observer would think that a temporary sheriff might be influenced by his hopes and fears as to his [prospective] advancement.

And this from Lord Reed:

> Judicial independence can be threatened not only be interference by the Executive, but also by a judge's being influenced, consciously or unconsciously, by his hopes and fears as to his possible treatment by the Executive. It is for that reason that a judge must not be dependent on the Executive, however well the Executive may behave: 'independence' connotes the absence of 'dependence'.

There has been, however, a retreat from Starrs, 1999. We have noted that in *Ruddy v Procurator Fiscal* even where a temporary sheriff should not have sat the doctrine of acquiescence can apply. Before getting to other aspects of these moves away from *Starrs* it is convenient to look at what has been said both at Strasbourg and in Canada where there has been much discussion of judicial independence. In *Stieringer v Germany* the Commission said:[127]

> It is the purpose of the requirement in Article 6(1) that courts shall be 'established by law' that the judicial organisation in a democratic society must not depend on the discretion of the Executive, but that it should be regulated by law emanating from Parliament. However [the] Article does not require the legislature to regulate every detail in this area by a formal Act of Parliament if the legislature establishes at least the organisational framework for the judicial organisation ... What is at stake is the confidence which the courts in a democratic society must inspire in the public.

But:

> Recourse to judges who, considering the possibility of their dismissal during the probationary period, do not fully benefit from the guarantee of personal independence must remain the exception, namely if a necessity to train judges or other imperative reasons, such as reinforcing courts, exist.

On the other hand, it said in *Steck-Risch v Liechtenstein*:[128]

127 *Stieringer v Germany*, 25 November 1996.
128 *Steck-Risch v Liechtenstein*, 19 May 2005, [39].

> The Court notes ... that the complaint is to be seen against the background of a part-time judiciary operating in a small country like Liechtenstein, where the same persons perform double functions as judges, on the one hand, and as practicing lawyers, on the other. The Court has no reason to doubt that legislation and practice on the part-time judiciary can be framed so as to be compatible with Article 6.

In Canada, in *R v Généreux* Lamer CJC said:[129]

> The independence of a tribunal is to be determined on the basis of the objective status of that tribunal. This objective status is revealed by an examination of the legislative provisions governing the tribunal's constitution and proceedings, irrespective of the actual good faith of the adjudicator. Practice or tradition ... is not sufficient to support a finding of independence where the status of the tribunal itself does not support such a finding.

And in *Gratton v Canadian Judicial Council* Strayer J added:[130]

> Independence of the judiciary is an essential part of the fabric of our free and democratic society. It is recognized and protected by the law and the conventions of the Constitution as well as by statute and common law. Its essential purpose is to enable judges to render decisions in accordance with their view of the law and the facts without concern for the consequences to themselves. This is necessary to assure the public, both in appearance and reality, that their cases will be decided, their laws will be interpreted, and their Constitution will be applied without fear or favour. The guarantee of judicial tenure free from improper interference is essential to judicial independence. But it is equally important to remember that protections for judicial tenure were 'not created for the benefit of the judges, but for the benefit of the judged'.

The language is not very different from that in the Strasbourg cases.

To return to the United Kingdom, in *Clancy v Caird*, 2000,[131] the Scottish court considered the appointment and tenure of temporary judges in contrast to temporary sheriffs. It held that they were convention compliant at least as regards purely private law litigation. Lord Sutherland said:

> While the general principles to be applied will remain constant, the actual decision in each particular case may vary, depending upon the way in which the principles are applied to the facts of that particular case. It is therefore of little assistance to consider the detail of cases involving military tribunals in Turkey or Belgium, probationary judges in Germany, Housing and Tenancy Courts in Sweden, and so on.

He noted that 'judges in the ECtHR itself are appointed for a fixed term of between three and nine years'[132] and went on:

---

129 *R v Généreux* [1992] 1 SCR 259 (SCC), 304.

130 *Gratton v Canadian Judicial Council* [1994] 2 FC 769 (Fed. TD), p. 782.

131 *Clancy v Caird*, 2000 SC 441, 2000 SCLR 526.

132 But see Coomber, 'Judicial, Independence-Law and Practice of Appointments to the European Court of Human Rights', [2003] EHRLR 486.

> In *Starrs* the court was concerned about the matter of reappointment ... The appointment of temporary sheriffs was for a period of one year only. When inviting applications to become temporary sheriffs it was made clear that the appointment would be regarded as to some extent a probationary period for the possible appointment of full-time sheriffs … As he was in effect on trial, it would certainly be arguable that an impartial observer would take the view that a temporary sheriff might be influenced, consciously or unconsciously, in his consideration of cases either involving the Executive or of public interest by consideration of the fact that the nature of his decision might endanger his prospects of reappointment. [But] … an impartial observer informed as to the method by which the system works, even if of a somewhat paranoid nature, would find difficulty in finding any possible breach of the requirement of impartiality and independence [of temporary judges].

Lord Penrose argued:

> As a matter of common sense, there is little difficulty in understanding the need for some provision to enable the courts to deal with fluctuating demand. Taking account of a reasonable provision for predictable absence from duty on holiday, or in servicing tribunals with a judicial membership, the proportion of each year that a full-time judge should work is, or ought to be, predictable ... However, judges are not immune from illness and other personal problems that may render them incapable of performing their duties from time to time. Abnormal and unanticipated demand for judicial services may be generated by circumstances thought at the time to be unique, such as a major disaster or an unprecedented rise in detected criminal activity ... But even ignoring that possibility there is no difficulty in identifying the need for some flexible system of response to unusual or unanticipated demand if the judicial system is to be able to provide for an appropriate hearing to decide parties' rights and obligations within a reasonable time.

But:

> If the aggregate use of temporary resources exceeded by a substantial margin the time commitments of full-time equivalents there could be a danger that the permanent establishment of the court would be reduced below the level required to meet the Convention criteria. Hitherto, the number of judges appointed as members of the permanent judicial establishment of the Court of Session has been determined by the Executive, as holder of the public purse, rather than by the independent and transparent application of any ascertainable objective criteria to the data bearing on demand for judicial services ... This inevitably creates a tension between the court and the Executive given the basic constitutional principles of the separation of powers and the rule of law.

He went on:

> The pursuer criticised the character of the appointment. There were two factors indicating that the appointment had a probationary character: the possibility of renewal of the temporary appointment, and the possibility of appointment as a permanent judge. A well-informed observer would expect that, as a matter of course, the temporary judge would be watched. The temporary judge himself must suspect that. The risk created pressures that ought not to exist in a judicial system. There was no reason why the temporary judge

> should not preside in cases of great importance to the Executive ... There was a colourable risk that the temporary judge would look over his shoulder at the possible response of the Executive to his performance. It would be wrong to suggest that, with a career path which was at the discretion of the Executive, he could be thought to be immune from such a risk.

However, 'This was a purely private dispute in which the Executive had no interest. There was no suggestion that the temporary judge had any connection with either party'.

In *Kearney v Her Majesty's Advocate*, 2006[133] *Clancy v Caird* was approved on a wider basis in relation to criminal trials. The distinction between *Starrs* and *Clancy* lies in the differences of the tenure of temporary sheriffs and temporary judges. Lord Bingham said:

> As the head of the Scottish judiciary, with overall responsibility (no doubt in conjunction, in practice, with the Lord Justice-Clerk) for the handling and dispatch of business in the higher courts, it is the Lord President who first recognizes and can best predict the need for temporary judges to supplement the permanent members of those courts. Thus the evidence shows, as one would expect, that it is he who instigates the making of a temporary appointment and he who suggests the names of suitable appointees. The process of appointment is not initiated by the Lord Advocate, as was the case with the temporary sheriffs ... the practice now is for the Lord Advocate to be informed but not consulted.

Lord Carswell said:

> Independence of a tribunal is required in order that the public, seeing this, may feel confidence in its ability to decide cases without any influence from the Executive being brought to bear or any feeling that it needs to have regard to the views or wishes of the Executive in reaching its decisions. That confidence is in addition and complementary to the need for the public perception of lack of bias or partiality. For this reason the concepts are separate and distinct, though closely linked both in their nature and in the underlying reason for the imposition of the requirements.

Starrs v Ruxton provides a baseline, but it is not one that condemns all part time appointments. Thus, in *Holder v Law Society*[134] the court could say:

> Taking into account all the circumstances, the nature of the Tribunal is entirely adequately independent and impartial for the purposes for which it is constituted. The reasonable by-stander, properly informed of the facts, could not consider otherwise. One might ask rhetorically, what more could be done in practice to ensure the independence of a domestic disciplinary tribunal such as this. The appointment and removal process is conducted under the auspices of a senior judicial officer. The Law Society does not and could not influence it. There is no link, actual or perceptible, between membership of the Tribunal

133 *Kearney v Her Majesty*'s *Advocate* [2006] UKPC D1.

134 *Holder v Law Society* [2005] EWHC 2023.

> and the career structure of any individual member. The objections identified in the *Starrs* case do not apply … to either the constitution or the operation of this Tribunal.

So, then, part-time, temporary appointments and no doubt the occasional engagement of retired judges are convention compliant so long as the numbers involved are not large compared to the full-time judiciary and they are not at the whim of an executive influenced either by the outcome of a decision or seeking to reduce costs. In particular, part-time appointments are permitted as part of a training or assessment process for full-time engagement. We may surmise, although the matter is less clear, that the occasional use of full-time judges at a higher level in the hierarchy than that for which they are appointed, for example, a circuit judge in the High Court or a puisne judge in the Court of Appeal, is also convention compliant, at least subject to the same conditions.

Listing and other considerations

Section 3(6) of the Constitutional Reform Act 2005 provides:

> The Lord Chancellor must have regard to –
>
> (b) the need for the judiciary to have the support necessary to enable them to exercise their functions;
>
> (c) the need for the public interest in regard to matters relating to the judiciary or otherwise to the administration of justice to be properly represented in decisions affecting those matters.

It also says in s. 7:

> (1) The Lord Chief Justice holds the office of President of the Courts of England and Wales and is Head of the Judiciary of England and Wales.
>
> (2) As President of the Courts of England and Wales he is responsible –
>
> (b) for the maintenance of appropriate arrangements for the welfare, training and guidance of the judiciary of England and Wales within the resources made available by the Lord Chancellor;
>
> (c) for the maintenance of appropriate arrangements for the deployment of the judiciary of England and Wales and the allocation of work within courts.

In England, apart from the new Supreme Court, the courts are run by Her Majesty's Court Service, an executive agency within the Department for Constitutional Affairs. The Department, through this agency, provides all the court staff. They, and indeed the staff of the Supreme Court, are civil servants.[135] The point has only to be made for it to be obvious that they are not, and thus cannot be seen to be, independent of the Executive. It is difficult to see how the Executive has any place in the micro-management of the system of justice. This is, of course, not to say that government, still less ministers, actually seeks to influence the business of the courts in particular cases. If it matters, s. 1 and s. 3(5) of the Constitutional Reform Act (and maybe the Lord Chancellor's new oath under s. 17) prohibit any attempt.

The actual processes of listing for trial and for constituting a panel for any appeal are obscure although not on that account necessarily sinister. As we have just seen the President of the Courts is responsible. Nevertheless, we may surmise that at some point members of staff of the Court Service are involved. It suffices to say that the appearance of the possibility of the executive being able to choose a particular judge for a particular case raises questions of a systemic lack of impartiality in the whole structure.[136] Lord Mackay himself acknowledged as much. The function of the judges, he said:[137]

> [it] is to decide cases and in so doing they must be given full independence of action, free from any influence. But in order to preserve their independence the judges must have some control or influence over the administrative penumbra immediately surrounding the judicial process. If judges were not, for example, in control of the listing of cases to be heard in the courts, it might be open to an unscrupulous executive to seek to influence the outcome of cases (including those to which public authorities were a party) by ensuring that they were listed before judges thought to be sympathetic to a particular point of view, or simply by delaying the hearing of the case if that seemed to advantage the public authority concerned.

Doubtless, the doctrine of necessity allows judges to refuse to recuse themselves because of systemic lack of impartiality. It is less clear that the court at Strasbourg is powerless to at least suggest that British arrangements be brought into line with the Convention requirements for the appearance of impartiality. The matter would be different if there were a plausible reason why the Court Service should be run out of the Department. It is notable that the Act expressly says that the staff of the new Judicial Appointments Commission are not 'servants or agents of the Crown'.[138] The question is why the difference?

---

135 Special arrangements are made for the new Supreme Court. However, both its Chief Executive and staff are civil servants. The explanatory notes prepared by the Department 'in order to assist the reader in understanding the Act' give s. 49 as authority. That section says:

> the civil service pension arrangements for the time being in force apply (with any necessary adaptations) to the chief executive of the Court, and to persons appointed under subsection (1), as they apply to other persons employed in the civil service of the State.

136 The plot of the popular television series, *Judge John Deeds*, is based on this appearance.

137 Lord Mackay of Clashfern, 'The Lord Chancellor in 1990s', (1991) 44 *Current Legal Problems*, 241 at p. 247.

138 CRA sched. 12 para. 22 (7).

In terms which remind us of Lord Mackay's problems with the EAT, an Australian judge argued:[139]

> A court in which those responsible to the Executive decide the way in which the operations of the court will be managed, the way cases will progress towards hearing, and which cases will be heard by which judge at which time, is not likely to produce the impartial strength and independence of mind which the community requires of its judges. The relationship between administrators and judges will tend to develop to one where the judges are well cared for and even prized, but are treated as senior staff who do specialized public work in the courts which the administrators run on behalf of the Executive.

In Canada, LeDain J in *Valente v The Queen* said:[140]

> Conceptions have changed over the years as to what ideally may be required in the way of substance and procedure for securing judicial independence in as ample a measure as possible. Opinions differ on what is necessary or desirable, or feasible. This is particularly true, for example, of the degree of administrative independence or autonomy it is thought the courts should have ... Professional and lay concern about judicial independence has increased with the new power and responsibility given to the courts by the Charter [for which, of course, in the United Kingdom, we may read the HRA].

And later:[141]

> When considering the independence of the judiciary, it is necessary to draw a careful distinction between independent adjudication and independent administration ... The position of the judiciary under the English and Canadian Constitutions is quite different from that under the American Constitution. In the United States the federal judiciary is a separate branch which includes judicial administration ... The degree to which the judiciary should ideally have control over the administration of the courts is a major issue with respect to judicial independence today ... In Ontario, the primary role of the judiciary is adjudication. The Executive on the other hand is responsible for providing the court rooms and the court staff. The assignment of judges, the sittings of the court, and the court lists are all matters for the judiciary. The Executive must not interfere with, or attempt to influence the adjudicative function of the judiciary. However, there must necessarily be reasonable management constraints. At times there may be a fine line between interference with adjudication and proper management controls. The heads of the judiciary have to work closely with the representatives of the Executive unless the judiciary is given full responsibility for judicial administration ... Judicial control over … assignment of judges, sittings of the court, and court lists – as well as the related matters of allocation of court rooms and direction of the administrative staff engaged in carrying out these functions, has generally been considered the essential or minimum requirement for institutional or 'collective' independence.

---

139 McGarvie, 'Judicial Responsibility for the Operation of the Court System', (1989) 63 ALJ, 79, quoted in Purchas, 'The Constitution in the Market Place', vol.143 (1993) NLJ, p. 1604.

140 *Valente v The Queen* [1985] 2 SCR 673, 25.

141 At 47.

But:[142]

> The essentials of institutional independence which may be reasonably perceived as sufficient for purposes of [the Charter] may be summed up as judicial control over the administrative decisions that bear directly and immediately on the exercise of the judicial function.

So also, *in re the Territorial Court Act* Vertes J developed four aspects to the constitutional imperatives of independence and impartiality:[143]

> (1) 'Individual independence,' defined as the 'complete liberty of individual judges to hear and decide the cases that come before them without interference from any outsider' ... This individual independence component is reflected in part by such matters as security of tenure and financial security.
>
> (2) 'Institutional independence,' defined as 'judicial control over the administrative decisions that bear directly and immediately on the exercise of the judicial function' ... The institutional independence of a court or tribunal is reflected in its institutional or administrative relationships to the executive and legislative branches of government as well as in such matters … as financial security on a collective basis.
>
> (3) 'Individual impartiality,' which connotes absence of bias, actual or perceived ... This relates to the state of mind of the decision-maker on a case-by-case basis.
>
> (4) 'Institutional impartiality' which, like institutional independence, will not be met if the objective conditions and structure of the system being examined create a reasonable apprehension of bias on an institutional level ... This requirement is not satisfied merely by the lack of bias of any particular judge in any particular case.

And:[144]

> One should not underestimate how concerns over administrative matters could compel judges to make difficult choices. These are not mere operational issues but go to the root of the role of the courts in a democratic society.

But in *Clancy v Caird* Lord Coulsfield citing *Stieringer* and *Valente* continued:

> I think that there is room for doubt whether institutional independence in the more extended sense discussed in the opinion in *Valente*, would or should be regarded, in a European context, as ideal or even as desirable.

And, Lord Penrose, quoting Vertes J's assessment of the Canadian Supreme Court, said:

---

142 At 52.

143 *Reference re Section 6(2) of the Territorial Court Act (NWT)*, 9 October 1997, 41.

144 *Reference re Section 6(2) of the Territorial Court Act (NWT)*, 9 October 1997, 125.

> [it] involves tests which have no parallel in Convention jurisprudence. The idea of 'institutional independence' ... involves the notion that judges should have control over the administration of the courts. The claim goes beyond the assignation of work, sittings of the court, court lists, the allocation of courtrooms and the control of administrative officers carrying out such functions.

He seemed to accept that judicial independence included 'the assignation of work, sittings of the court, court lists, the allocation of courtrooms and the control of administrative officers carrying out such functions'. This is not, and, even with the changes of Constitutional Reform Act, does not appear to be, the English system. Lord Penrose concluded:

> On the approach of the Canadian courts, it would be doubtful whether the Court of Session as a whole was institutionally independent ... We were not referred to any case which suggested that such an approach had been developed in the European jurisprudence.

We have, however, noted that the language in Canada is not very different from that used by the Commission in *Stieringer*. Such differences as there are between the UK (and Europe) and Canada do not seem to justify such different approaches. Among the characteristics that distinguish the Canadian system from the British are the facts that the Charter is not the same as the ECHR, Canada is a Federation and at least the bars in Scotland and England are much closer to their benches than is the Canadian bar. Individually or cumulatively these do not justify an outright rejection of the Canadian cases. As the ECtHR put it in *Piersack v Belgium*: 'In order that the courts may inspire in the public the confidence which is indispensable, account must also be taken of questions of internal organization.'

My argument need not, however, go as far as the adoption of the Canadian cases. My complaint is that the Court Service is part of the Department of Constitutional Affairs and its staff is members of the civil service. They are subject to transfer in and out of judicial support work. Their position is in contrast to the staff who serves the legislature. That staff is recruited along side the civil service but once appointed is part of an autonomous establishment under the control of the Speaker and Sergeant at arms. Why, of the three recognized powers in the state, is it only the judiciary that does not have its own staff? Is it an answer that the civil servants working in the courts do so under the direction of the President of the Courts and the Heads of the Divisions? Can these officers really serve two masters?[145]

Sir Isaac Hyatali (a former Chief Justice of Trinidad and Tobago) argued:[146]

> Industry can only prosper when it treads in the footsteps of peace and order ... The stark reality ... is that by reason of the total dependence on the Executive for its material and

145 Hollander, 'Conflicts of Interest and the Duty to Disclose Information', (2004) 23 CJQ 257, cited *Matthew* 6.24 as he discussed problems associated with 'double employment' of solicitors.

146 Hyatali, 'The Protection of Judicial Independence', (1983) CJQ, 76.

> human resources the constitutional independence of the judicial arm is susceptible of erosion by indirect but nevertheless effective means.

In a surprising passage in *Kearney v Her Majesty*'s *Advocate* Lord Bingham said:

> As was accepted in *Starrs v Ruxton* ... there is nothing inherently objectionable in the appointment of judges by the executive, which is the practice in much of the world: it makes practical sense that judges should be appointed by the body which is thereafter responsible for paying them, accommodating them and servicing their professional requirements.

It is surprising because by the time of *Kearney* the Constitutional Reform Act had been passed. It separates the bodies which appoint from those which service the judiciary.

One of the factors in *Clancy v Caird* was that the temporary judge only heard private law cases. Where there is judicial control of who hears what this is no doubt Convention compliant. Where the executive makes the decision, the situation may be different.

The practice raises a more fundamental problem. It is not discussed in either the cases or the literature. Given that the full-time judiciary have security of tenure, do they also have a right to have cases actually assigned to them?[147] Can the listing officers, in England, the Civil Service, simply not assign any, or any of a defined class of, case to a particular judge?

We have noted Lord Mackay LC's problems with the EAT. They occurred before the HRA brought rights back home. Whatever the detail of that dispute, there is not much doubt that there was the appearance of a lack of independence. The task of the Constitutional Reform Act 2005 is to separate, and be seen to separate, the three powers of government. It fails on that count. There is more. In s. 1, the Act says it:

> does not adversely affect –
>
> (a) the existing constitutional principle of the rule of law, or
>
> (b) the Lord Chancellor's existing constitutional role in relation to that principle.

And in s. 3 it goes on:

> (1) The Lord Chancellor, other Ministers of the Crown and all with responsibility for matters relating to the judiciary or otherwise to the administration of justice must uphold the continued independence of the judiciary.

---

147 The duty in s. 86 of the 2005 Act is scarcely of importance if a judge has no right to have cases assigned to him or her.

(4) The following particular duties are imposed for the purpose of upholding that independence.

(5) The Lord Chancellor and other Ministers of the Crown must not seek to influence particular judicial decisions through any special access to the judiciary.

Neither of these sections would prevent the mischief we have noted relating to the 1953 discussions on the scope of what was then called Crown Privilege.

Again, the Constitutional Reform Act 2005 fails in its purpose of creating a judiciary that is insulated from threats to its independence that are real and not theoretical or imaginary. The draftsman has taken a narrow and untenable view of judicial independence. The problem with s. 1 is while no doubt the rule of law includes such independence, the section refers to the 'existing' principle. It leaves no room for development in the light of, for example, decisions at Strasbourg or elsewhere. We have seen LeDain J in *Valente* arguing:[148] 'Conceptions have changed over the years as to what ideally may be required in the way of substance and procedure for securing judicial independence.' S. 1 sets independence in concrete. The Act itself is testimony that the idea is not static.

S.3 is built on the assumption that the only threat to independence from the executive is in individual cases. However, the use of any special access by ministers or anyone else to a judge in a particular case is already prohibited by the rules dealing with real and apparent bias. The more insidious threat, and one that is outside the section, comes from executive claims to influence the general state of the law by private and secret conversations, as it tried with Crown Privilege and again with the Employment Appeals Tribunal rules. I argue that the threat is no less when it comes from executive claims to control funding, resources and indeed the rules of court. Discussing the justifications for openness, I suggested 'Public debate and the rule of law combine to form the idea that justice should be done in public'. Dicey argued that the only proper way for the executive to talk to the judges is by an Act of Parliament passed after open debate. We need institutional safeguards to prevent Lord Mackay LC's problems with the EAT from arising ever again. Anything less shrouds justice in a cloak of secrecy.

Funding

In 1215, *Magna Carta* declared 'to no man shall we sell or deny justice'. From then or shortly after, the judges were paid a salary out of Royal revenues. Holdsworth said the judges augmented this income by taking 'pensions, rents and lands' from large landowners and fees from suitors in their courts and keeping the fines they imposed.[149] These extra-salary sources roughly doubled the incomes of the judges. By the end of the seventeenth century, the chief justices added the sale of minor and not so minor judicial offices to these sources. For these, income was generated from

148 *Valente v The Queen* [1985] 2 SCR 673, 25.

149 Holdsworth, *A History of English Law*, vol.1.

damages awarded and by charges for the steps in each action (the issue of the writ, the entry of other records, etc.).

The situation was regularized in the early and mid nineteenth century. In common with most of the rest of the central administration, servants of Crown including the judges and the associated minor offices, were no longer paid by what they could charge, or take or keep, but received salaries determined by statute. The legal system was nationalized.[150]

The judges then were and are still are different from other aspects of the central government in two major respects. First, under the Act of Settlement they have extensive security of tenure. Secondly, judicial salaries are charged to the Consolidated Fund rather than a departmental allowance. The advantage to the judges of their being paid in this way is that there is no annual debate in either House of Parliament about their salaries or their conduct or their decisions.

For much of the last century, litigants were required to pay fees for various court services but the amount of these fees was fixed in a random way bearing no relation to expenditure. They did not fund considerable parts of the legal system. In particular, judicial salaries (and pensions) were excluded. So also, other support costs of the judges were not the subject of detailed accounting.

The Department Discussion Paper 'Access to Justice – Civil Fees' of 1997 recalled:

> In 1994 the then Lord Chancellor announced, in setting out his Department's expenditure plans (Cm 2509), that judicial salaries would no longer be excluded from the definition of recoverable costs.

A right of access to a court is an implication of any legal system. As Lord Diplock said:[151]

> Every civilised system of government requires that the state should make available to all its citizens a means for the just and peaceful settlement of disputes between them as to their respective legal rights.

So too, under the Convention there is an obligation to provide a legal system. Court fees are permitted. As the ECtHR put it in *Kreuz v Poland*:[152]

> The Court once again recalls that it has never ruled out the possibility that the interests of the fair administration of justice may justify imposing a financial restriction on the individual's access to a court ... Furthermore, the Court considers that while under Article 6(1) fulfilment of the obligation to secure an effective right of access to a court does not mean merely the absence of an interference but may require taking various forms

---

150 Lord Evershed's word.

151 *Bremer, Vulkan Schiffbau and Maschinenfabrik v South India Shipping* [1981] AC 909, 977.

152 *Kreuz v Poland*, 19 June 2001.

> of positive action on the part of the State … a right to free proceedings in civil matters [cannot] be inferred from that provision.

It concluded:

> The Court accordingly holds that the requirement to pay fees to civil courts in connection with claims they are asked to determine cannot be regarded as a restriction on the right of access to a court that is incompatible per se with Article 6(1) of the Convention.
>
> It reiterates, however, that the amount of the fees assessed in the light of the particular circumstances of a given case, including the applicant's ability to pay them, and the phase of the proceedings at which that restriction has been imposed are factors which are material in determining whether or not a person enjoyed his right of access and had 'a … hearing by [a] tribunal'.

In *Jedamski and Jedamski v Poland*, it added:[153]

> [It] must be satisfied that the limitations applied do not restrict or reduce the access afforded to the individual in such a way or to such an extent that the very essence of that right is impaired.

And, speaking of the discretion vested in the Polish court to set an appropriate fee which could be proportionate to the amount claimed and the applicants' means, it concluded:

> The fee required from the applicants for proceeding with their action was excessive. It resulted in their desisting from their claim and in their case never being heard by a court.

So also in *Teltronic-CATV*, it said:[154]

> The requirement to pay fees to civil courts in connection with claims or appeals cannot be regarded as a restriction on the right of access to a court that is incompatible per se with Article 6(1) of the Convention. However, the amount of the fees assessed in the light of the particular circumstances of a given case, including the applicant's ability to pay them, and the phase of the proceedings at which that restriction has been imposed, are factors which are material in determining whether or not a person enjoyed that 'right of access … hearing by [a] tribunal'.

And later:

> The Court considers that restrictions on access to a court which are of a purely financial nature and which … are completely unrelated to the merits of the claim or its prospects of success, should be subject to a particularly rigorous scrutiny from the point of view of the interests of justice.

---

153 *Jedamski and Jedamski v Poland*, 26 July 2005.

154 *Teltronic-Catv v Poland*, 10 January 2006, [48].

In a passage that should now be read subject to this case-law, Brooke LJ in *Tanfern* rightly told us:

> Parliament is responsible for controlling the expenditure of public resources on the administration of justice (whether in relation to the direct costs of the courts, including the cost of the judiciary, or in relation to expenditure on what used to be called legal aid).

Apart from accommodating the very poor as required by *Witham*, the entire cost of the Court Service comes from fees paid by litigants. They cover not only the physical and human infrastructure of the courts but also the judges' salaries and pensions. The fees are determined largely by reference to the amount in dispute and the court in which a claim is to be heard. There is no attempt (beyond *Witham*) to determine whether a claimant can afford them. A minister argued:[155]

> Where people can afford to pay the fees involved in court proceedings the taxpayer should not be expected to pay ... Access to justice is an important principle for this government, but we need to balance this with the need to protect the interests of taxpayers. A balanced package of court fees is essential if we are to continue to invest in accommodation and IT and if we are to have a Court Service fit for the twenty-first century.

More recently, another minister said:[156]

> The Government's policy remains that court fees should generally be set to reflect (on average) the cost of the service provided. Where they can afford to do so, it is right that litigants using the civil courts, rather than the taxpayer, should meet the cost. This ensures that the taxpayers' contribution to the cost of the civil and family courts is focussed on funding the cost of the system of fee exemptions and remissions, in order to ensure that less well-off citizens are not denied access to justice. Setting fees generally at levels lower than the full cost would mean that corporations and other wealthy litigants would benefit from taxpayers contribution – increasing cost and putting pressures on other budgets like legal aid.

She also announced 'a fundamental review of the system of exemptions and remissions to ensure that it adequately protects access to justice and is operated consistently' and a review of:

> The structure of the system, that is the points at which fees are charged. The key objective will be to achieve a closer match of income and cost drivers, in particular through the introduction of trial fees. This is necessary both to make the system fairer as between different types of litigant, and make it easier to ensure that cost and funding remain in balance as workload changes.

---

155 *Press Release*, Court fees: balancing access to justice with value for money for the taxpayer, 5 May 2004.

156 Written ministerial statement by the Parliamentary Under Secretary of State, Department for Constitutional Affairs (The Baroness Ashton of Upholland), 10 January 2006.

It is doubtful whether this can meet the persistent complaints that fees deter claims, a problem made worse by their relativity high levels for small claims.[157]

In *De Cubber v Belgium*, the ECtHR recalled:[158] 'that the Contracting States are under the obligation to organize their legal systems 'so as to ensure compliance with the requirements of Article 6(1).' It is difficult to see how the United Kingdom can be complying with its Convention obligation to provide a civil court system while it does so at virtually zero cost.

At present, the fee structure is weighted so the County Courts provide some subsidy to the Senior Courts (as we must learn to call them) because part of the work of these involves setting precedents for the benefit of all court users.[159] This potential also means that all benefit from an effective county court system. This cross-subsidy recognizes that the court system does more than settle individual disputes. Senior court decisions benefit taxpayers generally and not only court users because every one is potentially a court user. Lord Falconer has claimed that the legal services market generates 'almost 2% of our GDP'.[160] The court system is the centre of this revenue. Those who do not litigate get a host of free rides.[161] The only real issue is the extent of these rides.

Although there is a copious literature on law and economics, it is mainly directed to the effect of individual rules of substantive law. I can trace nothing on the relation between a successful legal system and a successful national economy. We may hazard the guesses that the more effective a legal system is, the smaller is the black or barter economy and that the linkage is stronger in the service sector than in manufacturing. Of course, law has other interests beyond maximizing the economy. Nevertheless, the failure properly to fund the legal system may cause a shortfall in tax revenues and act as a break on the growth of national income.

The whole community, via the State, is under the obligation to have a system of civil justice. Further, as we have seen, the legal system as a whole tries to be sympathetic to litigants in person. Judges and even opposing lawyers give help with the presentation of their cases. This help is not free. It is a charge on the system (and the opponents). I have already suggested that it is a charge that costs more than legal

---

157 See e.g. Law Society, *Press Release: Raising Small-Claims Limit Will Block Access to Justice*, 28 February 2006.

158 *De Cubber v Belgium*, 26 October 1984, [35]. It cited *Guincho v Portugal*, 10 July 1984, [38].

159 For example, the Consultation Paper on Fee Changes, Code No CP 10/04, May 2004, 5.6, argued:

> Those cases resolved in the county courts benefit from decisions taken on appeal in other cases that by their nature are disproportionately costly. It would be unreasonable and would restrict access to justice if those claimants whose cases are resolved in the High Court were required to meet the full costs individually, despite the fact that all other litigants benefit from those decisions.

160 See above p. 6 n. 27.

161 Much of the Courts Service website is devoted to general information and not only court users.

aid would because judges, even at the lowest level in their hierarchy, are typically more expensive than legal aid lawyers. In so far as it is a cost falling on the Court Service, it is currently paid for not by the State or the taxpayer but by other court users. Assuming, as the system does, that we all gain from allowing individuals to litigate in person, those who do not use the courts get another free ride. Again, the Practice Direction to CPR Part 52, in order to facilitate appeals, allows the court to order that transcripts shall be made available 'at public expense' where a potential appeal might be stifled if they are not available. The expense in question is not the general exchequer, it is Court Service funds. Once again, other litigants are required to pay for a general public good.

It is difficult to see how a fee can be Convention compliant where it is levied in a system which does not allow for these general benefits. In total, fees in our system must be excessive because they ignore the public benefits and thus the extra costs incurred because of the interest of the public. The overall level of fees must be disproportionate to the purpose of providing a legal system. It may exceed the margin of appreciation permitted to States. For example, there is little doubt that open justice costs more than cloistered justice but it is insisted upon for a wider public good than mere dispute disposal.[162] Why, then, should it be paid for only by court users?

In discussing open justice and ADR, I objected to a system which imposes financial sanctions for proceeding with otherwise arguable cases. I suggested that it is in violation of the right to a public trial. The violation is worse when imposed by State rule rather than the discretion of a judge attempting a proportionate response to the case in hand.

It is notable that, as far as I can tell, the United Kingdom is alone in its policy. The State makes grants in aid for the civil justice system in places as far apart as Poland, Switzerland, France, Australia and the USA. Ideally, and actually at least in Australia, an independent officer (maybe the Chief Justice) receives a lump sum to be spent as he or she thinks fit. Indeed, the Constitutional Reform Act goes part of this way as regards the new Supreme Court.[163]

This is the main principled objection. There is another. The Court Service has estimated that around half of the claims issued are against defendants who are

162 We have seen Lord Hope, for example, saying in *R (on the application of Smith) v Parole Board*: *R (on the application of West) v Parole Board* [2005] UKHL 1, [64]: 'It is, of course, more costly and time-consuming to deal with cases by means of oral hearings,' (and see Lord Slynn, [48]).

163 See Scott, 'A Supreme Court for the United Kingdom', (2003) CJQ, 22 318, discussing the Consultation Paper which became the Act. He argued that the great expansion in executive power over the courts occurred as a result of the Beeching reforms of the 1970s, that 'the disadvantages inherent in an "executive-based" judicial administration system have indeed been mitigated to a degree by the fact that ... the Lord Chancellor ... was also head of the judiciary', but 'Now ... the official answer no longer suffices and the Government's proposals for the administration of the legal institution designed to replace the Appeal Committee look like a shameless grab for power by the executive branch of government'.

wrongly named or who do not live at the specified address.[164] In other words, the claims should not be issued and the Court Service should not receive a considerable part of its income. Its business plan is defective. Even if we assume that the virtual zero cost policy of the United Kingdom is Convention compliant in respect of existing fees, if these are adjusted upwards so the income does not include amounts in respect of claims which should not be brought, it is at least likely that fee levels will, as the ECtHR said in *Jedamski and Jedamski v Poland*, result in parties 'desisting from their claim and in their case never being heard by a court'.

The making of rules for civil procedure

The Civil Procedure Act 1997 defines by whom and how the Civil Procedure Rules are made. The Act has been heavily amended first by the Courts Act 2003 and most recently by the Constitutional Reform Act 2005. It is my argument that aspects of the scheme fall foul of the case law we have looked at. I have already argued that the absence of any claimant does not absolve the United Kingdom from the duties it has assumed under the Convention. Illegality is not dependent on the possibility of likely litigation.

The Act establishes a Rules Committee (including the Head and the Deputy Head of Civil Justice). Broadly it is made up of judicial members appointed by the Lord Chief Justice and non-judicial members appointed by the Lord Chancellor.[165] The Rules must be agreed by the Lord Chancellor. If he or she does not confirm them, written reasons must be provided explaining why not.[166] The Act gives the Lord Chancellor power to direct that rules be made to achieve specified purposes.[167]

My problem with these arrangements is the combination of judicial and executive inputs. We have seen that in *McGonnell v UK*[168] the ECtHR was concerned that the same person should not promulgate legislation and then decide its meaning. On its face, this might lead to the view that judges, especially those among the most senior, should have no part in framing the rules of court. Such a conclusion does not seem sensitive to the experience they can bring. On balance, it seems better to distinguish *McGonnell* on the basis that here we are considering procedural and not substantive rules.

But how with a fully independent judiciary can the executive have the influence the Act gives to the Lord Chancellor? He or she appoints around half the members

164 Court Service Consultation Paper, Register of Court Judgments, CS CP 01/03, June 2003. The New Civil Procedure Rules and the Register of Judgments Orders and Fines Regulations 2005 SI 2005 No. 3595 came into force on 6 April 2006. They are intended to cure these defects. It remains to be seen what effect they will have on Court Service income.

165 CRA 2005, Sched. 4 para. 263, amending CPA 1997 s. 1(3) as amended by Courts Act 2003 s. 82.

166 CRA 2005, Sched. 1 Part 1.

167 CRA 2005, Sched. 4 para. 266, inserting new s. 3A into the Civil Procedure Act 1997.

168 *McGonnell v UK*, 8 February 2000.

of the Committee, his or her consent is required for all rules that are made and directions can be given as to particular purposes to be achieved. As I discussed listing, I objected to the executive having power to micro-manage the system of justice. So also, I have objected to its powers both to fund (or underfund) the civil justice system and to fix fees for particular claims or steps in claims. My objection here is the same. This level of control is incompatible with an independent judiciary or its appearance.

But there is more here. There is power to override the Rules Committee even if it is independent: and power to compel it, including its senior judges, to do things it, and they, might choose not to. At best, the scheme is a recipe for negotiation, and not only on a macro level, but on detail. The judges cannot be seen to be independent. They are compromised.

Chapter 6

And So?

We have come a long way. Before seeking answers to the questions posed in Chapter 1, it is perhaps helpful if I summarize my argument. It is convenient to take it in reverse.

From what I have said at the end of the previous chapter it might seem that I am a disgruntled old man. Far from that. It seems to me that not only are our judges better than they have ever been but so also are both sides of the profession. They are all, at least as classes, better educated, more sober,[1] less remote and less pompous than they have ever been. My problem lies with modern government and its obsession with control to the apparent exclusion of all other factors which might be valued. We see it in the health service where officials in that Department cannot let clinicians be clinical. We see it in education where central officials seemingly do not trust teachers in schools to teach or our academies to research. And so we see it in the legal system. Government is now by numbers and this has as much relation to the art of governance as painting by numbers has to pictorial art. In general, I am saying that government must let go. There is too much, and too remote, micro-management.

My concern in this book is only with the legal system. And here, I argue, it is not only national policy that should inform the overarching rules. The United Kingdom has taken on obligations which I have argued are at odds with the way the Department for Constitutional Affairs, no doubt partly under Treasury influence, wants to run things.

The European Convention, like many other international instruments, imposes obligations which deny that government is unfettered. The Convention requires two central things of the system: that the executive does not interfere with the judiciary and that the right to a court is real and not illusory. It is in this context that I have argued the Department has no place in either determining the rules of court or providing the support staff (and other facilities) for the judges. Nor has it any place in fixing court fees, and particularly not at levels which render the right of access illusory. This level of control is, I say, incompatible with an independent judiciary, or its appearance, or the individual's rights of access all of which are required by Art. 6.

In discussing the appointment and tenure of the judges, I have been less than generous to the Constitutional Reform Act. It does go a long way in helping the English system to be Convention compliant. In particular, it takes any sting out of the denial that we do not have a career judiciary. In former times it was an almost

1 See Sir G Lightman, 'The Case for Judicial Intervention', p. 42, n. 161 above.

complete truth that the 'twelve men in scarlet' were equals headed only by the two chief justices and the Chief Baron. However, rank, and with it promotion, was introduced by the creation of the Court of Appeal and life peerages for members of the Judicial Committee. With the rise in numbers of judges at all levels throughout the last century, rank and promotion progressively became more important. Toward its end, there became an even greater emphasis as the possibility of promotion was opened up to judges at all levels in the hierarchy. The last step was taken with the creation of the office of Senior Law Lord (to become the President of the Supreme Court). It is the English way to assert that change is a shift backwards towards some supposed golden age. These reforms are no different. The pretense that there is no career has been maintained in defiance of the facts. Perhaps, one reason is that civilian systems happily acknowledge their career judiciary and we still, with remnants of the old fear of the juryless inquisition, pretend that we are different.

However, it has long been wrong to deny that we have a career judiciary. Judges are now entitled to hope for promotion and typically they spend more than half their working lives as judges. The new attachment to training and appraisal emphasize this. Once again the contrast with the civilian systems is diminishing. Until the Constitutional Reform Act judicial careers were in the control, if not of the Lord Chancellor, at least his Department. The separate Judicial Appointments Commission has taken over all this. It is notable that the Act says 'The Commission is not to be regarded … as the servant or agent of the Crown'.[2] There is now a new appearance of independence.

I have argued on the basis of *Kearney*[3] in 2006 that there has been a retreat from *Davidson*[4] of 2004, on the basis particularly of *Ruddy*[5] in 2006 but in part of *Clancy v Caird*[6] in 2000 that there has been a retreat from some wider conclusions that might have come out of *Starrs*[7] also of 2000. So also, I have said, on the basis of *Meerabux*[8] in 2005, that there has been a retreat from *Pinochet* (No.2)[9] reported in 2000. This much should go some way to appease Blom-Cooper.[10] These retreats do not, however, signal a rout. Rather, they show as I suggested in Chapter 1, the sincere anguish judges display when confronted with allegations of bias. They also establish positions more in accord with common sense. There is no rout because meantime the law has also found a new instrument with which to determine bias, the

2 CRA 2005, Sched. 12, para. 18.

3 *Kearney v Her Majesty's Advocate* [2006] UKPC D1.

4 *Davidson v Scottish Ministers* (No 2) [2004] UKHL 34.

5 *Ruddy v Procurator Fiscal, Perth* [2006] UKPC D2.

6 *Clancy v Caird*, 2000 SC 441, 2000 SCLR 526.

7 *Starrs v Ruxton* 2000 JC 208, 11 November 1999.

8 *Meerabux v Attorney General of Belize* [2005] UKPC 12.

9 *R v Bow Street Metropolitan Stipendiary Magistrate, ex p Pinochet* (No.2) [2000] 1 AC 119.

10 Blom-Cooper, 'Bias on Appeal', [2005] PL 225 above p. 186.

test in *Re Medicaments and Related Classes of Goods (No.2)*[11] as modified in *Porter v Magill*.[12] It is whether 'a fair-minded and informed observer would conclude that there is a real possibility tribunal is biased'. And the courts have moved quickly to describe who this fair-minded observer is and what he or she knows. This observer stands alongside the man on the Clapham omnibus as another guide to the standards set by law.

In Chapter 4, I described public interest immunity. There are three central problems. The power of the court to inspect documents creates two of them. Both have worried the ECtHR. Both have caused divisions among our judges. Comments of the ECtHR have caused changes in statute and practice. If a tribunal can inspect documents from one side, and perhaps take argument from it as to why they should remain confidential, the court infringes its elementary obligation to give both sides equal access. It creates what I called the contaminated judge. The eyebrows of the fair-minded observer are likely to be raised. If, on the other hand a cure is sought in the use of specially appointed counsel with access to the documents but not fully to his or her client, it is certainly not always clear that those eyebrows will not still be higher than normal. The process inevitably infringes the relationship that elsewhere the courts have been jealous to protect as when legal professional privilege is challenged.

The third issue raised by public interest immunity is the content of the claim. In the old days, the minister's certificate was sufficient. Now we have inspection. In this book and elsewhere I have argued it makes no sense that a court can say 'we have inspected the documents and find that no damage will come from disclosure yet it must not be disclosed'. I am arguing, in effect that the mortal blow to the class claim came when the courts asserted the right to inspect. As a matter of judicial statement we have had to wait for the HRA and the recognition that the ECtHR likes to decide cases on their particular facts.

Time and again, I have pointed to procedural forms of ours that are explicable only because once we had a jury. Legal professional privilege and the discussions of whether we still have adversarial proceedings is one such. There are times when our language is clothed in past and forgotten battles. So also, legal professional privilege is rare among the devices we have looked at in that, subject to statutory intervention (for example, compulsory disclosure to enforcement agencies of information that might disclose illegal activity), it is an absolute. Where it applies, there is no discretion and there is no balance. There is no sense of the proportionality essential to the philosophy of the Convention and the CPR.

Of course, beyond harmony, there is no reason why it should follow either of these instruments. To be sure, Art. 8 gives protection to privacy but this privilege is not founded in the Convention. It exists at common law. Nor, is it strictly procedural

---

11 *Re Medicaments and Related Classes of Goods* (2) [2001] 1 WLR 700. It is probably the HRA and the recognition of changing fairness that enables him to depart from an otherwise binding authority.

12 *Porter v Magill* [2001] UKHL 67.

or in any way connected with the CPR. It is substantive law. Nevertheless, it is ill at ease in a structure where so much else has either discretion or balance, where so much else calls for judgment. So also, much else does indeed depend on harmony. It is this which gives law its unity and at the end of the day makes it intelligible to lawyers and laity alike. Legal professional privilege giving blanket protection to the relationship of lawyer and client, in contrast to all other professional relationships, is likely to amaze the neutral observer. And this observer is unlikely to be happy to be told that it is none of his or her business.

The privilege purports to prioritize the rule of law over the openness of a trial. This is illogical because both these ideas serve the same purpose, the re-enforcement of tolerant democracy. To emphasize one with no balance is to distort the whole.

Chapter 3 discussed the extent of right to legal representation, how far judges can provide mitigation for litigants in person and the limited extent of the duty on the State to provide legal aid. It did so in the context of the right of access to the court.

More broadly, Chapter 3 (along with Chapters 4 and 5) discussed the adoption of the civilian doctrine of equality of arms and how far it is implicit in the common law before the advent of the HRA. That discussion was based in the well-known doctrines of what the common law calls natural justice, that both sides shall be heard and by an independent tribunal. For a while it seemed as if the common law might have adopted a third category – a notion of a constitutional right. At one time *Morgan Grenfell*[13] seemed to suggest that such rights could be recognized. That decision was, however, based in the interpretation of statute. Now, *Watkins v Secretary of State for the Home Department* makes it clear, that a constitutional right is not a free standing concept. It is an aid to statutory interpretation. As, for example, Lord Rodger put it:[14]

> It is in the sphere of interpretation of statutes that the expression … has tended to be used, more or less interchangeably with other expressions … the courts interpret the particular provision in this way because the substance of the rule is perceived to be so important that Parliament must squarely confront what it is doing when it interferes with it and must accept the political cost ... The term 'constitutional right' works well enough, alongside equivalent terms, in the field of statutory interpretation. But, even if it were otherwise suitable, it is not sufficiently precise to define a class of rights whose abuse should give rise to a right of action in tort without proof of damage.

Discussing the elements of the tort of misfeasance in public office, he concluded:

> Despite the encircling difficulties, it might be worth trying to deploy the concept of constitutional rights in the law of tort if it represented a way forward which best fitted the present state of the law. But it does not. Most of the references to 'constitutional rights' are to be found in cases dealing with situations before the Human Rights Act 1998 brought

13 *R (on the application of Morgan Grenfell) v Special Commissioner of Income Tax* [2002] UKHL 21.

14 *Watkins v Secretary of State for the Home Department* [2006] UKHL 17, [61]-[62], [64]. He cited Lord Hoffmann in *Wainwright v Home Office* [2003] UKHL 53.

> Convention rights into our law. In using the language of 'constitutional rights', the judges were, more or less explicitly, looking for a means of incorporation *avant la lettre*, of having the common law supply the benefits of incorporation without incorporation. Now that the Human Rights Act 1998 is in place, such heroic efforts are unnecessary: the Convention rights form part of our law and provide a rough equivalent of a written code of constitutional rights, albeit not one tailor-made for this country. In general, at least, where the matter is not already covered by the common law but falls within the scope of a Convention right, a claimant can be expected to invoke his remedy under the Human Rights Act rather than to seek to fashion a new common law right.

The flirtation with a free standing constitutional right may be over.

Chapter 2 described the most important principle of civil justice, openness and its ramifications. I have suggested it is the most important if only because if the public cannot see what is being done, any adherence to the rule of law achieved by the others matters less. Each of the discussions in both Chapters 3 and 4 of the various aspects of the equality of arms – the right of access to the court, the right to be heard and disclosure and evidence – is intended to reinforce the rule of law which, to repeat the words of the ECtHR,[15] 'the Contracting States undertook to respect when they ratified the Convention'. It is central to the Convention idea of a tolerant democracy. We have seen that at the heart of the impartial tribunal is the notion of the lay observer. Unless justice is open, this observer will not have much to do.

Given all this, what have we leaned? There are a number of things to be said. We have seen that *Lambeth LBC v Kay*; *Price v Leeds CC* suggested that the doctrine of precedent within the English hierarchy has priority over Strasbourg decisions.[16] This chapter, and indeed this book, is no place to indulge in an extended discussion of the modern doctrine of precedent. It suffices to say that strictly the House of Lords cannot, and could never, lay down the doctrine's extent for courts other than itself. This is because whether it affirms or reverses a lower court, the reason for its decision can only be on the basis of its own authorities. We cannot know whether there is a binding decision until a court says it does not like a rule but applies it because it is bound. *Kay* follows a previous House of Lords decision but on the basis that it got the law right first time. There was no reluctance. Strictly, and fortunately, what was said about precedent was *obiter*.

But the discussion itself is surprising. Much has changed in the 30 and more years since *Broome v Cassell* on which the House rested.[17] To name some:

1. the United Kingdom has joined what is now the European Union. It is now known that not only is the sovereignty of Parliament limited by membership of the Union but the final word on what its law means is in Brussels not in any

15 *Ryabykh v Russia*, 24 July 2003 [55].

16 *Lambeth London Borough Council v Kay*; *Price v Leeds City Council* [2006] UKHL 10.

17 *Broome v Cassell* [1972] AC 1027.

doctrine of precedent.

2. The HRA has been enacted. It is clear to me, at least, that the final word on what the Convention means is in Strasbourg.
3. It is as if the judges suddenly believe that they make law. We saw for example *Lord Browne-Wilkinson Barrett v Enfield LBC* spoke of an 'an area of the law which was uncertain and developing'.[18] No doubt law developing and law-making are more fun than law-applying. But the old way never sensibly denied that judges make law: long ago Dicey told us the constitution is judge-made. What has happened is that the period for development has been truncated. Ours is not a patient age. Instead of letting law develop as rock weathers over time, we want to sculpt it to its future shape and then change it again. I have complained that discipline has yet to be found in this new way.
4. There has been a great rise in the courts permitting and encouraging non-party interventions. The device itself is not new but the extent of its use is. These new interveners should be seen in light of these other changes. We saw the ECtHR used interveners in *Pizzati v Italy*.[19] The interventions there were because the other governments want guidance on how to order their own affairs. The new English interveners are interlopers seeking to influence other peoples' disputes. They are heard because the judges are too impatient, and too rational, to allow the slow haphazard accretion of case-law.

I began by asserting that modern civil justice is concerned with expediency and efficiency and that the ECHR has a different emphasis from the CPR. Thinking about human rights, I said, is, in part, an attempt to identify a rational system for the recognition of human dignity and equality. On that basis, I had expected the English cases to be fact specific and those at Strasbourg to be full of principle. The reverse is the case. Often, the English courts offer general guidance on how things should be done before descending into a specific application for the case to hand. The ECHR, by contrast, commonly refuses to discuss issues beyond those raised by the immediate facts. Our technique is transformed but not by the new human rights law. It is by the new desire to legislate.

It is unnecessary here to list all the changes the HRA has made to our civil litigation processes. There is a new idea of the independent court and a modification to the idea of bias. A new breed of specially appointed advocates has been created spawning a set of novel problems for only some of which have answers been attempted. Beyond the phrase, it is doubtful if Strasbourg has added much to our understanding of equality at arms. ADR is homegrown or at least certainly not imported from Europe. Art. 6 insists on the openness of legal proceedings. But so did the common law long before the Convention required it.

I asked whether Lord Woolf was right to worry shortly before the HRA came into force that the new civil procedure regime could be susceptible to numerous HRA

18 *Barrett v Enfield LBC* [2001] 2 AC 550, p. 117 above.

19 *Pizzati v Italy*, 29 March 2006 [GC].

challenges. I have identified some areas, but they are not many. Of them, the system of funding is the most important.

Does the different emphasis in the CPR and ECHR mask anything important? The two instruments have not collided. Does the HRA then add anything to the CPR? The answer at one level is no. In the great majority of cases the English and Strasbourg courts have similar conceptions of fairness. The HRA has moved our ideas of procedural justice but not by far. At another level the answer is more complex. And, it goes beyond the HRA and the ECHR into more general debate.

The enactment of the HRA has changed public discourse. There, the technical limitations of the legislation an irrelevant. The Act has propelled, in ways that have surprised me, consideration of human dignity and equality into public debate and policy deliberations. Our judges have a homegrown sense of justice. They do not need the HRA to tell them. But what the HRA does do is important. It gives an external legitimacy to that sense. It gives the judges greater confidence to apply it. In our age, which rejects tradition as a justification and history to explain anything, it also acts as a counterweight to the otherwise dominant ideas of consumerism and management. The ECHR via the HRA is the means by which procedural justice can remain intact.

At the outset, I suggested that procedure is not just dry rules but that it is the means by which we express our collective underlying sense of what matters, that is, of justice. This book has been about that sense.

Index